WHEN YOU MAKE FLOATING LINES LIKE WE DO, EVERYONE LOOKS UP TO THEM.

In 1945, we introduced Air Cel™ lines, the world's first modern floating fly lines. And for over 50 years, we've never stopped searching for ways to perfect them.

For example, we developed innovative taper designs for specific fish and specific fishing conditions. We pioneered new line coatings that are slicker, more durable, and require less dressing and care. And while all our floating lines are as effortless to pick up and cast as they are to mend and control, innovations like our Microballoon™ technology and chemically-hydrophobic coating have made them even more so. No wonder everyone looks up to them.

Check out our full range of floating fly lines, including the new Ultra 3 Multi-Color, the next time you visit your Scientific Anglers™ products dealer. For the name and number of the one nearest you, call 1-800-430-5000.

Scientific Anglers
THE METHOD TO THE MADNESS
3M *Innovation*

The key to the last great cottage industry...

Success, so they say, consists of finding a need and filling it. If the raves we've received for our first edition are any indication, we've achieved some measure of it. We've heard from anglers...outdoor writers and industry executives...virtually all of whom offered praise and encouragement.

Most notably, we've heard from fly tackle dealers. Hundreds of them. So many expressed delight at receiving, in effect, an entire industry in a neat 6" x 9" package, that we knew we had struck a responsive chord. So we embarked on some original research. And came up with some surprising results.

For example, conventional wisdom estimates that a quality list of fly tackle dealers nationwide would number about 1,500. *Black's Fly Fishing* has uncovered—and added to our circulation—another 1,000 dealers. By the time we're done we're fairly certain that the number of individual owners, managers and buyers on that list will total some 4,500 individuals.

We've concluded that fly tackle dealers are the key component in one of the last great cottage industries.

Think about it. There are hundreds and hundreds of fly fishing suppliers. Some are large corporations. Most are modest size companies that craft their products by hand or in small shops. And most sell direct to the tackle dealers, who are deluged with flyers, brochures and catalogs--marketing and sales materials that are glanced at, then often misplaced or discarded.

If you were to chart the key position these dealers hold in the fly fishing world, it would look like this:

| **Thousands of Suppliers** | **Fly Tackle Dealers** | **Millions of Anglers** |

Small wonder, then, that tackle dealers are among the most enthusiastic recipients of *Black's Fly Fishing*. Now they have a comprehensive buyer's guide, a single source of information on the entire industry. *Black's Fly Fishing* has become their desk top reference. Needless to say, we're delighted to serve this function for them, just as we do for anglers themselves. And--at the risk of sounding immodest--we'd like to suggest that savvy suppliers who want to influence tackle dealers can find no better medium than this directory.

That said, we offer to everyone who wrote or called to wish us well a heartfelt thank you.

Sincerely,

James F. Black, Jr., Publisher

Black's **1997** FLY FISHING

Publishing & Advertising Sales Office:
**P.O. Box 2029 · 43 West Front Street
Suite 11 · Red Bank, NJ 07701
(908) 224-8700 · Fax: (908) 741-2827**

PUBLISHING STAFF

James F. Black, Jr.	*Publisher*
Raymond Goydon	*Senior Associate Publisher*
Lois A. Ré	*Editor*
Amanda Santos	*Associate Publisher*
Ann N. Edmonds	*Associate Publisher*
Glenn J. J. Davidson	*Database Support*
David G. Hanson	*Contributing Writer*
Sir Harry Ré	*Director of Security*
Guerry Associates Middletown, NJ	*Cover Design*

CANYON CREEK · GUEST RANCH

AT ROAD'S END FIND TRUE PEACE AND QUIET.

If fly fishing is your dream, Canyon Creek Guest Ranch, in the awesome beauty of Montana Beaverhead National Forest, is the place for you.

Lakes and streams abound throughout this majestic, rugged wilderness area. Our guides know where the trout are "really jumpin" in this legendary fishing region.

There are few places remaining in the world where you can find the variety of Mountain Trout fishing opportunities that are available at Canyon Creek. Depending on where you fish, Native Brown, Rainbow, Cutthroat, Grayling and Brook trout, average anywhere from 8 to 24 inches.

A fly fisherman will relish the diversity of wading the Big Hole River one day and stalking the brushy narrows of a mountain stream the next. Our secluded alpine lakes provide another spectacular dimension for the fly fisherman.

Canyon Creek is the perfect place to take a trail ride. Our private log cabins have showers and baths, wood-burning fireplaces and com-fortable beds. Meals are served family style in the main lodge.

You will enjoy the finest fishing and hunting in Montana amid scenery so breathtaking that you will never forget the experience.

Please don't forget your camera. Do make reservations and arrangements well ahead of time. We'll pick you up in Butte.

Canyon Creek Guest Ranch "where at road's end, you'll find true peace and quiet."

CANYON CREEK · GUEST RANCH

"The only one of its kind in all outdoors."
For brochure, information & reservations:

800-291-8458

P.O. Box 126 • Melrose, Montana 59743

Eastern Coordinator
FRANK EICHMAN
610-436-0336

Make the Difference With
FLY◆TECH®

Neoprene Family of Waders

Men's 2041 (Regular, Tall, Short and King), Ladies 2042 (XS-L), Youth 2043 (XS-L)

- 2040 Series includes 33 sizes to fit men, ladies and youth
- High Back 3.5mm Neoprene
- Adjustable Neoprene suspenders
- Large handwarmer pocket

- Padded knee pads
- Hypalon® soles
- 3 D-rings for accessories
- Gravel guards & repair kit included

4mm "Polypropylene"/Neoprene Stocking Foot Chest Wader

- Coville "AM Microstop" polyolefin fleece lining transfers moisture and controls odors and bacteria
- High back 4mm Neoprene
- Adjustable Neoprene suspenders
- Extra large double Neoprene/mesh pocket

- New durable molded rubber knee pad
- New seamless sock design
- 3 D-rings for accessories
- Adjustable gravel guards & repair kit included

Premium quality waders, ultralight fly and spinning rods, reels, float tubes, caps, vests and other fishing products for fishing enthusiasts who demand the best and know the difference.

Semi "V" 1000

Semi "V" shape and dual keels allow this tube to track in the direction you want to go.

- Open front with stabilizer bar
- Cover made of 430 denier nylon with 1000 denier cordura bottom
- Durable polyurethane primary bladder
- Duo PVC back rest bladders
- All critical seams triple stitched
- Adjustable seat with quick release buckle
- Multi equipment/Accessory pockets

- Rod holders
- Fluorescent safety panels on all sides for visibility
- D-rings for accessory attachment
- Dry-Fly patch
Made in USA
Color: Navy/Black

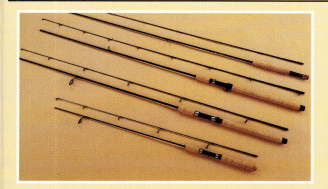

Supreme Fly Rods and Reels

7450 Whitehall • Fort Worth, TX 76118

OPEN YOUR OWN FLYTECH PRO SHOP OR DEPARTMENT!
For Details call Jesse at

800-590-2281

FEATURES

ARTICLES, CHARTS & DIAGRAMS

Exceptional Fishing

*S*porting vacations are all to precious for us to waste with an unsatisfactory experience due to the incompetence of the guide or host lodge. Over a decade ago, Orvis set out to make life easier for its fishing customers by seeking out the best fishing lodges, outfitters and guides in the country.

The result is the **Orvis-Endorsed** Lodge, Outfitter, Expedition and Guide Program. Operators in the program are located in exceptional fishing areas and have a reputation for superior client service. Each operation is run by people who can deliver a day or a week filled with the very best the outdoors has to offer. Each has its own character, but they all share the ideals of excellent service, great fishing and an experienced staff.

All operations are continually reviewed by the Orvis staff and must continue to meet rigorous requirements. Through annual training seminars sponsored by Orvis, each lodge, outfitter and guide continues to learn the latest in fishing techniques and client services. Orvis recommends these services with the utmost confidence.

Look for the words **Orvis-Endorsed** in listings and advertisements that appear in this book. Or call 1-800-778-4778 for help in making your choice.

ORVIS-ENDORSED

LODGES *Offer:*

- Complete extended stay service
- Excellent accommodations
- Quality cuisine
- Complete outfitting shop
- Knowledgeable guides

OUTFITTERS *Offer:*

- A full-service shop for all your needs
- A resident staff of quality guides
- In-depth knowledge of, and access to, area fishing

EXPEDITIONS *Offer:*

- Remote wilderness fishing trips
- Quality guides and wranglers
- Complete outfitting for extended stays

GUIDES *Offer:*

- A complete fishing experience
- Knowledge and insight into their region's fishing

EQUIPMENT

INSTRUCTION

DESTINATIONS

ACCESSORIES

ADSCO
3162 Baumberg Ave., Suite D
Hayward, CA 94545
(510) 786-1121
FAX: (510) 785-7461
Contact: Al Schneider
Get-It-Right® Fish Weight Chart–
Dealer Calls Welcome.

Abel
165 Aviador St.,
Camarillo, CA 93010
(805) 484-8789
FAX: (805) 482-0701
Est.: 1977   Staff: 40
President: Steve Abel
Sales Mgr: Gina Abel
Abel offers a full line of accessories including Abel Pliers™ (in two models: #2 & #4); Abel Liner Lock Knife, Angler's Versi-Pak, Abel Arm™, T-shirts, Flies, Reel Bags and Abelube System™. Abel skin care products. Call for brochure.

H. Abrams Manufacturing
51 Grace Ave., Lynbrook, NY 11563
(516) 593-6024
Contact: H. Abrams
Maker of linewinder and fly tying equipment.

R.A. Allen Co., Inc.
PO Box 221
Lincoln, MA 01773
(800) 722-5536
FAX: (617) 259-4116
Est.: 1995   Staff: 20
Contact: Richard Allen
The Rod Gripper; Allen's saltwater Tide-Guide; Allen's rod carrier for utility vehicles.

Angler's Engineering
Rt. 6, Box 27
Eureka Springs, AR 72632
(800) 752-7132
FAX: (501) 253-7850
Contact: Skip Halterman
Angler's manufactures Turn-on™ strike indicators; Yarn Anchors strike indicators; and The Ultimate Loop–a leader connections loop.

Angler's Expressions, Inc.
PO Box 3136, Boise, ID 83703
(208) 375-5242
FAX: (208) 376-6114
President: Janet Downey
Gifts featuring an outdoor theme–mugs, etched glass, pewter, dinnerware, note cards, t-shirts, etc.

Anglers Image Inc.
5714 Clark Rd., Sarasota, FL 34233
(800) 858-0903
FAX: (941) 927-0560
Est.: 1990   Staff: 5
Contact: Stan Sugerman
Manufacturers of "The Flyfishing Knife", Line Winder, world's best Line Clipper, Flyfishing Pliers & more.

Angling Designs, Inc.
820 S. Monaco, #264
Denver, CO 80224
(303) 750-3345
FAX: (303) 369-0495
Contact: Steve Schwartz
Manufacturer of the Quick-Seine, the net-handle seine that is stored and transported on your landing net handle. The patented design allows you to seine frequently and conveniently for more effective fly pattern selections. Awarded "Top Ten" new product at the 1996 International Fly Tackle Dealer Show. Available at your favorite fly shop or call 800-896-8998. Dealer inquiries invited.

Atlanta Fly Fishing Outfitters
5486 Chamblee-Dunwoody Rd.
Atlanta, GA 30338
(770) 698-0707
Contact: Rick Pettepher
Your strike indicator applies without kinking or gumming up leaders.

Caney Fork Outfitters
PO Box 1427, Franklin, TN 37065
(615) 790-7545
Contact: Rod Teague
Maker of midge twister.

Cardoza Creations/Scales
2541 5th Ave., Suite E
Oroville, CA 95965-5882
(916) 533-8692
FAX: (916) 894-8350
Contact: Kreg Brawley
No rust, no-fail fish scales and drag testers. 4 models ranging from 15 lbs. in 2 oz. increments up to 100 lb. scale in 1 lb. increments. Drops indicator off at peak weight.

John Chatillon & Sons, Inc.
83-80 Kew Gardens Rd.
Kew Gardens, NY 11415
(718) 847-5000
FAX: (718) 441-4365
Contact: Dick Zebler
Manufacture 11 streamside scales, 2 to 100 lb. range for weighing fish and line drag.

Compleat Angler, Inc.
1320 Marshall Lane
Helena, MT 59601
(406) 442-1973
FAX: (406) 442-9900
Sales Mgr.: Rob Deadmond
Fine quality wading accessories.
Felt sole kits, wading sandal, wader
repair kits, wader belts and sus-
penders, rod bags, wader pack,
Mt. Guides Boat Bag.

Cougar Products
Box 1153, Bothell, WA 98041
(206) 486-5011
FAX: (206) 486-5011
Contact: William J. Van Natter
Indestructible polyurethane coil re-
tractor bundled with nipper.
Quality economical fly threaders.
Wholesale.

Diamond Machining Tech.
85 Hayes Memorial Dr.
Marlborough, MA 01752
(508) 481-5944
FAX: (508) 485-3924
Manufacturers of diamond knife
and hook sharpeners.

**"Dinsmores" Removable
"Green Cushion" Tin Split
Shot & Tin & Lead Split Shot**
Distributed by Belvoirdale
PO Box 176, Wyncote, PA 19095
(215) 886-7211
FAX: (215) 886-1804
President: Grahame Maisey
Dinsmores—the only "high performance" shot. A divot, not "ears",
opens the shot, so it sinks faster,
doesn't snag or twist the line so...it
fishes better, longer.
NEW..."Green Cushion" tin coating
grips soft lines firmly without crimp-
ing. Dark olive color provides very
low visibility in water.

Dr. Slick
114 S. Pacific, Dillon, MT 59725
(406) 683-6489
FAX: (406) 683-5123
Contact: Becky Benzel
Surgical-quality instruments for anglers, including gift sets, scissors,
clamps, pliers, forceps, nippers, pin-
on-reels, etc. Call or write for
information.

Donnmar Enterprises Inc.
2111 SE Columbia Way, #100
Vancouver, WA 98661
(360) 694-7980
FAX: (360) 694-7969
Corp. Sales: Dan Madsen
Donnmar manufactures the Checkpoint line of stainless steel pliers,
hook and knife sharpeners, including the top-of-the line DONNMAR
CP850 series of stainless steel pliers. All Checkpoint products
feature state-of-the art design and
are engineered for years of dependable performance. Made in the
U.S.A. Dealer inquiries are welcome. Call for more information.
See Our Ad Pg. 9

Dream Makers Marketing
Box 1855, Evergreen, CO 80437
(303) 670-0496
VP/Sales & Mktg: Bruce Semler
The Right Fly Ready Reference System helps eliminate the mystery of
fly identification & selection for all fly
fishers with its 5 essential products.

East Coast Fisherman
530 Main St., Suite 750
New Rochelle, NY 10801
(914) 576-3733
Contact: Jeff Mancini
East Coast Fisherman "Big Water
Stripping Basket"

Elastic Products/Suspenders
PO Box 39, Marble, NC 28905
(704) 837-9047
Contact: Harry Baugh
The Hold-Up Gang—quality suspend-
ers and belts for waders.

THE SHARPENER PEOPLE

Eze-Lap Diamond Products
3572 Arrowhead Dr.
Carson City, NV 89706
(702) 888-9500
FAX: (702) 888-9555
Est.: 1973   Staff: 45
Sales Coordinator: Donna Long
Gen. Mgr: Ralph Johnson
Manufacturer and originator of the
finest patented Diamond knife and
fishhook sharpeners on the market
today.

Finsport
11410 NE 124th St., Suite 583
Kirkland, WA 98034
(206) 821-5227
FAX: (206) 821-5227
Contact: Gary Burtrim
Maker of the front-to-back fishing
pack and the new Finsport ultralight chest packs. Made in the U.S.

FINGER SOCK™
"The Best Way to Prevent Fly Line Burns"

Fly Presentations, Inc.
403 Brady Lane, Austin, TX 78746
(512) 327-8910
FAX: (512) 327-6580
Contact: Brian Slaga
Offering an innovative (Patent Pending) solution to irritating fly line
burns—The FINGER SOCK is made of
an elastic lycra material which comfortably conforms to your entire
finger and allows the fly line to
slide freely. Look for other innovative products coming soon from
the people who brought you the
FINGER SOCK.

Fly Tyer's Carry-All
Box 299, Village Station
New York, NY 10014
(212) 242-2856
FAX: (212) 989-2989
Contact: Joan Stoliar
Catch-A-Hatch—the vest-pocket in-
sect net—catch and release for the
insects. Fly Retreev—the vest-pocket
tree-branch hook.

Flyfisher Products
PO Box 370166, Denver, CO 80237
(303) 750-1831
FAX: (303) 750-1856
Contact: Ken Walters
Split-willow creel with a leather
latch strap, rustproof buckle and
cowhide harness. Hand woven in 3
sizes.

Haber's Export Agencies, Inc.
PO Box 436, Glens Falls, NY 12801
(518) 793-3517
FAX: (518) 793-0085
Contact: Eleanor Shaw
Quick release snap hooks—ideal for
attaching landing net to vest for
easy access.

HatchMatch™
Manufacturing Technologies, Inc.
PO Box 801, 3570 Highway 287
Sheridan, MT 59749-0801
(406) 842-5403
FAX: (406) 842-5204
Contact: Nick Savko

Fly or nymph? Choose the right one with HatchMatch, a light, durable, self-contained hatch monitor designed for quick set-up, ease of use and simple bag storage. Single unit construction features two compartments that monitor surface and base flow. Sturdy nylon netting, polymer injection molded frame, convenient cord handles. HatchMatch includes a rot- and mildew-resistant nylon carrying bag with drawstring tie. An invaluable accessory for veteran fisherman and novices alike. Phone or fax for free literature or location of nearest dealer/distributor.

KENNEBEC RIVER
FLY&TACKLE
C O M P A N Y

Kennebec River Fly & Tackle
39 Milliken Rd.
North Yarmouth, ME 04097
(207) 829-4290
FAX: (207) 829-6002
Est.: 1994   Staff: 4
Pres: John Bryan
Manager: Ashley Richards
The KR Linetender is the most versatile stripping basket available. Unique safety features for "big water" anglers. Tacklekeeper "unique corrosion protection" products. Free catalog.

King Tool, Inc.
5350 Love Lane,
Bozeman, MT 59715
(406) 586-1541
FAX: (406) 585-9028
Contact: Steven J. Emerson
Angler's accessories featuring "The Streamside" instant-update thermometer, "mini-THERM" multi-purpose thermometer, and our fly rod holder.

J. Frederic Latour
418 River Dr., Lolo, MT 59847
(406) 273-0559
Produces reel covers in elk or buck skin in three sizes; tippet and fly caddy; fly and streamer book and ribbed foam fly holders.

LOON OUTDOORS
7737 W. Mossy Cup St.
Boise, ID 83709
(800) 580-3811
FAX: (800) 574-0422
Contact: Ken Smith
Loon Outdoors produces and markets a unique line of accessories for fly fishing, fly tying and related avocations. Items not listed in other categories include: cleaners, lubricants for lines, flies, hands, tubes, waders and reels; vest caddies; and a very compact first aid kit. Call for information.

Mayfly
PO Box 8307, Holland, MI 49422
(616) 399-4673
FAX: (616) 399-8978
President: Scott Hoffman
Quality fly fishing accessories including lanyards, net releases, fly floatant holders, etc. Dealer catalog upon request.

Moose Creek Co.
PO Box 309, Lakeville, MN 55044
(612) 891-5159
FAX: (612) 463-8363
Hatchcards™ contains insect hatch information and are available for over 45 rivers and lakes.

Orvis Company
Rt. 7A, Manchester, VT 05254
(800) 333-1550 (Ext. 844)
(802) 362-3622
Orvis provides a full line of fresh and saltwater fishing accessories.

Palsa Outdoor Products
Pinch-On-Float
Box 81336, Lincoln, NE 68501
(800) 456-9281   (402) 488-5288
FAX: (402) 488-2321
President: Bill Harder, Jr.
VP/Sales: Ray Clatanoff
The ideal fly fishing strike indicator. Soft, light, highly buoyant, and colored for outstanding visibility, the Palsa Pinch-On-Float is the industry standard. Any combination of floats can be used to create the desired flotation. Easy to use—simply peel off the backing, position the float on the line or hook, and pinch it into place. Easy to remove when no longer needed.

R.W. Reinhold Co.
4446 Westridge Dr.
Williamsburg, MI 49690
(616) 938-9211
Contact: Ron Reinhold
Manufacturer and distributor of the world's only Hackyl Foldyr (hackle folders). Needle Weasel (needle in a tube). Yellowstone net releases.

Riverborn™

Riverborn Fly Company, Inc.
Box 65, Wendell, ID 83355
(800) 354-5534
FAX: (208) 536-6103
A full line of fishing and tying accessories for on the water or at the bench.

Roe Mfg. Inc.
PO Box 229, Benton, KY 42025
(800) 552-4331
FAX: (502) 527-5322
Contact: R.O. Johnson
Roe Mfg. offers quality products for the fisherman: the Tippet Dispenser, the Tweezie, the Zingeee and the Two-in-One Fisherman's Knot Tool. Call for information.

The Royal Wulff Wristlok
HCR1, Box 70
Lew Beach, NY 12758
(800) 328-3638
(914) 439-4060
FAX: (914) 439-8055
Contact: Doug Cummings

Sierra Stream & Mountain
PO Box 7693, Chico, CA 95927
(916) 345-4261
FAX: (916) 345-4261
Line of accessories, including knot
tyer, tool retractor, line clippers, pliers and folding scissors.

Sports Tools
8589 Nevada Ave.
West Hills, CA 91304
(818) 992-5747
FAX: (818) 992-4732
Contact: Barry Kustin
Retracto–all metal construction,
heavy-duty clamp, extra long 18"
nylon-covered steel cable. Private labeling available. FF-1 Plier–all
stainless steel combination cut-
ter/pliers. Optional nylon holster.
Made in the U.S.A.

Stone Creek, Ltd.
PO Box W, Greeley, CO 80632
(970) 351-6241
FAX: (970) 346-1384
Contact: Rocky Bloskas
Supplier of premium fishing flies,
gifts, classic split willow creels, creel
lamps and other quality fishing accessories.

Streamer Trunk Collection
51 Chestnut Grove Rd.
Shippensburg, PA 17257
(717) 532-9226
FAX: (717) 532-9226
Contact: Bill Ferris
Manufacturer of "Rod Case Mem-
ory Decals".

Sunsor, Inc.
1509 Rapids Dr., Racine, WI 53404
(414) 637-0608
FAX: (414) 637-3015
Contact: Troy Sorsen
Manufacturer of leader boxes.

Tamsco
PO Box 173, Lake Mills, WI 53551
(414) 648-8552
FAX: (414) 648-3056
Contact: Curt Loeffler
Manufacturers of a diverse selection of surgical-quality instruments,
scissors, pliers, forceps, etc. for anglers.

Ursus Enterprises
PO Box 9421, Missoula, MT 59807
(406) 542-2568
FAX: (406) 542-2568
Contact: Gus Serven

Maker of "Flot-Pak" and "Flot-Pak II"
floatant holders.

The Waterworks
73 California Ave.,
Orinda, CA 94563
(800) 435-9374
(510) 253-1664
FAX: (510) 253-1665
Contact: Ryan Harrison
The "Ketchum Release", available
for freshwater and saltwater offers
two significant benefits: it saves
fish and it saves flies.

Wind River
3982 Rolfe Ct.
Wheatridge, CO 80033
(303) 378-7287
FAX: (303) 420-1522
Est.: 1993   Staff: 3
Rod Ruler, Net Keeper, Boat Anchor Ditty Bag, sunglass case and
door mat. Distibutor of Johnson &
Johnson sun block and mageye's
magnifier. Four types of insect
seines, insect vials, and insect pre-
servative for serious anglers.

**Wooley Bugger
Entomology Co., L.L.C.**
PO Box 7571
Boulder, CO 80306-7571
(303) 444-7722
FAX: (303) 499-6091
Contact: Britt Clayton
Scientifc tools for collection, preser-
vation and display of aquatic and
terrestrial insects. Five different kits
designed specifically for the fly fish-
erman.

Zeppelin Products
3120 SW 19th St., #149
Pembroke Park, FL 33009
(800) 270-1477
(954) 989-8808
FAX: (954) 989-8578
Contact: Alan Granovsky
Manufacturer of quality American-
made embroidered leather belts
and accessories.

ACCESSORIES/
CHEST PACKS

All Angles Co.
PO Box 1533, Ashville, NC 28802
(704) 299-3995
Contact: Alan Geer
Two styles of chest packs retailing
for $38.95 and $69.95. Direct and
dealer calls welcome.

Bridger Mountain Pack Co.
333 Simmental Way
Bozeman, MT 59715

(406) 582-9637
FAX: (406) 585-9284
General Mgr: Dave Kosmatka
At Bridger Mountain Pack Co., we
design and build high quality
chestpack and backpack systems
for fly fishing.

Coldwater Packs Company
PO Box 19887, Seattle, WA 98109
(206) 572-5611
Co-owner: Daniel Marshall
Co-owner: Robert Pinnell
Producers of Chestpacks, Fanny
packs, Reel cases, winter
Salmon/Steelhead vests, and two
new products; a Wader pack and a
Boat bag. Made in the U.S.A.

FOW Fly Box
Flies On Water, Inc.
PO Box 4875
Ketchum, ID 83340-4875
(208) 726-7690
FAX: (208) 622-8040
Est.: 1995   Staff: 8
President: Dick Hare
The FOW Fly Box is made of high-
quality anodized aluminum and is
offered in 4 functional models–call
or write for free color brochure.

Predator Sporting Equip.
Box 1752, Sanford, ME 04073
(603) 749-0526
FAX: (603) 749-7112
Contact: Jim Coury
Replace your old fishing vest with
an Angler's Chest Pack from Predator. Pack comes with comfortable
padded shoulder straps and pockets—three in front, three in back
—designed to hold almost any size
fly box. Detachable pouch for rain
wear or jacket. Made in the U.S.A.
Comes with a lifetime warranty.

The Richardson Chest Box Co.
120 Dunlap St.
Bellefonte, PA 16823
(814) 353-3188
Contact: Bob Hegedus, Jr.
The Richardson Chest Box is made
of aircraft grade aluminum and is
available in 5 models. All boxes
come in 2,3,4 or 5 section models
with numerous options.

Steel Shadows, Inc.
Box 33239, Denver, CO 80233
(800) 248-9203
FAX: (303) 255-2907
Est.: 1993   Staff: 4
Contact: Jason Volmer
Manufacturer of lightweight fly
tackle; Tippet 'n Leader wallets, Fly
Fishing Wallets™, fly box storage
cases and Clip-On Fly Boxes™.

ACCESSORIES/ CLEANERS, CHEMICALS & DRESSINGS

Cortland Line Co.
3736 Kellogg Rd.
PO Box 5588, Cortland, NY 13045
(607) 756-2851
FAX: (607) 753-8835
Contact: Tom McCullough
Line cleaners & conditioners to en-
hance performance & add life to lines.

The Creek Company
PO Box 773892
Steamboat Springs, CO 80477
(800) 843-8454 (970) 879-5221
FAX: (970) 879-7577
President: Christopher Timmerman
Greased Lightnin'™ Line Dressing is
a non toxic line dressing that cleans
and lubricates both sinking and
floating lines without wax. Pure
Flote™ is a pure odorless 100% silicone fly floatant paste with
constant viscosity in any tempera

ture. Pure Sinc™ is a pure odorless
wetting agent that allows flies to
absorb water and sink naturally.

Guup Clip
PO Box 396, Fall City, WA 98024
(206) 222-7789
Guup Clip is the only fly floatant
that attaches to your rod.

**Kennebec River Fly &
Tackle Company**
39 Milliken Rd.
No. Yarmouth, ME 04097
(207) 829-4290
FAX: (207) 829-6002
Est.: 1994   Staff: 4
Pres: John Bryan
Manager: Ashley Richards
Tacklekeeper products protect your
tackle and tools from rust and fric-
tion. Unique dry film technology
that really works! Free catalog.
See Our Ad Below

Lexico, Inc.
4479 Brooks Vale Ct.
Harrisburg, PA 17110
(717) 541-0250 FAX: 0262
Contact: Alexis Kassnar
Mucilin brand fly dressing.

LOON OUTDOORS
7737 W. Mossy Cup St.
Boise, ID 83709
(800) 580-3811
Contact: Ken Smith
Loon Outdoors, known for "environmentally friendly fly fishing
products that perform," features
several distinctive items in this cate-
gory: a variety of floatants
—temperature stable gel, silicon
paste, powder and spray—strike indicators and wetting agent which are
biodegradable, lead-free weight,
and easy-to-use desiccant.

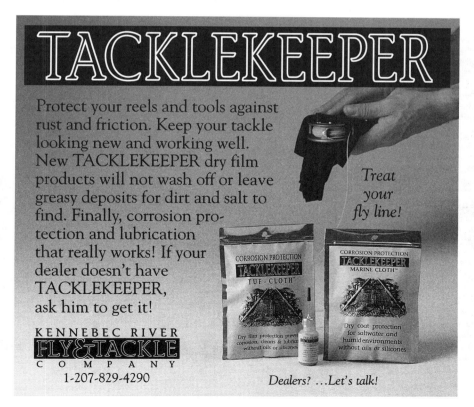

Multisorb Technologies, Inc.
325 Harlem Rd.
Buffalo, NY 14224-1893
(800) 445-9890
Contact: Michael Peters
Shur Float™ Dry Floatant

Path Silicones
Box 430, Elmwood Park, NJ 07407
(201) 796-0833
FAX: (201) 796-4845
Est.: 1990
Contact: Tom Buckley
Clear Fly is a clear, non-toxic fly floatant that leaves no oil slick, will not mat hackle and flows and coats hot or cold.

Scientific Anglers

3M Scientific Anglers
3M Center-Bldg. 223-4N-05
St. Paul, MN 55144-1000
(800) 525-6290
Scientific Anglers fly-fishing accessories—fly line dressing and cleaning pad improve floatability and shootability in both fresh and saltwater lines, and can be used and applied even on the water.
Fly Floatant was named one of the fly tackle industry's Top 10 new products for 1996, primarily because it flows evenly in both hot and cold weather. UltraFlex Adhesive easily repairs punctures, tears, holes, leaky seams and wear areas, and can be used on neoprene, rubber, felt, vinyl, canvas, leather and nylon. Dubbing Stick dries clear, has just the right tack for delicate jobs, and dabs onto a thread evenly.
See Our Ad Pg. 1

Superior Fly Products
PO Box 1411
Englewood, CO 80150
(800) 732-1947
(303) 788-1947
FAX: (303) 788-0192
Contact: Joe Martinez
The world's foremost supplier of fly & fly line treatments including floatants, leader sink, line cleaner, and fly waterproofers. We also supply a quality line of fly tying products including fly tying kits, head cement, dubbing wax, and a host of fly fishing accessories. Let us be your one stop supplier.

Tite Line Fishing
325 N. Pine
Townsend, MT 59644
(406) 266-3225
Contact: John J. Seidel
Tite Line provides a complete line of fly fishing chemical products to assist fishermen.

U-40 Rod Maintenance
Trondak, Inc.,11710 Airport Rd.
Everett, WA 98204
(800) 878-1492
FAX: (206) 355-9101
Cust. Svc: Matt Hulsey
Rod maintenance products for fishermen who meticulously care for and maintain their rods.

Vitek Research Corporation
251 Roosevelt Dr.
Derby, CT 06418
(203) 735-1813
FAX: (203) 735-1814
Est.: 1968   Staff: 25
Technical Dir: Armand Moscovici
President: Charles Evans
Available: Retail & Direct
A very thin encapsulation service for wet and dry flies, providing superior quality and long life.

ACCESSORIES/ CLIPPER-NIPPER

The Creek Company
PO Box 773892
Steamboat Springs, CO 80477
(800) 843-8454   (970) 879-5221
FAX: (970) 879-7577
President: Christopher Timmerman
Maker of Nip'n Knot™...the consumate streamside tool. Combines a leverless nipper, a guarded needle and a nail knot tyer's tool. Made of stainless steel.

Donnmar Enterprises Inc.
2111 SE Columbia Way, #100
Vancouver, WA 98661
(360) 694-7980 FAX: 7969
Corp. Sales: Dan Madsen
All Checkpoint products feature state-of-the art design and are engineered for years of dependable performance. Made in the U.S.A. Dealer inquiries are welcome. Call for more information.
See Our Ad Pg. 9

Sports Tools
8589 Nevada Ave.
West Hills, CA 91304
(818) 992-5747
FAX: (818) 992-4732
Contact: Barry Kustin
The ultimate clipper is here! Wide-opening resharpenable blades of surgical-grade (420) stainless steel. Easy-to-use front retractable needle cleans hook eyes and untangles leaders; the nail-knot tool easily ties three important knots. Resharpenable, fine-pointed needle guaranteed never to fall out. Made in the U.S.A.

ACCESSORIES/ FLY BOXES

Alexander's
3021 Power Dr.
Kansas City, KS 66106
(913) 236-9565
FAX: (913) 236-9565
Est.: 1977
Contact: Bill Alexander

Angler Sport Group
6619 Oak Orchard Rd.
Elba, NY 14058
(716) 757-9958
FAX: (716) 757-9066
President: Paul Betters
Extensive line of fly boxes, including Wheatley, Danica, Flambeau, Myran, Bonnand, Meiho and other quality products. Wholesale only.

The Box Co.
3462 Summerford Ct.
Marietta, GA 30062
(770) 565-0942
FAX: (770) 565-0942
Est.: 1991   Staff: 3
President: Robin Smyth
Manufacturer, distributor of adjustable, water-resistant, see-through fishing tackle boxes: The Box, The Foam Box, The Half and Half Box.

Cortland Line Co.
3736 Kellogg Rd.
PO Box 5588, Cortland, NY 13045
(607) 756-2851
FAX: (607) 753-8835
Contact: Tom McCullough
Wide variety of fly boxes, fly wallets and fly books. A size and compartment configuration for every type

of fly. Custom printed logos available on many boxes. Call or write for catalog.

DeWitt Plastic
Div. RPM Industries
PO Box 400, 26 Aurelius Ave.
Auburn, NY 13021
(315) 255-1105
FAX: (315) 252-1167

Diamonds & Fly's Ltd.
45 W. 47th St., Suite 501
New York, NY 10036
(888) DIA-FLYS   **(212) 944-2129**
Contact: Frank McNamara
Wheatley hand engraved fly boxes

Flambeau Products Corp.
15981 Valplast Rd.
PO Box 97, Middlefield, OH 44062
(800) 457-5252   **(216) 632-1631**
FAX: (216) 632-1581
Mktg. Coordinator: Steve Baisden
Manufactures and distributes 3
lines of fly boxes: the Mighty Tuff®
Series, Back Country Fly Box Series,
and Streamside Series.

The Fly Trap
by the Waterworks
73 California Ave., Orinda, CA 94563
(800) 435-9374   **(510) 253-1664**
FAX: (510) 253-1665
Contact: Ryan Harrison
The "Fly Trap" is a fully ventilated
lightweight anodized aluminum fly
box.

Fly-Mate®
by Janco, Inc.
PO Box 857, Dover, NH 03821
(603) 742-1581
FAX: (603) 749-0082
President: Andrew Janetos
Fly-Mate® line of molded foam fly
boxes in five convenient sizes for
fresh water and five sizes ("BIG
FLY") for bass, saltwater, etc. These
fly boxes out perform all others–
lightweight, buoyant, consistent
closure and crush resistant. Also, introducing a lightweight, buoyant,
protective eye glass case for the
outdoor enthusiast.

W.W. Grigg Co.
Box 204, Lake Oswego, OR 97034
(503) 636-4901
FAX: (503) 636-8942
Contact: Tom Grigg
Handmade aluminum fly boxes
with precision clear view compartments. Foam pads and stainless steel
sure grip clips. Wholesale only.

 **Mill Stream** ™

Mill Stream
60 Buckley Ave.,
Manchester, NH 03109
(800) 582-7408
(603) 647-4003
FAX: (603) 647-8097
President: Don Dobrowski
Line of accessories, including custom printed fly boxes, ripple foam
fly patches, strike indicators, the
"Fly Pak", replacement foam inserts,
fly tying materials, tackle bags and
much, much more....call or write
for our catalog today.

The Morell Company
315 West St.
Needham Heights, MA 02194
(617) 455-6905
FAX: (617) 455-6905
President: Bradford Voight
Each Morell box is made entirely of
high-tech, multidensity foams. The
result is a very light fly box that
floats and is shatterproof. Call for
more information. Dealer & distributor inquiries welcome.

Perrine Fly Boxes
Distributed by Orbex, Inc.
4444 Ball Rd., NE
Circle Pines, MN 55014
(612) 785-8885
FAX: (612) 785-2255
Offering a variety of fly boxes de-
signed for the serious fisherman.

Plano Molding Co.
431 E. South St., Plano, IL 60545
(708) 552-3111
FAX: (708) 552-9737
Complete line of tackle and stow-
away utility boxes.

Rose Creek Anglers
1946 Tatum St.
Roseville, MN 55113
(612) 647-1860   **(612) 786-5844**
FAX: (612) 636-8944
Contact: Rich Femling or
Dave Oliver
Aluminum "Streamside" Fly Boxes;
Hardwood "Presentation" Fly Boxes;
and Leather D-Ring Net Release

Rubbermaid Specialty Prod.
Box 6000, Wooster, OH 44691
(216) 264-6464
FAX: (216) 287-2298
VP/Sales: Tom Lombardo
VP/Mktg: Pat McCabe

Salt Creek Products
25086 Perch,
Dana Point, CA 92675
(800) 850-0108

Scherer Designs
1309 Arch St.
Berkeley, CA 94708
(510) 849-1703
FAX: (510) 849-1703
Owner: Jim Scherer
Supplier of the 'Tach-It™ Fly Box and
Fly 'n Hook holder. Call for dealer lo-
cations or more information.

 **Scientific Anglers**

3M Scientific Anglers
3M Center-Bldg. 223-4N-05
St. Paul, MN 55144-1000
(800) 525-6290
Scientific Anglers fly boxes–rustproof, lightweight and virtually
indestructible come in small, medium and large sizes with either
flat/ripple or flat/flat foam lining.
The foam lining provides easier fly
selection, and acts as built-in flotation in case you do the
"unthinkable."

Sierra Pacific Products
PO Box 276833
Sacramento, CA 95827
(916) 369-1146
FAX: (916) 369-1564
Est.: 1990   Staff: 9
Owner: Greg Vinci
We specialize in innovative state of
the art fly boxes, fly tackle accesso-
ries, fly tying materials & tools.

Spencer Tackle Inc.
Rt. 1, Box 18, Grafton, IL 62037
(618) 786-3866
FAX: (618) 786-3866
Contact: Don Spencer
Round fly boxes.

Wheatley Fly Boxes
Distributed by Angler Sport Group
6619 Oak Orchard Rd.
Elba, NY 14058
(716) 757-9958
FAX: (716) 757-9066
Sole U.S. distributor of world's fin-
est fly boxes.

ACCESSORIES/
KNOT TYING AIDS

FAS-N-AIDER

Fas-N-aider
Colby's, Inc., 3315 Gran Tara,
Ketchum, OK 74349
(800) 729-5668
FAX: (918) 782-2724
Est.: 1985   Staff: 8
CEO: Duane Colby
Fishermen everywhere are applauding Colby's Fas-N-aider, a unique tool that ties a perfect non-slip knot in monfilament or braided line...in seconds, even without bifoculs! Exclusive funnel design holds most hooks, lures, jigs and helps you thread a hook with ease, even ice-fishing wearing gloves! The Fas-N-aider is ideal for ALL anglers, including children, arthritis sufferers or even people with only one hand. It also has a built-in line cutter. For more information, or to order, phone 800-729-5668.

Koehler Industries
PO Box 265, Harltand, MI 48353
(810) 632-5552
FAX: (810) 632-7186
Contact: Ken or Helen Koehler
Solid brass "Cinch Tie" ties 14 fishing knots. New "Tru-Blood" ties perfect blood knots fast.

LPC Mfg., Inc.
14850 Downey Rd. (M-21)
Capac, MI 48014
(800) 726-3501   (810) 395-9100
FAX: (810) 395-8840
Mktg.: Ted Rusztowicz
Maker of the fishermen's "Knot Tying Tool by Charger", a small, lightweight, stainless steel & delrin tool to tie 16 popular knots, including the True Blood Knot.

Moodus Sports Products
PO Box B, East Haddam, CT 06423
Knot tying tool for fishermen

Quik-Tye
S and S Mfg. & Dist.
111 E. Drake Rd., Suite 7078
Ft. Collins, CO 80525
(800) 766-9034
Contact: Myron Schmidt
Quik Tye Tool is a fast and easy way to thread fishing line through the smallest eyelet of any fishing hook; ties clinch & turle knots too.

J.E. Sherry Co./Pro-Knot
635 Stanford Dr.
San Luis Obispo, CA 93405
(805) 544-3839
(800) 809-0341 Orders Only
FAX: (805) 544-3825
Contact: John Sherry
"Pro-Knot" plastic cards illustrate eight fly-fishing knots. Handy size. Waterproof. Call or write for information.

Sierra Stream & Mountain
PO Box 7693, Chico, CA 95927
(916) 345-4261
FAX: (916) 345-4261
Contact: Ron Lewis
The Tie-Fast Knot Tyer is a one-piece, stainless steel knot tyer–fast, safe, easy, sure. Call or write for more information.

Sports Tools
8589 Nevada Ave.
West Hills, CA 91304
(818) 992-5747
FAX: (818) 992-4732
Contact: Barry Kustin
The ultimate tying tool is here! Wide-opening resharpenable blades of surgical-grade (420) stainless steel. Easy-to-use front retractable needle cleans hook eyes and untangles leaders; the nail-knot tool easily ties three important knots. Resharpenable, fine-pointed needle guaranteed never to fall out. Made in the U.S.A.

TY-RITE
PO Box 4431, Boulder, CO 80306
(303) 442-6846   (303) 443-4030
FAX: (303) 442-2093
Owner: Don Brakhage
Easiest way to get that fly on the line. 2 sizes: TY-RITE SR. & JR. (for midges).

Zipon
101 Riverview Blvd., #C
Great Falls, MT 59404
(406) 453-0126
Contact: Grover R. Austad
Zipon, a "no-knot" fishing system includes Zipon forms for making no-knot flies and streamers. The Zipon connection is stronger than a knot.

Great Gift Idea!
Black's Fly Fishing makes a great gift for your favorite angler! Why not order one now? Call: 800-224-9464 (9am-5pm EST) to order.

ACCESSORIES/
LUGGAGE

Abel
165 Aviador St.
Camarillo, CA 93010
(805) 484-8789
FAX: (805) 482-0701
Est.: 1977   Staff: 40
President: Steve Abel
Sales Mgr: Gina Abel
Abel "Holds Everything" Tackle Bag, 10- and 15-Day Lodge Trip Bags, Wet/Dry Wader Bag, Versi-Pak and Rod Carriers.

BAD Bags
Best American Duffel
2601 Elliott Ave., #4317
Seattle, WA 98121
(800) 424-BAGS   (206) 448-7810
FAX: (206) 448-7422
Contact: Malcolm Vetterlein
Adventure duffel bags–dealer inquiries welcome.

Buck's Bags
2401 W. Main St., Boise, ID 83702
(800) 284-2247   (208) 344-4400
FAX: (208) 344-6244
Est.: 1979   Staff: 60
Contact: Dave Klein
Durable, water resistant wader bag, gear bag, and chest/fanny pack combos.

Cascade Designs, Inc.
4000 1st Ave., South
Seattle, WA 98134
(800) 531-9531
Makers of SealLine® dry bags.

Clear Creek Co., Inc.
15 S. Locust
New Hampton, IA 50659
(800) 894-0483
FAX: (515) 294-2048
Est.: 1991
Contact: Bob Hansen
Attention retailers: Clear Creek manufacturers over 150 different styles of bags for every sport, including soft-sided bags that are great for river and airline travel. Clear Creek specializes in custom work and can put your logo on anything it makes. A great way to advertise your store! Call today for more information.
See Our Ad Pg. 18

D.B. Dun Inc.
2801 W. Idaho, Boise, ID 83702
(208) 344-5445
FAX: (208) 344-4892
Contact: Dan Baumgardner
Component chest and fanny packs
constructed of 600 Denier Polyester
Duck, travel bags, tackle organizer,
and wading bags.

Fieldline
1919 Vineburn Ave.
Los Angeles, CA 90032
(213) 226-0830
FAX: (213) 226-0831
Gen. Mgr: Al Kavalauskas
Complete line of backpack, tackle
bags and fanny packs. Dealer inquiries only. Call for our 6-page color
brochure today.

C.C. Filson
PO Box 34020, Seattle, WA 98124
(800) 624-0201
FAX: (206) 624-4539
Contact: John DePalma

Fly Tech
7450 Whitehall
Ft. Worth, TX 76118
(817) 590-2282
FAX: (817) 590-2053
Est.: 1987   Staff: 23
Sales Mgr: Jesse Shetter
Available: Retail
Waterproof 4mm Neoprene fishing
gear bags. Call for more informa-
tion.

Holland Brothers
190 Napolean St.
San Francisco, CA 94124
(415) 824-5995
FAX: (415) 824-0265
Contact: Tom Sobolewksi
American manufacturer of high
quality leather and canvas travel
bags, hand bags, sporting equipment and accessories.

Leigh Outdoor Products
58 S. 950 West
Brigham City, UT 84302
(801) 734-0750
FAX: (801) 734-0750
Contact: Le Grand Leigh
Fly tyer bags, luggage and rod
cases.

G. Loomis, Inc.
1359 Down River Dr.
PO Box E, Woodland, WA 98674
(800) 662-8818
FAX: (360) 225-7169
Contact: Kris Leistritz
We offer 3 water-resistant travel
bags. Call for more information.

Precision Flyfishing Int'l
14109 Dartmouth Ct.
Fontana, CA 92336
(909) 428-2054
FAX: (909) 428-2058
Est.: 1990
Contact: Bob Montgomery
Superior quality and design, US-
made softgoods: duffle-style
luggage, fly-tying caddy, vest
caddy, net caddy and Tri-folds.

Predator Sporting Equip.
Box 1752, Sanford, ME 04073
(603) 749-0526
Contact: Jim Coury
Predator's Woodsmen Back Pack
System allows you to carry a float
tube, waders, boots, flippers, fishing tackle, sleeping bag, ground
pad, cookware and more—with
room to spare. The only travel bag
you may ever need! Carry it on
your back or like a duffel bag. Extra
heavy duty construction. Made in
the U.S.A.

Sage Tech
8500 NE Day Rd.
Bainbridge Island, WA 98110
(800) 533-3004   (206) 842-6608
FAX: (206) 842-6830
Contact: Bill Dawson
Sage GuideLine luggage, water-
proof tech bags and travel rod cases.

Scott Fly Rod Co.
200 San Miguel River Dr.
PO Box 889
Telluride, CO 81435
(800) 728-7208
FAX: (970) 728-5031
Contact: Todd Field
Satchels, rod cases, duffle bags, fly
reel cases, fly wallets and more in
latigo leather or an abrasion resistant wool. Call or write for more
information.

Sportline USA
3359 Fletcher Dr.
Los Angeles, CA 90065
(213) 255-8185
FAX: (213) 258-2001
Est.: 1979
Contact: John Gramatky
Wader bags, rod and reel cases
and accessories

Wood River Co., Inc.
2960 Saturn St., Suite G
Brea, CA 92821
(800) 897-FISH
(714) 996-5961
FAX: (714) 996-4807
Est.: 1980
Contact: Pete Ross
Maker of premium tackle bags.

ACCESSORIES/
FLY ROD HOLDERS

Blue Water Designs Inc.
205 Cross St.
Bristol, CT 06010
(860) 582-0623
FAX: (860) 585-8133
Contact: Tom Delekta or
Mike Stange
Manufacturer of the Delstang Fly
Rod Holder/Transporter

Indiana Marine Company
PO Box 408
Westfield, IN 46074
(317) 896-9531
FAX: (317) 867-0641
Marketing: Debbie Hamer
The Rod Buckle is a holding system
that's designed to be mounted in-
side the hull of a boat.

Sound Inventions, Inc.
PO Box 6665,
Lynnwood, WA 98036
(800) 338-4889   (206) 672-3328
FAX: (206) 672-3198
Contact: Mike Walker
Rod & net holder–straps securely to
inflatable boats and adapts easily
to solid-hull boats.

Water Otter, Inc.
112 Freeze Lane
Hamilton, MT 59840
(406) 363-2398
FAX: (406) 363-2398
Est.: 1985
Contact: Darryl Osburn
Fly rod holder for float tubes and
pontoon boats.

Among the Missing?
You're entitled to a free listing in Black's Fly Fishing if
you're an equipment sup-
plier (company or
individual)... a qualified fly
fishing school or instructor..or a marketing
oriented lodge, outfitter
or guide.

We've made every effort
to include everyone who
qualifies. But if we've over-
looked you, please let us
know. We'll make certain
that you're listed in our
next annual directory.

ACCESSORIES/
ROD & REEL CASES

Alexander's
3021 Power Dr.
Kansas City, KS 66106
(913) 236-9565
Contact: Bill Alexander

B&L Sport Products
2115 Center Rd.
Clinton, OH 44216
(330) 882-5362
FAX: (330) 882-5362
Contact: Theresa Walker
Offering three rod cases: Zoom-Lok (telescoping); Spin-Top (vented screw cap with security chain); Push-Top (pressure locking cap)—each is made of hi-impact styrene.

Benchmark Co.
179 Knapp Ave.
Clifton, NJ 07011
(201) 779-1389
FAX: (201) 773-2308
Est.: 1984   Staff: 2
Owner: Bruce Hollowich
Brass and aluminum, heavy wall 1 5/8" & 2" with solid brass fittings.

Boulder Landing Rod Case
3728 S. Elm Pl., Suite 532
Broken Arrow, OK 74011
(918) 455-3474
FAX: (918) 451-1802
Est.: 1993
VP: Merrieann Miller

Bridgeport Landing Net Co.
7813 S.E. Luther
Portland, OR 97236
(800) 275-1168   (503) 775-2247

FAX: (503) 775-1081
President: Dave Nelson
Heirloom rod cases featuring brass end caps available in 3 types of wood: figured anigre, tiger oak and bubinga.

Clear Creek Co., Inc.
15 S. Locust, PO Box 182
New Hampton, IA 50659
(800) 894-0483
(515) 394-2048
FAX: (515) 394-4278
Est.: 1991
Contact: Bob Hansen
Attention retailers, custom rod and rod manufacturers: Protect the rods you sell with Clear Creek's crush resistant, foam core, aluminum tubes. High quality at the right price! Private labeling, sewing, embroidery and silk screening also available. Clear Creek specializes in custom work and can put your logo on anything it makes. A great way to advertise your store or product! Call today for more information.
See Our Ad, Left

Country Cobbler Fly Cases
1031 12th St., Cody, WY 82414
(307) 527-6593
Contact: Tom Farnworth
Custom leather fly rod cases

Dart Manufacturing
4012 Bronze Way
Dallas, TX 75237
(800) 345-3278   (214) 333-4221
FAX: (800) 833-3278
President: Sam Kogutt
Custom vinyl and fabric products, including reel cases, fly wallets, and more.

Douglass-Arthur Casemakers
13825 Parks Steed Dr.
Earth City, MO 63045
(800) 846-6533
FAX: (314) 291-5329
Contact: Doug Meyer or James Arthur
The Douglass-Arthur Fly Rod Case is available in a variety of selected hardwoods and features a patent pending closure design that makes certain that this is the most elegant fly rod case on the market.

D.B. Dun Inc.
2801 W. Idaho, Boise, ID 83702
(208) 344-5445
FAX: (208) 344-4892
Est.: 1986
Contact: Dan Baumgardner
Complete line of rod cases with
many options and configurations.
Call for our color brochure today.
Dealer inquiries only.

Flambeau Products Corp.
15981 Valplast Rd.
PO Box 97, Middlefield, OH 44062
(800) 457-5252   (216) 632-1631
FAX: (216) 632-1581
Mkgt. Coordinator: Steve Baisden
Produce and distribute 3 types of
Bazuka™ cases and 3 rod tube
cases.

Fly Tech
7450 Whitehall
Ft. Worth, TX 76118
(817) 590-2282
FAX: (817) 590-2053
Est.: 1987   Staff: 23
Sales Mgr: Jesse Shetter
Available: Retail
Single and double fly rod cases and
padded nylon reel cases. Call for
more information.

Grand Rod & Tackle Co.
645 W. Oak St.
Oak Harbor, WA 98277
(360) 675-0444
FAX: (360) 679-6681
Contact: Craig Dixon

Greenheart Tackle Carriers
F.I. Sherman Company
10810 Hart Lane
Bainbridge Island, WA 98110
(360) 779-1456
FAX: (360) 779-1454
Contact: Donna Green
Greenhart premium fly rod cases.

W.W. Grigg Co.
PO Box 204
Lake Oswego, OR 97034
(503) 636-4901
FAX: (503) 636-8942
Contact: Tom Grigg
Custom made aluminum and
cordura PVC tubes. Wholesale only.

Harding & Sons
PO Box 195, Evergreen Dr.
Idleyld Park, OR 97447
(541) 496-3020
Contact: Etivise Harding
Carrying cases for rods, reel covers,
sports bags.

K.I.S. Rodcase
Dept. AA70, PO Box 618001
Dallas, TX 75261
(800) 747-6952
Est.: 1988   Staff: 20
Director: Magnus Ramsay
K.I.S. Rodcases are heavy-duty, air-
line proof and lock onto car roof
racks. $99.95

Landmark Co.
4350 Ryan Way, #1
Carson City, NV 89706
(800) 796-2626
FAX: (702) 885-9910
Contact: Allen Putnam
Industry's largest selection of rod
cases. Tubing of aluminum (anodized or powder coated), natural
hardwoods or plastic with ends of
aluminum, solid brass or plastic in 1
5/8", 2", 2 1/2" and 3" O.D.s. Custom screen print your logo at low
cost. Reel-on-rod-guard–neoprene
pouch for attaching and protecting
assembled flyrod and reel to rod
tube.

Mark Pack Works
230 Madison St.
Oakland, CA 94607
(510) 452-0243
Contact: Phil Mark
Saltwater tackle bags, rod, reel and
equipment cases.

Arne Mason
125 Wimer St., Ashland, OR 97520
(541) 482-2260
FAX: (541) 482-7785
Contact: Arne Mason
Makers of the finest in traditional
and contemporary hard leather
cases, fly wallets, and reel bags.

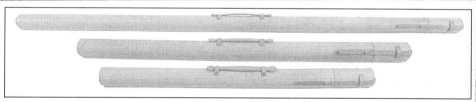

Leather Rod Cases handcrafted from select vegetable tanned hides protect your flyrod(s) in either anodized aluminum or non-metallic impact resistant protective tubing. Available in either a light natural color hide or dark brown hide. Like well traveled luggage, scratches and marks will add to the character of these cases imparting a unique identity through years of service. Hand selected hides, detailed workmanship, solid brass hardware, and nylon stitching create heirloom quality and lifelong protection for your most cherished fly rods. Standard and custom sizing available for single or multiple rods in various diameters and lengths depending upon the angler's needs. All cases are guaranteed against defects in materials and workmanship. Please call or write for pricing and ordering information.

Mills River Trading Company, Inc.

1800 Second Street · Suite 960
Sarasota, FL 34236-5992
941·366· 9331   Fax 941· 365· 6311
– Dealer Inquiries Invited –

Mills River Trading Co.
1800 2nd St., Suite 960
Sarasota, FL 34236-5992
(941) 366-9331
FAX: (941) 365-6311
Est.: 1996   Staff: 6
Contact: Mike Furtick
Leather Rod Cases for single or multiple rods in various lengths and diameters custom sized for the specific needs of discriminating anglers.
See Our Ad Pg.19

RioWest Carvers
PO Box 30592, Billings, MT 59101
(406) 245-8586   FAX: 8586
Contact: Bill Hawkins
Rod-Porter™—a shoulder sling that easily carries n up to 3 rod cases.

Rod Caddy
Bead Tackle, Inc.
600 Main St., Monroe, CT 06468
(203) 459-1213   FAX: 1215
Est.: 1990   Staff: 10
President: Peter H. Renkert
The Reel-On-Rod Caddy is a fleece-lined pouch with zipper access; holds two-piece rods up to nine feet long with reel attached. And, several plastic fly rod cases with lockable flip-tops.

Sack-Ups
Div. of Norco Textiles, Inc.
1611 Jamestown Rd.
Morgan, NC 28655
(704) 584-4579
Sales Mgr: Warren Norman

Sporting Specialties
Box 4405, Sunland, CA 91041
(818) 353-4035
Contact: Barry or Denis
Hardwood fly rod and reel cases. Also custom built fly rods.

Wachter Landing Nets
10238 Deermont Trail
Dallas, TX 75243
(214) 238-0823
FAX: (214) 238-1641   Est.: 1986
Contact: Kathy Wachter
Rod holders in solid cherry or oak hold 10 rod cases up to 2 1/2" in diameter.

Wind River
3982 Rolfe Ct.
Wheatridge, CO 80033
(303) 378-7287
FAX: (303) 420-1522
Est.: 1993   Staff: 4
Fleece reel bag, fish print rod bags.

World Gear, Inc.
24908 W. Fox Trail
Lake Villa, IL 60046
(708) 356-9885
FAX: (708) 356-9886
President: Julie Forster
Rod case accessory belt and non-spillable, floatable gear bags.

ACCESSORIES/ SUNSCREEN/INSECT PROTECTION

The ALL TERRAIN Co.
315 First St., Suite U-274
Encinitas, CA 92024
(619) 944-8507
FAX: (619) 944-6731
Contact: John Wheatley
ALL TERRAIN™ COMPLETE OUTDOOR PROTECTION™ is an all-in-one insect repellent, sunscreen and moisturizer. ALL TERRAIN™ HERBAL OUTDOOR PROTECTION™ is a moisturizing insect repellent without sunscreen. Other products available soon.

"Buzzoff" Outdoor Wear
Maryed Int'l., Inc.
5045 Lake Blvd.
Delray Beach, FL 33484
(561) 495-8258
FAX: (561) 499-5633
Contact: Mary L. Baltes
Clothing offering cool, comfortable, non-toxic protection from biting and stinging insects.

Dermatone Laboratories, Inc.
80 King Spring Rd.
Windsor Locks, CT 06096
(860) 292-1311
FAX: (860) 292-1459
Manager: Ingrid Friedman
Outdoor skin protection (regular scented, fragrance free, citronella scent (deet free) creams, waterfree ointment, sprays, zinc oxide/titanium oxide product that goes on clear. Sun protection factors from 10 to 33.

Shannon Outdoors, Inc.
Rt. 3, Box 77
Winnsboro, SC 29180
(800) 852-8058   (803) 635-3482
FAX: (803) 635-3265
Sales Mgrs: Ken or Marilyn Shannon
Bug Tamer™ parka, pants and mittens provide total protection against biting insects.

Shoo-Bug Insect Repellent Garments
Palsa Outdoor Products
PO Box 81336
Lincoln, NE 68501-1336
(888) SHO-OBUG
(402) 488-5288
FAX: (402) 488-2321
President: Bill Harder, Jr.
VP/Sales: Ray Clatanoff
Lightweight and easy to wear, ShooBug jackets, pants and head nets with Space Shield II ™ Repellent offers guaranteed protection for up to 1000 hours! Garments last for years and can be recharged with repellent. Field tested by the U.S. Armed Forces. Call for more information and to order.

SmartShield™
Skin Research Labs, Inc.
12800 Hillcrest, Suite 103
Dallas, TX 75230
(800) 343-1504
FAX: (800) 431-1568
Contact: Brad Bierman or Jim Astaff
Maker of non-oily, easy-to-apply, premium sunscreen designed for the sportsman.

Straight Arrow
2020 Highland Ave.
Bethlehem, PA 18017
(800) 827-9815
FAX: (610) 882-9688
Media Relations: Devon Katzev
Manufacturer of Body Guard personal insect repellent.

Sun Rise Distribution Co.
46 Lindstrom Ct.
Manchester, NH 03104
(603) 641-2800
FAX: (800) 829-9272
Contact: Ray Scott
Distributors of a complete line of bug protection products: bug caps, bug nets, bug baffler shirts, pants & ankle guards.

ASSOCIATIONS

The interests of America's sportsmen and sportswomen are served by a great number of associations and organizations. You will find valuable information about the largest and most influential of these groups in the four sections that follow:

ASSOCIATIONS/ CONSERVATION

American Fisheries Society
5410 Grosvenor, Suite 110
Bethesda, MD 20814-2199
(301) 897-8616
FAX: (301) 897-8096
Est.: 1870
Members: 8,500
Exec. Dir: Paul Brouha
A professional society to promote the conservation, development and wise utilization of fisheries, both recreational and commercial.

American Rivers
1025 Vermont Ave., NW
Suite 720, Washington, DC 20005
(202) 547-6900
FAX: (202) 347-9240
President: Rebecca Wodder
American Rivers is the nation's leading river conservation organization. Our mission is to protect and restore America's river systems and foster a river stewardship ethic in the United States.

American Sportfishing Assn.
1033 N. Fairfax St., #200
Alexandria, VA 22314
(703) 519-9691
FAX: (703) 519-1872
President/CEO: Michael Hayden
The American Sportfishing Association is a nonprofit industry association dedicated to ensuring healthy and sustainable fisheries resources, increasing sportfishing participation and providing valuable services to its members. In addition to ASA's strong government affairs efforts in Washington, DC, and across the nation, ASA members

and staff fulfill the association's mission through the Future Fisherman Foundation, an educational component; FishAmerica Foundation, a grassroots conservation projects component; and the ASA Fund, a component to assist in the funding of recreational fisheries research and management.

American Wildlands, Inc.
40 E. Main St., #2
Bozeman, MT 59715
(406) 586-8175
FAX: (406) 586-8242
Contact: Jeff Larmer
Non-profit conservation organization dedicated to efforts to ensure sportfishing, protection and restoration of fish habitat in the No. Rockies.

Anglers for Clean Waters
PO Box 17900
Montgomery, AL 36141
(334) 272-9530
FAX: (334) 279-7148
VP & Conservation Dir: Bruce Shupp
A non-profit organization dedicated to the stewardship of America's aquatic resources.

Atlantic Salmon Federation
PO Box 807, Calais, ME 04619
(506) 529-4581
FAX: (506) 529-4438
Members: 5,000
President: Bill Taylor
VP/Development: John Cameron
An international, non-profit organization consisting of members dedicated to promoting the conservation and wise management of the Atlantic Salmon and its environment.

Atlantic States Marine Fisheries Commission
1444 Eye St., NW, 6th Fl.
Washington, DC 20005
(202) 289-6400
FAX: (202) 289-6051
Info. Officer: Tina Berger
Coordinator: Richard Christian
ASMFC works at improving Atlantic coastal fisheries conservation and management.

California Trout
870 Market St., #859
San Francisco, CA 94102
(415) 392-8887
FAX: (415) 392-8895
Est.: 1971
California Trout is a statewide organization of anglers and conservationists who believe the survival of wild trout is a matter of personal responsibility.

Catch & Release Foundation
10 A Midway Lane
Pound Ridge, NY 10576
(800) 63-CATCH (914) 764-9655
FAX: (914) 764-1515
President: Paul Carpenter
Exec. Dir: Kyler Cragnolin
Board Advisor: Vin T. Sparano
A non-profit organization that was created to promote and preserve the sport of fishing throughout the United States. The Foundation serves to advise, educate and develop support for research and management programs designed to conserve and improve our aquatic resources.

Coastal Conservation Association (CCA-ME)
PO Box 239, Freeport, ME 04032
(207) 865-0396
Our primary mission is to restore and protect our marine resources and preserve recreational saltwater fishing now and for future generations.

Congressional Sportsmen's Foundation
1730 K St., NW, Suite 1300
Washington, DC 20006
(202) 785-9153
FAX: (202) 785-9155
Est.: 1989
Chairman: David B. Rockland, Ph.D.
President: G.J. Thomas Sadler, Jr.
The Congressional Sportsmen's Foundation is dedicated to "preserving and promoting our nation's outdoor heritage, in particular sport hunting and angling." The Foundation's programs closely parallel those of the Congressional Sportsmen's Caucus which is comprised of more than 40 percent of the U.S. Congress. Referred to as "the sportsmen's link to Congress," the Foundation works to ensure that sportsmen have a strong voice in the Nation's capital. The CSF is supported through membership dues.
See Our Ad Pg. 23

FFF Steelhead Committee
16430 72nd Ave. W.
Edmonds, WA 98206
(206) 742-4651
FAX: (206) 745-9478
Contact: Pete Soverel

The Federation of Fly Fishers.

Federation of Fly Fishers
502 S. 19th, Suite 1
PO Box 1595, Bozeman, MT 59771
(406) 585-7592
FAX: (406) 585-7596
Est.: 1965   Staff: 4
Members: 10,500
President: Tom Jindra
An international non-profit organization dedicated to conservation, restoration, and education through fly fishing.

Fish Unlimited
Box 1073, 1 Brander Pkwy.
Shelter Island, NY 11965
(516) 749-FISH
FAX: (516) 749-3476
Est.: 1989
Prog. Dir.: Mark Ketcham
Exec. Dir.: Bill Smith
National clean water/fisheries conservation group.

FishAmerica Foundation
1033 N. Fairfax St., #200
Alexandria, VA 22314
(703) 548-6338
FAX: (703) 519-1872
Pres/COB: Jim Hubbard
Treasurer: Andrew Loftus
The FishAmerica Foundation provides funding for community-based projects which directly improve fish populations and water quality. Since 1983, FishAmerica has assisted over 400 groups in North America to complete such hands-on projects as stream habitat improvement, sediment control, construction of marine and freshwater artificial reefs, fish stocking, hatchery construction and shoreline stabilization. Projects must be reviewed and endorsed by state natural resources agencies and be conducted by nonprofit, volunteer based organizations. FishAmerica is a 501(c)3 organization supported through a broad spectrum of environmentally concerned companies and individuals and is the conservation projects arm of the American Sportfishing Association.

Pass on the tradition.

Fly Fisher Apprentice Program
407 W. Seneca St.,
Ithaca, NY 14850
(607) 272-0002
FAX: (607) 272-7088
Exec. Dir: Phil Genova
Youth fly fishing and natural resources education.
Mission statement: "to identify, encourage and educate the future stewards of our resources through fly fishing." As a not-for-profit educational organization, FAP has broadened, popularized and redefined the role of fly fishing in natural resources education. We combine the educational, conservation and fly fishing communities into a unique collaboration that benefits our sport, our resources and our youngsters. "Absolutely the finest, most effective youth fly fishing program I have every witnessed", Gary LaFontaine. FAP relies on private and corporate funding sources. Inquries welcomed.

Future Fisherman Foundation
1033 N. Fairfax St., #200
Alexandria, VA 22314
(703) 519-9691
FAX: (703) 519-1872
The Future Fisherman Foundation is a 501(c)3 non-profit organization formed to promote participation and education in fishing and is the educational arm of the American Sportfishing Association. Future Fisherman provides leadership in the area of sport fishing and aquatic resource education and co-ordinates the popular "Hooked On Fishing - Not On Drugs" program that combines drug prevention, environmental education and fishing into a powerful package. Instructor and student manuals, videos and other support material on the subjects of sport fishing, aquatic resource education, and "Hooked On Fishing - Not On Drugs" are available through Future Fisherman.

The Theodore Gordon Flyfishers Inc.
PO Box 978, Murray Hill Station
New York, NY 10156-0603
FAX: (516) 766-3864

Est.: 1962
Pres.: Stanley Bryer
Membership: Walter Kaufman
Coordinator: Barbara Lituchy
TGF is a local, northeastern, conservation and flyfishing organization dedicated to protect the fine fishing waters in the Northeast.

International Association of Fish & Wildlife Agencies
444 N. Capitol St., NW
Suite 544, Washington, DC 20001
(202) 624-7890
FAX: (202) 624-7891
Est.: 1902   Staff: 12
Members: 450
Exec. VP: R. Max Peterson

International Game Fish Association (IGFA)
1301 E. Atlantic Blvd.
Pompano Beach, FL 33060
(954) 941-3474
FAX: (954) 941-5868
A non-profit organization which maintains and promotes ethical international angling regulations and compiles world game fish records for saltwater, freshwater and fly fishing. We certify record catches and scales. In 1981, flyrod-record tippet classes were standardized at: 1kg/2-lb, 2kg/4-lb, 3kg/6-lb, 4kg/8-lb, 6kg/12-lb and 8kg/16-lb. And in April 1991, the IGFA officially ratified a 10kg/20-lb tippet class.

International Women's Fishing Assoc. (IWFA)
PO Drawer 3125
Palm Beach, FL 33480
Members: 260
An association for sportfisherwomen that promotes angling competition among women anglers; encourages conservation; and fosters fishing tournaments of all kinds.

National Fish and Wildlife Foundation
1120 Connecticut Ave., NW
Suite 900, Washington, DC 20036
(202) 857-0166
FAX: (202) 857-0162
Exec. Dir: Amos Eno
A national non-profit organization whose resources are dedicated to making investments in nature by funding conservation projects.

National Forest Foundation
1099 14th St., NW
Suite 5600 W
Washington, DC 20005-3419
(202) 501-2473
FAX: (202) 219-6585
Est.: 1993

Chairman: Grant Gregory
President: J. Lamar Beasley
VP/Mktg. Dev. Events: Terry Austin

New England Salmon Association (NESA)

33 Bedford St.,
Lexington, MA 02173
(617) 862-0941
FAX: (617) 862-0952
Est.: 1983
Pres: Andrew V. Stout
NESA is a non-profit conservation organization dedicated to the restoration and conservation of wild Atlantic salmon back to their native New England Rivers.

No. American Fishing Club

PO Box 3405
Minnetonka, MN 55343
(612) 936-9333
FAX: (612) 936-9755
Est.: 1988
President: Steve Burke
NAFC is dedicated to helping serious fishermen increase their fishing skills and enjoyment.

Salmon Unlimited

4548 N. Milwaukee Ave.
Chicago, IL 60630
(773) 736-5757
FAX: (773) 736-8900
Est.: 1971
President: John Ohl
President Emeritus: Cass Sliwa
Members: 1,000
SU works to preserve and improve salmon and trout sportfishing on the Great Lakes, especially Michigan.

Steelhead Society of BC

240-1140 Austin Ave., Coquitlam
British Columbia, Canada V3K 3P5
(604) 931-8288
FAX: (604) 931-5074
Exec. Dir: Craig Orr
Join the Steelhead Society of BC and help protect, enhance and restore British Columbia's wild salmon and salmon habitat.

Trout Unlimited

1500 Wilson Blvd., #310
Arlington, VA 22209
(703) 522-0200
FAX: (703) 284-9400
Est.: 1959   Staff: 22
Chapter System: 470
Members: 95,000
President/CEO: Charles Gauvin
America's leading trout and salmon conservation organization, dedicated to conserving, protecting and restoring coldwater fisheries and their watersheds.

Trout Unlimited-Canada

PO Box 6270, Station D
Calgary, Alberta, Canada T2P 2C8
(403) 221-8360
FAX: (403) 221-8368
Managing Dir: Greg Shyba

U.S. Fish & Wildlife Service

PO Box 25486, Denver, CO 80225
(303) 236-7905
FAX: (303) 236-3815
Contact: Sharon Rose

United Fly Tyers, Inc.

PO Box 2478, Woburn, MA 01888
V.P. Membership: Robert Fownes
The United Fly Tyers Inc. has developed into an international non-profit organization spanning the United States, Canada, and 27 other countries. The "Roundtable" Magazine is respected as a publication devoted to the fly tyer's art, the people who developed the craft, and serves those who carry on the tradition. At monthly meetings, top name speakers and free fly tying instruction are featured.

Izaak Walton Fly Fisherman's Club

2400 Dundas St., Unit 6
Suite 283, Mississauga, Ontario
Canada L5K 2R8
(905) 855-5420
President: Ken Geddes

Izaak Walton League of America

707 Conservation Lane
Gaithersburg, MD 20878-2983
(301) 548-0150
FAX: (301) 548-0146
Est.: 1922   Staff: 27
Members: 40,000
Exec. Dir: Paul Hansen
Promotes the means and opportunities for educating the public to conserve, maintain, protect and restore our natural resources and the enjoyment and sustainable utilization of those resources.

Washington Trout

PO Box 402, Duvall, WA 98019
(206) 788-1167
FAX: (206) 788-9634
Est.: 1988
Exec. Dir: Kurt Beardslee
Washington Trout is a statewide, non-profit charitable and educational organization whose mission is to preserve, protect and restore Washington's wild fish and their habitats.

ASSOCIATIONS/ GUIDES & OUTFITTERS

Coastal Guides Association

Box 288, Island Heights, NJ 08732
(908) 929-9419
FAX: (908) 929-9419
Contact: Capt. Mike Corblies
National network for guides to address issues concerning guides. Public referral system is also available.

National Association of Fly-Fishing Guides

101 Hathaway Rd.
DeWitt, NY 13214
(315) 446-2624
FAX: (315) 446-2624
Founder: Jason P. LaManna
The National Association of Fly-Fishing Guides was established in late 1995 to promote professionalism in the rapidly expanding fly-fishing guide trade.

New Brunswick Outfitters Association

PO Box 74, Woodstock, New Brunswick
Canada E0B 2B0
(800) 215-2075
(506) 272-1091
FAX: (506) 444-6487
Est.: 1959
Contact: Leah Shaw
More than 30 quality fishing and hunting outfitters—Outdoor adventures are our specialty.

Newfoundland Outfitters' Association

PO Box 2430, Station C
St. John, A1C 6E7 Canada

ASSOCIATIONS/ MUSEUMS

American Museum of Fly Fishing

PO Box 42, Manchester, VT 05254
(802) 362-3300
FAX: (802) 362-3308
Est.: 1968
Exec. Dir: Craig Gilborn
A nonprofit museum to preserve and exhibit the treasures of American angling. Winter hours are M-F, 10-3; Summer hours are 7 days/week, 10-4.

Catskill Fly Fishing Center and Museum

PO Box 1295,

Livington Manor, NY 12758
(914) 439-4810
FAX: (914) 439-3387
Est.: 1981
Museum Dir: Lisa M. Lyons
A non-profit organization to preserve the heritage, enhance the present and protect the future of the sport of fly fishing. New museum and a variety of educational and recreational programs year-round.

Int'l Fly Fishing Center
215 East Lewis,
Livington, MT 59047
(406) 222-9369
Est.: 1996
Director: Bob Wiltshire
Email: iffc@alpinet.net
Operated by the Federation of Fly Fishers, the IFFH functions as a visitor and education center as well as a resource center.

The National Fresh Water Fishing Hall of Fame
Box 33, Hall of Fame Dr.
Hayward, WI 54843
(715) 634-4440
Dir: Ted Dzialo
The Fishing Hall of Fame is a public supported educational museum dedicated to the portrayal and conservation of the historic and contemporary aspects of freshwater sport fishing and its participants.

ASSOCIATIONS/
TRADE

The American Casting Association (ACA)
1773 Lance End Lane
Fenton, MO 63026
(314) 225-9443
Exec. Secretary: Dale Lanser
Members: 1,500
The ACA is the control organization for competitive casting in the USA. Its primary purpose is to sponsor and promote casting competition for distance and accuracy on the local, regional and national levels. Four kinds of tackle are covered: spinning, spin-casting, bait-casting and fly-casting; in all but some of the distance events, standard fishing tackle is used.

American Sportfishing Association (ASA)
1033 N. Fairfax St., #200
Alexandria, VA 22314
(703) 519-9691

FAX: (703) 519-1872
President/CEO: Michael Hayden
See our listing under "Conservation Associations."

European Fishing Tackle Trade Association (EFTTA)
Forde House, 51 Cloth Fair
London, EC1A 7JQ, England
011-44-171-606-0555
FAX:: 011-44-171-606-0226
Contact: Caroline Thomas
Public Relations Mgr: Nimrat Bains
Organizer of EFTTEX trade show, publishes International Fishing Tackle Trade Handbook and Fishing Dictionary. Represents European manufacturers and wholesalers.

International Float Tube Associationn (IFTA)
PO Box 80010
Rancho Santa Margarita, CA 92688
(714) 888-5859   FAX: 7000
Contact: Todd Schiedow
The IFTA is your connection to the float tubing world–we are the only club specifically designed for the float tube enthusiast. Call for membership information.

North American Fly Tackle Trade Association (NAFTA)
PO Box 248, Eugene, OR 97440
(541) 485-5373
FAX: (541) 345-2977
Administrator: Jerry Wiant

Outdoor Writers Assn. of America (OWAA)
2017 Cato Ave., #101
State College, PA 16801-2768
(814) 234-1011
Est.: 1927   Staff: 5
Exec. Dir: James W. Rainey
Public. Editor: Carol J. Kersavage
Members: 2,000

RodCrafters
C.T. Building, 444 Schantz Rd.
Allentown, PA 18104
Contact: Dale Clemens or
Rodcrafters is an international association of custom rod builders whose purpose is to improve the development of their craft through sharing. These methods all originate with other Associates, and come to you in the easily readable bi-monthly RodCrafters Journal.

Saltwater Flats Fishing Association (SFFA)
6786 Brentford Rd.
Sarasota, FL 34241-5705
(941) 379-4446
FAX: (941) 342-3492
Contact: Bob Nies
Flatsmaster Magazine published 8

times in 1997; 33 tournaments scheduled for '97–each has a fly fishing division.

The Sportfishing Promotion Council (SPC)
1033 N. Fairfax St., #200
Alexandria, VA 22314
(703) 519-9691 FAX: 1872
VP: Joe Kuti
The Sportfishing Promotion Council (SPC) is the marketing arm of the American Sportfishing Association. Two marketing programs the SPC manages are the Fishing Tackle Loaner Program and 1-800-ASK-FISH. The 1-800-ASK-FISH program offers FREE information to callers anywhere in the continental U.S. on where to fish, where to buy a license, where to launch a boat, handicap access sites and additional information regarding fishing. The other marketing program is the Loaner Program, which is also FREE. This program loans fishing equipment to anyone visiting a participating public library and/or parks & recreation department. The loaner program gives people the opportunity to experience the joys of fishing without initially investing into the sport. The goal of the program is to reach inner city settings, single-parent families, young children and their families and provide them with the necessary equipment to go fishing. This program truly exemplifies the effectiveness of a "true" working partnership. Partners involved with this program are the State Fish and Game Agency, Libraries, Parks & Recreation Departments, local Retailers and Civic Organizations.

Tackle/Shooting Sports Agents Association (TSSA)
1033 N. Fairfax St., #200
Alexandria, VA 22314
(703) 684-3202
President: Bill Cullerton, Jr.
Coordinator: Andy Martin
The Tackle/Shooting Sports Agents Association was founded in 1953 as the national trade association for independent manufacturers' rep agencies in the fishing tackle industry. Expanded in 1986 to include the shooting sports industry, the TSSA is composed of the leading agencies in the outdoor sporting goods market. Every member adheres to a strict Code of Ethics and has many years of experience selling in the fishing tackle/shooting sports industries.

BOATS & FLOATS/ DRIFT BOATS

Clacka Craft River Boats
13111 SE Hwy. 212
Clackamas, OR 97015
(800) 394-1345
FAX: (503) 657-4631
Est.: 1976   Staff: 10
Sales Mgr: Rick Atwood
Fiberglass drift boats and accessories—endorsed by guide schools and fishermen. Call for more information.

Clavey River Equipment
PO Box 180, 607 Second St.
Petaluma, CA 94953
(707) 766-8070
FAX: (707) 766-8072
Est.: 1983   Staff: 2
Contact: Tom Meckfessel
Supplier of the Avon Drifter and Pole Cat.

Fish-Rite, Inc.
1419 Justice Rd.
Central Point, OR 97502
(800) 575-2243   (503) 776-0621
FAX: (503) 776-3879
Contact: Mike Snow
Aluminum drift boats.

Ken Hankinson Associates
Box 272, Hayden Lake, ID 83835
(208) 772-5547
Contact: Ken Hankinson
Selection of wood & aluminum "build-yourself" driftboats.

Don Hill Riverboats
6690 Main St., PO Box CC
Springfield, OR 97477
(800) 878-5488 (541) 747-7430
FAX: (541) 747-7474
Contact: Don Hill
Custom wood, aluminum and fiberglass drift boats. Plans, kits and accessories and training.
See Our Ad Across

Hyde Drift Boats
1520 Pancheri Dr.
Idaho Falls, ID 83402
(800) 444-4933
(208) 529-4343
FAX: (208) 529-4397
Est.: 1981   Staff: 25
Contact: LaMoyne or Steve Hyde
Hyde Drift Boats—aluminum, fiber-

glass boats. Fly shop and outfitter at the North Fork & South Fork Snake River, Teton River & Yellowstone National Park.

Lavro, Inc.
16311 177 Ave., SE
Monroe, WA 98272
(888) 337-2980   (360) 794-5525
FAX: (360) 805-9277
Est.: 1973
Contact: Ron Lavigueure
Available: Retail & Direct
Lavro manufactures 14', 15', 16' & 18' drift boats. Highest quality, outstanding workmanship that surpasses all others for over 25 years. Excellent dealer program available U.S. & Canada for stocking & non-stocking shops.

Osprey Drift Boats
121 Andrea Dr., Bruce Industrial Pk.
Belgrade, MT 59714
(800) 428-9510   (406) 388-0077
FAX: (406) 388-7430
Contact: Carl Seelhoff
The design and quality of Osprey Drift Boats makes rowing less effortless and the boat more maneuverable. To meet customer demands, our 96 line will include a 16' Outfitter model, a 15' Prodrifter model and a 13' Daydrifter model. All models have high quality fiberglass construction. All our boats are lightweight, durable, beautiful and very functional. All inclusive pricing. Call for our free brochure.

Ray's River Dories
PO Box 19954
Portland, OR 97280-0954
(503) 244-3608
Est.: 1975
Contact: Cyrus Happy or Ray Heater
Wood-expoxy drift boats and easy to build boat kits in lengths from 8' to 18'. Builders of Oregon's original McKenzie river boat. Call or write for brochure.

Greg Tatman
Wooden Boats
1075 Clearwater Ln.
Springfield, OR 97478
(541) 746-5287
FAX: (541) 744-2190
Contact: Greg Tatman
Small wooden boats, boat kits and accessories for fishermen. Call or write for catalog and website address.

Willie Boats
1440 Justice Rd.
Central Point, OR 97502
(541) 779-4141

FAX: (541) 779-9346
Contact: Willie Illingworth
Aluminum drift boats.

Woodward Rangeley Boats
4544 6th Ave.,
St. Augustine, FL 32095
(904) 824-0642
FAX: (904) 824-7954
Contact: Richard Woodward
Seventeen foot, hand-made, Rangeley boat, constructed of a wood-glass-epoxy composite, specifically built for fly fishing in lakes or rivers. Call or write for more information.

BOATS & FLOATS/ FLOATS

Angler's Edge Kikkboat
3926 Westheimer,
Houston, TX 77027
(713) 993-9981
Contact: Brooks Bouldin

Anglers Craft Boat Builders
408 Prince St.,
Alexandria, VA 22314
(703) 549-6648
FAX: (703) 549-6649
Est.: 1995
President: Larry Hammick
Traditional mahogany fly fishing skiff

Boatman
6325 Borg Circle,
Ogden, UT 84403
(801) 479-3451 FAX: 3451
Contact: Bryan Redd
Boatman-the original open-frame, inflatable pontoon catcraft design. All models feature "no-tools-needed" assembly. Airline and bush plane friendly. Modular frame design allows custom configurations and your choice between the compact "Skiffer" for still water, the River Boatman for heavy fast water and steelhead fishing, the convertible Tandem Boatman, or for the long trip—Alaskan Boatman. All "For Your Fishing Freedom."

Browning Fishing
PO Box 270, Tulsa, OK 74115
(918) 831-6857
FAX: (918) 831-6938
President: Larry McIsaacs
Product Mgr: Andy Carroll
Browning offers a complete line of fishing tackle and accessories; including fly rods and fly reels–fly to baitcast to spinning; accessories–float tubes to waders, wading shoes to tackle systems.

Rowing a Drift Boat

Fly fishing from a well handled drift boat is a pleasure. But maneuvering one can be a challenge for the uninitiated. It's strenuous, so good physical condition is a "must." And experts suggest you master the skill in easy stages, preferably working with an experienced rower, and always exercising common sense. White water, they say, is no place for a beginner. Spend a season or two in slow waters before you row in fast ones.

Because even placid waters can present an unexpected rock or tree, avoidance of hazards is one of drift boating's fundamental concepts. It's accomplished by pointing your bow directly at the hazard and rowing backward. Once you have this skill in hand, the potential for trouble is greatly reduced.

Drift boating involves two basic strokes, straight backward for movement and speed control, and a cross stroke for positioning your craft. The backward stroke—used 95% of the time—calls for rolling your wrists slightly to pitch the top of the blades slightly forward, the bottoms slightly back. The trickier cross stroke is a simultaneous push and pull with the oars. Feathering is the use of very flat strokes in shallow waters. A lift stroke is used to gain maximum reduction in speed or to stop. It consists of digging your oars deep, then lifting the blades back and up.

Other tips from veteran drift boaters: Approach banks stern first; step out of the boat on the bank side; never drop anchor in a heavy current; use your anchor on shore when you beach your boat; and when you're rowing while fishing, make minor oar adjustments to keep the boat steady and parallel to the bank.

Buck's Bags
2401 W. Main St., Boise, ID 83702
(800) 284-2247   (208) 344-4400
FAX: (208) 344-6244
Est.: 1979   Staff: 60
Contact: Dave Klein
Quality float tubes and pontoon boats, fly fishing accessories and travel bags. Call /write for brochure.

Bullfrog Kick Boats
PO Box 9007, Nampa, ID 83652
(208) 463-8930
Contact: Marianne Baker
Our innovative features make our kickboats the most advanced, stylish and comfortable to fish in the industry. Four models available in a variety of colors. Call for a current price guide and color brochure.

Caddis Manufacturing Inc.
3120 N. Hwy. 99W
McMinnville, OR 97128
(800) 422-3347   (503) 472-3111
FAX: (503) 434-5038
Manufacturers of pontoon float boats and related equipment.

Clearwater Angler
620 Auburn Way, S., Suite J
Auburn, WA 98002
(206) 939-1484
FAX: (206) 939-1484
Est.: 1991
Contact: Brian Steele
Maker of the Super Cat, an innovative design that turns a back pack into a pontoon boat in minutes.

The Creek Company
PO Box 773892
Steamboat Springs, CO 80477
(800) 843-8454   (970) 879-5221
FAX: (970) 879-7577
Contact: Chris Timmerman
Maker of the original open-front float tube. The patented U-Boat® design positions the angler higher in the water. Guaranteed for life.

Fenwick Corp.
5242 Argosy Dr.
Huntington Beach, CA 92649
(714) 897-1066 Ext. 226
Contact: Dale Barnes
The Fenwick V-Hull Float Tube is radically different and proven better. It's stable, easy to launch, and stays on point...even in strong head winds. Built tough with an outer shell of 420 denier urethane-coated packcloth, it carries an ample 250 lbs.

The Fishing Cat
Fisheries West, Inc.
PO Box 7224, Boise, ID 83707
(800) 380-1991
FAX: (208) 344-6159
Est.: 1986
President: Barry Ross
VP: Mike Ross
Maker of inflatable catarafts, for use in up to Class II white water, fully adjustable frame.

Fly Tech
7450 Whitehall
Ft. Worth, TX 76118
(800) 590-2281
FAX: (817) 590-2053
Est.: 1987   Staff: 23
Sales Mgr: Jesse Shetter
Available: Retail
Offering two styles of float tubes– the Semi "V" 1000 and the Expert 1010. Call for pricing and information.
See Our Ad, Left

Gliderider
Wood River Co., Inc.
2960 Saturn St., Suite G
Brea, CA 92621
(800) 897-FISH   (714) 996-5961
FAX: (714) 996-4807
Est.: 1980
Contact: Greg Ross
Maker of the V shaped Gliderider™, a float tube with a patented design that allows it to slip through wind and waves with "stealth-like performance." Call for information or local dealers.

Hobie Outback
4925 Oceanside Blvd.
Oceanside, CA 92056
(619) 758-9100 Ext. 404
FAX: (619) 758-1841
Contact: Bill Horner

J.W. Outfitters
169 Balboa St.
San Marcos, CA 92069
(619) 471-2171
FAX: (619) 471-1719
Contact: Jeff Wieringa
Pontoon boats, float tubes and fly fishing accessories for the discriminating angler. Free brochure.

Jack's Plastic Welding
115 South Main Ave.
Aztec, NM 87410
(505) 334-8748
FAX: (505) 334-1901
Est.: 1982
Contact: Jack Kloepfer
Inflatable pontoon kayaks used primarily to get into rough, backcountry streams.

Kingfisher, Inc.
PO Box 1085, Sandpoint, ID 83864
(800) 726-3254
Contact: Ray Pelland
Maker of inflatable fishing products.

Leigh Outdoor Products
58 S. 950 West,
Brigham City, UT 84302
(801) 734-0750
FAX: (801) 734-0750
Est.: 1983
Contact: LeGrand Leigh
Maker of two float tubes; the Whisper, an open front tube for easy entry and exit, and the Roundabout, a round tube. Also available, a line of inflatable pontoon boats.

Outcast Sporting Gear
PO Box 3401, Boise, ID 83703
(208) 343-3281
FAX: (208) 345-1856
Est.: 1994
Contact: Jim Dean
The "most technologically advanced fishing inflatables available anywhere." 10 year warranty. Call for information.

Outdoor Engineering Inc.
4218 Iris Ave., Morgan, UT 84050
(800) 568-8366   (801) 876-3127
FAX: (801) 876-2419
Est.: 1993
Contact: Randell Heath
Providing high tech solutions to your fishing and hunting needs since 1993. Call for information on Versa-Vessel™ Kickboats and Mountain Master™ Fanny Pack Systems.

Outdoor Water Sports, Inc.
PO Box 5043, Missoula, MT 59806
(800) 239-7238   (406) 251-3337
FAX: (406) 251-3338
Contact: Hugh Frame
The world's finest kick boat, versatile and practical, one person floatation raft. Ideal for fishing, hunting, diving and general recreation. We also manufacture Water Master power hex fins, easy attach in 10 seconds and they float.

Predator Sporting Equip.
PO Box 1752, Sanford, ME 04073
(603) 749-0526
FAX: (603) 749-7112
Contact: Jim Coury
Makers of the Kodiak Float Tube. Our float tubes will carry up to 350+ pounds. THEY HOLD THE LOAD. All Predator products come with a full lifetime warranty. See our other listings.

Quiet Sport
26330 NE Kennedy Dr.
PO Box 1600, Duvall, WA 98019
(800) 243-0688
(206) 788-4481
President: Jerry S. Baker

Sea Eagle
Harrison Hoge Industries, Inc.
200 Wilson St.
Port Jefferson Station, NY 11776
(516) 473-7308
FAX: (516) 473-7398
President: Cecil Hoge, Jr.
Sales: Thomas McSwane
Inflatable boat, with a floorboard, which takes a small electric motor for use in all types of water.

Stillwater Fishing Systems
PO Box 506, Arvada, CO 80001
(800) 950-0197   (801) 269-0197
FAX: (801) 262-6897
Contact: Joe Banta
Stillwater offers 6 float tube models, 1 pontoon boat and accessories for boats.

Water Otter, Inc.
112 Freeze Lane
Hamilton, MT 59840
(406) 363-2398
FAX: (406) 363-2398
Est.: 1985
Contact: Darryl Osburn
Versatile, portable, stable, one person water crafts. Call or write for color brochures.

Water Wolf
PO Box 169, Telluride, CO 81435
(800) H2O-WOLF
FAX: (970) 728-3907
Est.: 1988
Contact: Joe Powell
Float tubes made of Kevlar nylon fiberglass fabric—light and extremely durable. Modular components allow single and multi-user configurations.

BOOKS & VIDEOS

Frank Amato Publications
PO Box 82112, Portland, OR 97282
(800) 541-9498   (503) 653-8108
FAX: (503) 653-2766

Angler's Book Supply
1380 West 2nd Ave.
Eugene, OR 97402
(800) 260-3869
FAX: (541) 342-1785
Owner: Mark Koenig
Sales/Cust. Svc: Jackie Hammerton
Distributors of books & videos–fly fishing, fishing & field sports.
The best selection of angling and sporting books, videos, maps, computer software, calendars, audio tapes and more. Over 2000 titles from more than 100 publishers. We offer guaranteed same day shipping, volume discounts and free freight on orders over 25 items. Please call for a free catalog and information on how we can help you (retail outlets only).
See Our Ad Pg. 30

Anglers & Shooters Bookshelf
Box 178, 49 Old Middle St.
Goshen, CT 06756
(860) 491-2500

The Anglers Art
PO Box 148, Plainfield, PA 17081
(717) 243-9721
FAX: (717) 243-8603
Contact: Barry Serviente

BT Direct
6703 River Hills Dr.
Greensboro, NC 27410
(910) 664-0006
FAX: (910) 664-0006
Est.: 1996
Owner: Ben Herndon
Available: Direct
Fly fishing instructional books and materials. Call 1-888-EAT A FLY. Free report available–call now.

Bennett/Watt Entertainment, Inc.
13101 244th Ave., SE
Issaquah, WA 98027
(800) 327-2893
FAX: (206) 392-4104
Contact: Nick Kinler

Over 104 fly fishing & fly tying instructional and adventure videos to choose from for only $19.95 plus $5 s&h per $40 ordered. Brought to you by the producers of ESPN's "Jim & Kelly Watts Fly Fishing Video Magazine" television series.

Judith Bowman Books
Pound Ridge Rd.,
Bedford, NY 10506
(914) 234-7543
Est.: 1979   Staff: 2
Contact: Judith Bowman
Hunting & fishing books—mail order only

Cortland Line Co.
3736 Kellogg Rd., PO Box 5588
Cortland, NY 13045
(607) 756-2851
FAX: (607) 753-8835

Contact: Tom McCullough
How-to books and videos on fly tying and fishing. Call or write for catalog.

The Countryman Press
PO Box 748, Woodstock, VT 05091
(800) 245-4151

Countrysport, Inc.
1515 Cass St.,
Traverse City, MI 49684
(800) 367-4114
FAX: (616) 929-9813
Dir. of Editorial: Art DeLaurier, Jr.
President: Charles Fry

Derrydale Press
226 Sunflower,
Clarksdale, MS 38614
(601) 624-5514

East Coast Fisherman
530 Main St., Suite 750
New Rochelle, NY 10801
(914) 576-3733
FAX: (914) 576-3733
Contact: Jeff Mancini
Producer of "Fly Fishing for Striped Bass". 123 minutes full feature film—retails for $29.95.

Flyfisher's Classic Library
Dartmoor View, Mary Street
Bovey Tracey, Devon, UK TQ13 9HQ
011-44-1626-834182
FAX: 011-44-1626-835-714

Foghorn Press
555 Deharo St., Suite 220
San Francisco, CA 94107
(800) FOG-HORN   (415) 241-9550
FAX: (415) 241-9648
Contact: Laurel Rivers
Outdoor publisher of fishing activity guides.

Greycliff Publishing Co.
PO Box 1273, Helena, MT 59624
(404) 443-1888
FAX: (406) 443-0788
Contact: Stan Bradshaw

Highwood Bookshop
Box 1246, Traverse City, MI 49685
(616) 271-3898 M-F, 9-5 EST
Contact: Lewis L. Razek
Large stock of back issues of fishing and other outdoor magazines. Mail order only.

In-Fisherman, Inc.
2 In-Fisherman Dr.
Brainerd, MN 56401
(218) 829-1648
FAX: (218) 829-3091
President: Al Lindner

Inter-Sports Books & Videos
790 W. Tenn., Denver, CO 80223
(800) 456-5842   (303) 778-8383
FAX: (800) 279-9196
Mktg: Johnny J. Jones
America's largest assortment of hunting, fly fishing and archer books, maps and videos. Please call for our 80-page catalog describing 1,500 titles (retail outlets only).

Just Good Books
PO Box 232, Belgrade, MT 59714
(800) 207-0799
FAX: (406) 388-7435
Est.: 1995
Contact: Tom Pappas or Harold Johnson
New, used, rare & out-of-print fly-fishing books–specializing in signed 1st edition & limited editions.

Kitty Creek Press, Inc.
PO Box 5222, Austin, TX 78763
(512) 349-7797
FAX: (512) 418-9147
Contact: Raye Carrington
Publisher of "HOOKED: Funny Quotes from Serious Anglers".

Lyons & Burford, Publishers
31 W. 21st St., New York, NY 10010
(800) 836-0510 Ext. 39
(212) 620-9580 Ext. 39
FAX: (212) 929-1836
Sales/Mktg: Jerry Hoffnagle
Sales/Mktg: Tony Lyons
Publishers of the finest books on fly fishing & wingshooting trade. Limited and deluxe editions. Over 500 titles currently in print.
See Our Ad Below

Penguin Productions
2625 Carissa Dr.
Vero Beach, FL 32960
(561) 562-3756
FAX: (561) 562-0171
Contact: Mary Castlow

Press of the Sea Turtle
Box 406, East Hampton, MA 01027
(413) 527-8557
FAX: (413) 527-6958
President: Alan Robinson

Pruett Publishing
2928 Pearl St., Boulder, CO 80301
(800) 247-8224 (303) 449-4919
FAX: (303) 443-9019
Publisher: Jim Pruett
Publishers of non-fiction outdoor books. We have 12 fly fishing books in the program ranging from guidebooks to the West's best fishable waters to books on fly tying to award-winning literary works.

3M Scientific Anglers
3M Center-Bldg. 223-4N-05
St. Paul, MN 55144-1000
(800) 525-6290
Scientific Anglers fly-fishing videos enable anglers to "mentally rehearse" what they may encounter before a day on the water. 3M Scientific Anglers offers an extensive line of instructional fly-fishing videos, including "Fly Fishing Made Easy," an award-winning video that's a great starting point for beginners. There are also videos available on fly casting, fly tying, steelhead, tarpon, and "everything you want to know" about trout.

Sportsmen's Closet
12 Main St., PO Box 180
Mainland, PA 19451-0180
(215) 256-6265 FAX: 9543
Owner: Bill Dromsky

Stackpole Books
5067 Ritter Rd.
Mechanicsburg, PA 17055
(800) 732-3669 (Orders)
(717) 796-0411
Outdoor Sales Mgr: Larry Johnson
Fly fishing books—call for catalog.

Stream Stalker Publications
Box 238, Woody Creek, CO 81656
(970) 923-4552
Contact: Bob Sterling

Tomorrow River Press
PO Box 1745, Wausau, WI 54402
(715) 842-9879
Contact: Nancy Borger
Publishing the award-winning books, videos and audios by Gary

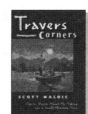
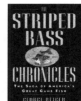
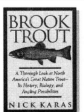

Borger: "Presentation" called by one reviewer, "the best fly fishing book I've ever read." "Designing Trout Flies," heralded as one of the most original books on tying. Fourteen video titles including "Nymphing" (still the industry standard). "My Madison," award winning nature music audio and more.

Vivid Publishing, Inc.
347 Rural Ave., PO Box 1572
Williamsport, PA 17701
(800) 326-9694
FAX: (717) 322-0912
Contact: Karl Ings or Larry Seaman

Wilderness Adventures Sporting Books
PO Box 627
Gallatin Gateway, MT 59730-0627
(800) 925-3339
FAX: (406) 763-4911
Contact: Chuck Johnson
World's largest selection of hunting & fishing books for the collector and enthusiast.

CLOTHING

This section contains informtion on fly fishing related apparel, including **VEST** *manufacturers. For clothing that is designed to repel insects or proviide protection from the sun, see* **ACCESSORIES**/*Skin Protection/ Insect Repellant. page 20.*

Aqua Design
Bluff Rd., RR#3, Box 9E
Newport, VT 05855
(802) 334-5994
FAX: (802) 334-5798
Est.: 1996   Staff: 15
President: Al Diem
Aqua Design™ is a unique, innovative concept in fishing apparel that makes it harder for fish to see the fisher. This means that when you wear Aqua Design™ apparel, you can get closer to the fish without frightening them.

Barbour, Inc.
55 Meadowbrook Dr.
Milford, NH 03055
(800) 338-3474
FAX: (603) 673-6510
Contact: Tom Hooven
Maker of high quality clothes and accessories for the angler.

Big Rock Clothing Co.
3075 S. 1030 W.
Salt Lake City, UT 84119

(801) 973-9350
FAX: (801) 570-9357
Est.: 1993
Contact: Tim Hammon
Silk-screened & embroidered T-shirts.

Bimini Bay Outfitters, Ltd.®
43 McKee Dr., Mahwah, NJ 07430
(800) OUT-FIT1 (688-3481)
FAX: (201) 529-0291
President: Robert Feldsott
Nat'l. Sales Mgr: Tom Cappy
Manufacturer of "outdoor friendly" sportswear, rainwear, gear and accessories. Sold under Bimini Bay Outfitters, Ltd.®, Yukon Traders®, PENN® Apparel for Fishermen & The Billfish Foundation®

Burke & Wills
Box 5222, Scottsdale, AZ 85261
(800) 532-2755
FAX: (602) 991-4651
Contact: David Michaels
Quality fishing and utility vests; beautiful embroidered sweatshirts.

Camp David
7920 Foster,
Overland Park, KS 66204
(913) 648-0573   FAX: 7444
Nat'l. Sales Mgr: Brian Austin
Apparel line includes full range of sportswear with embroidered designs of fly fishing and other wildlife/outdoor themes.

Columbia Sportswear
Box 83239, Portland, OR 97203
(800) MA-BOYLE   (503) 286-3676
FAX: (503) 289-6602
PR: Beth Gillespie

Dirt Roads & Damsels
1457 Nelson St.,
Lakewood, CO 80215
(303) 232-8298   (503) 667-6602
FAX: (503) 667-2917
Contact: Rhonda Sapp or D. Teeny
Designers of functional, high-tech fishing gear for women. These products are designed to offer style, color and fashion.

Eagle Athletic Manuf.
Box 2826, Great Falls, MT 59403
(800) 833-3313   (406) 452-8541
FAX: (406) 452-1031
President: Russell Corn
Fly fishing jackets that are weather resistant and functional for use in the fly fishing field and all outdoor activities.

Englands Fly Fishers
152 High St., Harborne,
Birmingham, B17 9PN England
Contact: Michael J. England-Kerr
Englands offers the "fishing jacket that saves lives," a stylish, light-

weight, multi-functional jacket that automatically inflates within 5 seconds of water immersion. Manufactured and tested to the highest standards, yet affordable. Please write for information.

Ex Officio
1419 Elliott Ave., W.
Seattle, WA 98119
(206) 283-1471
FAX: (206) 286-9012
Est.: 1986   Staff: 20
VP/Sales: Steve Bendzak
Engineered for the adventurous angler. Ex Officio offers lightweight, quick drying, sun protective clothing.

C.C. Filson
PO Box 34020, Seattle, WA 98124
(800) 624-0201
FAX: (206) 624-4539
Contact: John DePalma
Maker of fishing vests, tackle packs, wading jackets & fly rod travel cases.

Fly Tech
7450 Whitehall, Ft. Worth, TX 76118
(817) 590-2282
FAX: (817) 590-2053
Est.: 1987   Staff: 23
Sales Mgr: Jesse Shetter
Offering 18 styles of caps, four styles of rainwear, cotton shirts, gloves and accessories. Call for more information.

Fly by Night Fly Fishing Apparel
1025 Miller Dr., #105
Altamonte Springs, FL 32701
(800) 725-3761   (407) 339-2200
FAX: (407) 830-1001
Contact: Jamieson Thomas
Manufacturer, designer, printer & embroiderer of outdoor clothing lines with fly fishing graphics.

Flying Fisherman
PO Box 545, Islamorada, FL 33036
(800) 356-0607
FAX: (305) 664-8388
VP: Linda Sheldon
Line of T-shirts and sweatshirts featuring original, dynamic sport fishing designs. Free color catalog.

Go Fish Ltd.
618 NW Glisan, #303
Portland, OR 97209
(503) 224-3474
FAX: (503) 224-0166
Contact: Bart Bonime
Line of humorous, graphic inspired T-shirts and headwear; also fully constructed technical line of apparel from vests to rainwear.

Goldeneye
PO Box 6387, Bozeman, MT 59771
(406) 586-2228
FAX: (406) 587-0478
Est.: 1990
Contact: George Foster
Recipient of Fly Rod & Reel's 1995
KUDOS for fine tackle, Goldeneye
produces innovative and comfortable hand-crafted flyfishing vests
for men and women in Bozeman
Montana. Goldeneye uses only the
finest materials available, and backs
their commitment to quality and
customer satisfaction with a lifetime warranty. Call or write for
information.

Hamilton's
PO Box 2672, S. Vineland, NJ 08360
(800) 292-3695
FAX: (609) 691-0398
Contact: Timothy D. Hamilton
Sportsman's Jacket 100% Egyptian
waxed cloth, 5 pockets, 2-way
brass zipper, snap-on hood, tartan
lining, olive green. Sizes XS-XXXL.
Call for brochure.
See Our Ad Pg. 35

HEAD VEST

HeadVest
15030 Ventura Blvd., #716
Sherman Oaks, CA 91403
(800) 365-6294
Wear your vest on your head with
the new HeadVest. This khaki cap
has an elongated "Hemingway"-

type bill that increases shade, reduces water glare. The largest
patch of sheepskin on any fishing
hat is perfect for storing, hanging
and drying flies. Multiple pockets
with soft velcro closers. Inside
mesh flap for leader packets and
other flat items. Adjustable leather
band means one size fits all. The ultimate in convenience. Phone
toll-free to order.
See Our Ad Below

Helly-Hansen
Box 97031, Redmond, WA 98073
(800) 435-5901 (Cust. Svc.)
(206) 883-8823
FAX: (206) 882-4932
Est.: 1877
Sales Mgr: Roger Pawley
The Helly Hansen WeatherSystem™
of Dress product line includes jackets, vests, & wading trousers for
the angler.

Hook & Tackle™ Outfitters
6501 Northeast Second Ct.
Miami, FL 33138
(305) 754-3255
Est.: 1963   Staff: 500
VP/Sales: Abe Rudman
Authentic quality fishing apparel built for performance, comfort and long lasting. Creators of America's original BeerCan Island Short.

Labanu, Inc.
2201 F Fifth Ave.
Ronkonkoma, NY 11779
(516) 467-6197
FAX: (516) 981-4112
Contact: Naim Rahman
Quality fishing vests–3 models available.

Lewis Creek
1 Pine Haven Shore Rd.
Shelburne, VT 05482
(800) 336-4884   (802) 985-1099
FAX: (802) 985-1097
Contact: Kari Stolpestad
Extensive collection of waxed cotton fieldwear and 100% cotton sporting apparel, including the Silver Creek wading jacket and flyfishing shirts. Call or write for a free color catalog and the name of the dealer near you.

G. Loomis, Inc.
1359 Down River Dr.
PO Box E, Woodland, WA 98674
(800) 662-8818
FAX: (360) 225-7169
Contact: Kris Leistritz
We offer a variety of shirts, sweatshirts, jackets, hats and vests. Call for more information.

Orvis Company
Rt. 7A, Manchester, VT 05254
(800) 333-1550 (Ext. 844)
(802) 362-3622
Contact: Randy Carlson
Orvis, For Women by Women, is a complete line of fishing and outdoor clothing, waders and vests designed by angling women for the Orvis Company. From tropical flats to Alaskan rivers, the Orvis women's line of gear is unmatched in the industry today. For more information on the Orvis women's line, call 800-333-1550 (Ext. 844).

Outdoor Necessities
2414 NE 434th St.
Woodland, WA 98674
(360) 225-3442
FAX: (360) 225-6314
Contact: Jody Loomis-Brentin
Distributors of award winning "Nomad" rain garments.

Pacific Fly Group
730 E. Huntington Dr.
Monrovia, CA 91016
(800) 582-5145
FAX: (818) 305-6661
Est.: 1994
Contact: Edward Han
Two models of rain jacket are made with waterproof and breathable material, functional design, outstanding workmanship and exceptional value. Fishing vest made with strong and lightweight material, knit collar. We also carry Neoprene glove, Bunting glove, Neoprene socks, wading shoe, landing net, fly box and flies.

Patagonia
Box 150, 259 W. Santa Clara
Ventura, CA 93002
(805) 643-8616
FAX: (805) 653-6355
Est.: 1970
Product Dir: Bill Klyn
Comprehensive softwar layering system for anglers, including underwear, shirts, specialized fishing vests, hats and gloves.

Rainy's Flies & Supplies
690 N. 100 East, Logan, UT 84321
(801) 753-6766
FAX: (801) 753-9155
Contact: L. Rainy Riding
Manufacture Rainy's Versa-Vest– the ultimate chest fanny pack unit.

Sage Tech
8500 NE Day Rd.
Bainbridge Island, WA 98110
(800) 533-3004   (206) 842-6608
FAX: (206) 842-6830
Contact: Bill Dawson
The Sage Tech line has been carefully designed by anglers to meet the special performance needs of fly fishing. Sage quality and performance in technical flyfishing gear. Packable wading jacket, vests, shorts, shirts, pants and headware.

Salmo Salar
31 St-Barthelemy Sud,
Joliette, Quebec, Canada J6E 5N6
(514) 752-1057
FAX: (514) 752-4252
Contact: Gerves Dufour
Clothing manufacturer for the hunter and fisherman, bags and accessories.

Sea Harbour Inc.
9183 Pineridge Lane
Boulder, CO 80302
(303) 823-5977
FAX: (303) 823-9066
Est.: 1991
Contact: Currie Harbour
Credith Neptune
Cool, comfortable 100% cotton, prewashed clothing for all types of fishing. Designed solely for the fishing industry with both technical and non-technical garments, including hats, shirts, shorts, pants and vests. We also have a full line of water-resistant travel luggage & packs.

Simms Fishing Products
PO Box 3645, Bozeman, MT 59772
(406) 585-3557
FAX: (406) 585-3562
Simms provides superior products, from BiPolar™ Underwear to the high-tech Activent® Shell. Simms manufactures a complete line of high quality fishing vests, all made in Montana.

Solitude Fly Company
207 N. Stoneman Ave., Suite 10
Alhambra, CA 91801
(818) 458-6624
FAX: (818) 308-9068
Contact: John Bonk or Ray Chang
Makers of wading jackets & vests.

Spartan-Realtree Prod., Inc.
1390 Box Circle,
Columbus, GA 31907
(706) 569-9101
Contact: Bill Jordan
Maker of camouflage pattern clothing.

Sportif USA
1415 Greg St., Ste. 101
Sparks, NV 89431
(702) 359-6400
FAX: (702) 359-2098
Est.: 1965   Staff: 50
Sales Mgr: Steven Kirsch
Cust. Svc. Mgr: Diane Ducker
Technical nylon shorts, pants, zip-leg pants & shirts treated with Intera and ventilation for comfort!

Sporting Lives, Inc.
1510 N.W. 17th St.
Fruitland, ID 83619
(208) 452-5780
FAX: (208) 452-5791
Est.: 1985
President: Scott Swamby

Sospenders® World Class Inflatables is the high performance line of inflatable floatation devices. They are available in a variety of styles and colors: Shorty Vest; Fly Fisherman; Trimline Vest; and Pro Bass.

Sportline USA
3359 Fletcher Dr.
Los Angeles, CA 90065
(213) 255-8185
FAX: (213) 258-2001
Est.: 1979
Contact: John Gramatky
Solars™ Sun Protective Apparel, High Rise™ printed and technical Shirts. OEM, Private labeling available.

Stormy Seas, Inc.
PO Box 1570, Poulsbo, WA 98370
(206) 779-4439
FAX: (206) 779-8171
Est.: 1984
Contact: Mike Jackson
A full line of comfortable jackets and vests featuring a patented inflation system providing the ultimate in wearability and safety.

Stream Designs
Ausable, Div. of Amerex Outdoors
350 Fifth Ave., Suite 5515
New York, NY 10118
(800) 876-3366
FAX: (212) 967-2157
Est.: 1949
VP: Janie K. Davis
STREAM DESIGNS® is the Premier Manufacturer of innovative and technical fly fishing vests, apparel and accessories for the novice or professional fisherman. Our full range of vests include models for men, women and children.

Tarponwear
PO Box 2272, Jackson, WY 83001
(307) 739-9755
FAX: (307) 739-9817
Nat'l. Sales Dir: Terry Ross
Cool, comfortable, sun-protective clothing and accessories for fishing and active outdoor uses.

Todd Sportswear
PO Box 130413
Birmingham, AL 35213
(205) 802-7907
Owner: Dave Bennett
Manufacturer of outdoor sportswear. Custom embroidery for clubs and organizations.

Trout Tramp Gear
344 S. 68th, Boulder, CO 80303
(303) 494-5678
Contact: Bob Sweet
"Rainbow Trout" logo shirts

Versitex of America Ltd.
3545 Schuylkill Rd.
Spring City, PA 19475
(610) 948-4442
FAX: (800) 331-6406
Est.: 1985   Staff: 6
President: Frederic S. Claghorn, Jr.
Office Mgr: Nancy M. Ewing
Available: Retail & Direct
Shirts, vests, tackle belts, jackets and shorts for fresh and saltwater fly fishing. Our Freshwater and Drytex Vests are offered in a variety of styles made of lightweight material for the ultimate in fishing comfort.

Wasatch Dry Goods
Distributed by Spelcor
4130 S. 500 W., #1
Salt Lake City, UT 84123
(800) 574-4471   (801) 265-8113
VP: Kim Raymer
T-shirts and twill shirts featuring silk screened etchings by wildlife artist Mike Stidham.

Wind River
3982 Rolfe Ct.,
Wheatridge, CO 80033
(303) 378-7287
FAX: (303) 420-1522
Est.: 1993   Staff: 3
Quality outdoor gear made in Colorado USA. Fleece and Windstopper fingerless gloves and Convertamitts for fishing and hunting. Fleece cap, fleece hat and balaclava, T-shirts and fish print boxer shorts. Fly fishing accessory products including reel and rod bags, net keeper, rod ruler, mageye's magnifier and entomology products.

CLOTHING/HATS

HEAD╂VEST

HeadVest
15030 Ventura Blvd., #716
Sherman Oaks, CA 91403
(800) 365-6294
Convert your hat into a vest with the new HeadVest. This khaki cap has an elongated "Hemingway"-type bill that increases shade, reduces water glare. The largest patch of sheepskin on any fishing hat is perfect for storing, hanging and drying flies. Multiple pockets with soft velcro closers. Inside mesh flap for leader packets and other flat items. Adjustable leather band means one size fits all. The ultimate in convenience. Phone toll-free to order.
See Our Ad Pg. 33

Identity Headwear
5830 Woodson, Mission, KS 66202
(913) 677-4287
FAX: (913) 677-4288
Contact: Jim Thomure
Manufacturer of quality, fashion and functional headwear.

Imperial Headwear
5200 E. Evans, Denver, CO 80222
(800) 757-8538   (303) 757-1166
FAX: (303) 757-1515
Contact: Rod Rennick
Variety of longbill, winter, corduroy, washed cotton twill, and straw baseball and baseball style caps for the fly fisherman. Dealer inquiries welcome.

Jacobson Hat Co.
230 Sandstone Rd.
Columbia, SC 29212
(803) 749-2845
FAX: (803) 781-9019
Contact: Ed Walshe
Manufacturer/importer of custom logo embroidery on caps, straw, cotton & crushable felt headwear.

Outback Trading Co.
39 S. Third St., Oxford, PA 19363
(610) 932-5141
FAX: (610) 932-0227
Manufacturer and distributor of waterproof oilskin outerwear and headgear. Exclusive US distributor of Akubra Fur Felt Hats made in Australia.

Ultimate Products Inc.
4893 West Waters Ave.
Tampa, FL 33634
(813) 881-1575
FAX: (813) 881-1831
Contact: Don Bennett
Ultimate hats tie on, float, repel rain and mildew. Fabrics for all climates.

Watership Trading Co., Inc.
1025 Fraser St.,
Bellingham, WA 98226
(800) 676-4305
FAX: (360) 676-8809
Owner: Greg Frechette
Complete line of hats for the fly fishing shop. Call for our 16-page illustrated brochure. Wholesale only--thank you.

CLOTHING/GLOVES

Glacier Glove
4890 Aircenter Circle, #210
Reno, NV 89502
(800) 728-8235   (702) 825-8225
FAX: (702) 825-6544
Est.: 1982
Contact: Paolo Della Bordella
Neoprene gloves for hunting and fishing.

Hodgman Inc.
1750 Orchard Rd.
Montgomery, IL 60538
(630) 897-7555
FAX: (630) 897-7558
Est.: 1838
Mktg. Dir: Craig Foster
Maker of Lakestream® neoprene all-purpose gloves.

Kobuk Inc.
17950 E. Ajax Circle
City of Industry, CA 91748
(818) 965-8773
FAX: (818) 965-9634
Est.: 1982
Nat'l. Sales Mgr: Dan Reed
Maker of neoprene fishing gloves.

Springbrook Mfg./Mangrove
8115 Sovereign Row
Dallas, TX 75247
(800) 638-9052
Est.: 1990
Contact: Rick Pope
Sun Gloves® provide UV protection for fishing in bright sunlight. Glove material is thin yet tough and washable, never interfering with casting or other outdoor activities.

Sun Checkers
Fishing for Ideas, 9 Woodland Rd.,
Sewickley, PA 15143

(800) 588-8727
FAX: (412) 741-7713
Contact: Tom Potter
Sun Checker gloves provide UV protection for your hands and arms-a low cost alternative to unreliable lotions.

Thunderwear, Inc.
1060 C Calle Negocio
San Clemente, CA 92673
(714) 492-1141
FAX: (714) 492-3259
Est.: 1984
Contact: Katherine Mielke
Maker of neoprene gloves, water shoes and boots.

Wind River
3982 Rolfe Ct.,
Wheatridge, CO 80033
(303) 378-7287
FAX: (303) 420-1522
Est.: 1993
Owner: Dean Swanson
Fleece and Windstopper fingerless gloves and Converta-Mitts for fishing and hunting.

COLLECTIBLE TACKLE DEALERS

Adams Angling
1170 Keeler Ave.
Berkeley, CA 94708
(510) 849-1324
FAX: (510) 883-9257
Contact: Jim Adams
Purchase and sell fine fly fishing tackle, old & rare fishing books. Catalogs issued.

American Sporting Collector
Arden Dr., Amawalk, NY 10501
(914) 245-6647
Contact: Allan J. Liu
We buy and sell the finest sporting collectibles, specializing in 8' or shorter classic bamboo rods, collectible fly reels, fly fishing accessories and angling art.

Bill Ballan Reel & Rod Co.
230 Seaman Ave.
Bayport, NY 11705
(516) 472-0744   (516) 246-8004
FAX: (516) 472-0744
Contact: Bill Ballan

Lon Blauvelt
15 Town Landing Rd.
Falmouth, ME 04105
(207) 781-5235
Contact: Lou Blauvelt
Appraisal and antique rods bought and sold.

Pete Caluori
4370 Decatur Ave.
Castle Rock, CO 80104
(303) 660-3854
Contact: Pete Caluori
Collector of 19th century salmon fly fishing equipment.

Walt Carpenter Sporting Collectibles
Box 52, Huntington Mills, PA 18622
(717) 477-3571
Owners: Walt and Marcia Carpenter

Tom Clark
1308 West Washington
Jackson, MI 49203
(517) 783-1515

Classic Rods & Tackle, Inc.
Box 288, Ashley Falls, MA 01222
(413) 229-7988
Contact: Martin J. Keane
Deal in high quality bamboo rods.

Len Codella's Heritage Sporting Collectibles
2201 South Carnegie
Inverness, FL 34450
(352) 637-5454
FAX: (352) 637-5420
Contact: Len Codella
Collections and estates bought. Fishing tackle wanted. Bamboo fly rods and quality reels. We buy, sell and trade only the highest quality tackle and related items. Paying highest cash prices! Free catalog.

J. Garman
316 Hartford Rd.
Manchester, CT 06040
(203) 643-2401
FAX: (203) 647-7988
Contact: Joe Garman
Over 40 years of satisfied clients–appraisals and sales.

The Dave Inks Company
5629 Skyview Dr.
Florence, MT 59833
(406) 273-2678
FAX: (406) 273-2608
Contact: Dave Inks

The Jordan-Mills Rod Co.
11 Wesley Rd., Congers, NY 10920
(914) 268-9252 Est.: 1985
Contact: Carmine Lisella, Prop.
Classic bamboo rods of recent and older vintage. Reels both resale items and/or collectible. Fly fishing paraphernalia. Send for catalog.

Dave Klausmeyer's New England Angler
PO Box 105, Steuben, ME 04680
(207) 546-2018
Contact: Dave Klausmeyer

Lang's Sporting Collectibles
31 R Turtle Cove,
Raymond, ME 04071
(207) 655-4265
FAX: (207) 655-4265
Contact: Bob Lang
Decades of experience as an auction house, bonded & insured. Appraisals also available.

Tony Lyons' Rare Fly Fishing Books
108 W. 76th St., #4A
New York, NY 10023
(212) 580-7872
Contact: Tony Lyons
Rare books on fly fishing bought & sold. Inventory ranges from 30 to 300 titles. Call for current list.

Raptor Rod
2563 Kennedy Ave.,
Chico, CA 95973
(916) 894-2062
FAX: (916) 894-1230
Est.: 1995 Staff: 2
Owner: Jim Clarkson
5-page list of new & used rods–call today for list.

"The Reel Man"
6 Springwood St.
Cranston, RI 02905-3622
(401) 941-6853
Est.: 1988
Contact: Bruce Boyden
Antique, collectible & usable fishing tackle & related sporting paraphernalia. Mail order list of items issued periodically. Send business size S.A.S.E. for copy.

Rods & Reels
17 Massasoit Rd.,
Nashua, NH 03063
(603) 886-0411
Contact: Bob Corsetti
We buy, sell and trade cane fly rods and fine fly reels.

Andy Sekora Bamboo Dealer
3626 Theisen Rd.
Gaylord, MI 49735
(616) 546-3425
Est.: 1989
Contact: Andy Sekora or Bill McRoy
Quarterly mailing.

Shelly Spindel
231 Sykes Point Lane
Merritt Island, FL 32953

Vaden/French Rod Co.
2041 S. 380th St.
Federal Way, WA 98003
(206) 838-7939
Est.: 1994 Staff: 2
Proprieter: Charles F. Vaden
Finest bamboo flyrods at competitive prices. Lots of rods, reels, nets, and tubes in stock.

COMPUTER APPLICATIONS

All Outdoors, Inc.
Box 1906, Traverse City, MI 49685
(616) 947-8181
FAX: (616) 941-9019
Mktg. Dir: Charlie Janis
Broad based Internet site for hunting and fishing. Provides commercial access and marketing to fly fishing, general fishing and hunting clients including Orvis, Normark, Daiwa, Shimano, Rocky and many others.

America Outdoors Web Site
Operated by Outdoor Management Network, Inc.
4607 NE Cedar Creek Rd.
Woodland, WA 98674
(360) 225-5000
FAX: (360) 225-7616
Contact: Robert R. Knopf
http://www.americaoutdoors.com
Cyberspace Sales and Marketing for the Outdoors. Full Service Sales, Marketing, P-R Programs Full Service Internet/World Wide Web Consulting. E-mail - omni@americaoutdoors.com
America Outdoors Site Features: Fishing, Hunting/Shooting, Camping, General Outdoors, Photography, Boating, Hiking/Biking, Conservation, Travel and Wildlife. Offers listing and advertising service for game preserves, clays ranges, outdoor manufacturers, guides, outfitters, resorts Brochure Available

Clear Creek Productions
Box 1473, Oregon City, OR 97045
(503) 259-9609
FAX: (503) 777-4818
General Mgr: Kristi Beyer
Our computer mousepad is a reproduction of Vic Erickson's "Last Light" print, while the screensaver features Ron Pittard's trout images, deemed as authentic to the scale level by Dr. Robert Behnke.

Tim Damon's Fly Fishing Supply Co.
763 A State Hwy. 11B
Potsdam, NY 13676
(888) 265-1408   (315) 265-1408
FAX: (315) 265-1408
Est.: 1994   Staff: 3
Owner: Tim Damon
On-line catalog offering fly fishing, fly tying and rod building equipment, tools & materials at discount prices.

Elkwing Productions
PO Box 789, Waitsfield, VT 05673
(802) 496-4587
Contact: Bob Lang
Interactive CD-ROMs covering Trout and Saltwater fly patterns, authored by Dick Stewart and Farrow Allen. These CDs include full-motion video and step-by-step tying instruction as well as recipes, backround information, and detailed graphics. There are additional sections on streamside insects and coastal baitfish. The CD, Tying Flies for Trout, was voted a "Top Ten Best New Products" by FTD magazine.

FBN

FBN®
The Fly-Fishing Broadcast Network
12081 A Tech Rd.
Silver Spring, MD 20904
(301) 622-3090
FAX: (301) 622-3078
Contact: Avi Adler
FBN-The Fly-Fishing Broadcast Network features the most comprehensive, timely and interactive fly-fishing information and entertainment on-line. FBN offers many levels of advertising/merchandising opportunities and is the only on-line site delivering both the AOL and WEB communities. Professional Web site design and re-design are available (AOL keyword: Fly-fishing, Web: http://www.fbn-flyfish.com).
See Our Ad Across

FLYbase
Tom Dewey & Associates
PO Box 67, Coudersport, PA 16915
(814) 274-7981
FAX: (814) 274-0641
http://flyfish.com/FLYbase/
FLYbase for Windows is the only fly fishing software that deals specifically with the hatches. Over 1,000 pattern dressings are included. FLYbase will create a hatch chart for any fly fishing region, for any day of the year.

The Fishing Hole
3620 West 9th St.
Leawood, KS 66206
(800) 961-5554
Distributors of 2 software programs for the fly fisherman. Fly Tech offers 3 separate editions that educate the individual on fly tying. Virtual Streams provides the fly fisherman with information on interesting fly fishing streams.

Fishware
7354 Poudre Canyon Hwy.
Bellvue, CO 80512
(970) 224-5009
Contact: Kevin Rogers
FishScalz...essential weight determining software for the serious catch-and-release angler. Call for more information.

Fly Fish America
PO Box 408, Fryeburg, ME 04037
(888) 843-2359   (207) 935-4725
FAX: (207) 935-4726
http://www.flyfishamerica.com
Internet publication

Fly Fishing Network
Arden Dr. , Amawalk, NY 10501
(914) 245-6647
Contact: Allan J. Liu
Look us up today at http://www.fly-fishingnetwork.com
The Fly Fishing Network is the oldest on-line service dedicated solely to fly fishing.

Fly Fishing Resource Guide
10007 Eagle Pl.
Anderson Island, WA 98303
(206) 884-1555   (206) 878-6655
FAX: (206) 878-6657
Sales: Terry Thomas
World Wide Web site catering to fly fishers–flyfish.com.

FlyTy
c/o Amiable Instruction
1721 N. 1200 E., PO Box 281
Lehi, UT 84043
(801) 768-1280
FAX: (801) 768-1281
Contact: Clint Covington or Peter Maiden
Instruction by Mickey Anderson with 500 photos, 100 patterns (with journals) and 28 step-by-step tying lessons. Available on 3.5 or CD-ROM media.

Flyfishing.com
29 Gilley Rd., Perryville, MD 21903
(410) 642-0136
Contact: Dave Paris

Hatchmaster™
Tight Lines International
1627 W. Main St., Suite 204
Bozeman, MT 59715
(800) 786-8769 (Orders)
(406) 763-4515 (Voice)
FAX: (406) 763-4515
President: Matthew R. Field
Computer CD program that analyzes hatches and appropriate flies and equipment to use. Retails for $49.95.

HyperCompleat Angler
Dunworth and Hagen Co.
998 Center St., Suite 1
Boston, MA 02130
(800) 422-7698   (617) 983-9260
FAX: (617) 983-9260
Contact: Eamon Dunworth or Margaret Hagen
Software for fly fishermen

IntelliMedia Sports Inc.
Two Piedmont Center
Suite 300, Atlanta, GA 30305
(800) 269-2101   (404) 262-0000
FAX: (404) 261-2282
Contact: Dave Sack
Receive personal fly fishing instruction on CD-ROM from five world renowned professionals. Call for free catalog.

McDonald Horton Co.
PO Box 4051
Burlingame, CA 94011
(415) 615-8237

nevik Applications
PO Box 621666
Littleton, CO 80162-1666
(303) 643-1893
FAX: (303) 933-2081
The Fly Fisherman's Trout Stream Log keeps a computer record of your fishing trip including stream and trip information, and trout caught.

Reel-Time
2912 Claremont Ave., Suite 32
Berkeley, CA 94705
(510) 848-7261
Publisher: Thorne Sparkman
Website: www.reel-time.com
Reel-Time is an online publication devoted to saltwater and anadromous fly fishing containing regional reports and articles.

Rocky Mountain Flyfisher
7673 S. Harrison Way
Littleton, CO 80122
(303) 793-0488
Contact: John Baxter
The Rocky Mountain Fly Fisher PC compatible software offers complete information on 36 premiere

"Not AOL **or** The Web... AOL **and** The Web!"

What? **FBN** is the Fly-Fishing Broadcast Network. FBN puts the most current, reliable and interactive fly-fishing information at the fingertips of fly-fishing enthusiasts.

Where? **FBN** is featured on America Online **(Keyword: Fly-fishing)**, the world's largest online access service with over 6 million members and the World Wide Web at **http://www.fbn-flyfish.com**. As an FBN/AOL advertiser your business' advertising message will be carried over to our Web site *at no additional cost*. Not AOL *or* the Web...AOL *and* the Web!

How? **FBN** recognizes that "the build it and they will come" approach does not work online. The user must have incentive to come into the area. For this reason, FBN integrates your advertising message into daily updated and interactive content — driving traffic to your FBN advertisement and Web site. If you do not currently have a Web site, or feel you are paying too much for your current one, the FBN Web Team will create a custom designed demo for you — free of charge.

Who? **FBN's** seasoned professionals have over 20 of years collective marketing experience. We will serve as your "mini agency" to maximize the return on your online investment. For more information, **contact us at (301) 622-3090 or via email at FBN4Value@aol.com.**

 Not Just Another Fish Story!   AMERICA *Online.*

trout streams in the Rockies: Where to fish...what to use...effective patterns... stream photos and maps...and much, much more. Simple searching capability. Consumer and shop/guide versions available.

Sporting Adventures
15 River Rd., Wilton, CT 06897
(203) 834-2130
FAX: (203) 834-2781
Est.: 1995   Staff: 20
President/CEO: Peter M. Cholnoky
Editor-in-Chief: Jennifer T. Cholnoky
World Wide Web site for fishing, hunting and outdoor enthusiasts.
www.spav.com

Sporting Life Software Inc.
Box 4051, Burlingame, CA 94011
(415) 348-3313
FAX: (415) 348-3353
Est.: 1993   Staff: 5
Contact: McDonald Horton
Developer and distributor of fly fishing computer software games, related gifts and accessories.

Tite Line Fishing
325 N. Pine, Townsend, MT 59644
(406) 266-3225
Contact: John J. Seidel
This comprehensive software is windows based to make searching easy for any user. Information includes: printable maps, fish species, hatches, fly patterns, CFS flows, travel information, boat ramps, access points and local fly shops. Plan an entire fishing trip from your home or office computer–please call for more information.

Virtual Adventures
Tower Bldg., Suite 411
1809 7th Ave., Seattle, WA 98101
(800) 437-0005   (206) 292-1140
FAX: (206) 684-6977
Contact: Lynda Mills
CD Rom: Great rivers of the west. Sights, sound and beauty of six great western rivers.

FLY FISHERMAN's
the virtual flyshop
www.flyshop.com

The Virtual Fly Shop
3336 Sunningdale
Ft. Collin, CO 80525
(970) 484-8650
FAX: (970) 484-8256
Contact: Mike Tucker
One of the oldest and best known fly fishing related Web sites, The Virtual Flyshop offers a broad range of valuable information for the angler. In addition to articles from Fly Fisherman magazine, you can browse for information on fly fishing equipment and guided fishing trips. Other features include a page for fly tyers, a bulletin board, a chat room and an "Ask the Experts" page.
See Ad Inside Front Cover

Yellowstone Fishing Advisor
Management Systems Guild
9513 Ash Hollow Pl.
Gaithersburg, MD 20879
(301) 990-4076
Contact: Donald Marks
A software program that acts as a planning model for Yellowstone as well as a description of the streams and ponds.

EQUIPMENT/ GLASSES

Polarized Sunglasses

Action Optics by Smith
Box 2999, Ketchum, ID 83340
(800) 654-6428
(208) 726-4477
FAX: (208) 726-9584
Contact: Peter Crow
Action Optics provides the finest in polarized eyewear for the fly fisherman. Numerous frame styles, exceptional polarization combined with carefully chosen lens tints and 100% UV protection have made Action Optics the "Guides Choice" worldwide. Available in "ready to wear" and prescription single vision, bifocal and trifocals. Call or write for information.
See Our Ad Across

Angler Eyes
Division of Capo, Inc.
2 Sunshine Blvd.
Ormond Beach, FL 32174
(800) 282-7696   (904) 673-4966
FAX: (904) 672-8720
Mgr/Product Line: Jack Hewett
Lenses by Polaroid. 15 Fishing styles, 8 with side shields. Dealer inquiries welcome.

Costa Del Mar Sunglasses
123 N. Orchard St., Bldg. 1
Ormond Beach, FL 32174
(800) 447-3700   (904) 677-3700
FAX: (904) 677-3737
Est.: 1983
VP/Sales: Ron Dotson
VP/Operations: Ed Moody
Available: Retail
Maker of polarized sunglasses and polarized prescription sunglasses for sports enthusiasts.

Fisherman Eyewear
PO Box 261, Hollister, CA 95024
(408) 637-8271
FAX: (408) 636-9664
Est.: 1974
Contact: Rudy S. DeLuca
Sales Assoc: Jeff Tomasini
Complete line of polarized sunglasses from traditional fishing models to styles that double for everyday wear. Dealer inquiries only.

Floater Eyewear Inc.
7599 Kenwood Dr.
Cincinnati, OH 45236
(800) 769-3937   (513) 351-2020
FAX: (513) 891-0942
Est.: 1989
President: Clifford A. York
Polarized, virtually shatterproof sunglasses with a frame made of a material so light it floats. Frames USA made.

Flying Fisherman
PO Box 545, Islamorada, FL 33036
(800) 356-0607
FAX: (305) 664-8388
VP: Linda Sheldon
Polarized sunglasses, clip-ons & side shields for fishing and outdoor enthusiasts. Free full color catalog.

Hobie Sunglasses
Specialized Eyeware
5866 S. 194th St.
Kent, WA 98032
(714) 498-8828
FAX: (714) 498-8142
Contact: Dennis Bush
Optical quality polarized sunglasses.

Maui Jim
Polarized Sunglasses
930 Wainee St., Suite 9
Lahaina, HI 96761
(800) 848-3644 (888) MAUI-JIM
FAX: (800) 638-0351
Maui Jim "Polarized" Sunglasses provide a clearer view above and below the water. Their "Patented Lens" combines 99.9% polarization, bi-gradient and anti-reflectant glare absorption. Two lenses: Gray and new HCL (High-Contrast) bronze lens. Water-proof coating makes cleaning a snap on fresh and salt water. Over 20 styles. RX available.

Olympic Optical Co.
PO Box 752377
Memphis, TN 38175-2377
(800) 238-7120   (901) 794-3890
FAX: (901) 794-0676   Est.: 1976
Sales Mgr: Danny Holmes
Stren fishing eyewear

Orvis Company
Rt. 7A, Manchester, VT 05254
(800) 333-1550 (Ext. 844)
(802) 362-3622
Orvis sunglasses are designed by Orvis development specialists, specifically for fishing.

Premier Optics L.C.
2134 Sea Pines Way
Coral Springs, FL 33071
(305) 752-9717
FAX: (305) 752-0996
Contact: Alan Dinges
Maker of Fold Away Reading Glasses available in eight different focal ranges from +1.50 to +3.25. Unbreakable and scratch resistant, these glasses attach to cap or visor and can be used without removing sunglasses. Call or write for more information.

Revo, Inc.
1315 Chesapeake Terrace
Sunnyvale, CA 94089
(415) 962-0906
FAX: (415) 961-5486
Contact: Karen Palermo
Maker of the Revo H-2-O collection, featuring lenses designed especially for boaters and fishermen who need to see through the surface (polarized) glare of water.

Rocky Mountain
High Sports Glasses
8121 N. Central Park Ave.
Skokie, IL 60076-2992
(847) 679-1012
FAX: (847) 679-0184
Est.: 1991   Staff: 25
Div. Mgr: Eric L. Esson
VP/Sales & Mktg: Tibor Gross

Complete line of Polarized fishing/boating/glasses. Feature glass or plastic lenses. Styles and lense tints ideal for all fishing conditions. Dealer inquiries welcome.

Sunray Optical
2038 Massachusetts Ave.
Cambridge, MA 02140
(800) 323-2932
FAX: (617) 492-7918
Contact: Leslie Arslanian
Customized polarized prescription and non-prescription sunglasses, as well as name brand polarized sunglasses from Revo, Maui Jim and Serengeti.

EQUIPMENT/
LANDING NETS

Angler Accessories Ltd.
42 Maces Rd.,
Christchurch, New Zealand
011-64-3 3841477
FAX: 011-64-3 3265611
Contact: Marj Allan
Email: angler@sirranet.com
We handcraft top quality wooden
landing nets, custom design available. Knotless net fabrics on all
products.

Anglers Custom Products
1 Forest St., Hudson Falls, NY 12839
(518) 747-7458
FAX: (518) 747-6965
Est.: 1975
Owner: Marc Francato
High quality wood-frame landing
nets. Single strip and laminated.
Catch & release a specialty.

B.K. Products, Inc.
22227 S. Ferguson Rd.
Beavercreek, OR 97004
(503) 632-3622
FAX: (503) 632-3622
Gen. Mgr: Barry Bowler
Nationwide distributor of McLean
Angling (NZ) Ltd. nets. Weigh nets,
folding nets, extending and specialty high quality NZ made nets.

Benchmark Co.
179 Knapp Ave., Clifton, NJ 07011
(201) 779-1389
FAX: (201) 773-2308
Est.: 1984   Staff: 2
Owner: Bruce Hollowich
Handcrafted wooden nets with
catch & release or traditional cotton bags.

Bridgeport Landing Net Co.
7813 S.E. Luther
Portland, OR 97236
(800) 275-1168   (503) 775-2247
FAX: (503) 775-1081
President: Dave Nelson
High-quality landing nets with lifetime guarantee. Soft nylon catch &
release netting, six-lamination construction.

Brodin Landing Nets
300 Buffalo Jump Rd.
Three Forks, MT 59752
(406) 284-6320
FAX: (406) 284-3021
Contact: Chris Brodin
High-quality wood-frame landing
nets.

Christensen Networks LLC
5506 A Neilsen Rd.
Ferndale, WA 98248

(800) 459-2147
FAX: (360) 384-1446
Est.: 1988
Contact: Scott Christensen or
Cindy Robertson
Available: Retail & Direct
Landing net bags, insect seines, research fish handling netting
products.

Cortland Line Co.
3736 Kellogg Rd., PO Box 5588
Cortland, NY 13045
(607) 756-2851
FAX: (607) 753-8835
Contact: Tom McCullough
Hand crafted premium nets are
made from laminated hardwood
with distinctive finish. Broad weave
cotton mesh with brass French clip-
5 models. Plus S,M,L collapsible
aluminum trout nets in folding handle model or telescoping and
folding handle model.

Cuba Specialty Manuf. Co.
PO Box 195, Fillmore, NY 14735
(716) 567-4176
FAX: (716) 567-2366
Est.: 1903   Staff: 25
President: Dana R. Pickup
Quality fishing accessories and
nets. Used and endorsed by experienced fishermen for over 90 years.

Ed Cumings, Inc.
PO Box 90118, Flint, MI 48509
(810) 736-0130
President: Jeff Powell
Sales Admin.: Brenda Rutherford
World's largest net manufacturer offers a net for every fishing situation.

"Dinsmores" Catch and Release Landing Nets
Distributed by Belvoirdale
PO Box 176, Wyncote, PA 19095
(215) 886-7211
FAX: (215) 886-1804
President: Grahame Maisey
Bowlite featherweight 14" net.
Zero damage to fish's eyes, fins, scales; doesn't remove protective slime.

Fablok Mills, Inc.
140 Spring St.,
Murray Hill, NJ 07974
(908) 464-1950
FAX: (908) 464-6520
Contact: Laurie Green
Manufacturer of nets (OEM only)

The Fishing Line
65202 97th St., Bend, OR 97701
(800) 499-5420   (541) 317-1472
FAX: (541) 317-1514
Contact: Sheri Reynolds
Three sizes of landing nets available. Call for more information.

Hudson Woodworks
D.C. Angler Landing Nets
17744 Jones Ridge Rd.
Grass Valley, CA 95945
(916) 272-5606
FAX: (916) 272-5606
Est.: 1980
Contact: David Hudson
Manufacturer of fine handcrafted landing nets. 11 models, 72 styles and four price ranges. Catch-and-release or cotton netting.

LDH Landing Nets
530 W. Redwing St.
Duluth, MN 55803
(218) 724-6283
Contact: Lloyd D. Hautajarvi
Premium quality nets with handles crafted from highly figured North American hardwood. Available in a variety of styles and sizes. Handcut checkering and assorted inlays also available. Call for information.

Mengo Industries, Inc.
4611 Green Bay Rd.
Kenosha, WI 53144
(414) 652-3070
FAX: (414) 652-9910
Est.: 1966   Staff: 32
Sales: David A. Mengo

President: Gerald R. Mengo
Available: Retail
A complete line of fish landing nets - many styles including "Quick-Draw" folding, collapsible, telescopic nets.

Mid-Lakes Corp. (Loki Nets)
Box 5320, Knoxville, TN 37928
(423) 687-7341
FAX: (423) 687-7343
Est.: 1965   Staff: 30
Gen. Mgr: Bill Edwards
Knotless nylon netting and "Loki" brand catch & release trout nets.

Midstream
4721 Meldon Ave.
Oakland, CA 94619
(510) 532-8908
FAX: (510) 536-7384
Contact: Seth Norman
The Landing Hand is a knotless mesh glove that allows anglers to gently grasp fish with minimum loss of scales and protective slime.

Ranger Products
19669 John R, Detroit, MI 48203
(313) 368-0220
FAX: (313) 368-5680
Est.: 1960
President: David Golde
Deluxe, quality wood nets and aluminum catch & release trout nets of all sizes.

Signature Concepts
Box 1247, Ballston Lake, NY 12019
(518) 426-3214
FAX: (518) 426-4190
Est.: 1986   Staff: 25
President: Jeffrey R. Henry
All wood landing nets

Todd's
3962 Campo Ct.,
Boulder, CO 80301
(303) 443-3065
Est.: 1995
Contact: Todd Fosbenner
Manufacturer of premium quality handcrafted hardwood landing nets. Six wood styles to choose from. All sizes S, M, L and Boat are teardrop shaped. Includes French clip on small & medium, Edgin Handy Clip on large. Offering catch & release nylon, knotless nylon netting, or cotton net bags. Call for information.

Wachter Landing Nets
10238 Deermont Trail
Dallas, TX 75243
(972) 238-0823
FAX: (972) 238-1641
Est.: 1986
Contact: Kathy Wachter
Hand-crafted 3-ply wooden landing nets–3 series, 8 models, and 14 species of handle woods, including 6 burls.
See Our Ad Across

NET SILHOUETTES

The sizes and shapes of landing nets vary from manufacturer to manufacturer. Use the diagram below as a general reference when ordering nets from any of the companies listed in this section.

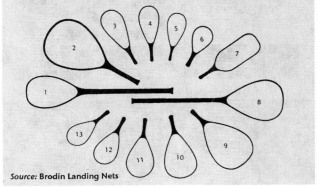

Source: **Brodin Landing Nets**

EQUIPMENT/
WADERS & BOOTS

Alexander's
3021 Power Dr.,
Kansas City, KS 66106
(913) 236-9565
FAX: (913) 236-9565
Est.: 1977
Contact: Bill Alexander
Manufacturers of lightweight waders and fishing accessories. Dealer inquiries only.

American Camper
14760 Santa Fe Trail Dr.
Lenexa, KS 66215
(800) 255-6061
(913) 492-3200
FAX: (913) 492-8749
President/CEO: Peter Boyle
Mktg. Dir: Dean Cost
Vulcanized rubber chest waders, rubber and insulated hip waders, vinyl stocking foot waders.

Bare Sportswear Corp.
Box 8110-577,
Blaine, WA 98230
(604) 533-7848
(800) 663-0111 Orders
FAX: (604) 530-8812
Dir/Sales & Mktg: Andy Leteta
Neoprene and nylon fabric fishing waders and accessories, carefully conceived and field tested.

L.L. Bean
1 Casco St.
Freeport, ME 04033
(800) 809-7057
FAX: (207) 552-3080
New Gore-tex® Waders with Kevlar® around the lower legs to help prevent pinholes and punctures. Call for more information.

Benik Corporation
9465 Provost Rd., NW, #204
Silverdale, WA 98383
(800) 442-8910 (Orders)
(360) 692-5601
FAX: (360) 692-5600
President: Tim Baumgartner
Benik offers chest, waist high and hip waders in a variety of colors. We also offer the versatile Seacoat, wader accessories and other products. Call for more information.

Browning Fishing
PO Box 270, Tulsa, OK 74115
(918) 831-6857
FAX: (918) 831-6938
President: Larry McIsaacs
Product Mgr: Andy Carroll
Browning offers a complete line of fishing tackle and accessories; including fly rods and fly reels–fly to baitcast to spinning; accessories– float tubes to waders, wading shoes to tackle systems.

Danner Shoe Mfg.
12722 NE Airport Way
PO Box 30148

Portland, OR 97230
(800) 345-0430
FAX: (503) 251-1119
Est.: 1932   Staff: 200
Contact: Renee Henry
River Gripper Series

DuPont SealSkinz®
1002 Industrial Rd.
Old Hickory, TN 37138-3693
(800) 868-2629
FAX: (615) 847-6044
SealSkinz® combine waterproof technology and a seamless design with the comfort of traditional socks.

FLY◈TECH®

Fly Tech
7450 Whitehall
Ft. Worth, TX 76118
(800) 590-2281
FAX: (817) 590-2053
Est.: 1987   Staff: 23
Sales Mgr: Jesse Shetter
Available: Retail
Quality fishing waders (neoprene, nylon, 3-ply canvas, and rubber), wading shoes for men, women, and youth. Call for a dealer in your area and for more information.
See Our Ads, Left & Right

Glacier Glove
4890 Aircenter Circle, #210
Reno, NV 89502
(800) 728-8235   (702) 825-8225
FAX: (702) 825-6544
Est.: 1982
Contact: Karen Moore
Neoprene and lightweight nylon chest waders, socks and wader accessories.

Gralite Outdoors
Div. of Standard Safety Equip. Co.
1407 Ridgeview Dr.
McHenry, IL 60050
(815) 363-8565
FAX: (815) 363-8633
Contact: Steve Medves
PVC waders

Grub Creek Wading Boots
3504 NE 109th St.
Vancouver, WA 98686
(800) 722-3542   (360) 573-7654
FAX: (360) 576-0341
Contact: Becky Iverson
Makers of Grub Creek wading boot, specializing in durability, comfort and value. All sales are being handled through Bare Sportswear Corp. at 800-663-0111.

Hodgman Inc.
1750 Orchard Rd.
Montgomery, IL 60538
(630) 897-7555
FAX: (630) 897-7558
Est.: 1838
Mktg. Dir: Craig Foster
For over 150 years, Hodgman has been making high-quality, carefully designed waterproof products for the outdoorsman who demands the very best. Call or write for information.

Kobuk Inc.
17950 E. Ajax Circle
City of Industry, CA 91748
(818) 965-8773
FAX: (818) 965-9634
Est.: 1982
Nat'l. Sales Mgr: Dan Reed
Neoprene and outerwear and accessories: hippers, overalls, chest waders, wader booties, gloves.

Korker's Inc.
Box 166, Grants Pass, OR 97526
(800) 524-8899   (541) 476-6823
FAX: (541) 479-1281
Est.: 1955
Contact: Doug Smith
Korkers offers easy-on, easy-off slip resistant soles for your shoes, boots and waders—for fishing and working. Durable and lightweight—fits any size.

LaCrosse Footwear, Inc.
PO Box 1328, LaCrosse, WI 54602
(800) 671-BOOT
FAX: (800) 658-9444
Est.: 1897
Mktg: Tiffany Olson
Mktg: Cheryl Dutton
Manufacturer of protective footwear for the sporting, occupational and industrial markets.

Landmark Co.
4350 Ryan Way, #1
Carson City, NV 89706
(800) 796-2626
FAX: (702) 885-9910
Contact: Allen Putnam
Wader belt: EZZ endless wader belt (pat. pend.) eliminates loose belt ends, fastest on and off for convenience and safety.

McNett Corporation
1405 Fraser St.
Bellingham, WA 98226
(360) 671-2227
FAX: (360) 671-4521
Contact: Cheryl Willis
Manufacturer of fishing accessories for repair & maintenance of waders.

O.S. Systems
PO Box 1088, 33550 SE Santosh St.
Scappoose, OR 97056
(503) 543-3126
FAX: (503) 543-3129
Contact: Paul Gunderson
Maker of "gravel tough and travel ready" waders—tough enough to slide down a gravel bank, but versatile and compact enough to be easily stowed in a convenient travel bag.

Orvis Company
Rt. 7A, Manchester, VT 05254
(800) 333-1550 (Ext. 844)
(802) 362-3622
Contact: Randy Carlson
All 23 models of Orvis waders are guaranteed for 4 years under the Orvis Unconditional Wader Guarantee. From our high-tech breathable "No Sweat" waders to our 4mm Guideweight, Orvis offers an incredible array of waders and hippers from $39.50 to $350 for men, women and children. For more information on Orvis waders, call 800-333-1550 (Ext. 844).

Outdoor Necessities
2414 NE 434th St.
Woodland, WA 98674
(360) 225-3442
FAX: (360) 225-6314
Contact: Jody Loomis-Brentin
Nomad Wayfarer Chest Waders are constructed of Ventflex, a breath-

able coated material. Available in 10 sizes and retail for around $185.

Pacific Fly Group
730 E. Huntington Dr.
Monrovia, CA 91016
(800) 582-5145
FAX: (818) 305-6661
Contact: Edward Han

Quiet Sport
26330 NE Kennedy Dr.
PO Box 1600
Duvall, WA 98019
(800) 243-0688   (206) 788-4481
President: Jerry S. Baker
Offers a line of high-quality custom-designed fishing and hunting products, led by float tubes and neoprene waders. The company's innovative "As You Grow" program offers waders with inseams that can be lengthened and booties that can be enlarged (for a nominal fee) to fit young, growing flyfishers.

Rogue Sandals/Pure Juice
4151 Avenida De La Plata
Oceanside, CA 92056
(619) 945-8880
FAX: (619) 945-8897
Est.: 1971   Staff: 15
President: Greg Johnson
Mktg. Mgr: Jeff Warwick
The world's finest flyfishing sandal– a great alternative to standard waders.

W.C. Russell Moccasin Co.
285 S.W. Franklin, Berlin, WI 54923
(414) 361-2252   FAX: 3274
Est.: 1889   Staff: 30
Pres: Ralph Fabricius
Hand lasted custom made fishing, shooting boots and shoes. Any size, any width, color, height. Specializing in special orders and hard to fit boots.
See Our Ad Below

Simms Fishing Products
PO Box 3645,
Bozeman, MT 59772-3645
(406) 585-3557
FAX: (406) 585-3562
Mktg: Diane Bristol
Simms, innovators in fishing gear technology, manufacture the world's greatest waders and boots to fit every anglers needs. Whether you're fishing days are warm or Ex-Stream-ly cold, Simms has the gear.

Springbrook Mfg./Mangrove
8115 Sovereign Row,
Dallas, TX 75247
(800) 638-9052
FAX: (214) 638-8143
Est.: 1990
Contact: Rick Pope
Springbrook offers a full line of waders from neoprene to breathable.

Stream Line Inc.
7865 Day Rd., W., Bldg. B
Bainbridge Island, WA 98110
(206) 842-8501
FAX: (206) 842-0307
Contact: Schuyler Horton
Streamline offers the finest mens and womens neoprene and waterproof breathable waders, available in stocking foot or boot foot (lug or flat) in a wide variety of styles and sizes.

Top Line Manufacturing Co.
901 Murray Rd.
E. Hanover, NJ 07936
(201) 560-9696
FAX: (201) 560-0661
Contact: John Duncan
Manufacturer of a complete line of rubber, canvas and neoprene hip and chest waders.

The Waterworks
73 California Ave.,
Orinda, CA 94563
(800) 435-9374   (510) 253-1664
FAX: (510) 253-1665
Contact: Ryan Harrison
Worn under your waders, "Underwaderwear", is made of a "moisture transport" fabric that wicks moisture away from the skin to the outer layer of the fabric but does not allow it to pass back. The result is a garment that remains comfortably dry no matter how much the flyfisher perspires.

Weinbrenner Shoe Co.
108 S. Polk St., Merrill, WI 54452
(800) 826-0002   (715) 536-5521
FAX: (800) 569-6817
Est.: 1892   Staff: 450
Contact: John Schenzel
Available: Retail
Maker of the high quality, ultra-lightweight Ultimate® wading shoes designed by Gary Borger.

EQUIPMENT/ WADING STAFF

Angler Accessories Ltd.
42 Maces Rd.,
Christchurch, New Zealand
011-64-3 3841477
FAX: 011-64-3 3841477
Contact: Marj Allan
Top quality laminated wading and
hiking staffs.

Cascade Designs, Inc.
4000 1st Ave., South
Seattle, WA 98134
(800) 531-9531
Tracks® Fish Stick is a shock-corded
staff for stream fishing and wading. Snaps together quickly and is
available in three lengths.

Ed Cumings, Inc.
PO Box 90118, Flint, MI 48509
(810) 736-0130
FAX: (810) 736-7701
Est.: 1927
President: Jeff Powell
Sales Admin.: Brenda Rutherford
Tubular fiberglass wading staffs
with rubber crutch tip, deluxe grip
and cord.

Fly Tyer's Carry-All
Box 299, Village Station
New York, NY 10014
(212) 242-2856
FAX: (212) 989-2989
Contact: Joan Stoliar
Designed specifically for wading,
Folstaf® folds easily and compactly
to only 9", yet springs open instan-
taneously and locks into a sturdy
shaft that can't collapse–Tungsten
carbide tip for positive bottom grip.
Folstaf® models are available for
every type of wader and wading situation.

Flycatcher Fishing Co.
38 Don Gabriel Way
Orinda, CA 94563
(800) FLY-STAF (415) 362-1214
FAX: (415) 433-4456
Contact: Marc Ericksen
The Flycatcher Wading Staff is a
sturdy double tubed light weight
wading staff that has the ability to
extend eight feet with a folding
hook. Ideal for retreiving flies and
lures tangled in trees. "It's the only
wading staff that pays for itself."

Leki-Sport USA
60 Earhart Dr., #18
Williamsville, NY 14221
(800) 255-9982
FAX: (716) 633-8063

Contact: Debbie Cramp
High-tech, lightweight adjustable
wading staffs featuring carbide
tips, various grip options, accessories and attachments.

FLIES

Accardo/Peck's Poppers
3708 Conrad St.
Baton Rouge, LA 70805
(504) 355-0863
FAX: (504) 355-0420
Est.: 1950   Staff: 19
Contact: Tony or Matthew Accardo
We are the fly fishing people–everything for the avid fly fisherman. We
only sell and specialize in fly poppers and accessories.

Angling Specialties
3731 Stucky Rd.
Bozeman, MT 59715
(406) 587-7246
FAX: (406) 587-7246
Est.: 1979   Staff: 3
Owners: Bob and Jean Granger
Flies of all types, specializing in
bead head nymphs. Sales to con-
sumers as well as fly shops across
SW Montana.

B-17 Fly Tackle Ltd.
9164 Brady, Redford, MI 48239
(313) 255-2838
FAX: (313) 531-4233
Est.: 1989   Staff: 3
Founder: Thom. Hnizdor
Diving, deep-diving, floating, sinking, riffling, finning, popping,
waking, chugging, jumping, revolving, counter-revolving, keeling,
wiggling, wobbling, scenting and
neutral buoyancy flies. Over
130,000 flies in stock. Call for our
12-page, 4-color catalog of unique
flies.

Otto Beck Co.
1208 Bower Hill Rd.
Pittsburgh, PA 15243
(800) 323-3083 (412) 276-4112
FAX: (412) 276-7397
Contact: Gretchen Beck
750 stock patterns immediately
available in both salt and freshwater. We are also happy to do
custom tying for your fly shop.
Dealer inquiries only–thank you.

Bighorn Fly Trading Co.
1517 14th St., W.
Suite 229, Billings, MT 59102
(406) 652-1557
FAX: (406) 652-1557
Contact: Roger Lee
Manufacturer and wholesale distributor of superb quality flies for
discriminating shops. Own two
overseas factories. Custom orders
welcome.

Black Canyon Flies & Supplies
91 Market St.
Wappingers Falls, NY 12590
(800) 544-7343 (914) 297-0098
FAX: (914) 297-0142
Est.: 1990
Contact: Janet Zito
Peter Zito
Manufacturer and distributor of fly
tying material and American-made
flies. Wholesale catalog available.
Dealer inquiries only–thank you.

Blue Ribbon Flies
Box 1037,
West Yellowstone, MT 59758
(406) 646-7642
Contact: Craig or Jackie Mathews
Blue Ribbon offers a variety of fly
patterns, Yellowstone and saltwater flies, and numerous new fly
selections. Call for more information.

Mr. Bob's Lucky Day Lures
15759 Widewater Dr.
Dumfries, VA 22026
(800) 962-2682
Featuring new soft bodies & do-it-
yourself kits for novice, master
maker of the popular "Prissy Miss &
Mr. Jet" bugs.

Brookside Flies
Distributed by J.S. Marketing Inc.
8200 E. Pacific Place, #202
Denver, CO 80231
(303) 369-8839
FAX: (303) 369-8938
Contact: Jerry R. Schreiber

Bud's Bugs
Hand Crafted Flies
26183 Chambers Ave.
Sun City, CA 92586
(909) 679-1647
FAX: (909) 679-1647
Est.: 1988
Owner: Robert (Bud) J. Nichols, II
Handcrafted flies & custom fishing
rods.

Bunyan Bug Co.
PO Box 33, Grennough, MT 59836
(406) 543-4408
FAX: (406) 543-4282
Contact: Richard Rose
The Bunyan Bug Dry Fly

Castlerock Tackle Company
PO Box 8977, Chico, CA 95927
(916) 894-2201
Contact: Lance Gray
Saltwater flies and poppers

Catskill Creations
RR1, Box 201, DeBruce Rd.
Livingston Manor, NY 12758
(914) 439-3934 (after 6pm)
Est.: 1994
Contact: Dave Catizone
Quality fly collectibles, presentation
salmon, steelhead and Catskill flies.
Angling related appraisals/fly au-
thentications. Mail order only.
Brochure upon request.

Catskill Flies
309 Mt. Cliff Rd.
Hurleyville, NY 12747
(914) 434-2268
Est.: 1990   Staff: 5
Owner: Dennis Skarka
Fine quality flies tied in the traditional manner by local tiers–nothing
imported! Guaranteed delivery.

Caylor Custom Flies
251 Sawmill Rd.
Todd, NC 28684
(704) 297-5426
FAX: (704) 297-5426
Est.: 1990
Contact: Roger Caylor
Specializing in trout flies. Mail order
catalog available.

Check Your Fly
3141 Beaver Lane
Trappe, MD 21673
(410) 476-3342
Est.: 1996
Contact: Steven V. Culver
Saltwater flies proven for the Chesapeake region as well as the rest of
the East Coast.

Cypert's Waterbugs, Inc.
Rt. 1, Box 128A
Aquilla, TX 76622
(817) 694-3422
Est.: 1990
Contact: Charlie Cypert
High quality foil pencil poppers &
flies. Retail & wholesale–fresh & salt-
water. Also retail tying supplies and
materials.

Kennebunkport, Maine

Dirigo Flies
PO Box 2066
Kennebunkport, ME 04046
(207) 967-5889
FAX: (207) 985-4955
Contact: Jim Dionne
Fresh and saltwater flies using on
the finest hooks and materials.
Over 75 selected patterns that
work anywhere. Tarpon, southern
and northeast fly selections a spe-
cialty.

Donner & Blitzen Fly Co.
9931 NE Mason
Portland, OR 97220
(503) 256-2637   (406) 243-1044
FAX: (503) 254-0744
Est.: 1996
Contact: Jeff Morgan
Custom top quality trout, steel-
head, bass and panfish flies, both
for commercial & individual buyers.

**Edge Water Fishing
Products Inc.**
35 N. 1000 W.
Clearfield, UT 84015
(800) 584-7647   (801) 825-8982
FAX: (801) 825-0624
Contact: Ed Miya
Manufacturers of closed-cell foam
flies and shaped component parts
of various sizes.

Edgewater Company
35 North 1000 West
Clearfield, UT 84015
(800) 584-7647
Contact: Ed Miya

Scott Eno Tackle Co.
PO Box 29, Parish, NY 13131
(315) 625-4064
Contact: Scott Eno
Produce molded bodies on hooks.
Use hard plastics and soft foams.
Originator of the En Razorback
Streamer. Very unusual designs.

Farlow & MacPhail, Inc.
Angler's Choice Flies™
5121 W. 98th Ave.
Westminster, CO 80030
(303) 438-6770
FAX: (303) 438-6765
Contact: Larry Farlow
Value-priced fishing flies–available
in bulk or prepackaged assort-
ments. Dealer inquiries
welcome–thank you.

Fischer's Flies
1417 Orr Dr.
Castle Shannon, PA 15234
(412) 884-2838
Est.: 1994
Contact: David Fischer
Custom specialized flies, jewelry
and art.

Flatwater Flies
7 Thompson St.
East Patchogue, NY 11772
(516) 447-1713
Contact: Bob Lindquist
Flatwater Flies is a unique company
offering both classic and original
saltwater fly patterns. We able to
develop designs which are fished
continually all season long–and
proven to produce!

Flies by Ilene
9630 Basher Dr.
Anchorage, AK 99507
(907) 338-7552
Contact: Ilene Hirsh
Manufacturer and distributor of cus-
tom flies for the Alaskan angler.
Tied in Alaska, by Alaskans.

New World Design . . . Old World Craftsmanship

Fly Pros Fishing Flies
19039 Killoch Way
Northbridge, CA 91326
(818) 360-4946
FAX: (818) 366-7433
Est.: 1993
Contact: Eric Berry, Proprietor
Because we fish all year round, we
know the critical value of well-
crafted flies. Try us–for Quality,
Value and Service. Thank you. Deal-
ers only please.

Fly of the Month Club™
Box 325, Lake Zurich, IL 60047
(800) 895-7036
FAX: (847) 726-7331   Est.: 1994
Contact: Lorraine Grobarek
The club designed by fishermen...for fishermen. Monthly
mailings of high quality flies, fishing
information and a periodic member
newsletter. Additional flies may be
purchased at special value prices.
Membership is tailored to your specific fishing interests. Also makes a
great gift. Call, fax or write for a
free brochure and membership application.

Frontier Flies, Inc.
PO Box 384, Corvallis, OR 97339
(800) 357-5408
FAX: (800) 357-5408
Est.: 1995   Staff: 45
President: Troy A. Bachmann
Offering hundreds of trout, steelhead and saltwater flies, as well as flyfishing accessories.

Gaines Fly Rod Products
Box 35, Gaines, PA 16921
(814) 435-2332
FAX: (814) 435-3474
Est.: 1947
Contact: Tom Eggler
Large selection of fresh and saltwater poppers. Dealer inquiries welcome.

Ted Godfrey's
3509 Pleasant Plains Dr.
Reisterstown, MD 21136
(410) 239-8468
Est.: 1972   Staff: 2
Owner: Ted Godfrey
Flies for Atlantic salmon, steelhead and trout.

HR Legacy Fly Goods
1033 E. Moorhead Circle
Boulder, CO 80303
(800) 872-8498
(303) 449-1510
FAX: (303) 449-1510
President: Penny Roberts
Manufacturer of trout, salmon, bass saltwater and steelhead flies.

Headwaters Fly Company
106 Paisley Ct.,
Bozeman, MT 59715
(406) 585-1743
Custom tied flies of the highest quality.

Hill Country Flyfishers
Box 2393, Wimberley, TX 78676
(512) 847-5421
Contact: Kevin
We specialize in custom hand tied bass and saltwater flies.

Holly Flies
Box 46, 518 N. Walnut St.
Mt. Holly Springs, PA 17065
(800) 451-5644   (717) 486-4646
Contact: Vic DeLan
We specialize in high-quality flies for the fly fishing specialty shop. Dealer inquiries only–thank you.

J.S. Marketing Inc.
8200 E. Pacific Place, #202
Denver, CO 80231
(303) 369-8839
Contact: Jerry R. Schreiber
Distributors of Brookside Flies and fly tying materials. 24 hour turnaround, large inventory. Tied with Daiichi Hooks and Hoffman Hackle; blend our own dubbings. Choice of the guides since 1989.

Jackson Cardinal Flies
Box 1280, Jackson, WY 83001
(307) 733-4877
FAX: (307) 733-7791
Contact: Kirk L. Stone
Flies, free display boxes, vest reels & clippers and floatants. Color catalog. Dealers only–thank you.

John's Custom Flies
PO Box 379, Sanford, MI 48651
(517) 687-9202
FAX: (517) 687-7103
Contact: John Kilmer
Manufacturer and international distributor of quality trout, steelhead and salmon flies. Specializing in custom orders for local patterns.

Knauff Hackle & Flies
1763 Blue Run Rd.
Lucasville, OH 45648
(614) 820-2650
Contact: Roger Knauff
Knauff Hackle & Flies; Distributor of quality flies specializing in saltwater patterns tied with our own quality saltwater hackle.

LP Fly Co.
12 Raemar Ct., Bethpage, NY 11714
(516) 931-6714
FAX: (516) 931-6714
Contact: President
LP Fly Co. produces large, realistic baitfish patterns, specially designed for use in saltwater.

Lisk Lures
Box 10116, Greensboro, NC 27404
Contact: Eva Lisk
Manufacturer of fly rod and spinning lures for over 40 years.

LOON OUTDOORS
7737 W. Mossy Cup St.
Boise, ID 83709
(800) 580-3811
FAX: (800) 574-0422
Contact: Ken Smith
A unique variety of dries, wets and saltwater flies which are tied in Idaho and feature Loon fly tying components–cements, lacquers, epoxies and dubbing materials are available.

Lords of the Fly
PO Box 189, Monroe, WA 98272
(360) 794-2392
Contact: Mark Broer
Five different fly box kits for specific
regions of the country. Each kit contains 24 finished, professionally tied
flies for $34.95.

Lure & Feather Co.
400 Pantigo Rd.
East Hampton, NY 11937
(516) 267-6307
FAX: (516) 267-3631
Contact: Gabriele Brouillaud
Saltwater flies, retail and wholesale
available.

Maxwell MacPherson, Jr.
PO Box 141, Bristol, NH 03222
(603) 744-6514
Atlantic salmon flies classically
dressed for the collector.

Mayfly Enterprises
Waterwisp Flies
Box 151028,
Chevy Chase, MD 20815
(301) 652-3848
FAX: (301) 652-8224
CEO: James Greene
Manufacturers of the patented line
of Waterwisp dry flies-35 patterns
for selective trout.

McKenzie Fly Tackle
1075 A Shelley St.
Springfield, OR 97477
(541) 741-8161
FAX: (541) 741-7565
Est.: 1971   Staff: 20
Sales Mgr: Dale Williams
Manufacturer and distributor of
high-quality flies, materials and fly
tackle. Dealer inquiries only–thank
you.

Muley Brand Inc.
713 Colt Dr., Loveland, CO 80537
(970) 622-0147
FAX: (970) 622-0147
Contact: Dan Mommer
US distributor of Mouches Neptune
Flies of Canada. 300+ patterns with
700,000 flies in stock. Dealer Inquries Only–Thank You.

Mystic Bay Flies
Box 1080, 39 Rodoalph Way
Dennis, MA 02638
(800) 255-4310 (508) 385-3965
FAX: (508) 385-3186
Owner: Kenneth Nelson

Owner: Maura Murphy
From our outstanding SeaFoam™
Poppers to variations on the classic
Deceiver, Sandeel and Tarpon patterns, Mystic Bay Flies utilizes
premium, saltwater sturdy materials and painstaking craftsmanship
to produce superior saltwater flies.
Prompt service, large inventories
and same-day shipping. Custom tying
available with reliable lead times.

Northwest Ties, Inc.
48582 McKenzie Hwy.
Nimrod, OR 97488
(800) 334-8437
(541) 896-3781
FAX: (541) 896-3906
Est.: 1985   Staff: 4
Contact: Ann Bono
A full line of freshwater and saltwater flies, anglers' corner fly tying
materials, fly tying kits and high
gloss fly tying cements.

ORVIS®

Orvis Company
Rt. 7A, Manchester, VT 05254
(800) 333-1550 (Ext. 844)
(802) 362-3622
Orvis product development specialists search the world over for new
and innovative fly patterns and
offer hundreds of patterns, sizes
and innovations such as Orvis Big
Eye™ hooks and barbless patterns
for catch & release anglers. From
trout to tarpon, no matter what the
fish Orvis has the fly that will catch it.
For more information on Orvis flies
call 800-333-1550 (Ext. 844).

Pacific Fly Group
730 East Huntington Dr.
Monrovia, CA 91016
(800) 582-5145
FAX: (818) 305-6661
Est.: 1994
Contact: Edward Han
The Best Source for
Your Next Fly Order
*Premium Quality
* Fantastic Program
* Great Service
We use Daiichi Hooks and Hoffman
Hackle, 300 patterns in stock, pres-
sure free buying program,
reasonable price, no minimum

quantity, on-time delivery, excellent
fill rate. We stand behind our flies.

Phantom Flies
International, Inc., PO Box 90568
Henderson, NV 89009-0568
(702) 558-0088
FAX: (702) 564-3961
Contact: Russell Schultheiss
Tying operation specializing in quality WoolHead Streamers and
unique trout style patterns of
proven performance. Dealer inquiries only–thank you.

Phone Flies
24 Blades Run Dr.
Shrewsbury, NJ 07702
(800) 367-3543
Phone Flies offers you color photos
of over 600 flies and 25 fly selections at the best prices in the
nation. Call for a free catalog, 6
days a week, 10am-9pm EST.

Premier Fly Company
Sales Office:
1100 Summit Ave., Ste. 102
Plano, TX 75074
(972) 424-5585 FAX: 3491
Contact: Brad Kottinger
Every fly we produce is tied to the
quality expectations of your customers. With a large inventory of trout,
steelhead, warm and saltwater flies
on hand, and a dedicated sales
staff ready to share their experience, we can match the hatch at
any time. Dealer Inquiries Only–
Thank You.

Riverborn™

Riverborn Fly Co., Inc.
Box 65, Wendell, ID 83355
(800) 354-5534
FAX: (208) 536-6103
Est.: 1987   Staff: 6
Pres/Owner: Warren E. Schoth
VP/Owner: Steve Hunter
Riverborn manufactures and distributes quality flies second to none in
performance, design and original-
ity. All styles and types are
represented in our catalog, including our own popular Black Ear
Rubber Legs, Super Prawns, Neon
Nymphs, and Rocky Road Caddis.
Strict continuous quality control
and the best materials available in-
sure confidence when your
customer demands the best in flies
for trout, steelhead, bass or saltwater action.
See Our Ad Pg. 49

Hank Roberts Flies

Sales Office: 1100 Summit Ave.,
Ste. 102, Plano, TX 75074
(972) 424-5585
FAX: (972) 424-3491
Contact: Brad Kottinger
Headquarters:
313 W. North St., Arkon, OH 44303
1-800-252-5873
Fax: 216-253-1251
Manufacturer and distributor of
top quality flies, fly tying tools, kits
and display boxes. Dealer Inquiries
Only–Thank You.

Rogan of Donegal

Bridge End, Ballyshannon
Co. Donegal, Ireland
011-353-72-51335
011-353-72-52784
Mgng. Dir: David Feely
Established by Michael Rogan in
1830, Rogan of Donegal has been
tying Atlantic salmon flies by hand
for over 160 years. Available direct
from company. Call or fax for our
brochure.

Al Rogers Flies

PO Box 297, Etowah, NC 28729
(704) 891-7179   **(704) 891-7345**

Est.: 1985   Staff: 2
Contact: Al Rogers
Top grade mail order trout flies–
price list at a wholesale price.

Round Rocks Fly Fishing

3663 North Hwy. 91
Smithfield, UT 84335
(800) 992-8774
FAX: (801) 755-3311
Contact: Kohn Smith

Royal Coachman

PO Box 423, Lexington, TX 78947
(512) 273-2545
Est.: 1982   Staff: 3
Contact: Frank or Don Perry
Presentation grade flies for all species. Hand tied leaders. Bulletin
type catalog available.

Royal Wulff Products

HCR1, Box 70
Lew Beach, NY 12758
(800) 328-3638   **(914) 439-4060**
FAX: (914) 439-8055
Contact: Doug Cummings

Shamrock Flies

Umpqua Feather Merchants
PO Box 700, Glide, OR 97443
(800) 462-9336   **(541) 496-3512**

FAX: (541) 496-0150
Contact: Gus Wunderly

Shasta Fly & Rod

4204 Shasta Dam Blvd.
Shasta Lake, CA 96019
(916) 275-6221
FAX: (916) 275-2655
Est.: 1972
Owner: David Stammet
Owner: Jean Stammet
Owner: John Stammet
Manufacturer of high quality flies:
dries, nymphs, steelhead, Alaskan,
saltwater, and the main source for
single egg patterns. Distributor of
McFLYFOAM products.

Cam Sigler

Box 656, Vashon Island, WA 98070
(206) 567-4836
FAX: (206) 567-4940
Contact: Cam Sigler
Produces a line of big game flies,
mini tubes and silicone flies. Dealer
inquiries welcome.

Skykomish Flies

McKenzie Fly Tackle Co.
PO Box 70165, Eugene, OR 97401
(541) 741-8161

ANATOMY OF A FLY

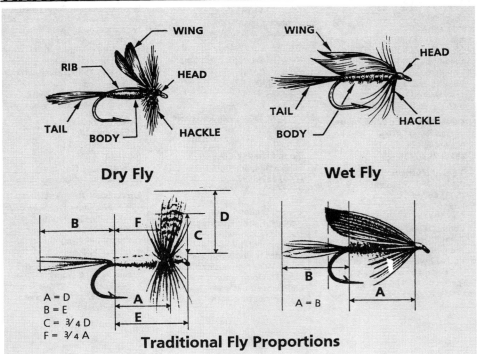

Dry Fly   Wet Fly

A = D
B = E
C = ¾ D
F = ¾ A

A = B

Traditional Fly Proportions

FAX: (541) 741-7565
Contact: Dale Williams
Est.: 1971
A complete line of wholesale fly fishing accessories and fishing flies. UPC Standard.

Solitude Fly Company
207 N. Stoneman Ave., Suite 10
Alhambra, CA 91801
(818) 458-6624
FAX: (818) 308-9068
Est.: 1995
Contact: John Bonk or Ray Chang
We offer quality flies and accessories: standard & parachute dry flies, terrestrials, nymphs, streamers, and the Brooks' fly series.

Spirit River
423 Winchester St.
Roseburg, OR 97470
(503) 440-6916
FAX: (503) 672-4309
Contact: Bill Black or Richard Wolfe
Manufacturer and distributor of pro-shop quality flies, materials, dispensers, boxes and streamside accessories. Please send SASE to request a color brochure.

Springbrook Mfg./Mangrove
8115 Sovereign Row
Dallas, TX 75247
(800) 638-9052
FAX: (214) 638-8143
Est.: 1990
Contact: Rick Pope
Springbrook has the widest possible variety of flies in stock-now. We've got 'em all! And when your order arrives in our office-via phone, fax or mail-we get it out as quickly as possible. Because, when it comes to flies-we deliver!

Doug Swisher Fly Fishing
29 San Remo Circle
Naples, FL 34112
(941) 793-7438

Teeny Nymph Company
PO Box 989, Gresham, OR 97030
(503) 667-6602
FAX: (503) 667-2917
Est.: 1971
Contact: Craig Inglesby
Teeny Nymphs, Teeny Leeches and Teeny Flash Flies. The Teeny Nymph holds 22 world records. An effective pattern on a wide variety of species that can be used year round.

Temple Fork Outfitters
196 South 100 East
Logan, UT 84321
(801) 753-1823
FAX: (801) 752-4074
President: Dennis Brown
Contact: Breon J. Robertson
Specialty and Beaded flys developed by professional fly fishing guides and tiers. Each pattern extensively field tested. Call or write for information.

Teton Flies
Div. of Jackson Cardinal
PO Box 1280, Jackson, WY 83001
(307) 733-4877
FAX: (307) 733-7791
Contact: Kirk L. Stone
Flies tied with American hackle and chemically sharpened hooks. Pro-shop quality, catalog–dealers only.

Thunderhead Swimming Flies & Lures
2984 Lostwood Dr., Sandy, UT 84092
(801) 572-0872
FAX: (801) 572-0872
Contact: Jim Perrick
Each Thunderhead Lure has a secret plastic lip that provides life-like action and fish calling vibrations.

Tight Lines
1100 Main St., PO Box 362
Housatonic, MA 01236
(413) 274-6143
Contact: Chris Windram
Wholesale and retail custom saltwater flies.

Traditionally Tied Flies
PO Box 80293
Portland, OR 97280
(503) 452-7624
Contact: Peter Rapport
We offer carefully chosen collections of proven patterns (wet, dry & nymph) directly to the fisherman.

True Life Fly Co.
PO Box 444, Smethport, PA 16749
(800) 488-3597
FAX: (814) 887-1975
Est.: 1951   Staff: 15
Owner: Gordon Colton
Heritage Fishing Flies are tied by artisans in Northwestern Pennsylvania and upstate New York using domestic materials and Mustad hooks. We produce high quality traditional flies of uniform pattern, size, color and silhouette. We are about catching fish, not fishermen.

Turrall USA
45 Knobhill St.
Sharon, MA 02067
(617) 784-3732
FAX: (617) 784-3732
Contact: Steven Pransky
Makers of quality flies. Hand-made high-carbon hooks. Fly-tying materials, kits and tools.

U.S. Fly Tyers
Box 4374, Harrisburg, PA 17111
(717) 657-9717
Contact: Robert Markowski
All flies are tied in the U.S. 375 different patterns: sizes #3/0 to #28. A wide variety of flies are available including Saltwater Flies. Call or write for free catalog.

Umpqua Feather Merchants
PO Box 700, Glide, OR 97443
(800) 322-3218   (541) 496-3512
FAX: (541) 496-0150   Est.: 1972
Nat'l. Sales Mgr: Gus Wunderly
In the specialized world of fly fishing, Umpqua is the name that's best known for flies. With more than 1,100 fly patterns in our list, Umpqua offers not only the classic, time-tested patterns, but also the hottest new flies from our great fly tyers. Even better, Umpqua flies are tied to last. Our quality control is the toughest in the industry. That means every Umpqua fly matches the original pattern exactly in color; materials and proportions. Look for Umpqua flies & other great products at the fly tackle dealer nearest you.

Under Water Fly's
3713 Clover Lane
Madison, WI 53714
(608) 221-4744
Contact: Jay R. Horner
Manufacturer of salmon flies

Upstream Innovations
406 Beaver Creek Rd., Suite 352
Oregon City, OR 97045
(503) 557-7064
FAX: (503) 557-3022
Contact: Rick Hagan
Exclusive manufacturer of Upstream fly tying products. Broad array of catch-and-release landing nets. Unique/comprehensive series of Western lake flies.

Versitex Of America

Versitex of America Ltd.
3545 Schuylkill Rd.
Spring City, PA 19475
(610) 948-4442
FAX: (800) 331-6406
Est.: 1985   Staff: 6
President: Frederic S. Claghorn, Jr.
Office Mgr: Nancy M. Ewing
Available: Retail & Direct
Extensive stocked selection of salt-
water and freshwater flies.
See Our Ad Page 102

IMPORTERS & EXPORTERS

Vjender International
PO Box 8432, Delhi 110052 India
011-91-11-7428903
FAX: 011-91-11-7252857
Contact: Kishan Singh
Est.: 1900
Fancy feathers, peacock feathers,
cock necks, saddles, hackles, cock
feathers. Fly tying material, fly tying
tools, Indian flies & fishing flots. Exporter & importer worldwide. Large
stock of feathers for wholesale
only. Call for a free catalog.

Warsa Flies
1820 Canterbury Dr.
Valdosta, GA 31602
(912) 253-9072
FAX: (912) 249-9475
Contact: Joe Branham
Available: Retail & Direct
Email: jbranham@surfsouth.com
Umpqua contract tyer
Catalog available and on-line cata-
log available

Water Wisp Flies
Distrib. by Raymond C. Rumpf & Son
PO Box 319, Sellersville, PA 18960
(215) 257-0141
FAX: (215) 453-9758
Contact: Cindy Novack

Willie Fishing Flies Ltd.
PO Box 7422, Nakuru, Kenya
011-254-037-45861
Est.: 1986   Staff: 2
FAX: 011-254-037-42809
Director: Wilson Mungai Ndagatha
Presently selling in the UK, capable
of providing 10,000 dozen a month.
Looking to expand into the US.

Yellowstone Fly Goods
5350 Holiday Ave.
Billings, MT 59101
(800) 262-1098   (406) 256-0799
FAX: (406) 256-3353
Est.: 1988
Contact: Mike Hoiness
Wholesale distributor of some of
the finest flies available today. Our
primary focus is on trout flies, but
we also carry a line of pike, bass,
steelhead and saltwater patterns.

FLY TYING AIDS

"Dinsmores" Modular Boxes
Distributed by Belvoirdale
PO Box 176, Wyncote, PA 19095
(215) 886-7211
FAX: (215) 886-1804
President: Grahame Maisey
Small and large modular boxes
make ideal hook and material orga-
nizers. Convenient sizes and
modularity.

Donegan Optical Co.
15549 W. 108th St.
Lenexa, KS 66219
(913) 492-2500
FAX: (913) 492-2503
Est.: 1952
Sales Mgr: Bill Donegan, Jr.
Manufacture the Optizisor™, which
is a binocular head band magnifier.

Goodwin Mfg. Company
241 Main St., PO Box 378
Luck, WI 54853
(800) 282-5267
FAX: (715) 472-2810
Est.: 1991   Staff: 5
President: Mark McGarraugh
The Giraffe™ Lighting & Magnify-
ing System is compatible with all
types of fly tying vises. Call for information on the best fly tying lighting
system available today.

Jiffy Steamer
PO Box 869, Rt. 3
Union City, TN 38261
(901) 885-6690
Manufacturers of professional
feather and hat steamers, Model
J1...costing about $120.

King Tool, Inc.
5350 Love Lane
Bozeman, MT 59715
(406) 586-1541
FAX: (406) 585-9028
Contact: Steven J. Emerson
The RoughNeck™ quality industrial

grade inspection light and magnifier for fly tying. Also streamside
digital thermometers and accessories.

Lap Trap Aprons
Fishing for Ideas, 9 Woodland Rd.
Sewickley, PA 15143
(800) 588-8727   (412) 741-7622
FAX: (412) 741-7713
Contact: Tom Potter
Lap Trap fly-tyer's apron, magnetic
hook keepers, easy to use hair-
stackers, and other innovative
products.

Luxo Lamp Corp.
36 Midland Ave.
Port Chester, NY 10573
(800) 222-5896
Manufacturer of the Luxo
Illuminated Magnification system
that uses a primary lens for most
tasks, and a secondary lens for increased magnification. Call or write
for more information.

MFD Enterprises, Inc.
222 Sidney Baker St., #204
Kerrville, TX 78028
(210) 896-6060
FAX: (210) 896-6064
Contact: Mary Frances Sherlock
MagEye's is a hands-free head-
mounted magnifier with visor.

Mag Eye's
222 Sidney Baker South
Suite 204, Kerrville, TX 78028
(800) 210-6662
FAX: (210) 896-6064
Contact: Mary Francis Sherlock
Head-mounted, hands-free magnifier.

Selden Craft, Inc.
1157 Highland Ave.
Cheshire, CT 06410
(203) 272-0559
FAX: (203) 272-0559
Contact: Tony Selden
Magni-Tyer (a magnifier-light combination); Enlarger-Lite (a rimless
magnifier lens & separate lamp). All
SeldenCraft products are fully guaranteed.

Spirit River
423 Winchester St.
Roseburg, OR 97470
(503) 440-6916
Contact: Bill Black
Specialize in dispensing & organiza-
tional tools for tyers. Wholesale
only–thank you.

Zelco Industries
630 South Columbus
Mt. Vernon, NY 10551
(914) 699-6230
Manufacturer of fly tying lamps.

FLY TYING/
DESKS/TABLES/CASES

Andras Flyfishing Enterpr.
3-1 Park Plaza, Suite 185
Old Brookville, NY 11545
(516) 671-7376
FAX: (516) 676-6849
Contact: Andrew Laszlo
Handcrafted, hand cut, hand polished fly-tie benches realistically
conceived by a fly fisherman for fly
fishermen like you. Also available:
The HATCH, a tough, functional,
affordable, and truly portable fly-
tying bench. Dealer inquiries
welcome. Call or write for information. Free brochure available.

Bench in a Box
2181 South Alton Way
Denver, CO 80231
(800) 645-6432   (303) 369-8239
Contact: Lou Halsell
Now...tie flies anywhere with
Bench in a Box–the perfect home
and travel bench. Sturdy, easy and
quick to set up and complete.
Write or call for a free brochure or
the dealer nearest you.

Brookhoppers
115 Industrial Dr.
Northampton, MA 01060
(413) 586-3528
President: Walter Price
Fly-fishing history, art and elegance
all rolled into one: The Fly Tyer's
Rolltop Desk–a fly-tying desk wor-
thy of the tradition of the sport.
Exquisitely crafted from red oak or
American black cherry. A classic addition to any living room or or
study. Call or write for more information.

The Bug Box™

D&T Enterprises, 20518 Meadow
Lake Rd. Snohomish, WA 98290
(360) 805-9231
FAX: (360) 794-2031 Est.: 1992
Contact: Doug Cooper
The Bug Box™ is an excellent, organized, all-in-one unit for all your
fly tying needs "in the home or on
the road." Handcrafted and built to
last. Quality and craftsmanship are
evident throughout. The Bug Box™
is used by hundreds of satisfied anglers including Poul Jorgensen,
Chuck Stranahan and endorsed by
Trout Unlimited. Call today to get a
free color brochure that fully describes this affordable necessity.
See Our Ad Above

Dannick Design
1762 E. State St., Eagle, ID 83616
(208) 939-8275
FAX: (208) 377-4056
Contact: Dan Seniw
The fly tying table holds 12 tools
and 9 thread spools; arms have
magnetic strips to hold hooks and
flies; movable glue pot to avoid
spills; vise arm adjusts & can be easily switched for right or left-handed
fly tying.

D.B. Dun Inc.
2801 W. Idaho, Boise, ID 83702
(208) 344-5445
FAX: (208) 344-4892
Est.: 1986
Contact: Dan Baumgardner
D.B. Dun offers a ruggedly constructed, portable, fly tying kit bag
that includes 27 pockets and a rigid
vice platform. Exceptionally well organized. Leather and brass
appointments. Contact your local
dealer or call directly.

Evets & Co.
5825 Dover St., Oakland, CA 94609
(510) 652-9387
FAX: (510) 654-0557
Line of quality products for the avid
angler and fly tyer, including the
Evets Travel-Ty® a soft-pack stor-
age/travel system designed
specifically for fly-tying tools & materials. Write or call for free brochure.

Fly Tye Designs
7732 Lemhi, Boise, ID 83709
(208) 327-0601
FAX: (208) 327-0909

Contact: Brad Shoebridge
Fly Tye Designs offers the finest in
tying tables and portable fly cases.

Fly Tyer's Carry-All
46 Jane St., New York, NY 10014
(212) 242-2856
FAX: (212) 989-2989
Contact: Joan Stoliar
The Carry-All with Mini-Vac Vise
Base is a handsome, portable canvas case for holding fly-tying
materials and work board.

The Flyfishing Company
491 N. 1100 E., Bountiful, UT 84010
(800) 600-0272
FAX: (801) 295-3932
Contact: Doug Jansen
Windriver, Rocky Mountain or Grand
Canyon Series flytying tables.

Fort Shockley
3711 Crooked Creek
Diamond Bar, CA 91765
(909) 595-0612   Est.: 1993
Contact: Greg Shockley
Noel's box is an affordably priced,
beautifully crafted oak box providing a fully self-contained and
portable fly tying station. Call or
write for free literature.

Freestone Design
202 Nutwood Dr.
Jamestown, NC 27282
(910) 454-4151
Est.: 1995
Owner: Larry Currie
Distinctive fly tying desks in the tradition of fine furniture–freestanding
or bench.

H. Gerstner & Sons
20 Cincinnati St., Dayton, OH 45407
(513) 228-1662
FAX: (513) 228-8557
Est.: 1906 Staff: 20
Contact: Jack Campbell
Manufacturer of finely crafted hardwood chest designed specifically
for the serious fly tyer. Made in
America since 1906. Call for information.

J.W. Outfitters
169 Balboa St.
San Marcos, CA 92069
(619) 471-2171
FAX: (619) 471-1719
Contact: Jeff Wieringa
J.W. Outfitters T.O.T.L. (Top of the
Line) fly tying valise is the most advanced organizer in the industry.
Our new foam forming design with
its unique modular pocket system
will please even the most articulate
fly tyer. See your nearest dealer or
call for a free brochure.

LOON OUTDOORS
7737 W. Mossy Cup St.
Boise, ID 83709
(800) 580-3811
FAX: (800) 574-0422
Contact: Ken Smith
Our economical tying bench and storage base features quality solid oak construction. Measuring 24" by 12", the Desktop includes an adjustable vice arm, magnets for hooks, and handy places for spools, tools and bottles. The oak pedestal base stores hackle, dubbing and more...comes with a Loon bench kit and an assortment of fly tying accessories. Contact Loon for information.

Perry Design
7401 Zircon Dr., SW
Tacoma, WA 98498
(206) 582-1555
Contact: Jack E. Perry
Small benches

Pockit Sports
7235 Syracuse Dr., Dallas, TX 75214
(214) 553-1845
FAX: (214) 533-0347
Contact: Larry Notley
Pockit Sports Company offers 2 portable tying stations for beginners to experts which are also excellent for home or travel. In addition we offer a vise caddy and a tool chest which is designed to hold pliers, clippers and alike.

Probox Tackle Co.
1347 White Pine Dr.
Eagle River, WI 54521
(800) 545-3995 (715) 479-6194
Est.: 1981
Contact: Chester Meyers
Probox Tackle Co., manufactures the Fly 'N' Ty Tackle Box for the dedicated fly fisher. Fully functional, strong, light-weight and beautiful, this box allows you to carry all your tackle and tying needs directly to streamside. Write or call for information.

George D. Roberts, Inc.
4801 A. Tholozan
St. Louis, MO 63116
(800) 747-1897 (314) 351-8988
FAX: (314) 752-2114
Contact: George D. Roberts
Fine wood products for the fly tyer, including cabinets, benches and storage seats crafted from Grade 1 hardwoods. Call or write for a free catalog.

Sespe Supplies
925 A Calle-Puerto Vallarta
Santa Barbara, CA 93103
(805) 966-7263
Contact: Ted Long
Hand-built fly tying boxes in limited editions for the fly fisher who demands the best.

Signature Concepts
PO Box 1247
Ballston Lake, NY 12019
(518) 426-3214
FAX: (518) 426-4190
Est.: 1986   Staff: 25
President: Jeffrey R. Henry

Spruce Creek Wood Works
HC01, Box 94
Spruce Creek, PA 16683
(814) 632-8613
Contact: Jim Brown
Manufacturer of a beautiful, functional fly tyer's desk in either oak, walnut or cherry.

Tri-Angle Products, Inc.
Box 2414, Longmont, CO 80502
(303) 772-8992
Est.: 1987
Contact: Robert Konkle
Line of portable tying benches and cases, including a steering wheel tying bench. Dealer inquiries welcome. Call or write for brochure.

Wachter Landing Nets
10238 Deermont Trail
Dallas, TX 75243
(972) 238-0823
FAX: (972) 238-1641
Est.: 1986
Contact: Kathy Wachter
High quality, versatile fly tying desks made of solid cherry or oak.

Worrywood Fishing Prod.
Box 91943, Tucson, AZ 85752
(520) 744-0011
FAX: (520) 744-0011
Contact: Mike Giggy
This organized workstation has an unbelievable amount of room–"U" shaped layout keeps tools and material organized and within reach.

FLY TYING/ EQUIPMENT

A.K.'s Fly Tying Tools
PO Box 6250, 2162 Renard Ct.
Annapolis, MD 21401
(410) 573-0287 (800) 942-5359
FAX: (410) 573-0993
Est.: 1994
Contact: Tom Dougherty or Mike Busada
Simply "The Best" in fly tying tools and vises. Manufacturer of high quality fly tying vises, and a complete line of tying tools. Products include several proprietary designs available only from A.K.'s Fly Tying Tools, as well as enhanced version of many standard tying tools.

Angler's Choice™
by Suncoast of America, Inc.
PO Box 150250
Cape Coral, FL 33915
(941) 458-8411
FAX: (941) 458-1805
Contact: John Horky
Fly-tying tools and kits. Wholesale only–thank you.

Angling Surgeon
12515 SE 74th St.
Newcastle, WA 98056
(206) 255-6794
FAX: (206) 682-3309
Est.: 1990
Contact: L. Troy Hatch
Angling Surgeon provides advanced, top quality, innovative fly tying tools.

Anvil Industries
860 Repp Dr., Columbus, IN 47201
(812) 376-2775
FAX: (812) 372-7605
Contact: Donald E. Vogel
Anvil makes Taperizer scissors, the 80-T Super Taperizer and the 90-T Taperizer. The Taperizer features a multi tooth blade specially designed for thinning and blending natural and synthetic fibers.

Bill Ballan Vise
230 Seaman Ave.
Bayport, NY 11705
(516) 472-0744
FAX: (516) 472-0744
Est.: 1985
Contact: Gail Ballan

Three models, with granite or marble bases. Solid brass stems and fittings. The most attractive and functional vise on the market. Immediately available. Call today.

Bedford Sportsman South
3405 Frederica Rd.
St. Simons Island, GA 31522
(912) 638-5454
Contact: Larry Kennedy
Distributor of the Xuron vise parts.

Bhagwati Impex (P) Ltd.
PO Box 16052, 27, Circus Ave.
Calcutta 17 India
011-91-33-2407820
FAX: 011-91-33-2401165
President: Kailash Tibrewal
A complete line of fly tying equipment and material.

Blue Mountain Angler
1375 Barleen Dr.
Wallawalla, WA 99362
(509) 529-8733
FAX: (509) 529-8149
Contact: Max Rutzer
MAGNUM rotating vise, G-CAP and a tying table.

Cortland Line Co.
3736 Kellogg Rd., PO Box 5588
Cortland, NY 13045
(607) 756-2851
FAX: (607) 753-8835
Contact: Tom McCullough
Pro Class and Limited Class tying tools are made in America of highest quality. Call or write for catalog featuring our full line of fly tying equipment.

Crest Tools
Cascade/Crest Tools
13290 Table Rock Rd.
Central Point, OR 97502
(541) 826-4030
FAX: (541) 826-4698
Est.: 1978
Contact: Pat Dunlop

Dr. Slick
114 S. Pacific, Dillon, MT 59725
(800) 462-4474   (406) 683-6489
FAX: (406) 683-5123
Contact: Becky Benzel
Surgical quality fishing tools, including scissors, clamps, pliers, plier-cutters and accessories, for today's discriminating angler. Call or write for information.

Dyna-King
Abby Precision Mfg. Co.
70 Industrial Dr.,
Cloverdale, CA 95425
(800) 396-2546   (707) 894-5566
FAX: (707) 894-5990

Est.: 1981   Staff: 20
Hand-crafted fly-tying vises and accessories. All standard model Dyna-King vises give you state-of-the-art craftsmanship and performance in the field of hook holding capability. Call for more information and ask for Lenora.

EDGIN MANUFACTURING

Edgin Manufacturing
21321 L W. Airport Way
North Bend, OR 97459
(541) 756-1269
FAX: (541) 756-1694
Est.: 1989
Contact: Charlene Edgin
Innovative, functional tying tools and fly-fishing accessories. Our products are warranted against defects. All products are made entirely in USA. Please call for free brochure.

See Our Ad Across

The Fishing Line
65202 97th St., Bend, OR 97701
(800) 499-5420   (541) 317-1472
FAX: (541) 317-1514
Contact: Sheri Reynolds
Complete line of fly tying equipment. Call for more information.

Griffin Enterprises, Inc.
PO Box 754, Bonner, MT 59823
(406) 244-5407
FAX: (406) 244-5444
President: Bernard Griffin
Manufacturer of quality fly tying tools, vises and accessories. Our products carry a lifetime warranty.

Grizzley Tackle, Inc.
Box 2219, Bellingham, WA 98227
(360) 650-9141
Sales Mgr: Tom McGinnis
Fly tying equipment including vises, forceps & tweezers, scissors, pliers and miscellaneous tools. Wholesale only–thank you.

Grizzly Knife & Tackle
1821 Valencia St.
Bellingham, WA 98226
(360) 650-9141
FAX: (360) 676-1075
Est.: 1994   Staff: 5
Nat'l. Sales Mgr: Chris K. McBride
Exec. Ass't: Denise Amos
Wholesaler and importer of fly tying tools and fine cutlery.

HMH

HMH Vise
Kennebec River Fly & Tackle
39 Milliken Rd.
North Yarmouth, ME 04097
(800) 335-9057
(207) 829-4290
FAX: (207) 829-6002
Contact: John Bryan
The HMH Vise has set the "standard" for performance and reliability since 1974. It features unique interchangeable jaws, full rotary benefits and lifetime warranty. Free catalog.

Hornet Fly Tying Vises
PO Box 2558
Grand Junction, CO 81502
(970) 242-8038 (Dealer Orders)
FAX: (970) 245-1276
Contact: Jim Shults
Foot control, variable speed, two directions, motorized vise.

Integra Fly Fishing Products
309 Swarthmore Ave.
Gaithersburg, MD 20877
(301) 990-0095
FAX: (301) 990-3903
Est.: 1984
Contact: Anil S. Gautam or Arlene Moreno
Flies, fly tying vises, tools, kits, hackle, materials, accessories, rods, reels, line, leaders, nets and gifts. Waders, vests, tippets, rod tubes and boots.

Matarelli Tools
4426 Irving St.
San Francisco, CA 94122
(415) 564-2091
Contact: Frank Matarelli
Maker of fly tying bobbins, whip finishers and dubbing tools.

Matthias
4554 Campbell Rd.
Pennsbury, PA 18073
(215) 679-8988
Contact: Richard Matthias or Hillary Matthias
Rotary fly vise

Miltex Instrument Co.
6 Ohio Dr., Lake Success, NY 11042
(516) 775-7100
FAX: (516) 775-7185
Sales Mgr: Robert Pugliesi
Manufacturers and importers of scissors.

Norlander Company
PO Box 926, Kelso, WA 98626
(360) 636-2525
FAX: (360) 636-2558
Contact: Norm Norlander
"Tie better flies faster" with Norlander's revolutionary fly tying tools and products.

Pamola Fly Tool Co.
Box 435, Upton, MA 01568
(508) 529-6086
FAX: (508) 529-3828
Contact: Pam Newton
Manufacturer of the Pamola Fly Lathe, a unique fly tying vise that functions as a static or in-line rotary vise; holds hooks from size 28 to 6/0. Optional pedestal and vise extension. Designed and made in the U.S.

Perry Design
7401 Zircon Dr., SW
Tacoma, WA 98498
(206) 582-1555
Contact: Jack E. Perry
Perry Design tools are handcrafted from only the best materials and are tested by professionals in the field before being put on the market.

Pockit Sports
7235 Syracuse Dr., Dallas, TX 75214
(214) 553-1845
FAX: (214) 553-0347
Contact: Larry Notley

Prime Line Tools USA
Div. of Jackson Cardinal
Box 1280, Jackson, WY 83001
(307) 733-4877
FAX: (307) 733-7791
Contact: Kirk L. Stone
Vises, scissors, hackle pliers, bobbins, miscellaneous tools and accessories. Catalog available. Dealers only.

Rainy's Flies & Supplies
690 N. 100 East, Logan, UT 84321
(801) 753-6766
FAX: (801) 753-9155
Contact: L. Rainy Riding

Regal Vise
Regal Engineering Inc.
RFD2, Tully Rd., Orange, MA 01364
(508) 575-0488
Contact: Tea Doiron
The Regal Vise offers easy to open action jaws–no jaws adjustment needed. Holds hook sizes from 6/0 to 32, and the head adjusts 180 degrees up and down. Rotary model available with 360 degree rotation and 220 degree up and down movement. Please call for more information.

Renzetti, Inc.
6080 Grisson Pkwy.
Titusville, FL 32780
(610) 486-6711
FAX: (610) 486-6713
Est.: 1974
Contact: Andy Renzetti
A line of true rotary vises, vise accessories, attachment, including the top-of-the-line Master's Vise, and a full line of tying tools. Call for more information.

Question or problem?
Give Black's Fly Fishing a call 9 am - 5 pm E.S.T.
(908) 224-8700.

thread spools. The only adjustable tension bobbin, made in U.S.A.

The Roby Bug Master
S.M. Roby Custom Flies
866 Roosevelt St.
Hazelton, PA 18201
(717) 454-4554
Est.: 1935
Contact: Stan Roby
The Roby Bug Master has a heavy pedestal base with a fully adjustable neck for proper jaws position; offering a selection of jaws for different hook sizes and rotating jaws.

Seattle Saltwater
PO Box 19416, Seattle, WA 98109
(206) 283-3590
FAX: (206) 283-1340
Contact: Peter Hylander
Makers of tube fly vises as well as tube fly tying adapters for both Renzetti and Regal vise owners for larger saltwater flies. Call, write or fax for our latest brochure.

Shurkatch F&A, Inc.
PO Box 850
Richfield Springs, NY 13439
(315) 858-1470
FAX: (315) 858-2969
Contact: Kelly Mandia
Complete line of fly tying equipment.

Sunrise Tools
Lotus Import Export, Inc.
260 W. Arrow Hwy., Unit C
PO Box 421
San Dimas, CA 91773
(909) 394-9676
FAX: (909) 394-0747
President: Chaman Hirani
Sunrise Tools offers a complete range of fly tying tools.

Thomason Products
PO Box 750573
Petaluma, CA 94975
(707) 763-7759
FAX: (707) 763-7759
Contact: Tom Thomason
Manufacturer and distributor of Hackle-Back, "your third hand," an innovative fly tying tool.

D.H. Thompson
200 Industrial Dr., #1
Hampshire, IL 60140
(847) 683-0051
FAX: (847) 683-0052
Est.: 1919
Contact: Paul Jacobsen
Complete line of fly tying vises, tools, materials and accessories.

Tool Tron
10-3 Parkway, Boerne, TX 78006
(210) 249-8277
(800) 293-8134 (Fax Orders)
FAX: (210) 755-8134
Contact: Thomas Love
Tool Tron offers several sizes and configurations of tools: scissors, pliers, clamps, combination scissor/plier, and nippers.

Toro Imports
1022 Avenue M
Grand Prairie, TX 75050
(214) 602-1723
FAX: (214) 602-1725
Contact: Zahoor Ellahi
Importer of fly tying tools. Dealer inquiries only.

Turrall USA
45 Knobhill St., Sharon, MA 02067
(617) 784-3732
FAX: (617) 784-3732
Contact: Steven Pransky
Complete line of vises & fly tying tools.

Tweezerman
55 Seacliff Ave.,
Glen Cove, NY 11542
(800) 645-3340
FAX: (516) 676-8788
Contact: Jay Katz
Manufacturers of several useful tweezers, clippers and scissors for fly tying.

Universal Vise Corp.
PO Box 626, Westfield, MA 01086
(413) 568-0964
FAX: (413) 562-7328
Est.: 1969   Staff: 12
President: Chet Cook
Manufacturer and distributor of fly tying tools, kits, materials and fly fishing tackle.

IMPORTERS & EXPORTERS

Vjender International
PO Box 8432
Delhi 110052 India
011-91-11-7428903
FAX: 011-91-11-7252857
Contact: Kishan Singh
Est.: 1900
Fancy feathers, peacock feathers, cock necks, saddles, hackles, cock feathers. Fly tying material, fly tying tools, Indian flies & fishing flots. Exporter & importer worldwide. Large stock of feathers for wholesale only. Call for a free catalog.

Walker Enterprises
PO Box 1294
Wheat Ridge, CO 80034
(303) 431-4899
FAX: (303) 431-4899

FLY TYING EQUIPMENT

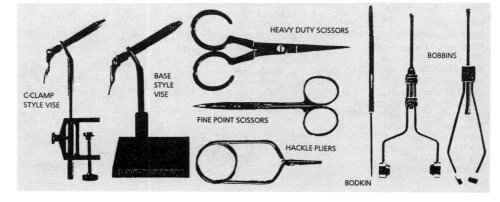

C-CLAMP STYLE VISE
BASE STYLE VISE
HEAVY DUTY SCISSORS
FINE POINT SCISSORS
HACKLE PLIERS
BODKIN
BOBBINS

Contact: Larry Walker
"DUBBIT" fly tying tool–comes in 3
types–standard, loop spin and hair
spin. Video Available.

Worrywood Fishing Prod.
Box 91943, Tucson, AZ 85752
(520) 744-0011
FAX: (520) 744-0011
Contact: Mike Giggy
Hair stackers of solid brass and bod-
kins with removable needles;
hackle gauge and palettes.

Zulco International
151-21 West Industry Ct.
Deer Park, NY 11729
(516) 242-8161
FAX: (516) 242-0920
Contact: Sylvia Farina
Surgical instruments for fly
tyers...scissors, forceps, pliers.
Dealer calls only.

FLY TYING/KITS

Superior Fly Products
Box 1411, Englewood, CO 80150
(800) 732-1947   (303) 788-1947
FAX: (303) 788-0192
Contact: Joe Martinez
We supply a quality line of fly tying
products including fly tying kits,
head cement, dubbing wax and a
host of fly tying accessories. Call
today for a complete catalog.

FLY TYING/ MATERIAL

Al's Grizzly Farm
73 Old Enfield Rd.
Belchertown, MA 01007
(413) 323-7748
Contact: Albert Brighenti
Grower and supplier of genetic grizzly, hackle–dyed and natural. Also
supplier of capes, saddles and body
feathers.

**Angler's Choice
Fly Tying Materials**
PO Box 466, Custer, WA 98240
(360) 366-5894
FAX: (360) 366-5894
Contact: Shim Hogan
Manufacturer of Super Floss™,
Angel Hair™, EZ-Body Dubbing™,
Mohair Plus™ and other natural
fiber and synthetic tying materials.
Wholesale only.

Angler's Workshop
PO Box 1010, 1350 Atlantic Ave.
Woodland, WA 98674
(360) 225-9445 (Orders)
(360) 225-8641 (Fax-Worldwide)
FAX: (800) 278-1069
Web Site: http://www.an-
glersworkshop.com
Angler's Workshop is celebrating
its 17th year supplying the rod
builder and fly tyer with hard-to-
find materials. Worldwide shipping.
Shop in Angler's Workshop catalog
to find rod blanks and components as well as an excellent
supply of fly tying materials, rods,
reels, lines, flies and more. We are
cork specialists supplying manufacturers and retailers with the finest
cork rings and preform handles. As
the North American distributors for
Hopkins and Holloway, we supply
the best fly guides made to the largest fly fishing market.
See Our Ad Pg. 61

AuSable Hackle
10719 Brush Rd.
Roscommon, MI 48653
(517) 275-5839
Contact: Jerry Smock
Wholesale & retail saddles and
necks.

B-17 Fly Tackle Ltd.
9164 Brady, Redford, MI 48239
(313) 255-2838
FAX: (313) 531-4233
Contact: Thom. Hnizdor
Custom body inserts, braided tubing, eyes, popping heads.

Dan Bailey's Fly Shop
Box 1019, Livingston, MT 59047
(800) 356-4052   (406) 222-1673
FAX: (406) 222-8450
Contact: Scott Sanchez
Complete line of fly tying tools and
materials. Distributors of Body Fur
& Wingfiber.

Bestco Enterprises
56 Elmwood Dr.
North Kingstown, RI 02852
(401) 884-3862
FAX: (401) 884-3862
Est.: 1991
President: Stuart M. Dickens
Lead dumbell eyes, non-lead
dumbell eyes–5 styles. Bead heads,
cone heads.

Bestway Outdoor Inc.
1649 Romain Dr.
Columbia, SC 29210
(803) 926-0545
FAX: (803) 926-0546
Contact: Paul Rowe
Artificial hairs and furs marketed
under Super Hair and Neer Hair.
Various tinsel products & 3-D eyes.
Dealer inquiries only.

Bill's Bodi-Braid
Narragansett Bay Flies
87 Lisa Terrace
Portsmouth, RI 02871
(401) 683-5346
Est.: 1989
Contact: Bill Peabody
Bill's Bodi-Braid is an 1/8 wide re-en-
forced mylar braid which has
become popular with tyers of flies
for fresh and saltwater. Many
shades available.

Black Canyon Flies
91 Market St.
Wappingers Falls, NY 12590
(800) 544-7343   (914) 297-0098
FAX: (914) 297-0142
Contact: Janet Zito or Peter Zito
Manufacturer and distributor of fly
tying material and American-made
flies. Wholesale catalog available.
Dealer inquiries only–thank you.

Bob's Hackle Farm
362 Cedar Valley Rd.
New Park, PA 17352
(717) 382-4402
Contact: Jan Pickel
17 colors–brochure available.

Burton Materials, Inc.
1945 Vance St., #
Lakewood, CO 80215
(303) 274-5394
Contact: Craig L. Burton
Offering Ultra Chamois™, an ultra
thin natural chamois and a cutting
method developed especially for fly
tying with no need to twist strips.

Cascade/Crest Tool
13290 Table Rock Rd.
Central Point, OR 97502
(541) 826-4030
FAX: (541) 826-4698
Contact: Pat Dunlop
Manufacturer and originator of
such products as V-Rib, GSP, Kelvar,
Spacklace, etc. and the list goes on
and on and on. Call for catalog and
pricing.

**Castle Arms, Fishermen's
Furs & Feathers**
Box 30070, Springfield, MA 01103
(413) 567-8268
FAX: (413) 731-1292

Contact: Phil Castleman
Breeds and distributes exotic feathers for salmon flies such as jungle cocks, argus, bustard, etc. and distributes Japanese silk, ceramic dubbing, rakes, ceramic hook sharpeners, silk gut, partridge hooks, saltwater hackle, books on salmon fishing and salmon flies.

Collins' Hackle Farm
436 Kinner Hill Rd.
Pine City, NY 14871
(607) 734-1765
Contact: Charlie Collins
Specializing in genetically bred fly tying capes for the discriminating fly tyer. For a free sample and complete information, send a stamped envelope to the above.

Corsair Products
33 Carroll Rd.
Woburn, MA 01801
(617) 932-0558
Contact: Kate Lavelle
The source for Corsair–the revolutionary new tubular fly tying material for imaginative fly tyers!

Danville Chenille Co., Inc.
Rt. 111A, PO Box 1000
Danville, NH 03819
(603) 382-5553
FAX: (603) 382-2133 Est.: 1954
Contact: Laura Farley
Manufacturer of the chenille and distributor of thread, floss and tools. Dealer inquiries only–thank you.

Dersh Feather & Trading Co.
62 W. 36th St., NY, NY 10018
(212) 714-2806
FAX: (212) 239-1407
Contact: Jay Dershowitz
Dealer inquiries only–thank you.

EZ Shape Sparkle Body
Box 362, Housatonic, MA 01236
(413) 274-6143 (Chris)
(413) 594-9686 (Al)

Edge Water Fishing Prod. Inc.
35 N. 1000 W.
Clearfield, UT 84015
(801) 825-8982
Contact: Ed Miya
Manufacturers of closed-cell foam flies and shaped component parts of various sizes.

Edgewater Company
35 North 1000 West
Clearfield, UT 84015
(800) 584-7647
Contact: Ed Miya
Manufacturer of poppers and popper heads.

Elite Products
12 Plants Dam Rd.
East Lyme, CT 06333
(860) 739-8185
Contact: John McBride
Bozo Hair–extra long (10") synthetic fly tying material. Available in many colors. Bug eye-mono stem eyes for shrimp and crab flies.

Ewing Feather Birds, Inc.
912 Waterville Rd.
Waterville, IA 52170
(319) 535-7682 FAX: 7708
Contact: Douglas Ewing
Hackle producer

Feathers Co.
S. 12315 Sands Rd.
Valleyford, WA 99036
(800) 442-2553
Contact: Dr. Michael Perry
50 natural colors of chicken feathers. Full color catalogue available

for $3.00 which is refundable with first purchase.

Finnish Fur Fly
68100 Himanka, Finland
A source for fur materials is Finnish Fur Fly providing brown bear, polar bear, raccoon, fox, marten tails, polecat zonkers, muskrat, deer hair, mink blend and dubbing threads.

Fish Hair Enterprises, Inc.
1484 West County Rd. C
St. Paul, MN 55113
(612) 636-3083
Contact: Deborah Steinback
Synthetic hair for fly tying–available both wholesale and retail. Call for information.

Fisheries West Inc.
PO Box 7224, Boise, ID 83707
(800) 380-1991
FAX: (208) 344-6159 Est.: 1986
President: Barry Ross; VP: Mike Ross
M.I. Minnow Bodies are preformed minnow bodies for streamer patterns. Available in traditional, inverted and saltwater patterns.

FLASHABOU®

Flashabou®
Hedron, Inc., 402 N. Main St., Stillwater, MN 55082
(612) 430-9606   FAX: 9607
Contact: Donald S. Mears
Prime manufacturer of fly tying and lure skirting materials. Specializing in synthetic, metallic fibers in a wide range of styles and colors. Dealer inquiries only.
See Our Ad Below

Fli Yarns
2005 East Holiday
Springfield, MO 65804
(888) MAK-AFLY
(417) 883-0974
FAX: (417) 883-5046
Contact: Sterling Blocker
Fli Yarns sells premium fly-tying materials and fly fishing related equipment to tackle dealers, licensed fishing guides and fly-in lodges only. Full color brochure. Call today for information.

Fly-Rite, Inc.
7421 S. Beyer
Frankenmuth, MI 48734
(517) 652-9869
FAX: (517) 652-2996
Contact: Judith G. McCann
Distributor of dubbing materials and tying tools.

Flycraft
PO Box 60582, Greendale Station
Worcester, MA 01606
(508) 853-3676
FAX: (508) 853-3676
Contact: Randy Swanberg
Manufacturer of foam terrestrial bodies and tying tools. Dealer inquiries only.

For Your Flies Only!
Box 51215, Idaho Falls, ID 83641
(208) 522-6227
Contact: Frank Sparkman
We have developed an attaching, dimensioning, weighting and colorization process for fly tying. Patent pending.

Gateway Feather Mfg.
Box 447, Holmen, WI 54636
(608) 526-4490
FAX: (608) 526-9699
Contact: Richard O. Vaaler or Jason A. Vaaler
Manufacturer and distributor of fine feather accessories for fly tying.

Gone Fishin' Ent.
PO Box 466, Custer, WA 98240
(360) 366-5894
FAX: (360) 366-5894
Super Floss™, Angel Hair™, Easy Body Dubbing .

Gordon Griffiths Fishing Tackle
1190 Genella, Waterford, MI 48328
(810) 673-7701
FAX: (810) 673-7701
Contact: Phil Griffiths
Distributors of fine quality fly tying materials & threads.

Gudebrod, Inc.
PO Box 357, Pottstown, PA 19464
(610) 327-4050
FAX: (610) 327-4588
The revolutionary Gudebrod Fly Tying System includes thread in sizes 8/0, 6/0 and 3/0 matched to the Gary Borger Color System. Completing the system is the all new, compact, and economical Gudebrod Thread Holder Tool which offers greater thread tension control, one hand thread rewinding and easy to use finger tip accuracy. Call or write for details.

Hareline Dubbin Inc.
24712 Territorial Rd.
Monroe, OR 97456
(503) 847-5310
FAX: (503) 998-6166
Est.: 1984 Staff: 12
Contact: Robert Borden
Manufacturer and distributor of fly tying materials and tools. Dealer inquiries only–thank you.

Hebert Genetic Hackle
8990 Garrison Rd., Box 237
Laingsburg, MI 48848
(517) 651-5109
FAX: (517) 651-2875
Contact: Ted Hebert
High grade dry fly hackle raised from the original Andy Miner hackle stock.

Hobbs Feather Co., Inc.
Box 187, West Liberty, IA 52776
(319) 627-4258
FAX: (319) 627-6529
Est.: 1962
Contact: Dorothy J. Hobbs
Wholesale supplier of fly tying and lure making material. Sells both bulk and pre-packaged.

Hoffman Hackle
c/o Whiting Farms, Inc.
PO Box 100, Delta, CO 81416
(970) 874-0999
FAX: (970) 874-7117
Contact: Dr. Thomas Whiting

Hunters North Country Angler
Box 516, North Conway, NH 03860
(603) 356-6000

Innovative Flyfishing Prod.
Kuferzeile 19, S. 4810
Gmunden, Austria
Contact: Roman Moser
Unique fly tying materials including Plushille®, Furabou™, Artfur® and Wooley Chenille.

Integra Fly Fishing Prod.
309 Swarthmore Ave.
Gaithersburg, MD 20877
(301) 990-0095
FAX: (301) 990-3903
Est.: 1984
Contact: Anil S. Gautam
Flies, fly tying vises, tools, kits, hackle, materials, accessories, rods, reels, line, leaders, nets and gifts.

Inter-Tac/Larva Lace
Box 6340,
Woodland Park, CO 80866
(800) 347-3432   (719) 684-2272
FAX: (719) 687-9820
Contact: Joan Camera or Phil Camera
Fly tying materials and other fly fishing products. Wholesale only.

J.A. Enterprises
PO Box 1051, Slatersville, RI 02876
(401) 765-0659
FAX: (401) 769-8688
Est.: 1994
Owner: John C. Archambault
Email: FFISH@aol.com
E-Z Body® is an American-made monofilament polyester tubing that's designed to make rugged, realistic fresh or saltwater flies. Available in four sizes and seven colors.

J.S. Marketing Inc.
8200 E. Pacific Place, #202
Denver, CO 80231
(303) 369-8839
FAX: (303) 369-8938
Est.: 1989
Contact: Jerry R. Schreiber
Distributors of Brookside Flies & fly tying materials. 24 hour turn-around, large inventory. Tied with Daiichi Hooks and Hoffman Hackle; blend our own dubbings. Choice of the guides since 1989.

Kennebec River Fly & Tackle
39 Milliken Rd.
North Yarmouth, ME 04097
(207) 829-4290
FAX: (207) 829-6002
Pres: John Brian
Manager: Ashley Richards
Fly tyers tubes made from brass or copper, aluminum and plastic.

Keough Hackles
23392 Hwy. M-60
Mendon, MI 49072
(616) 496-7464
FAX: (616) 496-8186
Contact: Bill Keough
Genetic dry fly hackle–13 natural colors.

Kreinik Manufacturing Co.
3106 Timanus Lane, Suite 101
Baltimore, MD 21244
(800) 354-4255   (410) 281-0040
FAX: (410) 281-0987
Contact: Jim Cargo
Hi Luster braids and ribbons; Micro Ice chenille, silk floss, metallic wrapping threads, silk dubbing and Flash in a Tube.

Lagartun, Ltd.
16741 S. Old Sonoita Hwy.
Vail, AZ 85641

---

(520) 762-5900
FAX: (520) 762-5959
Est.: 1988
Contact: Urch Gultepe
Manufacturer of tinsel, wire and silk floss. Dealer inquiries only.

LOON OUTDOORS
7737 W. Mossy Cup St.
Boise, ID 83709
(800) 580-3811
FAX: (800) 574-0422
Contact: Ken Smith
"Environmentally friendly fly fishing products that perform," Loon offers head cements and finishes both solvent- and (non-toxic) water-based. Hard Head water-base, no mix finishes come in a variety of 15 colors. Dubbing waxes and a new line of dubbings–Llama, shiny nylon, cotton and more–round out the offering.

Mangrove Feather Co.
468 Greenwich St.
New York, NY 10013
(212) 431-5806
Contact: Bob Davis
Wholesale, bulk feather order inquiries only.

Mazza Signature Hackle
2609 Genesee St., Utica, NY 13501
(315) 733-4593
Contact: Del Mazza
Signature hackle

McKenzie Fly Tackle
1075 A Shelley St.
Springfield, OR 97477
(541) 741-8161
FAX: (541) 741-7565
Est.: 1971   Staff: 20
Sales Mgr: Dale Williams
Manufacturer and distributor of high-quality flies, materials and fly tackle. Dealer inquiries only–thank you.

Metz Feathers
Div. of Umpqua
PO Box 700, Glide, OR 97443
(800) 322-3218   (541) 496-3512
FAX: (541) 496-0150
Est.: 1972

Nat'l. Sales Mgr: Gus Wunderly
Metz Feathers, a division of Umpqua, produces a wide selection of colors and types of genetic hackle for fly tying. Metz necks are renowned for their range of colors, small sizes of flexible hackle and consistent overall quality. Metz saddles produce the finest streamers, bass and saltwater flies available. New Microbarb saddles now available.

Mystic Bay Flies
PO Box 1080, Dennis, MA 02638
(800) 255-4310   (508) 385-3965
FAX: (508) 385-3186
Contact: Kenneth Nelson
FlyFur™ acrylic fur available in 26 colors. Convenient, practical and very popular. Flashabou tubing. Satellite City C/A glues in 3 viscosities, Crystal Clear epoxies, SS popper hooks and a hugh inventory of hard to find prism tape, animal and doll eyes. Saltwater sturdy, available variety.

Native American Nymphs & Flies
58 Circle Dr., Chicopee, MA 01020
(413) 594-9686
Contact: Al Niemiec
Limited quantities of Australian possum and iridescent dubbing blends & dubbing kits; Imitation Mottled Oak Turkey feathers available.

Nature's Spirit
7552 E. Greenlake Dr., N.
Seattle, WA 98103
(206) 527-1600
FAX: (206) 527-7202
Contact: Terry Ball
Nature's Spirit offers natural materials and accessories for the discrminating flyfisher. All of our products are processed with pure, natural green oil, "nature's finest conditioner," extracted from the glands of water fowl. Natural preen oil processed materials possess resilience, sheen, and a benign scent that are visually and functionally in a class of their own.

North American Fly Ltd.
PO Box 67, Strum, WI 54770
(715) 695-3533
FAX: (715) 695-3515
Complete line of fly tying materials

SWAFFARCO's Preen Oil Process Enhances Feathers and Fibers To Produce Exceptional Flies

Ducks are protected from the elements by feathers rich in waxes and natural preen oils. These substances are removed when feathers used to produce flies are prepared for dying.

Now they're being replaced. And the result is Cul de Canard flies that combine natural appearance with exceptional durability. What's more, the patented preen oil replacement process—the consequence of an intensive collaborative effort—is also used to enhance the qualities of natural fibers that are also employed in fly tying.

Credit for the process goes to SWAFFARCO Feather-N-Trading, a family enterprise founded in 1972 that produces 98,000 pounds of feathers per month and is operated by Loy and Donna Swaffar and their son Jeff in Springdale, Arkansas; and to Rene and Bonnie Harrop, whose patient, time-consuming research and testing culminated in the improved conditioning.

Replacing Dry Hackle

The quest for better fly materials began in 1990 when Loy and Donna visited Umpqua Feather Merchants of Glide, Oregon, and Umpqua's Bill Black predicted that the fine, wispy Cul de Canard feather would replace dry hackle in many production flies if supply and pricing improved.

Recognizing opportunity, the Swaffars soon established CDC production from 6.5 million ducks per year. And as production capacity surged, the price for CDC feathers plummeted by a dramatic $55 per ounce. At this point, the Swaffars enlisted the aid of Rene Harrop in testing and improving dyed CDC. The author of articles on the advantages of these feathers, Harrop rose to the challenge.

The Swaffars and Harrop realized that removal of natural waxes and oils--a necessary prelude to dying—compromised the integrity and longevity of feathers and any natural fiber. They realized, as well,

that these substances had to be chemically stripped so dye will distribute evenly, a "must" if the end product—a fly—is to accurately resemble an insect in color. So the question became obvious: Could the waxes and oils be replaced?

Natural Conditioner

The answer was "Yes." After tedious trial and error it was determined that natural oils could be retrieved and replaced. The result is SWAFFARCO's Natural Preen Oil Conditioner, with which all of the company's fly tying products are treated.

Another characteristic of SWAFFARCO products—extraordinary duplication of natural insect colors—is the result of using House of Harrop (HOH) color formulas developed by Terry Ball. And one of the most remarkable products to evolve from the preen oil research is a fine natural dubbing. This is produced by scouring a fine-fibered fleece to remove water-absorbent Lanolin, the application of gentle protein dyes, carding carefully to align the fibers, then adding preen oil.

SWAFFARCO supplies distributors and select fly tying companies only. Additional information about the firm's products and their availability is available from SWAFFARCO Feather-N-Trading, 5083 Dearing, Springdale, AR 72762. Telephone (501) 756-8898; fax (501) 756-8828.

Other SWAFFARCO Products

- Ozark Oak Mottled Turkey Quill
- Ozark Original Mottled Turkey Quill
- Micro Fleck Turkey Flats
- Turkey Hackle (Micro Fleck or Barred)
- Barred CDC
- Prime Marabou
- Turkey Biot Quill
- Micro Fleck Duck Quill
- Mottled Canada Goose Quill
- Spey Hackle
- Cul de Canard
- Cul de Canard Oiler Puffs

including hair, fur, feathers and synthetics available in bulk or pre-packaged.

Organic Dyestuffs
PO Box 14258
E. Providence, RI 02914
(401) 434-3300
Contact: Lori Mirandi
Supplier of fly tying dyes

Palsa Outdoor Products
Box 81336, Lincoln, NE
68501-1336
(800) 456-9281   (402) 488-5288
FAX: (402) 488-2321   Est.: 1982
President: Bill Harder, Jr.
VP/Sales: Ray Clatanoff
50 combinations of self-adhesive lure eyes. Product lines are Add-A-Glo™ and Add-N-Eye™. Eye sizes range from 1/8" to 3/8" and come in five metallic prism colors, five metallic foil colors and five colors.

Partridge of Redditch
Mount Pleasant
Redditch, Worcestershire
B97 4JE England
011-44-527-543555
011-44-527-550575
FAX: 011-44 527 546956
Contact: Alan Bramley
SLF dubbing material for fly tyers.

Quality Fishing Flies
PO Box 294, Lawrence, PA 15055
(412) 746-3511
Contact: Rod Yerger
Supplier of McMurray bodies in many colors and sizes, variations of these for making bees and wasps; also balsa cylinders for making your own. Selling direct to anglers only–thank you.

Rainy's Flies & Supplies
690 N. 100 East
Logan, UT 84321
(801) 753-6766
FAX: (801) 753-9155
Contact: L. Rainy Riding
Complete line of foam products.

Rocky Mountain Dubbing
Box 1255, 7Lander, WY 82520
(307) 332-2989
FAX: (307) 332-2989
Contact: Steve Kennerk
We tan and dye all our own hairs for fly tying and are the source for elk, deer, moose, antelope, muskrat, beaver, rabbit, Australian

possum; our new product is "Perfect Cut Wings" pre-cut wings.

M. Schwartz & Son, Inc.
45 Hoffman Ave.
Hauppauge, NY 11787
(516) 234-7722
Contact: Michael Schwartz
Feathers for fly tying. Wholesale inquiries only–thank you.

Seattle Saltwater
Box 19416, Seattle, WA 98109
(206) 283-3590
FAX: (206) 283-1340
Owner: Peter Hylander
Synthetic saltwater fly tying materials– striped popper kits in 5 colors & 3 sizes; "Flexo" braided tubing, available in 6 colors & 4 sizes. Call, write or fax for our latest brochure or a dealer near you.

Sol Shamilzadeh
103 Lexington Ave., #4C
New York, NY 10016
(212) 686-0545
Atlantic salmon fly tying materials and rare 19th Century salmon angling and salmon fly tying books. Mail order only.

Shannon's Fancy Hackle
Rt. 2, Lamar, AR 72846
(501) 885-3598
Shannon's Fancy Hackle has the essential qualities demanded by discriminating fly tiers: natural colors, maximum usable length, thin supple stems, stiff barbs, maximum barb counts, high feather count. Available at selected fly tackle dealers.

Sierra Pacific Products
PO Box 276833
Sacramento, CA 95827
(916) 369-1146
FAX: (916) 369-1564
Est.: 1990   Staff: 9
Owner: Greg Vinci
We specialize in innovative state of the art fly boxes, fly tackle accessories, fly tying materials & tools.

Spencer's Hackle
100 Deemer Creek Rd.
Plains, MT 59859
(406) 826-3644
FAX: (406) 826-3644   Est.: 1974
Contact: Hugh Spencer
Producers of premium hackle–eight natural colors of capes & saddles and 21 colors of dyed grizzly and white. Dealer direct and through selected distributors.

Spirit River
423 Winchester St.
Roseburg, OR 97470
(800) 444-6916 (Orders)

(503) 440-6916
FAX: (503) 672-4309
Contact: Bill Black or Richard Wolfe
Manufacturers of dubbing dispensers, Lite Brite, all types of dubbing, synthetics, feathers and hairs. Sold at dealers worldwide. Wholesale only–thank you.

Superfly, Inc.
11710 Kingsway Ave., #203
Edmonton, Alberta, Canada T5G 0X5
(800) 661-FLYS   (403) 429-1838
FAX: (403) 425-1828
Est.: 1990   Staff: 10
Operations Mgr: Bill Robertson
Manufacturer and distributor of fly tying tools, materials, kits and flies. Dealer inquiries only–thank you.

Swaffarco Feather-N-Trading
1409 Buena Vista
Springdale, AR 72764
(501) 756-8898
FAX: (501) 756-8828
Contact: Loy Swaffar
Superior flies result from using SWAFFARCO's Cul de Canard feathers or natural fibers treated with the company's Natural Preen Oil Conditioner to restore natural oils and waxes. These premium quality materials combine natural appearance with exceptional durability that any fly tying angler will value. SWAFFARCO also offers a complete line of turkey quill and hackle, duck and goose quill, barred CDC, prime marabou and CDC oiler puffs. Phone or fax for additional information or the location of your nearest SWAFFARCO distributor.
See Our Ad Pg. 63

W.W. Swalef & Son, Inc.
PO Box 3175, Pinedale, CA 93650
(209) 439-9602
FAX: (209) 439-9166
All manner of feathers for the fly tying trade–wholesale only.

Techflex, Inc.
PO Box 119, 50 Station Rd.
Sparta, NJ 07871
(201) 729-3944
FAX: (201) 729-9320
Contact: Bill Dermody, IV
Manufacturers of Flexo material and Flexo mirror braid. The tubing is available in four diameters and 16 colors.

D.H. Thompson, Inc.
200 Industrial Dr., #1
Hampshire, IL 60140

(847) 683-0051
FAX: (847) 683-0052
Est.: 1919
Contact: Paul Jacobsen

tiewell
PO Box 720, Newport Beach
NSW 2106, Australia
011-61-29973-1107
FAX: 011-61-29973 1953
Director: Deidre Sheldon
Exporter of fly tying material including: Fish Bodz, Mara-Wool, Mega Hair, Lazerlights Dubbing, Saltwater Strung Saddle Feathers, Reflections, Sparkleflash, Sparkleflash Maxibraid and Mottled Nymph Rib.

Turrall USA
45 Knobhill St., Sharon, MA 02067
(617) 784-3732
FAX: (617) 784-3732
Contact: Steven Pransky
Complete selection of the finest quality fly tying materials.

Ultimate Materials
494 San Mateo Ave.
San Bruno, CA 94066
(415) 583-8519
Contact: Frank Perasso
Dubbing in five colors and plummage to match for tying the birdsnest patterns, or any nymph or wet fly.

**Umpqua
Feather Merchants**
Box 700, Glide, OR 97443
(800) 322-3218   (541) 496-3512
FAX: (541) 496-0150   Est.: 1972
Nat'l. Sales Mgr: Gus Wunderly
To tie a great fly, you need the best materials. Umpqua Feather Merchants distributes the most respected lines of fly tying materials you can find: Metz Feathers, Tiemco hooks and fly tying tools, as well as a complete selection of the natural and synthetic materials preferred by fly tyers around the world.

Uni Products Inc.
561 Rue Principale
Ste-Melanie, Quebec
Canada J0K 3A0
FAX: (514) 889-8506

Universal Vise Corp.
PO Box 626, Westfield, MA 01086
(413) 568-0964
FAX: (413) 562-7328
Est.: 1969   Staff: 12
President: Chet Cook
Manufacturer and distributor of fly tying tools, kits, materials and fly fishing tackle. Dealer inquiries only.

IMPORTERS & EXPORTERS

Vjender International
PO Box 8432, Delhi 110052 India
011-91-11-7428903
FAX: 011-91-11-7252857
Contact: Kishan Singh
Est.: 1900
Fancy feathers, peacock feathers, cock necks, saddles, hackles, cock feathers. Fly tying material, fly tying tools, Indian flies & fishing floats. Exporter & importer worldwide. Large stock of feathers for wholesale only. Call for a free catalog.

Wagman Primus Group
10 Strawberry St.
Philadelphia, PA 19106
(215) 923-8090
FAX: (215) 925-0811
Trader: Adam Reisboard
Trader: Cathe Olson
Email: trading@wagprim.com
Distributor of "exotic" fly tying materials. Specializing in saltwater fly tying materials.

Wapsi Fly, Inc.
27 CR 458,
Mountain Home, AR 72653
(501) 425-9500
(800) 425-9599 (FAX)
FAX: (501) 425-9599
Est.: 1945   Staff: 30
G.M.: Karl Schmuecker
Sales Mgr: T.L. Lauerman
Wapsi manufactures and distributes a complete line of fly tying materials, tools and accessories.

White Fox Fur & Feather
PO Box 3, Pemberton, MN 56078
(800) 387-8646
FAX: (507) 869-3878
Contact: Jay A. DeLeon
Manufacturer and distributor of natural tying material. Hard to find and unusual material also available. Dealer calls only–thank you.

**Whitetail Fly Tieing
Supplies**
7060 White Tail Ct.
Toledo, OH 43617
(419) 843-2106
FAX: (419) 843-2106
Contact: Christopher Helm
Wholesale deer, elk and other hair for tying. The Brassie hair packer in three sizes.

Whiting Farms, Inc.
PO Box 100, Delta, CO 81416
(970) 874-0999
FAX: (970) 874-7117
Contact: Jerry Toft
Producers and world-wide distributors of Hoffman Hackle

Witchcraft Tape Products
Box 937, Coloma, MI 49038
(800) 521-0731   (616) 468-3399
FAX: (616) 468-3391
Est.: 1973
Contact: Ron Warczynski
Makers of prismatic tape products and stick-on prismatic fish eyes in numerous patterns, colors & sizes.

YLI Corporation
482 N. Freedom Blvd.
Provo, UT 84601
(800) 854-1932   (801) 377-3900
FAX: (801) 375-2879
Contact: Steve Butler
YLI offers its Success Serging Yarn in 12 colors.

Yellowstone Fly Goods
5350 Holiday Ave.
Billings, MT 59101
(800) 262-1098   (406) 256-0799
FAX: (406) 256-3353
Est.: 1988
Contact: Mike Hoiness
A complete selection of top quality tying materials, tools, necks, etc. We also stock Daiichi and Mustad hooks, along with many other accessory items.

Zucker Feather Products
PO Box 289, 512 North East
California, MO 65018
(800) 346-0657
FAX: (573) 796-2278

HOOKS

AvaLon Hooks
Distributed by Angler Sport Group
6619 Oak Orchard Rd.
Elba, NY 14058
(716) 757-9958
FAX: (716) 757-9066
President: Paul Betters
High-carbon steel, needle sharp
points and small barbs, combined
with "State-of-the-Art" production
quality and exact tempering, are
the features of AvaLon's, America's
new premium quality hooks.

B-17 Fly Tackle Ltd.
9164 Brady, Redford, MI 48239
(313) 255-2838
FAX: (313) 531-4233
Contact: Thom. Hnizdor
A unique line of black nickel-plated
keel hooks featuring long working
shanks with a keeling bend, large
bite, superb line of pull. Ideal for
fresh and saltwater tying. Sizes 1,
1/0, 2/0 and 5/0. Also available:
10XL Carrie Stevens hooks, sizes 2
and 2/0. Excellent for fresh and salt
patterns. All hooks produced to B-17
specs. Available wholesale and retail.
Phone for information, pricing.

Berkley Gold Point
1 Berkley Dr., Spirit Lake, IA 51360
(800) 237-5539
(712) 336-1520 (Consumer)
FAX: (712) 336-5183

The Trey Combs
Big Game Hook Series
Div. Bighorn Fly Trading Co.
1517 14th St., W.
Suite 229, Billings, MT 59102
(406) 652-1557
FAX: (406) 652-1557

Contact: Roger Lee
New series of hooks featuring
nickel-plated carbon-steel construction and a rounded point, and
come in sizes 2 to 10/0.

Dai-Riki High Carbon
Fly Hooks
Distributed by Dan Bailey
Box 1019, Livingston, MT 59047
(800) 356-4052   (406) 222-1673
FAX: (406) 222-8450
Contact: Scott Sanchez
Premium grade fresh & saltwater
hooks. Chemically sharpened.

Daiichi Hooks
Distributed by Angler Sport Group
6619 Oak Orchard Rd.
Elba, NY 14058
(716) 757-9958   FAX: 9066
President: Paul Betters
World's sharpest hooks with over
50 fly hook patterns.
See Ad Inside Back Cover

EAGLE CLAW®

Eagle Claw®
Wright & McGill Co.
4245 E. 46th Ave.
Denver, CO 80216-0011
(303) 321-1481
FAX: (303) 321-4750
Est.: 1925
Product Mgr: George Large
Eagle Claw® Lazer Sharp® fly
hooks take hook performance to a
new level with our Micro Grind™
and high-tech laser-sharpening process. Mini barb and small eye are
manufactured to rigid specifications. The first hook will be the
same as the last.
See Our Ad Across

Easy Set Hook Co.
2550 S. Campbell, #200
Springfield, MO 65807
(800) 906-6866   (417) 882-2725
FAX: (417) 882-2565
President: Trent Dixon
Mktg: Bobby Johnson
Easy Set produces a line of Midge
Fly and Salmon Egg hooks made of
the finest quality steel with a special Teflon ® coating. Easy Set
Teflon® coated hooks need less
force to penetrate from point past
the barb. Allows fly fisherman to
fish with lighter line!

Fenwick Corp.
5242 Argosy Dr.
Huntington Beach, CA 92649
(714) 897-1066 Ext. 226
FAX: (714) 891-9610
Contact: Dale Barnes
Fenwick Triple Sharpened fly hooks
are made of HC80™ high carbon
steel, forged and tempered to produce a super strong hook with a
smaller diameter. Treated in an IRP
cleaning process, each hook is
chemically sharpened to create the
finest needle point.

Fish Hair Enterprises, Inc.
1484 West County Rd. C
St. Paul, MN 55113
(612) 636-3083
Contact: Deborah Steinback
FisHair will custom dress hooks to
your specifications. Any combination of hair color, feathers or tinsel
can be added. With our patented
mold dressing process, the hair
ends are molded into one solid
piece. For added strength, a tough
apoxy finish covers the head result-
ing in a more durable lure
component. Call today. Private labeling available.

HOOKS

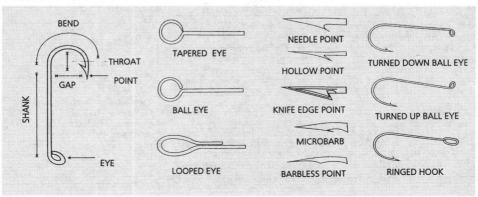

SHANK — BEND — THROAT — GAP — POINT — EYE
TAPERED EYE — BALL EYE — LOOPED EYE
NEEDLE POINT — HOLLOW POINT — KNIFE EDGE POINT — MICROBARB — BARBLESS POINT
TURNED DOWN BALL EYE — TURNED UP BALL EYE — RINGED HOOK

EAGLE CLAW®

Eagle Clay is proud to announce the introduction of their new Lazer Sharp Fly Hooks. These hooks are manufactured with vanadium High Carbon Steel. They feature Eagle Claw's famous Lazer Sharp points and new micro barbs for smooth penetration and positive hook up. This new line is offered in 15 different styles and 5 finishes and 18 sizes. A size and style for every application.

EAGLE CLAW FISHING TACKLE

P.O. BOX 16011

DENVER, CO 80216

Fuji Toki California, Inc.
1673 Donlon St., #208
Ventura, CA 93003
(800) 336-0669 (Orders)
FAX: (805) 644-0431
Contact: Toshio Nishioka
Fuji Toki offers a line of 25 different styles of high-carbon, chemically sharpened fly hooks. Sizes range from 2-24. Styles offered include dry, nymph, streamer, salmon and steelhead. Hooks are finished in bronze, gold or nickel chrome.

"Gaelic Supreme" Handmade High Carbon Hooks
Distributed by Belvoirdale
PO Box 176, Wyncote, PA 19095
(215) 886-7211
FAX: (215) 886-1804
President: Grahame Maisey
The finest handmade hooks from Redditch, England featuring optimum tempering for strength and reliability, with chemically etched points, smooth finishes and precision formed eyes. Trout Hooks are designed in the USA with custom styles, color finishes and half-raised eyes. Salmon hooks classically styled in black finish feature custom shanks, wire sizes and bends.

Gamakatsu USA
PO Box 1797, Tacoma, WA 98401
(206) 922-8373
FAX: (800) 223-9383
Est.: 1983　　Staff: 7
Nat'l. Sales Mgr: Bob Funk
Gen. Mgr: Shingo Tsuoka
Gamakatsu fly hooks are made from high carbon steel and are needle honed.

Hayabusa
c/o Composite Developments (NZ)
PO Box 100063, N. Shore Mail Ctr.
Auckland 10, New Zealand
011-649-415-9915
FAX: 011-649-415-9965
Sales/Mktg: Hamish Murray

Alec Jackson Spey Fly Hooks
c/o Yorkshire Fly Fisherman
PO Box 386, Kenmore, WA 98028
(206) 488-9806
FAX: (206) 806-9902
Contact: Alec Jackson
Specialty steelhead and salmon hooks available in choice of 5 finishes and 4 sizes.

Lazer Sharp Fly Hooks/Eagle Claw
Distributed by Gudebrod, Inc.
PO Box 357, Pottstown, PA 19464
(610) 327-4050
FAX: (610) 327-4588
Sales Mgr: Robert Graham

Maruto Fly Hooks
Dohitomi & Co., Ltd.
Sinjyo, Tojo-Cho, Kato-Gun
Hyogo-Pref., Japan
011-81-0795-46-0001
Fax: 011-81-0795-46-0303
Japanese hooks

O. Mustad & Son (USA), Inc.
PO Box 838, 247-253 Grant Ave.
Auburn, NY 13021
(315) 253-2793
FAX: (315) 253-0157
Est.: 1832
Sales Mgr: John DeVres
World's largest manufacturer of fish hooks, offering new premium 80,000 series fly hooks, standard fly hooks and fly collections.

Orvis Company
Rt. 7A, Manchester, VT 05254
(800) 333-1550 (Ext. 844)
(802) 362-3622
Contact: Randy Carlson

Owner American Corp.
17165 Von Karman, Suite 111
Irvine, CA 92614
(714) 261-7922
FAX: (714) 261-9399
Distributors of "Owner" hooks popular for a variety of saltwater and big game fishing.

Partridge of Redditch
Mount Pleasant, Redditch,
Worcestershire, B97 4JE England
011 44 1527 543555
011 44 1527 541380
FAX:: 011 44 1527 546956
Contact: Ole Bjerke
Offering the finest fish hooks especially with the "grey shadow" nylon finish.

TIEMCO®

Tiemco
Distributed by Umpqua
PO Box 700, Glide, OR 97443
(800) 322-3218　(541) 496-3512
FAX: (541) 496-0150　Est.: 1972
Nat'l. Sales Mgr: Gus Wunderly
When you need the best hooks for fly fishing, look no further than Tiemco. The originators of chemical sharpening for extra penetration, Tiemco produces a full line of hook styles for all types of fly fishing. The best fly tyers in the world insist on Tiemco hooks and precision Tiemco fly tying tools.

Turrall USA
45 Knobhill St., Sharon, MA 02067
(617) 784-3732
Contact: Steven Pransky
Hand-forged, high-carbon Sheffield steel hooks. Chemically sharpened needle points and double bronzed.

VMC Fly Hooks
Riverborn Fly Company, Inc.
Box 65, Wendell, ID 83355
(800) 354-5534
FAX: (208) 536-2355
Est.: 1987　　Staff: 6
Pres/Owner: Warren E. Schoth
VP/Owner: Steve Hunter
Exclusive distributor of the revolutionary new Vanadium Steel fly hooks from VMC of France. These hooks are 25% stronger and 25% lighter than the best high carbon steel hooks. Exclusive features include precision "UniSET" tempering, "Low Angle" microbarb, "Tru-Angle" eyes, "Full form" forging, hyper sharp "needle cone" points and double process finishing. Also available are superior quality HC80 carbon steel and stainless steel hooks for fresh and saltwater flies.
See Our Ad Pg. 49

Bob Veverka's Classic Salmon Hook
PO Box 353, Underhill, VT 05489
(802) 899-2049
Contact: Bob Veverka
Classic salmon & steelhead hook–sizes 2, 4, 6, & 8 in black, blue or gold finishes. Dealer Inquiries Welcome.

INDUSTRY CONSULTANTS

R. Valentine Atkinson
Atkinson Photography Studio
1263 6th Ave.
San Francisco, CA 94122
(415) 731-4385
FAX: (415) 731-7712
Representative: Susan Rockrise
Internationally acclaimed angling
and sports photographer who can
provide stock and assignment photo
services for the fly fishing trade.

Battenkill Press
PO Box 159, Cambridge, NY 12816
(518) 677-2019
FAX: (518) 677-8066
Contact: Chris Belnap
Packaging consultant and manufac-
turer of paper packaging for
leaders, hooks and material.

Buy the World, Inc.
6477 Fairview Ave., Suite H
Boise, ID 83704
(800) 636-7881 (208) 375-1800
FAX: (208) 375-1866
President: John Matteson
Internet consultants and designer

**Campbell Lacoste
Marketing & Advertising**
640 W. Washington, Suite B
Madison, WI 53703
(608) 256-3474
FAX: (608) 256-3848
Mktg. Dir: Harry Campbell
A full service marketing and adver-
tising agency specializing in
outdoor products.

Catalyst Marketing Services
120 W. LaSalle, Suite 503
South Bend, IN 46601
(219) 289-1331
FAX: (219) 289-1441
President: John Mazurkiewicz
Public relations agency specializing
in outdoor recreation and fishing
products.

Cunningham Mfg. Co.
Box 2437,
Huntington Beach, CA 92649
(714) 840-3900
FAX: (714) 840-5676
Contact: Wade Cunningham

**Eagle Recreational
Consultants**
PO Box 926, Lincoln, MT 59639
(406) 362-4270
Contact: Alan Kelly
Consulting service for wingshooting
and flyfishing lodges.
See Our Ad Pg. 71

Export/Import Managers Co.
3140 Harbor Lane, Suite 227
Minneapolis, MN 55447
(612) 559-3850
FAX: (612) 559-3852
Contact: Thomas Kalgren
Export mgmt. company represent-
ing manufacturers of fly fishing
equipment on international basis.

Extex Company
2363 Boulevard Circle, Suite 104
Walnut Creek, CA 94595
(510) 988-0190
FAX: (510) 988-0192 Est.: 1982
Pres: Ted Bamberger
Export USA-made sportfishing products to trade distributors
worldwide.

The Gillie, LLC
47 Farrington Rd.
Montauk, NY 11954

(888) 244-5543
Contact: Mike Grossman
The Gillie™ is a catalog of fly fishing vacations worldwide giving the
fly fisher only the best.

W.S. Hunter & Co.
PO Box 59, 223 South Hill Rd.
New Boston, NH 03070
(603) 487-3944
FAX: (603) 487-3940
Contact: Bill Hunter
Discreet problem solving based
upon 25 years of success in the fly
fishing industry.
* Extensive retail sales, start-up
and mail order experience
* Product design, testing and assis-
tance in marketing new products
and programs for manufacturers
* Destination development, design
and promotional assistance
* Acquisition review and
counseling
See Our Ad Above

Inter-Fluve, Inc.
25 N. Willson Ave., Suite 5
Bozeman, MT 59715
(406) 586-6926
FAX: (406) 586-8445 Est.: 1983
Principal/Hydrologist: Dale E. Miller
Inter-Fluve, Inc. is a professional
consulting firm that specializes in
aquatic resources. Our team of experts pioneered the integration of
biology, hydrology, engineering,

and landscape architecture, to become the leader in innovative aquatic resource enhancement.

Brad Jackson
Consultant to the Fly Fishing Industry
107 Village Dr., Redding, CA 96001
(916) 244-9314
FAX: (916) 244-9314
Contact: Brad Jackson
Brad offers 7 years experience providing advice and consultation to fly tackle dealers, private waters programs, lodges and manufacturers. Expertise: management, operations, marketing; all facets of how to grow & operate fly fishing businesses.

Tim Leary
PO Box 844, Franconia, NH 03580
(603) 823-5558
FAX: (603) 823-5779
Contact: Tim Leary
Clothing design specialist and freelance photographer/writer for the flyfishing industry. 7 years experience reviewing softgoods for the flyfishing industry; 10 years experience photographing and writing.

Nichols Boyesen & Zino
194 Valley View Rd.
New Hartford, NY 13413
(315) 797-0700
FAX: (315) 738-0224
Est.: 1987   Staff: 3
Contact: Hans Boyesen
Creative advertising and marketing services for the outdoor industry.

Perry, Inc.
2725 Cantrell, #201
Little Rock, AR 72207
Contact: Scott Perry

The Product Detective®
PO Box 1162, Blackfoot, ID 83221
(208) 785-5319
FAX: (208) 785-1553
Contact: Kitty Pearson
Packaging design, sourcing, marketing, photography, corporate identities.

Rainbow Packaging South
227 W. Seaview Circle
Marathon, FL 33050
(800) 747-5350   (305) 743-5350
FAX: (305) 743-0096
Contact: Charles McClelland
Specialize in packaging and labeling of fly rods and reels.

Reel Resources, Inc.
1600 Prince St., #103
Alexandria, VA 22314
(703) 683-5666
FAX: (703) 683-5667

Contact: Fred Rehbier
Video production firm

Scott Agency
Box 3310, Ketchum, ID 83340
(208) 726-9675
FAX: (208) 726-9759
Contact: Ford Scott Rollo
Advertising, marketing, packaging, graphic, Internet, catalogs, logos, etc.

Cam Sigler
Box 656, Vashon Island, WA 98070
(206) 567-4836
FAX: (206) 567-4940
Contact: Cam Sigler
Specialzies in international trade, product development and sourcing for the fly fishing industry.

The Speakers Bureau
6730 E. 91st Place South
Suite 2, Tulsa, OK 74133
(918) 491-0826
FAX: (918) 491-6675
Contact: Joan Whitlock
Agent for a list of speakers and instructors who are available to speak for club functions.

T-Winds Corporation
1819 South Central
Suite 104 & 110, Kent, WA 98032
(206) 854-3853
FAX: (206) 854-7354
Est.: 1994   Staff: 4
President: Hisa Iwasaki
Email: iwasaki@accessone.com
Export, import and market research

Trade Management Services
3140 Harbor Ln., #220
Plymouth, MN 55447
(612) 550-9170
FAX: (612) 550-0157
Contact: Mary Olson
International freight forwarder specializing in the transport of fly fishing equipment to foreign markets.

Video Wisconsin
18110 W. Blumound Rd.
Brookfield, WI 53045-2917
(414) 785-1110
FAX: (414) 785-9827
Contact: Jeff Utschig
International producer of outdoor marketing and training tapes; multi-million dollar teleproduction center located in Milwaukee.

Woodland Advertising
5100 Presbyterian Dr.
Conway, SC 29526
(803) 347-6862
Creative Director: Paul A. Olsen

A full service advertising agency dedicated to serving outdoor oriented businesses. We offer a full line of creative services including corporate identity programs, advertising campaigns, media planning, photography, Internet advertising and marketing. No matter what your business needs, turn to Woodland Advertising for the solution.

Wurtmann Advertising
938 Santa Florencia
Solana Beach, CA 92075
(619) 794-0101
FAX: (619) 794-0606
Contact: Jon Wurtmann

INSURANCE

BHJ, Inc.
PO Box 507, Buffalo, WY 82834
(307) 684-5529
FAX: (307) 684-9039
Contact: Tenley Spear
General liability insurance for outfitters and guides.

Bartlett, Baggett & Shands Insurance Agency
1204 S. First St.
PO Box 9, Lufkin, TX 75901
(800) 324-8452   (409) 632-4496
FAX: (409) 632-1125
Contact: Ben Bartlett

Bishop Insurance Center of Whitefish
Holiday Plaza, 6406 Highway 93 S.
Whitefish, MT 59937
(800) 775-2958   (406) 862-4480
FAX: (406) 862-0470
Contact: Mark Kuhr
General liability insurance for guides and outfitters.

Gwaltney & Gwaltney, Inc.
701 Sesame St., #200
Anchorage, AK 99503-6641
(907) 561-7468
FAX: (907) 561-4889
Contact: Chuck Weir
All lines of insurance specializing in guides, outfitters, & aviation insurance.

Jacobi Group, Ltd.
PO Box 54625, Phoenix, AZ 85078
(800) 355-4868   (602) 867-8422
FAX: (602) 867-3979
Contact: Ruth Jacobi
Full range of coverages for outfitters and guides.

Outdoor Underwriters, Inc.
1117 Chapline St.
Wheeling, WV 26003

(800) 738-1300
FAX: (304) 233-1732
Contact: Tim Reed

The Outdoorsman Agency, Inc.
PO Box 61127, Columbia, SC 29260
(800) 849-9288
FAX: (803) 799-6609
Contact: Steve Murray or Andrew Woodham, Jr.
Specialists in commercial insurance programs for outdoor-oriented businesses, to include: Fishing guides, outfitters and lodges; fly fishing schools and instructors; wilderness pack trip outfitters; canoeing, kayaking and backpacking guides. Also contact us for program information on wingshooting preserves, private hunting/fishing clubs and large landowners leasing to multiple clubs.
See Our Ad Above

Tournament Fishing Assn.
8350 N. Central Expwy., #730
Dallas, TX 75206
(800) 446-1885 (214) 691-6911
FAX: (214) 373-1619
Exec. Dir: Max Rhodes
Tournament fishing prize insurance

LEADERS & TIPPETS

Airflo Leaders
Distributed by Main Stream
65 New Litchfield St.
Torrington, CT 06790
(860) 489-4993
FAX: (860) 496-0267
Contact: Iain Sorrell
Airflo's award winning new Poly-Leaders & PolyTips have "zero" memory and are capable of turning over incredible tippet lengths making mono leaders and sink tip fly lines obsolete! Airflo's extensive leader range includes Tapered Braid leaders for trout, Salmon and Saltwater applications with leader sink rates up to an incredible 13 in/sec! All leaders come ready looped for ease of use and Total Depth Control.

American Fishing Wire
205 Carter Dr.,
West Chester, PA 19380
(800) 824-9473 Ext. 122
(610) 692-1971
FAX: (610) 692-2190
Est.: 1976
Sales Mgr: Mike Shields

Manufacturer's of extra flexible, miniature stainless steel tippet material. Premium quality tippet material is kink and bite resistant and provides more than mono and braided lines. Breaking strengths from 6.5 to 90 lbs. Excellent for pike, muskie, barracuda, bluefish, kingfish, shark, tuna, etc. Available nylon coated and bare in bright

Ande Monofilament
1310 53rd St.
West Palm Beach, FL 33407
(561) 842-2474
FAX: (561) 848-5538
Contact: Bill Munro
For over 30 years Ande monofilament fishing line has always stood up under every conceivable fishing condition. Available in two monofilaments: Premium and Tournament, 2 to 400 lb. Ande monofilament holds more than 1000 current IGFA World Records. Call, fax or write for information.

AvaLon Leaders
Distributed by Angler Sport Group
6619 Oak Orchard Rd.
Elba, NY 14058
(716) 757-9958
FAX: (716) 757-9066
President: Paul Betters
The finest designed knotted leaders available today. Tippet material is always the finest fluorocarbon and each leader comes with the most indispensable cross reference chart ever produced.

Blue Water Designs Inc.
205 Cross St., Bristol, CT 06010
(860) 582-0623
FAX: (860) 585-8133
Contact: Tom Delekta/Mike Stange
Various length wire shock tippets with specially designed fly snaps to facilitate quick fly changes; adjustable length wire shock tippets for everything from bluefish to blue sharks.

Burns Outfitters
PO Box 2632, Carlsbad, CA 92008
(619) 720-1108
FAX: (619) 720-6248
Contact: Carl Burns
Importers of the Softsteel fluorocarbon leader (3 to 27 lbs.)

Climax Systems USA
3736 Kellogg Rd.
Cortland, NY 13045
(607) 756-2851
FAX: (607) 753-8835
Contact: Tom McCullough
Climax is recognized as the world's leading manufacturer of specialty

leaders and tippets. High abrasion resistance, tough co-polymer material is supple enough to make knot tying easy. New fluorocarbon material virtually disappears in water! A full range of leaders and tippets for every fly fishing pursuit.

Cortland Line Co.
3736 Kellogg Rd., PO Box 5588
Cortland, NY 13045
(607) 756-2851
FAX: (607) 753-8835
Contact: Tom McCullough
A series of precision, knotless leaders and high-tech tippet materials including IGFA. True strength to diameter ratios in all materials from lightest tippet up through heavy butt material.

Dai-Riki
c/o Dan Bailey's Fly Shop
Box 1019, Livingston, MT 59047
(800) 356-4052   (406) 222-1673
FAX: (406) 222-8450
Est.: 1938
Contact: Scott Sanchez
Dai-Riki tippet features the exclusive tippet yoke system with a built-in leader straightener. Dai-Riki has leaders with powerful butts for turnover.

Elite Products
12 Plants Dam Rd.
East Lyme, CT 06333
(860) 739-8185
FAX: (860) 739-0680
Contact: Kathy McBride
Hand-tied leaders–saltwater/salmon steelhead, wire bite guard.

Fenwick Corp.
5242 Argosy Dr.
Huntington Beach, CA 92649
(714) 897-1066 Ext. 226
FAX: (714) 891-9610

Fin-Nor
5553 Angler Ave.
Ft. Lauderdale, FL 33312
(305) 966-5507
Contact: Bill Preuss
Fin-Nor Fluoro-Carbon leaders virtually disappear under water, are stronger with higher knot strength, sink faster and are more abrasion resistant.

Gudebrod, Inc.
PO Box 357, Pottstown, PA 19464
(610) 327-4050
FAX: (610) 327-4588
President: Robert Marquardt
Sales Mgr: Robert Graham
Guderod's Super G Loop-The-Loop Fly Fishing System offers you the ability to build your line expertly

and the convenience of quick, easy changes so you can adapt to fishing conditions. System includes: Mini Lead Heads, Braided Butt Leaders and Loop Connectors, Splicing Kits, Shooting Line, & Flyline Backing.

Jinkai
Distributed by High Tech Tackle
Box 308, Burlingham, NY 12722
(800) 888-5758
FAX: (800) 274-7071
Popular big game, shock or bite tippet mono.

Krema Corp. of America
420 Lexington Ave., #2740
New York, NY 10170
(212) 867-7040
FAX: (212) 953-0025
Contact: Koji Suyama
Seaguar fluorocarbon fishing line; Riverge tapered leaders

Mason Tackle Co.
PO Box 56, Otisville, MI 48463
(800) 356-3640
(810) 631-4571
FAX: (810) 631-8695
Contact: Richard Powell
Manufacturer of "Super Soft" leader material; "Hard Type" tippet material; "Lead Core" sinking leader; "Presentation" knotless tapered; "New Technology" knotless tapered fly line backing

Orvis Company
Rt. 7A, Manchester, VT 05254
(800) 333-1550 (Ext. 844)
(802) 362-3622
Contact: Randy Carlson

RIO International Products
180 Ridge St., PO Box 684
Blackfoot, ID 83221
(800) 553-0838   (208) 785-1244
FAX: (208) 785-1553
Contact: Jim Vincent or Kitty Vincent
RIO Products–The Leader & Tippet Specialist™. 200+ fresh & saltwater knotless & hand-tied tapered leaders. 4 types of tippet: Powerflex™, Salmon/Bass/Steelhead, IGFA Hard Mono Saltwater & supple IGFA

Roman Moser Leaders
c/o Davy Wotton, 1098 Randville Dr.,
Palatine, IL 60067
(847) 359-0297
FAX: (847) 359-0297
Contact: Davy Wotton
The original Roman Moser fly leaders with their special functions are constructed either conically braided, woven, spun or mono-tapered made out of Polypropylen, Polyamid, Dyneema, PU or Fluoro Carbon–as well as high-floating and rapid-diving. These leaders fit all situations and type of fish in fresh and saltwater.

X-RATING OF TIPPETS

The chart below will help you understand the relationship of a tippet's X-rating to its size, or more specifically to the diameter of the monofilament used. The important thing to notice when you are looking at a leader package is the diameter and the tippet pound-test rating.

Tippet Size	Diameter	Fly Size	Pound Test*
0X	.011	#4 - #6	6.5
1X	.010	#4 - #8	5.5
2X	.009	#4 - #10	4.5
3X	.008	#6 - #12	3.8
4X	.007	#6 - #14	3.1
5X	.006	#14 - #20	2.4
6X	.005	#18 - #26	1.4
7X	.004	#20 - #28	1.1
8x	.003	#20 - #28	.75

*Approximate—a leader's *X-Rating* and *Pound Test Rating* varies from brand to brand.

Scientific Anglers

3M Scientific Anglers
3M Center-Bldg. 223-4N
St. Paul, MN 55144-1000
(800) 525-6290
The final connection between you and the fish, Scientific Anglers leaders offered in freshwater and saltwater versions, are available in a range of strengths, lengths and butt diameters for almost all fly fishing situations. Scientific Anglers leaders and tippet material feature the best balance of properties, including high knot strength and abrasion resistance.
See Our Ad Pg. 1

Seafarer
Fishing Products, Inc.
200-30 Industrial Park Blvd.
Sebastian, FL 32958
(561) 587-1145
President: Albert Johnson, Jr.
Produce the Momoi's Hi-Catch IGFA line designed to break just under IGFA's specifications. Also produces low visibility fluoro-carbon monofilament called Seguar.

Stren Fishing Lines
c/o Remington Arms Company
PO Box 700, 870 Remington Dr.
Madison, NC 27025-0700
(910) 548-8546
Public Relations: Michael Fine

TEENY NYMPH CO.
QUALITY FLY FISHING PRODUCTS

Teeny Nymph Company
PO Box 989, Gresham, OR 97030
(503) 667-6602
FAX: (503) 667-2917   Est.: 1971
Contact: Craig Inglesby
Teeny Nymph Co. leaders are designed to help you to make smoother and more accurate presentations. They have low visibility and are very durable. Available in three types of leaders:
Salmon/Steelhead (durable for bigger fish)–9 ft. & 12 ft.;
MultiPurpose (low visibility green/trout, bass panfish)– 7 1/2 ft. & 9 ft.; T-Series (designed to match up specifically with T-Series or heavy flylines)–4 ft.
See Our Ad Pg. 77

Terminal Tactics, Inc.
Box 455, Sauk Rapids, MN 56379
(320) 251-9479
FAX: (320) 259-8719
Contact: Dutch Schaefers
Makers of Tippet in a Tube.

U.S. Line Company
16 Union Ave.,
Westfield, MA 01086
(413) 562-3629
Makers of braided backings and lead core lines.

Umpqua Feather Merchants
PO Box 700, Glide, OR 97443
(800) 322-3218   (541) 496-3512
FAX: (541) 496-0150
Est.: 1972
Nat'l. Sales Mgr: Gus Wunderly
Umpqua leaders help you present your fly better in a range of conditions, in both freshwater and saltwater fishing situations. Over the years, the Umpqua name on both tapered leaders and tippet materials has established a reputation in fly fishing as the standard for both toughness and ease of use. The Deceiver tapered leaders and tippet material, is made from a low-visibility material that is incredibly tough.

Ursus Enterprises
PO Box 9421, Missoula, MT 59807
(406) 542-2568
FAX: (406) 542-2568
Contact: Gus Serven
Maker "Deep Dive" leaded leaders.

LINE

Accardo/Peck's Poppers
3708 Conrad St.
Baton Rouge, LA 70805
(504) 355-0863
FAX: (504) 355-0420
Est.: 1950   Staff: 19
Contact: Tony or Matthew Accardo
Level & weight forwards tapers.
5,6,7,8 weight in green.

Airflo Fly Line
Distributed by Main Stream
65 New Litchfield St.
Torrington, CT 06790
(860) 489-4993
FAX: (860) 496-0267
Contact: Iain Sorrell
Airflo's award winning new Gold & 7000Ts series Fly Lines offer exceptional performance and quality–backed by a 5 year "non-crack" guarantee! The wide range of models and tapers includes the Highest Buoyancy Floaters, Clearest Intermediates and the Fastest Sinking Lines available. Airflo also offer a choice of either regular Traditional Stretch or the Latest "Hi-Sense" core for maximum sensitivity and hooking power.

Aquanova Flyline
c/o Northern Sport Fishing
Products, Ltd., 53 Victoria Rd., S.
Unit 4, Guelph Ontario
Canada N1E 5P7
(519) 824-4023
FAX: (519) 824-1439
Contact: Rick Tramer
Manufacturer of private label fly lines and Canadian-made Aquanova fly line.

Berkley Specialist©
1 Berkley Dr., Spirit Lake, IA 51360
(800) 237-5539
(712) 336-1520 (Consumer)
FAX: (712) 336-5183
Berkley Specialist© floating lines are offered in a variety of weights and tapers that suit every application. Berkley Select Advanta™ fly lines offer both floating and sinking lines in a variety of weights.

Gary Borger Signature Series Fly Lines
1075 A Shelley St.
Springfield, OR 97477
(541) 741-8161
FAX: (541) 741-7565
Est.: 1971   Staff: 20
Sales Mgr: Dale Williams
Supplier of the Gary Borger Signature Series fly lines. These lines are tailored to modern graphite rods and are available in four specialty tapers. Dealer and consumer inquiries welcome, call today.

Climax Systems USA
3736 Kellogg Rd.,
Cortland, NY 13045

Choosing The Right Line

No single piece of equipment in your fly tackle system is more important than fly line. That's because to present a fly successfully in a given fishing situation, you must use a line of the right weight, taper, color and buoyancy.

Weight

A typical spool of fly line will run anywhere from 80 to 110 feet or so in length. The line's weight designation, however, is arrived at by weighing the first 30 feet of line and seeing where that weight falls on a standard scale developed by the American Sportsfishing Association or ASA (formerly AFTMA or the American Fishing Tackle Manufacturers Association). The ASA scale ranges from a 1-weight, the lightest line, to 15-weight, the heaviest line. Most fly fishing situations call for a line in the 3 to 12 weight range, with 5, 6 & 7 weights being the most widely used.

Taper

A fly line's performance is not entirely based on its weight, however. Taper, or the line's thickness, also plays an important role. Here's a rundown of the typical line tapers you'll encounter [see accompanying chart]:

Level - Usually the least expensive line available, level line, as the name suggests, has the same diameter from end to end. The absence of a taper makes level line far more difficult to cast, and almost impossible to cast with style and finesse.

Weight Forward (WF) - Again, as the name implies, the weight in a weight forward line is concentrated in the first 30 feet, with the balance of the line consisting of a thinner and lighter material. One of the more popular tapers currently in use, weight forward line works well for short to long distance casts and with a wide variety of flys. (Bug or salt tapers carry the code WR and are variations of the weight forward design that concentrate even more weight up front. They are designed to cast heavier leaders and flies.)

Double Taper (DT) - Tapered at both ends, the double taper is considered by many experts to be the best taper for all around fishing and a good choice for the novice angler. The thicker mid-section of this line, however, makes it difficult to cast over long distances. One advantage of the mirror image taper is the ability to reverse the line as one end becomes worn.

Shooting Taper (ST) - This specialty taper is really two lines in one--a heavy forward section followed by a separate thin shooting line. Shooting taper lines are most often used when fishing salmon, steelhead or bass or in any situation requiring long casts. Difficult to use, these lines are not recommended for beginners.

Triangle Taper (TT) - One of the newest line designs to catch the fancy of the fly fishing world, the triangle taper works in a wide range of fishing situations. Starting >

LINE TAPERS

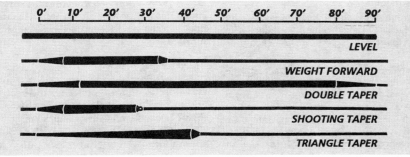

| 0' | 10' | 20' | 30' | 40' | 50' | 60' | 70' | 80' | 90' |

LEVEL

WEIGHT FORWARD

DOUBLE TAPER

SHOOTING TAPER

TRIANGLE TAPER

from a relatively fine tip, the line thickens to the 40-or-so foot mark where the taper reverses quickly in the next 10 feet to a thin running line. Proponents of the design claim it offers the greatest delicacy of any fly line.

Color

Read a dozen books on fly fishing and you'll get a dozen different theories on what color fly line works best. Some experienced anglers think that bright colored lines—especially sinking lines—scare fish; others say it's the line's shadow above, on or below the surface, not the color, that spooks them. The most authoritative anyone can be on the subject is to say that no one really knows for sure what works and why.

So what color line should you choose? For floating line (more on this below), go with a bright color. The reason is simple: When casting it is often very difficult to see where your fly is--and what you can't see you can't control. The end of a brightly colored line, however, is much easier to pick out in the water and can provide some clue about where and how you've presented

Front & Back: A Brief Guide to Leaders & Backing

Leader - a tapered, mono-filament—usually, nylon line—that connects the front end of the fly line to the fly (or sometimes to a tippet which connects to the fly.) Its low-visibility and taper are designed to make the fly appear as natural as possible when presented, floating or sinking. The three main parts of a leader are:

Butt - the thickest section of the leader that attaches directly to the fly line and continues the line's taper.

Body or Midsection - continues the leader's taper and connects the butt section to the tip of the leader.

Tip - the narrowest part of the leader and usually 12-24" long. Sometimes referred to as the tippet if a separate tippet section is not used.

Backing - Extra nylon or Dacron line added to the back end of the fly line. Backing is used to prevent a running fish from pulling off more than the 80-120' of fly line used in most fishing situations. The amount of backing used is determined by the capacity of the reel/spool, the size of the fly line used and the typical running distance of the fish being sought.

the fly. A bright line will also make it easier for you to pick up and correct casting errors.

Buoyancy

All fly line carries a code—again standardized by the ASA—that designate its function, which is to say, whether it floats or sinks. These functional categories are:

F - Floating line

S - Sinking Line

I - Intermediate Line

F/S - Floating with Sinking Tip

Floating lines are by far the most commonly used, primarily, though not always, with dry flies. They are generally considered the line of choice for beginners because of the ease with which they cast and handle on the water.

Sinking lines are designed, not surprisingly, to sink, though some at faster rates than others. They do this to pull a fly down to the level where fish are feeding in fresh or saltwater, anywhere from one or two to over 30 feet deep. Generally speaking, the deeper you want the fly to drop, the faster the sink rate you'll need.

Intermediate line is just heavier than water and sinks very slowly, making it a good alternative to full sinking line in weedy or choppy water where dropping the fly just below the surface is required. Intermediate line is also popular with some anglers because, when dressed with line floatant, it functions as a floating line.

Floating sink tip lines are used in specialized fishing situations where it is advantageous to have a portion of the line—through the tip, taper or belly—sink, while the remainder of the line floats. F/S is a popular choice as a second line and, because it is easier to handle than full sinking line, is often recommended for use by beginners.

What's Your Line

Expert advice on buying line is simple and close to unanimous: "Buy the best." Or, at the very least, the best you can afford. Why? Because, all other factors being equal, the better the line, the better your fly presentation. And better presentation results in better fishing.

(607) 756-2851
FAX: (607) 753-8835
Contact: Tom McCullough
Climax is offering the new, ready-to-fly line. Our factory spliced loop makes leader connections fast and easy. The contrasting "pickup" mark gives you an instant reference for precise rod loading, allowing quick, long, accurate shots with minimal false casting. And the unique taper design delivers positive turnover every time. Fresh and saltwater fly lines available.

Cortland Line Co.
3736 Kellogg Rd., PO Box 5588
Cortland, NY 13045
(607) 756-2851
FAX: (607) 753-8835
Contact: Tom McCullough
Over 400 fly lines for every fishing situation. From beginners through experienced professionals, Cortland makes a fly line for virtually all fresh and saltwater species. Plus Micron fly line backing is the standard choice for anglers all over the world.

Dai-Riki Shooting Line
Distributed by Dan Bailey
Box 1019, Livingston, MT 59047
(800) 356-4052   (406) 222-1673
FAX: (406) 222-8450
Contact: Scott Sanchez
Dai-Riki shooting line combines the narrow diameter of Dai-Riki line with a "slime line coating" and shoots like mono and handles like flyline.

Fenwick Corp.
5242 Argosy Dr.
Huntington Beach, CA 92649
(714) 897-1066 Ext. 226
FAX: (714) 891-9610 Est.: 1952
Contact: Dale Barnes

Flow Tek, Inc.
Box 2018, Boulder, CO 80306-2018
(303) 530-3050
Manufacturer of a clear and opaque saltwater floating line. Intended to be used in temperatures above 60 degrees.

Hardy (USA) Inc.
10 Godwin Plaza
Midland Park, NJ 07432
(201) 481-7557
FAX: (201) 670-7190
Contact: Jay White
Hardy fly lines have been the benchmark of quality and performance for almost a century. The current range of superb lines is manufactured to our own exacting specification, taper and density. Call or write for catalog.

The Teeny Nymph Co., leader in specialized flylines, received a KUDOS award from *Fly Rod & Reel* magazine in 1996, recognizing the T-Series & TS-Saltwater Series flylines as one of the best fly fishing products in the world. The Professional Series flylines are designed by some of the world's finest fly fishermen: Lefty Kreh, Gary LaFontaine, Flip Pallot, and Dave Whitlock.

For a free catalog contact us at:
PO Box 989, Gresham, OR 97030
Tel: 503-667-6602 Fax: 503-667-2917
Email: tnymph@transport.com
www.teeny-nymph.com

"Limestoner" Floating Fly Lines
Distributed by Belvoirdale
PO Box 176, Wyncote, PA 19095
(215) 886-7211
FAX: (215) 886-1804
President: Grahame Maisey
Nearest to a silk fly line. Best casting and presentation. Most durable. Chosen by the best guides.

The McKenzie STST
1075 A Shelley St.
Springfield, OR 97477
(541) 741-8161
FAX: (541) 741-7565
Est.: 1971
Sales Mgr: Dale Williams
The STST has a 25 foot sink tip with a large diameter running line which creates less line recoil memory. The tapered section between the floating running line and the sink tip make the STST cast without any hinging.

Monic Lines
Flow tek, Inc.
PO Box 2018, Boulder, CO 80306
(303) 530-3050
Contact: Bob Goodale
Makers of clear floating warm and coldwater fly lines.

Orvis Company
Rt. 7A, Manchester, VT 05254
(800) 333-1550 (Ext. 844)
(802) 362-3622
Contact: Randy Carlson
Orvis professionals design and extensively field test every Orvis fly line to offer you the most comprehensive series of fly lines available. From delicate one-weight double tapers to 600 grain Depth Charge lines, Orvis offers over 22 different fly lines and shooting head systems for the fly fisherman. For more information on Orvis fly lines, call 800-333-1550 (Ext. 844).

"Phoenix" Handmade Pure Silk Fly Lines
Distributed by Belvoirdale
PO Box 176, Wyncote, PA 19095
(215) 886-7211
FAX: (215) 886-1804
President: Grahame Maisey
10 ft. tapers, extra fine tips, thinner belly, give Phoenix ultimate presentation and distance. Unequalled durability.

RIO International Products
180 Ridge St., PO Box 684
Blackfoot, ID 83221
(800) 553-0838   (208) 785-1244
FAX: (208) 785-1553
Contact: Jim Vincent
RIO Products' specialty fly lines for spey/two handed rods: Accelerator™ & WindCutter™ with floating, sinking or interchangeable tips.

Head wallet, spey manual & video. For single handed rods: VersiTip™ for line weights WF7 to WF12 for fresh or saltwater fly fishing.

Royal Wulff Products
HCR1, Box 70
Lew Beach, NY 12758
(800) 328-3638   (914) 439-4060
FAX: (914) 439-8055
Contact: Doug Cummings
Award winning Royal Wulff Saltwater and Big Game Triangle short front tapers and thinner running line. See your dealer or contact Royal Wulff.

Ryobi Masterline Limited
Cotteswold Rd., Tewkesbury
Glosglow, UK GL20 5DJ
011-171-01684-299000
FAX: 011-171-01684-292557
Managing Dir: Dick Tallents
Complete line of fly lines including, Jubilee, Advantage, Challenge, Target and Pioneer.

3M Scientific Anglers
3M Center-Bldg. 223-4N-05
St. Paul, MN 55144-1000
(800) 525-6290
Scientific Anglers fly lines—more than 500 different fly lines are offered by 3M Scientific Anglers, including Ultra 3 floating and Ultra 3 Wet Tip™ lines, specialty bonefish/tarpon, steelhead and bass bug/saltwater tapers, and the Wet Cel™ and Uniform Sink full sinking line series. Specialty sinking lines including Monocore™ and Deep Water Express™ shooting tapers are also available.
Scientific Anglers Mastery Series fly lines, "A line for every water—A taper for every condition," are offered in twenty different tapers designed to excel in three performance categories—castability, shootability, durability. They are available exclusively from Scientific Anglers Mastery Series dealers. Call for your nearest location.
See Our Ad Pg. 1

Skyline™
Distributed by Skykomish Flies
Box 70165, Eugene, OR 97401
(541) 741-8161
FAX: (541) 741-7565
Est.: 1971
Sales Mgr: Dale Williams
Full length 83' weight forward flyl-

ine. Specialized taper and low friction coating for increased casting distance.

South Bend/Crystal River
1950 Stanley St.,
Northbrook, IL 60065
(847) 564-1900
Fly line, backing, leaders and flies marketed under the Crystal River trade name.

Statech™ Spinfly Lines
by Angler's Engineering, Rt. 6, Box 27
Eureka Springs, AR 72632
(800) 752-7132
FAX: (501) 253-7850
Contact: Skip Halterman
Use your spinning reel to cast like a fly rod. Call for our 12-page booklet that describes it all.

Teeny Nymph Company
PO Box 989, Gresham, OR 97030
(503) 667-6602
FAX: (503) 667-2917 Est.: 1971
Contact: Craig Inglesby
The T-Series and TS-Saltwater Series flylines have weighted heads smoothly attached with no loops or splices to a floating running line. T-Series have 24 ft. sinking head and TS-Saltwater Series has 30 ft. sinking head. Both series are made in grain weights so you can fish any level of the water. Professional Series flylines designed by some of the top flyfishermen in the world. Lefty Kreh-Distance casting line, Gary LaFontaine-Delicate trout line, Flip Pallot-Saltwater flats line, Dave Whitlock-Bass line & Midge/Nymph heads.
See Our Ad Pg. 77

Versitex of America Ltd.
3545 Schuylkill Rd.
Spring City, PA 19475
(610) 948-4442
FAX: (800) 331-6406
Est.: 1985   Staff: 6
President: Frederic S. Claghorn, Jr.
Office Mgr: Nancy M. Ewing
Available: Retail & Direct
Distributor of "Battle Line" fine diameter Gel Spun Poly backing.
See Our Ad Pg. 102

Woodstock Line Company
91 Canal St., Putnam, CT 06239
(860) 928-6557
FAX: (860) 928-1096
Est.: 1946   Staff: 15
VP & GM: Richard Rodensky
Offering our "PRESENTATION" series of fine, high quality floating fly lines, in flourescent lime color, on 30 yard spools, in 4" peg board display boxes. Sizes available: 5, 6, 7, 8 & 9 in Level, Weight Forward and Double Taper. We also offer fly line backing available in 12-15-20-30 pound tests, of nylon, dacron or vectran, and in natural, flourescent lime, orange and sand.

MAIL ORDER

Mail order shopping is a time-honored fly fishing tradition. Indeed, the oldest mail order company in the country began serving the fisherman five years before Abe Lincoln moved into the White House. Today catalog/mail order houses offer the fly fisherman a vast array of functional and reliable products. The companies listed below are among the best offering the fly fishing enthusiast a wide range of apparel, accessories, fly fishing gear and equipment.

A.A. Pro Shop
RD1, Box 78, White Haven, PA 18661
(800) 443-8119 (Orders)
(717) 443-8111
Bulletin-style catalog featuring a broad range of fly fishing equipment, clothes and accessories.

American Angling Supplies & Services
23 Main St., PO Box 987
Salem, NH 03079
(800) 264-5378 (Orders)
(603) 893-3333
FAX: (603) 898-8141
Contact: Dave Beshara
Full range of fly tackle, clothes and accessories featured in 70+ page catalog.

Angler's Catalog Co., L.L.C.

PO Box 111, Twin Falls, ID 83344
(800) 657-8040
FAX: (208) 735-8758
Contact: Scott Roberts
Gift catalog for fly fishermen. Includes art, bronzes, furniture, sculptures, clothing, misc. gifts.

Angler's Workshop

PO Box 1010, 1350 Atlantic Ave.
Woodland, WA 98674
(360) 225-9445 (Orders)
(360) 225-8641 (Fax Worldwide)
FAX: (800) 278-1069
Web Site: http://www.anglersworkshop.com
Angler's Workshop is a major mail order company celebrating its 17th year supplying the rod builder and fly tyer with hard-to-find materials. Worldwide shipping. Shop in Angler's Workshop catalog to find rod blanks, rod kits and components as well as an excellent supply of fly tying materials, rods, reels, lines, flies and more. We are cork import specialists supplying manufacturers and retailers with the finest cork rings and preform handles. As the North American distributors for Hopkins and Holloway, we supply the best fly guides made to the largest fly fishing market.
See Our Ad Pg. 61

Anglers Image Inc.

5714 Clark Rd., Sarasota, FL 34233
(800) 858-0903
FAX: (941) 927-0560
Est.: 1990   Staff: 5
President: Stan Sugerman
Manufacturers of "Anglers Image all stainless Flyfishing Knife", Line Winder, the worlds best Line Clipper with retractable needle, the only 100% Flyfishing Plier tool and more. Free full catalog featuring: The best in flyfishing equipment, gifts, gadgets, cutlery, apparel, books, videos, etc. A totally unique catalog.

Atlantic Rancher

89 Front St.
Marblehead, MA 01945
(617) 639-7700
Contact: Jennifer Chaisson

Dan Bailey's Fly Shop

Box 1019, Livingston, MT 59047
(800) 356-4052   (406) 222-1673
FAX: (406) 222-8450
Est.: 1938
Contact: John Bailey
Catalog features Dan Bailey's Fly Shop's line of the world's finest hand-tied flies, fly fishing tackle and great products for fly fishers around the world.

The Bass Pond

PO Box 82, Littleton, CO 80160
(800) 327-5014   (303) 798-3647
FAX: (303) 730-8932
Contact: Lori Tucker-Eccher
The one and only bass fly fishing catalog.

Bass Pro Shops

1935 S. Campbell
Springfield, MO 65898-0300
(800) 227-7776
Complete catalog & destination retailer in Springfield, MO and Duluth, GA, featuring top quality flyfishing gear at affordable prices.

L.L. Bean

Casco St., Freeport, ME 04033
(800) 809-7057
FAX: (207) 552-3080
Est.: 1912   Staff: 3800
Offering you more new, innovative fishing products than ever before. Call for a free flyfishing catalog.

Belvoirdale

PO Box 176, Wyncote, PA 19095
(215) 886-7211
FAX: (215) 886-1804
President: Grahame Maisey
Importer and distributor of the world's finest sporting equipment from England.
Gaelic Supreme Premium Handmade Fly Hooks
Phoenix handmade pure silk flylines
Limestone floating flylines
S. Maisey handmade rod components
Elephant silk rod winding thread
Modular boxes for hooks, fly tying and flyfishing
Dinsmores catch and release

landing nets
Coming in 1997!!!
Graphite rods
Wading jackets

Blue Ribbon Flies

Box 1037
West Yellowstone, MT 59758
(406) 646-7642
Our mail order catalog also features news and information on our guide services and lodging. The Blue Ribbon Fishing Report is a weekly update for Yellowstone Country—one year subscriptions available for $40.

Blue Ridge Rod Company

PO Box 6268, 2162 Renard Ct.
Annapolis, MD 21401
(410) 224-4072
FAX: (410) 573-0993
Est.: 1989
Contact: Tom Dougherty
Blue Ridge Rod Company is the only supplier in the US of blanks, components and tools exclusively for the fly rod builder. We feature Sage, Scott, Redington, Hexagraph and Blue Ridge by Diamondback blanks, and a complete line of components by Struble, Bellinger, REC, Fuji, Pacific Bay, Gudebrod, etc.

Cabela's

812 13th Ave., Sidney, NE 69160
(800) 237-4444
FAX: (308) 254-2200
Est.: 1961   Staff: 1000
Catalog features a full range of fly fishing tackle, tools, clothes and accessories of the "world's foremost outfitter."

Cast-A-Ways

45 Longwood Lake Rd.
Oak Ridge, NJ 07438
(800) 977-3999
Contact: Don Storms
Fly tying and fly fishing products.

The Classic Outfitters

1880 Mountain Rd.
Stowe, VT 05672
(800) 353-3963
Contact: Roger Ranz
Direct'to consumer—Lewis Creek wax cotton outerwear for fishing & hunting. Call for catalog.

Dale Clemens Custom Tackle

444 Schantz Rd.
Allentown, PA 18104
(610) 395-5119
FAX: (610) 398-2580
Catalog of rod building supplies and components.

Cold Spring Anglers
419 E. High St., Suite A
PO Box 129, Carlisle, PA 17013
(800) 248-8937   (717) 245-2646
FAX: (800) 553-9943
Est.: 1986   Staff: 8
Owner: Herb Weigl
48-page catalog featuring tackle
and tying supplies. $3.00 refund-
able with first order. We pride
ourselves on prompt service and
complete orders.

Crow's Nest Trading Co.
PO Box 3975, 208 N. Tarboro St.
Wilson, NC 27895-3975
(800) 900-8558   (919) 291-5577
FAX: (800) 900-3136
Contact: Doug Tennis
Full color catalog offers gift and ac-
cessory items with a distinctive
"sporting character" for the den,
game room or office.

Custom Tackle Supply
2559 Hwy. 41-A South
Shelbyville, TN 37160
(615) 684-6164
FAX: (615) 684-1755
Contact: Steve Abel
Catalog of rod building, travel accessories, fly and general tackle,
and fly tying products.

Damselfly
3450 Palmer Dr., Ste. 7-191
Cameron Park, CA 95682-8253
(800) 966-4166
FAX: (916) 676-7450
Est.: 1994
Contact: Joanne Harvey-Hill

Doug's Bugs
Box 14472, Santa Rosa, CA 95402
(707) 579-3474
FAX: (707) 527-8360
Contact: Doug Brutocao
Fly-fishing books, videos and fly-an-
gling accessories. Catalog for retail
dealers only.

Duranglers Flies & Supplies
801 B Main Ave.
Durango, CO 81301
(970) 385-4081   (506) 632-5952
Contact: John Flick

Egger's
PO Box 1344, Cumming, GA 30128
(770) 882-8066
FAX: (770) 889-8665
Est.: 1979   Staff: 2
Owner: Gene Hansard
Complete line of the finest quality
fly tying, fly fishing supplies and ac-
cessories.

English Angling Trappings
Box 8885, New Fairfield, CT 06812
(203) 746-4121
FAX: (203) 746-1348 Est.: 1984
Contact: Jim Hagen
Large selection of natural fly tying
materials available, including hard
to find feathers, silks and hairs, via
mail.

Feather-Craft Fly Fishing
8307 Manchester Rd.
Box 19904, St. Louis, MO 63144
(800) 659-1707   (314) 963-7876
FAX: (314) 963-0324
Est.: 1955
A series of "fun to read" bulletin-
type catalogs that will keep you
informed on new products, fly
tying patterns, rigging help and
more. Call to get your name on
mailing list.

C.C. Filson
PO Box 34020, Seattle, WA 98124
(800) 624-0201
FAX: (206) 624-4539
Est.: 1897
Contact: John DePalma
Full color catalog features our complete line of rugged outdoor wear
including our flyfishing vests, tackle
packs, wading jackets, caps and fly
rod travel cases. Call for free catalog.

Fishing Creek Outfitters
RD#1, Box 310, Benton, PA 17814
(800) 548-0093   (717) 925-2225
FAX: (717) 925-5644
Contact: Dave & Donna Colley
Catalog featuring the products and
services of the "most complete outdoor shop" in the region. Call or
write for information.

Float Tubers Unlimited
PO Box 80280
Rancho Santa Margarita, CA 92688
(888) 488-2377   (714) 888-5859
FAX: (714) 888-7000
Contact: Todd Schiedow
The ultimate float tube and acces-
sory catalog–call for a free copy.

Fly & Field
560 Crescent Blvd.
Glen Ellyn, IL 60137
(800) 328-9753   (708) 858-7844
FAX: (708) 790-0810
Contact: Marcos
Color catalog offering unique prod-
ucts and SLF dubbing for fly tyers.

The Fly Box
1293 NE 3rd St., Bend, OR 97701
(503) 388-3330
FAX: (503) 388-3330
Est.: 1982
Contact: Alan Stewart

Catalog offering a full range of fly
fishing tackle, clothing, accessories
and services from "Central
Oregon's Fly Fishing Headquarters."

The Fly Fishing Shop
PO Box 368, Welches, OR 97067
(503) 622-4607
FAX: (503) 622-5490
Contact: Mark or Patty
"The Wish Book" catalog of trips,
flies and supplies for the discriminat-
ing angler.

The Fly Shop
4140 Churn Creek Rd.
Redding, CA 96002
(800) 669-3474
FAX: (916) 222-3572
Est.: 1976
Owner: Mike Michalak
America's Flyfishing Outfitter since
1976. Call or fax for information to
order 106-page international guide
and fly fishing catalog.

Fly-Rite, Inc.
7421 S. Beyer,
Frankenmuth, MI 48734
(517) 652-9869
FAX: (517) 652-2996
Contact: Judith G. McCann
Quality dubbing, fishing gear, tools
and more.

Flyfisher's Paradise
2603 E. College Ave.
State College, PA 16801
(814) 234-4189
FAX: (814) 238-3686
Partner: Steve Sywensky
Partner: Dan Shields
Catalog features fly tying and fly
fishing products and books.

Foust's Fly Fishing
PO Box 583, Hamilton, MT 59840
Contact: John & Elna Foust
Large selection of unique fly tying
tools and material. Evazote and
closed cell foam available.

Frontier Anglers
680 N. Montana St.
Dillon, MT 59725
(800) 228-5263   (406) 683-5276
FAX: (406) 683-6736
Outfitters of fine fly fishing supplies. Catalog includes rods, reels,
vests, clothes, accessories, flies, fly
tying tools, and accessories.

Global Flyfisher
2849 W. Dundee Rd., Suite 132
Northbrook, IL 60062
(800) 457-7026 (Orders)
FAX: (847) 291-3486
The Global Flyfisher specializes in fly
fishing equipment for the traveling
flyfisher whether you travel around

the world or just down the road. Equipment from the finest fly fishing manufacturers including, Orvis, Thomas & Thomas, Abel, Ross, DB Dun and many more. Order toll-free 24 hours.

Ted Godfrey's
3509 Pleasant Plains Dr.
Reisterstown, MD 21136
(410) 239-8468
Est.: 1972   Staff: 2
Owner: Ted Godfrey
Co-Owner: Faye Godfrey
Custom hand-made reels, rods (Sage blank); 2-hand rods and flies for Atlantic salmon, steelhead and trout.

The Golden Hackle Fly Shop
329 Crescent Place
Flushing, MI 48433
(810) 659-0018
FAX: (810) 659-0018
Owner: Gordon A. Hall
Free catalog with 2,700 fly tying items at lower prices. Example: Mustad hooks #94840, sizes 2-20, $5.45 per 100; Tiemco #TMC100, sizes 8-26, 100 hooks $11.95. Comparable values on other Mustad and Tiemco hooks.

Gorilla & Sons
Box 2309, Bellingham, WA 98227
(800) 246-7455
FAX: (800) 647-8801

Est.: 1994   Staff: 13
Manager: Tom McGinnis
Lead Operator: Michelle Thomas
Available: Direct
Mail order for fly tying tools, accessories and fine cutlery.

Hareline Dubbin Inc.
24712 Territorial Rd.
Monroe, OR 97456
(503) 847-5310
FAX: (503) 998-6166
Contact: Robert Borden
Importer and exporter of quality fly tying materials and tools.

Capt. Harry's Fishing Supply
100 N.E. 11th St.
Miami, FL 33132
(800) 327-4088 (Orders)
(305) 374-4661
FAX: (305) 374-3713
President: Carl Liederman
Mktg. Dir: Chandra Whitehouse
Free color catalog offering fly rods, fly reels, flies, fly tying materials, clothing and gifts.

The Hodgson Hook Co.
7116 W. Rowland Ave.
Littleton, CO 80123
(303) 979-5206
FAX: (303) 979-5206
Contact: Bert Hodgson
Catalog offering hooks by Mustad, Dai-Riki, Partridge, and more.

The Hook & Hackle Company
7 Kaycee Loop Rd.
Plattsburgh, NY 12901
(800) 552-8342   (518) 561-5893
FAX: (518) 561-0336
Catalog featuring fly fishing outfits, rods, reels, line, fly tying tools, materials and accessories, clothes, books and more.

Hunters Angling Supplies
1 Central Square, Box 300
New Boston, NH 03070
(800) 331-8558   (603) 487-3388
FAX: (603) 487-3939
Contact: Leila Wilder
"The Fly Tyers Catalog" and our general fly tackle catalog.

Interior Alaska Custom Built and Accessories Catalog
6399 Cahill Ave., E.
Inver Grove Heights, MN 55076
(800) 455-5593   (612) 455-5583
Owner: Cedric A. Knuckey
Interior Alaska Custom Built and Accessories Catalog offers a full line of fly fishing products from name manufacturers. They include custom built rods, fitted waders, accessories, reels and lines. Call today for our catalog and reference list. Thank you.

BURST SPEED FOR AVERAGE-SIZE FISH

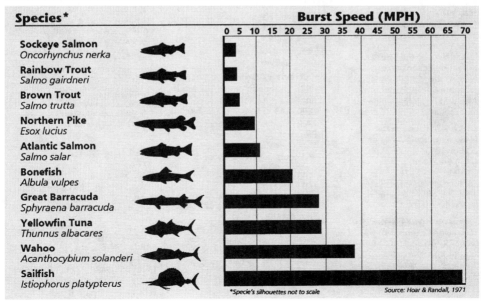

Species*	Burst Speed (MPH)
Sockeye Salmon *Oncorhynchus nerka*	
Rainbow Trout *Salmo gairdneri*	
Brown Trout *Salmo trutta*	
Northern Pike *Esox lucius*	
Atlantic Salmon *Salmo salar*	
Bonefish *Albula vulpes*	
Great Barracuda *Sphyraena barracuda*	
Yellowfin Tuna *Thunnus albacares*	
Wahoo *Acanthocybium solanderi*	
Sailfish *Istiophorus platypterus*	

*Specie's silhouettes not to scale   Source: Hoar & Randall, 1971

International Angler
501 Freeport Rd.
Pittsburgh, PA 15215
(800) 782-4222   (412) 782-2222
FAX: (412) 782-1315
Contact: Tom Ference
50-page, full color catalog for the
traveling angler.

J.W. Outfitters
169 Balboa St.,
San Marcos, CA 92069
(619) 471-2171
FAX: (619) 471-1719
Contact: Jeff Wieringa
Four color catalog featuring quality
fly fishing equipment and accessories, including bags, rod tubes and
carriers, floats, pontoon boats and
fly tying kits.

The Jealous Trout
306 Ginger Ave., Millville, NJ 08332
(609) 825-5256
FAX: (609) 825-3935
Est.: 1990   Staff: 6
President: Susanne Flickinger

Just Reels
PO Box 493, Big Bend, WI 53103
(414) 662-3626
Contact: Jim Williams
Just Reels features high quality fly
reels from over two dozen
reelmakers. From trout to billfish,
we have what you'll need. Call
today for catalog.

Kaufmann's Streamborn, Inc.
Box 23032, Portland, OR 97281
(800) 442-4359   (503) 639-6400
FAX: (503) 684-7025
Est.: 1971
Contact: Jerry Swanson
http://www.kman.com
112+ page color catalog features
"everything for the flyfisher." Worldwide fly selection in color. Also
featured from our travel department are 80 destinations from
Alaska to Argentina to the Bahamas to Russia.

Dave Klausmeyer's
New England Angler
PO Box 105, Steuben, ME 04680
(207) 546-2018
Est.: 1986   Staff: 2
Contact: Dave Klausmeyer
A full line of fly tying and fly fishing
materials.

Madison River Fishing Co.
109 Main St., Ennis, MT 59729
(800) 227-7127   (406) 682-4293
FAX: (406) 682-4744
Contact: Tom DiMeola

Manhattan Custom Tackle
913 Broadway, 2nd Floor
New York, NY 10010
(800) 219-2000   (212) 505-6690
FAX: (212) 505-1922
Contact: Phil Koenig

Bob Marriott's
Flyfishing Store
2700 W. Orangethorpe
Fullerton, CA 92833
(800) 535-6633 (Orders)
(714) 525-1827 (Info)
FAX: (714) 525-5783
http://www.bobmarriotts.com
Email: bmfsinfo@bobmarriotts.com
Designed to be a "tool for all fly fishers", this 400 page catalog
comprises 21 separate catalogs–everything from accessories to
waders. Informative articles and
special travel section included.

The Martin Company
Flyfishing Outfitters
PO Box 1461, Kamiah, ID 83536
(800) 705-0367
FAX: (208) 935-1465
Owners: Greg or Kathy Martin
The Martin Co. offers a 40-page,
color catalog of the finest in fly fish-
ing equipment, apparel and gifts.
Many items brought to you exclu-
sively. Call or write for free catalog.

Murray's Fly Shop
PO Box 156, 121 Main St.
Edinburg, VA 22824
(800) 984-4895 (Orders)
(540) 984-4212
FAX: (800) 984-4895
Est.: 1962   Staff: 4
President: Harry Murray
Catalog featuring rods, blanks,
reels, waders, vests, tools, accesso-
ries, and books. Call for your free
catalog today.

Offshore Angler
1935 S. Campbell
Springfield, MO 65898
(800) 463-3746   (417) 863-2499
FAX: (417) 873-5060
President: John L. Morris
Catalog featuring fishing, clothing
and equipment for all types of saltwater angling.

On the Fly
3628 Sage Dr., Rockford, IL 61114
(800) 232-9359   (815) 877-0090
FAX: (815) 877-4682
Contact: Dave and Jean Chadoir
Catalog features full range of fly
fishing products– rods, reels, flies,
waders, vests, fly tying equipment
and material.

Orvis Company
Rt. 7A, Manchester, VT 05254
(800) 333-1550 Ext. 844
Est.: 1856   Staff: 400
Discover the world's best and most
complete source of fly fishing products in the Orvis Fishing and
Outdoor Catalog, with over 140
pages of fly rods, reels, vests, waders, flies, gadgets, and outdoor
clothing. Most of these items are
exclusive and found nowhere else.
Call for a free catalog.

Patrick's Fly Shop
2237 Eastlake Ave. E.
Seattle, WA 98102
(800) 398-7693 (Orders)
(206) 325-8988 (Shop)
FAX: (206) 328-3474
Owner: Jim Lemert
Free rod building and fly tying catalog.

Round Rocks Fly Fishing
3663 North Hwy. 91
Smithfield, UT 84335
(800) 992-8774
FAX: (801) 755-3311
Contact: Kohn Smith
Catalog offering products constructed with the finest quality
materials, design and detail. Call for
our catalog.

Spring Creek "On the Fly"
13764 NW Klahanie Pl.
Bremerton, WA 98312
(360) 830-0815
FAX: (360) 830-0815
Contact: Shauneen or Jim Wheeler
Lightweight fiberglass prams and
accessories; rods and blanks; nets;
clothing; spiderweb watchbands.
Free catalog.

Tackle-Craft
Box 280, Chippewa Falls, WI 54729
(715) 723-3645
FAX: (715) 723-2489
Contact: Linda Woll
Complete line of fly and lure mak-
ing materials. Write for free
catalog.

The Tying Bench
PO Box 466, Custer, WA 98240
(360) 366-5894
FAX: (360) 366-5894
Contact: Shim Hogan
Fly tying materials, tools & fly
boxes.

Urban Angler Ltd.
118 E. 25th St., 3rd Fl.
New York, NY 10010
(800) 255-5488   (212) 979-7600
FAX: (212) 473-4020
Est.: 1988   Staff: 8

Contact: Steve Fisher
Email: urbang@panix.com
http:///www.urban-angler.com
Handsome 100+ page catalog featuring the finest fly fishing rods, reels, lines, clothing, fly tying equipment, and accessories.

IMPORTERS & EXPORTERS

Vjender International
PO Box 8432, Delhi 110052 India
011-91-11-7428903
FAX: 011-91-11-7252857
Contact: Kishan Singh
Est.: 1900
Fancy feathers, peacock feathers, cock necks, saddles, hackles, cock feathers. Fly tying material, fly tying tools, Indian flies & fishing flots. Exporter and importer worldwide. Large stock of feathers for wholesale only. Call for a free catalog.

Westbank Anglers
PO Box 523/Dept. BFF
Teton Village, WY 83025
(800) 922-3474   (307) 733-6483
FAX: (307) 733-9382
Contact: Stephen & Kim Vletas
Free catalog features tackle & flies for fresh and saltwater anglers. Also offers worldwide travel destinations.

World Wide Sportsman
82245 Overseas Hwy.
Islamaorada, FL 33036
(800) 327-2880
FAX: (305) 664-3692
Complete catalog & destination retailer, full line of top quality, custom fly fishing gear and adventure travel service for serious fly fishers.

OVERSEAS SUPPLIERS

Airflo
Unit 18, Industrial St.
Brocon, U.K.
Est.: 1970   Staff: 65
011-44-1874-611633
FAX: 011-44-1874-625889
Contact: P. Burnes
Airflo fly lines, braided leaders and poly leaders & many other Airflo items including fly fishing glasses, fly box systems, etc.

All England Ltd.
Chettisham Business Park
Ely, Cambridgeshire
CB6 1R4 England
Est.: 1982   Staff: 20
011-44-1353-666342
FAX: 011-44-1353-666423
President: Robert Altham
Chairman: Julian Pardoe
Floats, leaders, rigs & terminal tackle

Bando Sports Ltd.
409-3 Chungchua-Dong,
Pupyung-gu, Inchon
Republic of Korea
82-32-501-7383
FAX: 82-32-501-7391
President: Jeun Jong-O

Giorgio Benecchi Products
Via Giotto 279,
41100 Modena, Italy
011-39-59-341190
FAX: 011-39-59-342627
Manufacturer, importer and exporter of flies and fly tying tackles.

Bickton Flies
23, Southdown Rd., Thatcham,
Berks., RQ19 3BF England
Est.: 1974   Staff: 46
011-44-1635-523223
FAX: 011-44-1635-48169
Contact: Vince Lister
Hand tied fishing flies. Premier quality at affordable prices.

Coret Ltd.
Forchstrasse 59
Zurich, Switzerland 8032
011-41-1271-65-88
FAX: 011-41-1273-12-50
Contact: Daniel Pillen
General importer for Europe of Marryat flyfishing products.

Deepson's Trading Co.
91/39/D/1, Bose Pukur Rd.,
Calcutta-700 042, India
011-91-33-442-8582
Est.: 1971   Staff: 10
FAX: 011-91-33-442-5218
Managing Partner: Sushil K. Patodia
A complete line of fly tying equipment.

Dragon Tackle, Ltd.
29 Redland St., Newport, South
Wales, NP9 5L2 U.K.
Est.: 1985   Staff: 5
011-44-1633-821228
FAX: 011-44-1633-854261
Sales Mgr: Terry Clease
Europe's largest supplier of high quality fishing flies, specialists in own brand packaging.

Fishermens Feathers
Hill End Farm, Station Rd., Bransford
Worcs., WR6 5JJ U.K.
Est.: 1978   Staff: 6
011-44-1905-830548
FAX: 011-44-1905-831810
Contact: Ron Taylor
Producers of rare feathers from exotic birds bred domestically.

Flyfishing Brinkhoff
Auf Der Liet, Noennesee
Delecke, 59519 Germany
011-49-2924-637
FAX: 011-49-2924-332
Leader in flyfishing distribution, wholesaling, mail order, own and franchise stores, over 200 page catalog.

Fulling Mill Ltd.
Unit 5, 46 Croydons Rd.
Reigate, Surrey, RH2 ONH UK
Est.: 1980   Staff: 200
011-44-1737-243991
FAX: 011-44-1737-221594
President: Barry Unwin
Europe's top brand of quality fishing flies always in stock and shown in superb catalog/reference book.

Graham Trout Flies
Eastcombe Garway
Herefordshire HR2 BRE, England
Est.: 1985   Staff: 74
011-44-1600-750-288
FAX: 011-44-1600-750-380
Contact: Mike Dawes
Suppliers of the very highest quality trout and salmon flies. Also books: Flytiers manual & Flytiers companion by Mike Dawes.

Gordon Griffiths Fishing Tackle Ltd.
Unit 1/8, Lifford Way
Binley Industrial Way
Coventry England CV3 2RN
011-44-1203-440859
FAX:: 011-44-1203-635694
Contact: R. Griffiths
Threads, fancy flosses–tools, game-angling accessories and clothing.

Rudi Heger GmbH
Hauptstrasse U, 83313
Siegsdorf, Germany
011-49-8662-7079
FAX: 011-49-8662-2711

Innovative Flyfishing Products
Kuferzeile 19, S. 4810
Gmunden, Austria
Contact: Roman Moser

Lureflash Products, Ltd.
Victoria Street, Kilnhurst,
Rotherham, South Yorkshire,

S62 5SQ England
011-44-1709-580081
FAX: 011-44-1709-586194
Contact: Stephen J. Gross
Est.: 1985Staff: 20
The Lureflash brand is famous for innovative synthetic fly dressing materials and quality flies.

Pozo' by A. Pozzolini
Via Trento 2/A
25014 - Castenedolo (BS), Italy
011-39-30-2732027
FAX: 011-39-30-2732415
Manager: A. Pozzolini
Est.: 1992
High quality, custom-made rods and components; fly reels all with briarwood insert; high technology and elegance made in Italy at competitive prices.

Brian Rowe
Unit 2 Rocklands, Exeter Rd.
Kingsteignton, Devonshire
TQ12 3HX England
Est.: 1973   Staff: 43
011-44-1626-51461
FAX: 011-44-1626-55877
Contact: Brian Rowe
Manufacture top quality fishing flies and fishing rod guides

Shakespeare Company (UK) Ltd.
PO Box 1, Broad Ground Rd.
Lakeside, Redditch, Worcester
B98 8NQ England
Est.: 1897   Staff: 40
011-44-1527-513800
FAX: 011-44-1527-517507
Contact: John Tomsett
Rods, reels, fly lines and accessories

Sigma Industries
GPO Box 2051
Calcutta - 700 001, India
011-91-33-2200219
Est.: 1987   Staff: 12
FAX: 011-91-33-2200219
President: Sujit Majunder
Full line of fly tying equipment.

Siman Ltd.
Siman-Rybarsky Sport, Kpt. Jarose 1
30707 Plzen, Czech Republic
0042-19-7242207
FAX: 0042-19-7242207
Director: Jan Siman

Suiza Exports
PO Box 816, 89 Netaji Subhas
Calcutta A700 001 India
91-033-243-2237
FAX: 91-033-243-3120
Contact: SK Munot

Ultimate Fishing Supplies
72 Derwent St., Chopwell
Tyne & Wear, NE17 7HY England
011-44-1207-560931
FAX: 011-44-1207-562338
Contact: T.M. Hughes
Manufacturers of top quality fly tying kits and fly tying materials.

E. Veniard Ltd.
138 Northwood Rd.
Thornton Heath, Surrey
CR7 84G U.K.
Est.: 1923   Staff: 20
011-44-181-653-3565
FAX: 011-41-181-771-4805
Contact: P.J. Veniard
Suppliers of a complete range of fly tying materials and tools for manufacture and resale.

IMPORTERS & EXPORTERS

Vjender International
PO Box 8432, Delhi 110052 India
011-91-11-7428903
FAX: 011-91-11-7252857
Contact: Kishan Singh
Est.: 1900
Fancy feathers, peacock feathers, cock necks, saddles, hackles, cock feathers. Fly tying material, fly tying tools, Indian flies & fishing flots. Exporter and importer worldwide. Large stock of feathers for wholesale only. Call for a free catalog.

Wychwood Tackle
The Old Brewery, Priory Lane
Burford, Oxfordshire, UK 0X18 4SG
Est.: 1989   Staff: 25
011-44-1993-822822
FAX: 011-44-1993-824100
Contact: Dennis Moss/Bruce Vaughan
High quality luggage, breathable waterproof clothing and a wide selection of fly fishing accessories from rods to line.

PRIVATE LABEL MANUFACTURERS

Alexander's
3021 Power Dr.
Kansas City, KS 66106
(913) 236-9565
FAX: (913) 236-9565
Contact: Bill Alexander

Arapaho Trading Co.
990 A Bright Ct.

San Dimas, CA 91773
(909) 599-6504
FAX: (909) 592-7359
Contact: Patrick Lee
Private label manufacturer of soft sided tackle and accessories.

Clark Leather Products, Inc.
500 Lucerne Lane,
Bolivar, TN 38008
(901) 658-7103
FAX: (901) 658-7104
Contact: David Pistono
Private label manufacturer of rod & reel cases using woven fabric (OEM calls only).

Cunningham Mfg. Co.
PO Box 2437,
Huntington Beach, CA 92649
(714) 840-3900
FAX: (714) 840-5676
Contact: Wade Cunningham

Dart Manufacturing
4012 Bronze Way, Dallas, TX 75237
(800) 345-3278   (214) 333-4221
FAX: (800) 833-3278   Est.: 1965
President: Sam Kogutt
Custom vinyl and fabric products, including reel cases, fly wallets & more.

J.C. Rods
PO Box 370, Pine Grove, IA 95665
(209) 223-3217
FAX: (209) 223-3217
Contact: John Christlieb
Private label manufacturer of high-quality custom fly rods for retailers.

Lake King Rod Co.
3530 SE 4, Topeka, KS 66607
(913) 233-9541
Contact: Craig or Glen Thurber
Private label rod manufacturer

Micro Precision Corp.
PO Box 485, Mountville, PA 17554
(717) 285-5938
FAX: (717) 285-5960
Contact: Bill Brown
Private label manufacturer of fly fishing reels.

Northern Sport Fishing Prod.
53 Victoria Rd., S.
Unit 4, Guelph Ontario
Canada N1E 5P7
(519) 824-4023
FAX: (519) 824-1439
Contact: Rick Tramer
Private label manufacturer for fly lines.

Pacific Eagle USA
2443 Seaman Ave.
El Monte, CA 91733
(818) 455-0033
FAX: (818) 455-0035
Contact: Joyce Chan
Private label waders.

Raptor Rod
2563 Kennedy Ave.,
Chico, CA 95973
(916) 894-2062
FAX: (916) 894-1230
Est.: 1995   Staff: 2
Contact: Jim Clarkson
Private label graphite rod maker

Rebrod, Inc.
Box 475, Flippin, AR 72634
(501) 453-8500
FAX: (501) 453-8600
Private label assembler of fly rods

Talon
736 Davidson, PO Box 907
Woodland, WA 98674
(360) 225-8247
FAX: (360) 225-7737   Est.: 1990
Contact: Janis Schmahl
U.S. fishing blank/rod manufacturer, specializing in private labels, custom colors, over 400 actions.

Two Seeds Co., Inc.
2325 West Vancouver
Broken Arrow, OK 74012
(918) 259-5051
FAX: (918) 259-5050
Sr. VP: Don Beaulieu

PUBLICATIONS

American Angler®
Abenaki Publishers, Inc.
Box 4100, Bennington, VT 05201
(802) 447-1518
FAX: (802) 447-2471 Est.: 1977
Publisher: Joe Migliore
Editor: John Likakis
Advertising: Larry Kenney
Circulation: 60,000 Paid
Frequency: Bimonthly
Every issue of American Angler brings you a mix of practical information–from improving your skills to understanding entomology to tying better flies to catching all sorts of gamefish. No fluff, no hype; just solid information you can use on the stream, at the pond, and at your tying desk. Subscribe today!
See Our Ad Below

The American Fly Fisher
PO Box 42, Manchester, VT 05254
(802) 362-3300
FAX: (802) 362-3308
Exec. Dir: Craig Gilborn
Editor: Kathleen Achor
The American Fly Fisher is a scholarly magazine that preserves the history of fly fishing in the world in original articles, reprints, photographs and art. Now in its 23rd year, it appears quarterly and is published by the American Museum of Fly Fishing.

The Angler's Journal
Auger Enterprises, Inc.
Box 1427, Livingston, MT 59047
(800) 935-9347   (406) 222-2802
FAX: (406) 222-7767
Est.: 1993
President: Bob Auger
Editor: Neil M. Travis
Circulation: 10,000
Frequency: 4 Times/Yr.
The Voice of Quality Angling.

The Angling Report
Oxpecker Enterprises, Inc.
9300 S. Dadeland Blvd., Suite 605
Miami, FL 33156-2721
(305) 670-1918

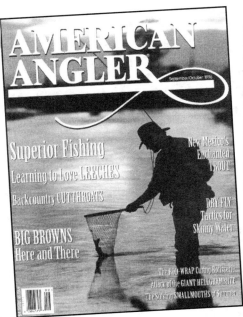

FAX: (305) 670-1376
Publisher/Pres: Don Causey
Prod. Mgr: Nilton E. Aquino
Circulation: 4,500
Frequency: Monthly newsletter
Serving the angler who travels

Aqua Field Publishing Co.
39 Avenue of the Common
Shrewsbury, NJ 07702
(908) 935-1222
Editor & Publisher: Steve Ferber
Managing Editor: Robert Illes
Publishers of Flyfishing Quarterly
Frequency: 4 Times/Yr.
Fly Fishing Made Easy
Frequency: 2 Times/Yr.
Fly Fishing for Trout
Frequency: Annual

**The Atlantic
Salmon Journal**
Box 429, St. Andrews,
New Brunswick, Canada E0G 2X0
(506) 529-4581
FAX: (506) 529-4985   Est.: 1952
Editor: Philip Lee
Advertising: Mary Ellen Nowlan
Mbrshp. Svcs: Rob Beatty
Frequency: 4 Times/Yr.
The Atlantic Salmon Journal is the
official publication of the Atlantic
Salmon Federation—an interna-
tional non-profit organziation.

**Bass Pro Shops
OUTDOOR WORLD**
1227 W. Magnolia
Ft. Worth, TX 76104
(800) 856-8060
FAX: (817) 921-9313   Est.: 1995
Publisher: Hal A. Brown
Editor: Eddie Lee Rider, Jr.
Frequency: Bi-Monthly
Circulation: 200,000
Where-to and how-to features tar-
geting serious sportsmen. Editorial
featuring fresh & saltwater fly fishing.

Black's **1997**
FLY FISHING

Black's Fly Fishing
43 West Front St., Suite 11
PO Box 2029, Red Bank, NJ 07701
(908) 224-8700
FAX: (908) 741-2827
Est.: 1991
Publisher: James F. Black, Jr.
Editor: Lois Re'
Sr. Assoc. Publisher: Ray Goydon
Asst. Publisher: Amanda Santos
Frequency: Annual
The complete angler's guide to
equipment, instruction and destina-
tions. The one-stop source of
information on anything and every-
thing that's fly fishing.

California Fly Fisher
Box 40429, San Francisco, CA 94140
(415) 284-0313
FAX: (415) 284-0321
Publisher: Stoakes Anderson
Editor: Richard Anderson
Frequency: Bimonthly
California Fly Fisher is a tabloid magazine that explores the wide
diversity of fly-fishing opportunities–
coldwater, warmwater and
saltwater–available in and near the
Golden State. Aside from features
on where and how to fly-fish, the
editorial mix includes angling es-
says, short fiction, science,
interviews and reviews of books of
regional interest. We strive to be informative, provocative and
entertaining.

Daniel Publishing Group
713 Pearl St., Boulder, CO 80302
(303) 442-2609
FAX: (303) 442-2399
Contact: Joseph E. Daniel
Publishers of the twice yearly Wing
& Fly cooperative card deck and
sporting directory.

FFish Book
PO Box 370, Camden, ME 04843
(800) 766-1670   (207) 594-9544
FAX: (207) 594-5144
Contact: Bill Anderson
Annual directory of fly fishing indus-
try suppliers.

Field & Stream
Times Mirror Magazines, Inc.
2 Park Ave., New York, NY 10016
(212) 779-5000
FAX: (212) 686-6877
Est.: 1895
Publisher: Michael Rooney
Editor: Duncan Barnes

Advertising: Jeff Paro
Circulation: 1,750,000
Frequency: Monthly
Magazine of the outdoors focusing
on the fishing/hunting experience
and man's relationship with nature.

Fishing Collectibles Magazine
2 Oak St., PO Box 2797
Kennebunkport, ME 04046
(207) 967-8044
FAX: (207) 967-2671
Est.: 1988
Editor/Publisher: Brian J. McGrath
Frequency: Quarterly
Circulation: 2,000

Fishing Tackle Retailer
B.A.S.S., Inc.
5845 Carmichael Rd.
Montgomery, AL 36117
(334) 272-9530
FAX: (334) 279-7148
Est.: 1980
President: Helen Sevier
Circulation: 21,338
Frequency: 11 Times/Yr.

Fishing Tackle Trade News
PO Box 370, Camden, ME 04843
(800) 766-1670   (207) 594-9544
FAX: (207) 594-5144
Est.: 1952
Sales Rep: Scott Ansley
Editor: Hugh McKellar
Circulation: 22,510
Frequency: 12 Times/Yr.
Trade magazine that serves the gen-
eral and fly-fishing industry.
Quarterly issues address products
sharing the same trade distribution
channels.

Fly Fish America
PO Box 408, Fryeburg, ME 04037
(888) 843-2359   (207) 935-4725
FAX: (207) 935-2746
Publisher: Dick Stewart
Editor: Bill Battles
Ad Sales Coord.: A. Tony Martineau
Advtg. Dir: Kevin Muse
Circulation: 100,000 per issue
Frequency: 6 Times/Yr.
http://www.flyfishamerica.com
Internet publication

Fly Fisherman
Cowles Magazines
6405 Flank Dr.,
Harrisburg, PA 17112
(717) 540-6619
FAX: (717) 540-6706
Est.: 1969
Editor/Publisher: John Randolph
Advertising: Linda Wood
Circulation: 151,302
Frequency: 6 Times/Yr.
For sportsmen who have an involve-

ment in fly fishing. Written for anglers who fish primarily with a fly rod and for other anglers who would like to learn more about fly fishing.

Fly Fishing Worldwide
c/o Ocean Arts Inc.
9121 SW 103rd Ave.
Miami, FL 33176-1609
FAX: (305) 274-2436
Editor: Bob Stearns
Frequency: Quarterly
FlyFishing Worldwide is a newsletter for fly fishers who like to travel.

Fly Fishing in Salt Waters
Hook and Release Publishing, Inc.
2001 Western Ave., #210
Seattle, WA 98121
(206) 443-3273
FAX: (206) 443-3293
Est.: 1994   Staff: 4
Publisher: R.P. Van Gytenbeek
Sales Manager: Julia Day

Circulation: 44,000
Frequency: 6 Times/Yr.
The premier saltwater magazine covers the world of our sport. Great text, photography, and the top guns, Lefty Kreh, Nick Curcione, Trey Combs, Tom Barnhardt, Flip Pallot, Lou Tabory, Charlie Waterman and more. Plus fly tying, new products, resource, boating, budget trips, video & book reviews and lots more.

Fly Rod & Reel
The Down East Outdoor Group
PO Box 370, Camden, ME 04843
(800) 766-1670   (207) 594-9544
FAX: (207) 594-5144   Est.: 1979
Sales Mgr: Bill Anderson
Editor: Jim Butler
Circulation: 54,103
Frequency: 6 Times/Yr.
Fly Rod & Reel is aimed at the fly-fishing consumer. Editorial emphasis is on in-depth equipment reviews, flyfishing travel, conservation and the sporting way of life.

Fly Tackle Dealer
The Down East Outdoor Group
PO Box 370, Camden, ME 04843
(800) 766-1670   (207) 594-9544

FAX: (207) 594-5144
Editor: Jim Butler
Sales Mgr: Bill Anderson
Circulation: 11,000
Frequency: 6 Times/Yr.
The trade magazine for makers and sellers of fly fishing products and services.

Fly Tyer
Abenaki Publishers, Inc.
Box 4100, Bennington, VT 05201
(802) 447-1518
FAX: (802) 447-2471 Est.: 1995
Publisher: Joe Migliore
Editor: Art Scheck
Advertising: Kate Fox
Circulation: 30,000 Paid
Frequency: Quarterly
Fly Tyer explains every aspect of the craft–latest techniques, materials and innovations, and patterns–with articles, beautiful photographs and illustrations. For novice fly tiers to the 30-year veterans. Subscribe today!
See Our Ad Below

Fly Tying

Frank Amato Publications
PO Box 82112, 4040 SE Wister
Portland, OR 97282
(503) 653-8108
FAX: (503) 653-2766
Est.: 1995
Publisher: Frank Amato
Editor: Nick Amato
Advertising: Carmen Macdonald
Frequency: Quarterly
Fly tying information and
techniques for the beginner and ad-
vanced fly tyer.

The Flyfisher

Keokee Co. Publishing
PO Box 722, Sandpoint, ID 83864
(208) 263-3573
FAX: (208) 263-4045
Editor: Chris Bessler
Managing Editor: Richard Wentz
Advertising: Chris Bessler/Richard
Wentz
Frequency: 4 Times/Yr.
The Flyfisher is the official publica-
tion of The Federation of Fly
Fishers, featuring news of the
organization's education and con-
servation efforts, plus
general-interests stories on fly fish-
ing and fly tying.

Gray's Sporting Journal

Morris Communications, Inc.
735 Broad St., Augusta, GA 30901
(706) 722-6060
Est.: 1975
Publisher: William S. Morris, III
Editor: David C. Foster
Circulation: 49,160
Frequency: 7 Times/Yr.
Literature and art edited for the ad-
vanced angler, hunter, shooter and
conservationist.

The Inside Angler

PO Box 31282
San Francisco, CA 94131-0282
(415) 586-7668
FAX: (415) 586-7668
Editor/Publisher: Michael Fong
Circulation Dir: Christine Fong
Frequency: Bimonthly
The Inside Angler is a newsletter
that lists and recommends lodging,

campgrounds, dining, guides and
outfitters at productive angling destinations from Alaska to Mexico,
and from the Rockies to the Pacific
Ocean. A one-year subscription is
$40 in the U.S.; $50 for Canadians
and $60 for all others.

Mid Atlantic Fly Fishing Guide

The O Boys Publishing Co., Inc.
PO Box 144
Allenwood, PA 17810-0144
(717) 523-0485
FAX: (717) 322-8191
Editor/Publisher: Mike O'Brien
Editor/Publisher: Jerry Stercho
Frequency: 10 Times/Yr.
The Mid Atlantic Fly Fishing Guide
is published 10 times each year,
serving the PA, NY, MD, NJ, DE, VA
and CT states.

Midwest Fly Fishing

4030 Zenith Ave., S.
Minneapolis, MN 55410
(612) 926-5128
FAX: (612) 925-2602
Est.: 1994   Staff: 3
Editor/Publisher: Tom Helgeson
Frequency: 5 Times/Yr.
Website: http://mm.com/mwflyfish-
ing Email: mwflyfishing@mm.com
Midwest Fly Fishing is a tabloid
magazine that covers the Midwest
fly fishing experience exclusively,
presenting unique information on
the sport of fly fishing and on the
rivers and lakes where fly fishing
takes place for fly anglers who live
or fly fish in the Midwest. We have
regular features on entomology,
travel, fly casting, fly fishing tactics
and techniques and fly tying; features book and video reviews and
product evaluation. We also report
aggressively on environmental
threats and issues.

Outdoor Life

Times Mirror Magazines, Inc.
2 Park Ave., New York, NY 10016
(212) 779-5000
FAX: (212) 686-6877
Est.: 1898
Publisher: Michael Rooney
Advertising: Jeff Paro
Circulation: 1,350,000
Frequency: Monthly
Outdoor Life is an information
source for the active outdoor enthusiast. Articles provide the fishing
and hunting sportsmen with the
"how-to", "where to go" and "what
to bring" on an outdoor adventure.

The PanAngler

180 North Michigan Ave.
Chicago, IL 60601

(800) 533-4353   (312) 263-0328
Est.: 1974
Owner: Jim Chapralis
Frequency: Monthly
Monthly international fishing news-
letter which costs $29 per annum.

Salmon Trout Steelheader

Frank Amato Publications
PO Box 82112, 4040 SE Wister
Portland, OR 97282
(800) 541-9498
FAX: (503) 653-2766
Est.: 1967
Publisher: Frank Amato
Editor: Nick Amato
Advertising: Sherry Gullings
Circulation: 30.845
Frequency: Bimonthly
Salmon Trout Steelheader covers
sport fishing techniques (fly, spin,
bait, casting, boating, etc.) and
best places to fish in the Great
Lakes and Pacific Coast states.

Saltwater FLY FISHING

Saltwater Fly Fishing

Abenaki Publishers, Inc.
Box 4100, Bennington, VT 05201
(802) 447-1518
FAX: (802) 447-2471
Publisher: Joe Migliore
Editor: Joe Healy
Advertising: Brendan Banahan
Circulation: 20,000 Paid
Frequency: 5 Times/Yr. ('97)
If you fly fish in coastal or off-shore
waters then Saltwater Fly Fishing is
for you. Features and columns
packed with solid information are
delivered in a useful, no-nonsense
style to help you become a better
fly fisher and tyer in the brine. Subscribe today!

See Our Ad Across

Southern Outdoors

B.A.S.S. Inc.
5845 Carmichael Rd.
Montgomery, AL 36117
(334) 277-3940
Est.: 1968
Publisher: Helen Sevier
Editor: Larry Teague
Advertising: Mike Swain
Circulation: 206,803
Frequency: 9 Times/Yr.
An outdoor oriented magazine pub-
lished for the sportsman. Articles
and departments cover freshwater
fishing, saltwater fishing, hunting,
boating, travel and camping.

Sporting Classics
Box 23707, 9330 A Two Notch Rd.
Columbia, SC 29224
(800) 849-1004   (803) 736-2424
Est.: 1981
Publisher: Art Carter
Circulation: 31,128
Frequency: Bimonthly

Sports Afield
The Hearst Corporation
250 W. 55th St.,
New York, NY 10019
(212) 649-4000
Est.: 1887
Publisher/Editor: Terry McDonell
Assoc. Publisher: Michael P. Wade
Circulation: 450,000
Frequency: 10 Times/Yr.
Sports Afield delivers hard-core
hunting and fishing information
that translates easily from the page
to real life. Established in 1887, SA
is the authority on traditional sporting activities, such as camping and
shooting sports, as well as survival
skills, gear and conservation issues.

Trout
1500 Wilson Blvd., #310
Arlington, VA 22209
(703) 284-9412
FAX: (703) 284-9400
Est.: 1959
Editor: Peter A. Rafle, Jr.
Circulation: 95,000
Frequency: Quarterly
The Journal of Coldwater Fisheries
Conservation is edited for the con-
servation-minded trout and salmon
angler, and for the members of
Trout Unlimited.

Warmwater Fly Fishing
Abenaki Publishers, Inc.
PO Box 4100, 160 Benmont Ave.
Bennington, VT 05201
(802) 447-1518
FAX: (802) 447-2471   Est.: 1997
Publisher: Joe Migliore
Advertising: Brendan Banahan
Frequency: 6 Times/Yr.
The magazine for warmwater en-
thusiasts brings you the latest tech-
niques, the best places, the newest
flies and the detailed how-to infor-
mation you need to catch species

ranging from bass and muskel-
lunge to carp and catfish. Subscribe
today!

Western FlyFishing
Frank Amato Publications
PO Box 82112, Portland, OR 97282
(503) 653-8108
FAX: (503) 653-2766 Est.: 1978
Publisher: Frank Amato
Editor: Marty Sherman
Advertising: Joyce Sherman
Circulation: 40,228
Frequency: 5 Times/Yr.
Western FlyFishing is a magazine
for the action-oriented west of the
Rockies fly fisherman. Articles cover
both fresh and saltwater flyfishing
and fly tying.

Wild Steelhead & Salmon
4105 E. Madison St.
Suite 2, Seattle, WA 98112
(206) 328-8760
FAX: (206) 328-8761
Publisher/Editor: Thomas R. Pero
Circulation: 14,959
Frequency: Quarterly

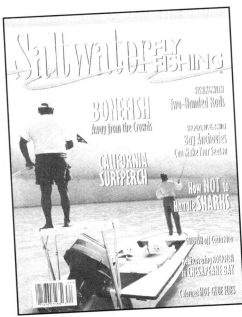

Choosing a Reel

A fly reel is a relatively simple mechanical device used to store leader, fly line and backing. It consists of a seat or foot to secure it to the rod, a handle to retrieve spent line, a frame, a spool, and some type of drag system that puts tension on the revolving spool to tire a fish making a run. Depending on how it's designed, what material it's made of, and what features it offers, a fly reel may cost anywhere from $25 to more than $5,000!

Reel Types

There are three types of fly reel:

- **Single-action** - The single-action fly reel is light, easy to maintain and by far the most popular choice among fly fishers. One complete turn of the handle of a single-action reel results in one complete turn of the spool.

- **Multiplying** - Similar in design to the single-action models, a multiplier reel is geared so that a single turn of the handle results in one-and-half or more turns of the spool. This feature is especially handy in fishing situations where fast or long line retrieves are common.

- **Automatic** - This type of reel uses a coil-spring mechanism, which tightens as line is pulled from the reel and then unwinds to retrieve line automatically. Generally heavier and far more prone to mechanical failure than the other types of reel, automatics are rarely used by serious anglers.

Drag Systems

The drag system of a fly reel serves two basic purposes: 1) it helps keep your line from tangling when you strip out line for casting; 2) it also helps tire a running fish by exerting tension on the spool. The relative importance of the drag system to the angler tends to increase with the size and the fight of the fish being played. A reel's drag system, for example, might not be used at all on small trout, which may be played entirely by hand. But the smoother more uniform tension provided by a mechanical drag—especially that of a disk drag—helps prevent leaders from breaking on hard running fish such as tarpon or bonefish.

As you shop for a reel, you'll come across two types of adjustable tension drag systems. First is the ratchet-and-pawl or, as it is called because of the clicking sound it makes as the spool revolves, the click drag. Experts agree that the simple, reliable design of click drag systems make them a good choice for most fishing situations. The second type of system is the disk drag, which generally uses cork or synthetic pads to exert pressure directly on the spool. Smoother than click drags and usually silent when engaged, disk drag systems can make larger, feistier fish easier to land. (Note: some manufacturers market reels that include both click and disk drags systems). In addition to these built-in drag systems, many reels feature an exposed spool rim that allows an angler to increase

continued on page 92>

TYPICAL REEL

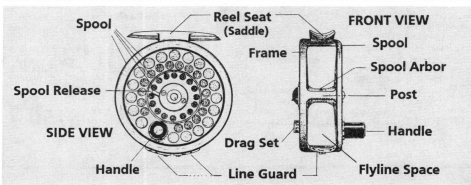

REELS

AYR Corp.
PO Box 783, Evergreen, CO 80437
(303) 670-1143
FAX: (303) 530-9511
Est.: 1997   Staff: 3
President: Bill Varner
AYR is entering the market with three new reels this year. Some exciting features include interchangeable large and small arbor spools, sealed delrin disk drag system, CNC machined 6061 T6 aerospace aluminum, stainless steel internal components for saltwater compatibility and all wrapped up in a traditionally early 1900's reverse tear drop look. A reasonable price for a high end reel: MSRP $240 to $290.

Aaron Reels
10141-9 Evening Star Dr.
Grass Valley, CA 95945
(800) 437-3578   (916) 272-7375
FAX: (916) 272-8549
Est.: 1990
Contact: Cherie or Wayne Grimm
Innovative engineering and manufacturing are the hallmarks of every Aaron Reel. Beautiful to hold. Tough and durable. Anodized, corrosion resistant, and saltwater capable. Unique Pop-Off, Pop-On spool mechanism for quick response to changing conditions. Adjustable right or left hand retreive. No reels offer more performance for the price than Aaron reels. Two models, in 7 sizes for virtually any line capacity, weight, taper and tippet. Prices range from $275-$545.

Abel
165 Aviador St.,
Camarillo, CA 93010
(805) 484-8789
FAX: (805) 482-0701
Est.: 1977   Staff: 40
President: Steve Abel
Sales Mgr: Gina Abel
The 21 sizes of Big Game, Anti-Re-verse, Rapid Retrive and Trout model Abel fly reels are performance-proven and the standard of the world. Fully machined, super anodized and user serviceable. Unequalled smooth as-silk drag and the choice of anglers from Alaska to Argentina. Available from Authorized Dealers only. Free catalog.

Abu Garcia
c/o Outdoor Technology
1 Berkley Dr., Spirit Lake, IA 51360
(800) 237-5539   (712) 336-1520
FAX: (712) 336-5183
Contact: Judy Sitzmann

Adams Reels
PO Box 183, Cambridge, NY 12816
(518) 677-2276
Est.: 1992
Contact: Bill Adams
Available: Direct
The Adams Improved American Classic is crafted in the USA. Unique engineering & design features, rim control, interchangeable spools, reversible wind, adjustable drag with the Traditional look of the past in two sizes moderately priced at $325. Call for additional information.

ATH - USA
130 Grant Ave., #202
Santa Fe, NM 87501
(505) 988-4730
FAX: (505) 988-3283
Technical & Service: Mark Gruber
We manufacture quality fly reels in four series of reels: the F-Series, the S-Series, the Remco and the Gallatin Series.

Ari't Hart International
Antoni Fokkerweg 14
1422 AG Uithoorn, Holland
011-31-297-567973
FAX: 011-31-297-540325
CFO: Edwin Hagebeuk
New series of reels, 2 round and 2 triangle.

Ascent Reels
Box 366, Walnut Creek, CA 94597
(510) 930-9225
Contact: Chip Flor
Manufacturer of high quality, light, bar-stock reels.

Bill Ballan Reels
230 Seaman Ave.,
Bayport, NY 11705
(516) 472-0744   (516) 246-8004
FAX: (516) 472-0744
Est.: 1985
Contact: Gail Ballan
Ballan's classic-styled reels are handmade, one at a time, of the highest quality anodized aluminum using the finest tooling available. Over 20 models to choose from. Price range: $295-$650.

Bauer - Premium Fly Reels
401 Corral de Tierra Rd.
Salinas, CA 93908
(408) 484-0536
FAX: (408) 484-0534
Contact: Jon Bauer
Precision large arbor reels with a cork disc drag that engages instantly and smoothly with no backlash. The large arbor spool provides quick line retrieval and consistent drag pressure so critical in protecting light tippets. Available in 7 sizes, from 2wt to 12wt.

Baum Flyfishing Products
1199 Blue School Rd.
Perkasie, PA 18944
(215) 249-0780
FAX: (215) 249-0599
Contact: Joel Baum

Baum Reels, manufactured entirely from aircraft quality aluminum, offer a multitude of high-performance features that assure ease of use, including dual drag adjustments, teflon-impregnated hardcoat finish, and medium arbor design for quick retrieval while maintaining higher line capacity. Exposed palming rim for additional braking and control. Large diameter cork-composite drag system provides smooth operation with low break-away pressures. Lifetime warranty. Phone or fax for more information, or to order.

L.L. Bean
1 Casco St., Freeport, ME 04033
(800) 809-7057
FAX: (207) 552-3080
The new Wide Arbor Reel with the most up-to-date technology and materials–three sizes available.

Berkley Reels
1 Berkley Dr., Spirit Lake, IA 51360
(800) 237-5539
(712) 336-1520 (Consumer)

drag by "palming the spool" (that is, running a palm or finger across the spool) as the fish takes out line.

Saltwater Reels

If saltwater fly fishing is in your plans, you'll need a reel expressly designed for the purpose. Saltwater reels are generally heavier, sturdier and have greater line capacity than their freshwater counterparts. In addition, the frames and internal parts of these reels are often constructed of materials such as anodized aluminum to resist the corrosive effects of salt air and water. When you're looking at a saltwater reel, check to see if its drive is direct or anti-reverse. In direct drive, the handle of the reels turns as line runs out; in anti-reverse drive models, a special mechanism allows the spool to turn independently of the reel handle (a nifty feature that'll keep your knuckles from being punished by a hard running fish).

Reel Shopping

Shopping for a reel—especially your first—needn't be difficult. Begin by asking yourself the question that should start most fly fishing equipment purchases: What kind of fish are you after? If the answer is smaller fish—panfish, smaller trout and bass—a good, inexpensive single action, click drag reel will serve you well. If you're thinking of fishing larger fresh and saltwater varieties, a more expensive reel might be in order.

Whatever price reel you feel comfortable with, there are several things most experts urge you to consider before you buy: First, is the reel's capacity—that is , the type of line and the amount of backing it can hold. A typical description of a reel's capacity will look like this: WF8F/125 yds. This means that the reel will hold weight forward, 8-weight floating line with 125 yards of backing. Use this information to ensure that the reel you're buying matches your rod and is right for the type of fish you'll be after.

Another important consideration is whether the reel is set up for a right- or left-handed angler. The difference is in the direction the drag tension is applied. Years ago many reels had to be set up one way or the other by the manufacturer. Today, however, most reels can be switched from left to right retrieve with ease. Read the manufacturers specs or ask your dealer before you buy.

If after doing your homework, you're still concerned about making the right choice, remember this: It's at the extremes of fly fishing that you're most likely to make a buying mistake. That means that you should be extra careful when buying ultra light or very heavy reels. In most other cases, a little background reading and the guidance of a reputable fly shop dealer is all you need to buy smart the first and every time you're in the market for a new reel.

Conservation Assures Continued Fine Fishing

Not so long ago, anglers often kept fish as a memento of a successful outing. Today, with fly fishing growing in popularity, the need to protect lakes and streams from depletion is increasingly apparent. And conscientious fly fishers are resorting to simple practices that help maintain fish populations. Among them:

Catch and Release - when you land a large fish, take a photo to record the moment and return your catch to the water.

Gentle Handling - use a soft mesh net to increase the number of fish you land, and to shorten handling time. Avoid squeezing fish too hard when you try to release the hook.

Strong Tippets - use the strongest tippet you can. When fishing in fast waters, or wet fly fishing, a stronger tippet won't be seen, fewer fish will break off, and you'll land them faster.

Barbless Hooks - barbless hooks test your ability and permit speedy release of fish. Several manufacturers make barbless hooks, and it's easy to pinch down barbs with fishing pliers.

The allure of fly fishing lies more in the challenge than in the results. And by helping preserve the quality of our wild fisheries, we make certain the challenge will endure.

FAX: (712) 336-5183
Contact: Judy Sitzmann
Berkley's one-piece frame Advanta fly reel is constructed of graphite-impregnated nylon, featuring an adjustable disc drag, left- or right-handed retrieve; will carry 4- to 9-weight lines.

Bogdan Reels
33 Fifield St., Nashua, NH 03060
(603) 883-3964   Est.: 1940
Contact: Stanley E. Bogdan
Trout and salmon reels.

Browning Fishing
PO Box 270, Tulsa, OK 74115
(918) 831-6857
FAX: (918) 831-6938
President: Larry McIsaacs
Product Mgr: Andy Carroll
Browning offers a complete line of fishing tackle and accessories; including fly rods and fly reels–fly to baitcast to spinning; accessories–float tubes to waders, wading shoes to tackle systems.

Bruce & Walker
Huntingdon Road, Upwood
Huntingdon, Cambridgeshire
PE17 1QQ England
011-44-171-487-813764

CRC Fly Reels
C. Beard Co., PO Box 2525
Loveland, CO 80538
(970) 227-4707
FAX: (970) 667-9425
Contact: Tom Clinkenbeard
CRC Reels (3 models available) feature a counter balanced spool, exposed spool rim and double click pawl drag that will perform smoothly for many years. They have a super hard, no glare finish that will keep looking good too! Comes with a protective draw string cloth bag.

Charlton Outdoor Technologies, Inc.
Charlton Reel, 1179 A Water Tank Rd., Burlington, WA 98233
(360) 757-2608
FAX: (360) 757-2610   Est.: 1991
Contact: Jack Charlton
Excepting the smallest trout reel, Charlton reels utilize a multiple disk, double sided, carbon fibre drag system. It automatically adjusts for disk wear over a lifetime and is fully o-ring sealed. Charlton makes several "Configurable" reels which allow fishing 6 or more different line weights by simply quick changing to different spools. Free color brochure.

Climax Systems USA
3736 Kellogg Rd.,
Cortland, NY 13045
(607) 756-2851
FAX: (607) 753-8835
Contact: Tom McCullough
Epic fly reels are precision die cast from high strength aluminum with secondary machining to precise tolerances. Dual pawl adjustable drag, palming rim, smooth single action retrieve. Easier convert from right to left. Light line sizes only.

Cortland Line Co.
3736 Kellogg Rd., PO Box 5588
Cortland, NY 13045
(607) 756-2851
FAX: (607) 753-8835
Contact: Tom McCullough
Cortland offers the angler eight different types of reels and over 20 models to choose from at prices ranging from $35.95-$395.95. Most convert easily from right to left hand retrieve. Anti-reverse reels are available.

Daiwa Corp.
7421 Chapman Ave.
Garden Grove, CA 92641
(714) 895-6645
FAX: (714) 898-1476
Est.: 1965   Staff: 150
Mktg. Mgr: John C. Weatherell
Product Spec: Adrain Dare
Freshwater reels, 4-6 wt., 7-9 wt.
lightweight alloy frame.

Giorgio Dallari Briar Reels
Giorgio Benecchi's Products
Via Giotto 279, 41100 ,
Modena, Italy
011-39-59-341190
FAX: 011-39-59-342627
Contact: Stefania
Giorgio Dallari briar reels–objects characterized by beauty and high technology.

Dennison Fly-Lite Reels
Dennison Research
2220 SW Troy, Portland, OR 97219
(503) 246-6576
Contact: Susan Dennison
2" machined aluminum Fly-Lite reels--the ultimate answer for light and delicate fishing situations. Small and lightweight, yet strong enough to use 3 and 4 weight lines for plenty of distance.

EAGLE CLAW®

Eagle Claw®
Wright & McGill Co.
4245 E. 46th Ave.
Denver, CO 80216-0011
(303) 321-1481
FAX: (303) 321-4750
Est.: 1925
Product Mgr: Chris Doenges
Offering three series of fly reels–
A.D. McGill® model comes in 2 versions, 4/6 and 6/8 line size–re-

tail price $129.95; Brave Eagle™ model comes in 3 versions, 4/5, 6/7, and 7/8 line size–retail price $14.95-$17.45; Granger® Medallion model comes in 3 line sizes- -4/5, 6/7 and 7/8–retails from $41.95-$44.45.

Elite Products
12 Plants Dam Rd.,
E. Lyme, CT 06333
(860) 739-8185
FAX: (860) 739-0680   Est.: 1987
Contact: John McBride
The die-cast aluminum reels feature secondary machining, rim control spool, adjustable-pawl drag, left/right winding, and a baked-on, non-glare finish in gun-metal gray. Handles lines ranging from 2 through 9. Prices range from $49.95 to $64.95. "New" diecast disc drag fly reels for 1997.

Fenwick Corp.
5242 Argosy Dr.
Huntington Beach, CA 92649
(714) 897-1066 Ext. 223
FAX: (714) 891-9610   Est.: 1952
Contact: Dale Barnes
Fenwick's World Class fly reels are built to provide years of consistent performance, featuring die-cast aluminum bodies and smooth running disc-drag systems. Prices range from $89.99 to $159.99.

Fin-Nor
5553 Angler Ave.
Ft. Lauderdale, FL 33312
(305) 966-5507
FAX: (305) 966-5509   Est.: 1933
Contact: Bill Preuss
The word "reel" doesn't adequately describe the precision, thought and hand craftsmanship that has made Fin-Nor a respected name in the sport. One-piece housing and spools, machined to fine timepiece tolerances, combine with extra large drag discs to offer a level of performance that no other fishing "reel" has been able to duplicate. Call or write for more information.

FLY◆TECH®

Fly Tech
7450 Whitehall, Ft. Worth, TX 76118
(800) 590-2281
Est.: 1987   Staff: 23
Sales Mgr: Jesse Shetter
Available: Retail
Fly reels available in graphite, aluminum and machined aluminum. Call for more information.

See Our Ad Pg. 93

FLYLOGIC.

FlyLogic, Inc.
PO Box 270, Melba, ID 83641-0270
(208) 495-2090
FAX: (208) 495-2064
FlyLogic™ introduces a breakthrough in performance and price with its new line of high quality U.S. made FL*Premium™ and FL*Optimum™ Series Reels. Quick engage disc drag systems, wide adjustment ranges, easy spool exchange, simple left-to-right hand retrieve conversion, lightweight design, ample line capacity and more.

J. Austin Forbes Ltd.

J. Austin Forbes, Ltd.
24 Pine St., East Hartland, CT 06027
(800) 827-6199   (860) 653-5181
FAX: (860) 653-9986
Est.: 1990
Contact: Timothy O'Connor
Compact rods, reels and equipment for international travelers.
See Our Ad Across

Galvan Fly Reels
14340 North Ridge Rd.
Sonora, CA 95370
(209) 588-1809
Est.: 1993
Contact: Bonifacio Galvan
Trout reels

Ted Godfrey's
3509 Pleasant Plains Dr.
Reisterstown, MD 21136
(410) 239-8468
FAX: (410) 239-8468
Est.: 1972   Staff: 2
Owner: Ted Godfrey
Co-Owner: Faye Godfrey
Custom, hand-made Atlantic salmon & trout reels by Ted Godfrey. These are classic designed 1.9:1 and 2.5:1 gear ratio multipliers. Price Range: $600-$800.

W.W. Grigg Co.
Box 204, Lake Oswego, OR 97034
(503) 636-4901
FAX: (503) 636-8942
Contact: Tom Grigg
Argus graphite titanuium and aluminum fly reels–wholesale only.

HT Enterprises, Inc.
139 East Sheboygan St.
Campbellsport, WI 53010
(414) 533-5080
FAX: (414) 533-5147
Est.: 1974
President: Paul Grahl
VP: Kenneth L. Grahl

Sales Mgr: Nate Grahl
Promotions Dir: Tom Gruenwald
HT offers a complete line of affordable, custom-designed fly rods, reels, components and terminal tackle. Our premium rods and reels range from basic entry-level equipment to high modulus graphites in a variety of lengths and line weights.

Hardy (USA) Inc.
10 Godwin Plaza
Midland Park, NJ 07432
(201) 481-7557
FAX: (201) 670-7190
Est.: 1842
Contact: Jay White
Hardy uses the latest materials and engineering in its quest to develop innovative fishing tackle. Nearly 50 different models to choose from in prices ranging from $182-$451. See your House of Hardy dealer today.

C.A. Harris Co.
986 East 10 Mile Rd.
Hazel Park, MI 48030
(810) 543-9909
FAX: (810) 543-7147
Est.: 1993
President: Craig Harris
Every Solitude reel features an enclosed, water- and dirt-proof drag system which delivers unrivaled smoothness and eliminates any discernible start-up resistance. Engineered and manufactured with the latest CAD/CAM technology, Solitude reels provide high performance and contemporary styling at surprisingly affordable prices. Saltwater safe, all parts anodized and coated aluminum or stainless steel. Available in four sizes: 5/6 weight, 7/8 weight, 9 weight, 10/11 weight and 12/13 weight. Retail price range $210 to $345. Call, write or fax for more information.

Henschel Reels
BreitackerstraBe 12/1
7622 Nurtingen, Germany
011-49-07022-34608
FAX: 011-49-07022-34608
Est.: 1992   Staff: 2
Contact: Karl-Heinz Henschel

The Heron Reel
c/o P/S Engineering & Manufacturing
Rt. 2, Box 243
Eureka Springs, AR 72632
(501) 253-7695
FAX: (501) 253-6930
Contact: Peter Bogner
Offering two models–the Heron 57

and Heron 810, retailing for $135 and $150 respectively.

The Dave Inks Company
5629 Skyview Dr.,
Florence, MT 59833
(406) 273-2678
FAX: (406) 273-2608
Contact: Dave Inks
Multi-piece construction with gold-anodized frames, sculptured stainless steel cross pillars, and black anodized one-piece spools. Every component is hand polished. The drag system is oil impregnated cork disc. All reels are serialized, available in matched sets, and backed by our lifetime warranty.

Islander Reels
6771 Kirkpatrick Crescent
Saanichton, British Columbia
Canada V8M 1Z8
(250) 544-1440
FAX: (250) 544-1450
Est.: 1990
Contact: Jack Foster/Heather Eisenhuth
Islander manufactures 21 of the finest disc drag fly reels on the market today. They are all available in two immaculate saltwater proof finishes--gloss black and rich gold. New to the line up this year are the Trout Series--3 sizes of fly reels engi-

neered to balance trout weight outfits wherever you choose to fish. Also new is our website--reel us in--on the water or your computer.
Internet: http://www.islander.com

Kensington/Crystal River
1950 Stanley St.
Northbrook, IL 60065
(708) 564-1900
Est.: 1906
Crystal River offers the Coachman series with a disc-drag system, easy right- to left-hand conversion that carry lines from 3- to 10-weight. Prices from $30 to $60.

Lamiglas

Lamiglas, Inc.
1400 Atlantic
PO Box U, Woodland, WA 98674
(360) 225-9436
FAX: (360) 225-5050
Sales Mgr: Mike Wardian
email: lamiglas@pacifier.com
"Stillwater" fly reels LF34 and LF56 with classic British styling. Two models offer a 3/4 and 5/6 weight lines. There is a traditional double click/pawl drag system and the reels have a generous backing capacity.

Lamson
Division of Sage
18080 NE 68th St., Bldg. C
Redmond, WA 98052

(206) 881-0733
Contact: John Harder
Extensive experience in machining and design enables Lamson to provide the fly angler with high-quality reliable fly reels at a moderate price. All reels backed with an unconditional guarantee. Lamson offers real performance and value in an American-made reel. Call for more information.

G. Loomis, Inc.
1359 Down River Dr.
Woodland, WA 98674
(800) 662-8818
FAX: (360) 225-7169
Contact: Kris Leistritz

Loop Reels
c/o Umpqua Feather Merchants
PO Box 700, Glide, OR 97443
(800) 322-3218   (541) 496-3512
FAX: (541) 496-0150
Est.: 1972
Nat'l. Sales Mgr: Gus Wunderly
Loop Reels are designed to take on the toughest fish--like steelhead, Atlantic salmon, bonefish and permit. Their large diameter spools provide much faster line retrieval, fewer tangles and more distance on your casts. That's why Umpqua distributes the full line of Loop Reels from Sweden.

Maclin Custom

Box 975, Londonderry, NH 03053
(603) 437-3076
Contact: Ron McKinley
Tribute Reel offered in one model, 3 sizes. All metal parts are nickel silver and side plates are black hard rubber.

Marryat USA

1104 NE 28th Ave., #A275
Portland, OR 97232
(800) 578-6226   (503) 233-3826
FAX: (503) 233-3850
President: Dave Nelson
Marryat offers 5 models of high-quality machined reels with one of the smoothest disc-clutch drag systems available. Extremely lightweight, corrosion resistant. Prices range from $214 to $244.

Martin

PO Box 270, Tulsa, OK 74115
(918) 831-6857
FAX: (918) 831-6938
President: Larry McIsaacs
Product Mgr: Bob Scudder
Martin, created in 1884, continues to apply our years of practical fly fishing experience to equip value-conscious anglers with a complete line of high-quality reels, rods and pre-packaged fly fishing outfits.

McNeese Reel Company

1191 Third St., NW
Salem, OR 97304
(503) 375-6288
Est.: 1990
Contact: Dave McNeese
High quality, hand-crafted anti-reverse fly reels. Six models: trout, salmon, bonefish, permit, tarpon, billfish. Prices range from $525-$695. Call/write for a free catalog.

Mitchell Reels

JWA Fishing & Marine
1326 Willow Rd.
Sturtevant, WI 53177
(800) 227-6433
FAX: (414) 884-1600
Contact: Bill Kelly
Mitchell offers 3 models in the 7000 Series fly reels, in which the frames, spools and feet are made from lightweight graphite for durability and corrosion resistance.

Mt. Rainer Reel

305 Jewel St.,
Enumclaw, WA 98022
(360) 825-9767
Contact: Monte Schroeder
Ball bearing drive, anti-reverse with unique padless cone drag. Reversible right to left hand wind. Comes

with extra spool & leather pouch. Reels made from 6061-T651AL or CP4-Titanium.

M. Noel Reels

200 Montee St. Claude
St. Philippe, Quebec, Canada J01 2K0
(514) 659-6410
FAX: (514) 659-6410
Est.: 1993   Staff: 2
Contact: Maurice Noel
Aluminum classics and titanium Vom Hofe style salmon reels, special two handed rods.

ORVIS®

Orvis Company

Rt. 7A, Manchester, VT 05254
(800) 333-1550 (Ext. 844)
(802) 362-3622
Contact: Randy Carlson
Orvis fly reels encompass 36 models from the heirloom quality tradition of the CFO to the high-tech wizardry of the Odyssey Series. From $29 to $470, there's an Orvis reel for every budget, every angler and every fishing hole from Maine to Madagascar. For more information on Orvis reels call 800-333-1550 (Ext. 844).

Billy Pate Fly Reels

Tibor Reel Company
900 NE 40th Ct.
Oakland Park, FL 33334
(305) 566-0222
FAX: (305) 566-9847
Est.: 1972
Contact: Tammy Randolph
Since their introduction in 1972, Billy Pate Reels have established a reputation for being extremely dependable, durable reels that render flawless, virtually maintenance free performance. Six models available in either direct or anti-reverse modes-cover the entire range of fly fishing pursuits. Prices range from $325 to $750.

E.F. Payne Rod Co.

Box 1994, Sisters, OR 97759
(541) 549-1544
Contact: Dave Holloman

Peerless Reel Company

427-3 Amherst St.
Suite 177, Nashua, NH 03063
(603) 595-2458
FAX: (603) 595-2458
Contact: Bob Corsetti
Angler's looking for top quality, classic design and the best modern

technology can find them all in Peerless hand crafted trout and salmon reels. Peerless: Simply the finest. Call or write today for catalog and dealer information.

Penn Fishing Tackle Mfg. Co.

3028 W. Hunting Park Ave.
Philadelphia, PA 19132
(215) 229-9415
FAX: (215) 223-3017
Est.: 1932
Contact: Ed Mesunas
Known for decades as a maker of first-rate trolling, casting, offshore and jigging reels, Penn has added a family of saltwater fly reels to its product line. Four models holding 6 to 8WT, 8 to 10WT and 10 to 12WT line are available. Retail price $330-$450. See your nearest dealer for more information.

Pflueger Fly Reels

3801 Westmore Dr.
Columbia, SC 29223
(803) 754-7000
Public Relations: Mark Davis
Pflueger-one of the oldest and most recognized names in fly fishing-offers reels at entry level prices. Eighteen models ranging in price from $25.99-$45.99 are available. Product lines are called Medalist and Supreme.

Phos Flyreels

601 Maple Ave.
Carpinteria, CA 93013
(805) 684-7727
FAX: (805) 684-6863
Est.: 1974
Contact: Keith Mojarro
Phos Flyreels offers a machined, corrosion-resistant, anodized, innovative drag. Lifetime warranty, beautiful finish, 5 models available.

Walton Powell Reel

1329 W. Lindo Ave.
Chico, CA 95926
(916) 895-8923
FAX: (916) 895-8946
Contact: Diane Powell

Precision Reels

113 Walters Ave.
Ewing, NJ 08638
(800) 555-2603
FAX: (609) 538-0510
Contact: David W. Lewis
Designed and built to meet your demands, Precision Reels offer the stopping power of full size disc drag, an exposed rim for added control, and the ease and convenience of a quick release spool. Four models made from solid 6061-

T6 Aircraft Aluminum and 316 Stainless Steel available.

RST Fishing Tackle
Schwaninger Strasse 31
89352 Ellzee, Stoffenried, Germany
011-49-8283-461-2074
FAX: 011-49-8283-2054
Contact: Reinhardt Steiner

Redington, Inc.
906 South Dixie Hwy.
Stuart, FL 34994
(800) 253-2538
FAX: (407) 220-9957
Contact: Jim Murphy

Regal Engineering Inc.
RFD2, Tully Rd., Orange, MA 01364
(508) 575-0488
Contact: Tea Doiron
Regal offers a unique four point brake system, anti-reverse fishing reel. Call or write for a free brochure.

Right Angle Reels
14 Perry Ave., Norwalk, CT 06850
(888) 803-5400 (Orders)
(203) 847-9398
FAX: (203) 846-2878
Est.: 1993
Contact: Glenn Holcomb
The Right Angle Reels AR Series are available in 3 sizes, 6-, 8-, and 10-weight.

Robichaud Reels
Box 119, Hudson, NH 03051-0119
(603) 880-6484
Est.: 1980
Contact: Dave Robichaud
Manufacturer of affordable classic fly fishing reels. Champagne color, black side covers. Many options. Call for information.

Ross Reels
1 Ponderosa Ct.
Montrose, CO 81401
(800) 336-1050   (970) 249-1212
FAX: (970) 249-1834
Est.: 1973   Staff: 40
Contact: David S. Heller
Manufacturer of the finest machined fly reels in the world. Guaranteed for life.

J. Ryall Fly Reels
993 E. San Carlos Ave.
San Carlos, CA 94070
(415) 592-8277
Est.: 1991
Contact: Jim Ryall
Patented drag system, hard-anodized finish and lifetime warranty combine to make a superior product.

S.J. Designs
15 Kearny Ave., Apt. 3-B
Edison, NJ 08817
(908) 985-1809
FAX: (908) 985-1809
Proprietor: Scott James
100% American-made from aluminum barstock. All reels are available in two colors–burgundy with black trim or all black. Outside screws are plated with 24 carat gold.

STH Reels (USA) Inc.
3736 Kellogg Rd.
PO Box 5588, Cortland, NY 13045
(607) 756-2851
FAX: (607) 753-8835
Contact: Tom McCullough
STH offers affordable, lightweight, high strength reels with the innovative interchangeable polycarbonate Cassette® spare spool system. Eight systems and over 20 models to choose from. Limited lifetime warranty to original owner. Write or call for more information on the Cassette® or reels.

Sage
8500 NE Day Rd.
Bainbridge Island, WA 98110
(800) 533-3004   (206) 842-6608
FAX: (206) 842-6830
Est.: 1980   Staff: 150
VP/Sales & Mktg: Marc Bale
Mktg. Mgr: Bill Dawson
Premium producer of high quality, performance fly rods, reels and accessories.

Scientific Anglers

3M Scientific Anglers
3M Center-Bldg. 223-4N
St. Paul, MN 55144-1000
(800) 525-6290
Scientific Anglers™ offers a range of fly reels to meet the needs of most anglers. Long recognized for their dependability and durability, System™ fly reels deliver great performance at an affordable price. Mastery Series fly reels are machined from bar stock aluminum and offer specially designed drag systems, components and features for specific-fishing situations. Available in 4 models exclusively from Scientific Anglers Mastery Series dealers.

Seamaster
16115 S.W. 117th Ave.
Suite A-8, Miami, FL 33177
(305) 253-2408
FAX: (305) 253-5901 Est.: 1950
Contact: Robby Jansen
Manufacturer of fine handcrafted angling equipment–4 models available. Retail price range $1,000-$4,000.

Shakespeare Co.
3801 Westmore Dr.
Columbia, SC 29223
(800) 334-9105   (803) 754-7000
FAX: (803) 754-7342
Public Relations: Mark Davis

Sharpe's of Aberdeen
Devercon Mill Glass, By Huntly
Aberdeenshire AB54 4XH
011-01466 700257
FAX: 011-01466 700333
Man. Dir: D.A. (Don) Mackenzie
Looking for US representative.

Sievert Engineering
3805 N. Brehler, Sanger, CA 93657
(209) 875-4868   Est.: 1986
Owners: Ron Geis & Steve Sievert
Patented direct drive and anti-reverse simultaneously engaged drive system–the best of both systems in one reel.

South Bend
1950 Stanley St.
Northbrook, IL 60065
(847) 715-1400
FAX: (847) 715-1411
VP/Sales & Mktg: Randy Lemcke
Quality fly reels marketed under the South Bend and Crystal River trade names.

Fly Reels

Stratos Fly Reels by ATC
21615 SW T-V Hwy.
Beaverton, OR 97006
(503) 642-9853
FAX: (503) 591-7766
Contact: Scotte Hughes
Reel Smooth...That's what professional and experienced anglers say when they use the Stratos Fly Reel. Five models made from precision machined aluminum and featuring a silky smooth, cork-free drag system are available in prices from $285-$440. Easy right to left conversion. Lifetime warranty. For a closer look contact ATC for the nearest dealer to you.

Stream Line Inc.
7865 Day Rd., W., Bldg. B
Bainbridge Island, WA 98110
(800) 553-5763
(206) 842-8501
FAX: (206) 842-0307
Contact: Schuyler Horton
Stream Line's reels are precision machined from a single block of aluminum alloy and hard anodized for maximum protection against the elements. A fully enclosed double disc drag system is a departure from conventional cork designs. Six models perfect for fresh and saltwater applications are available. Priced from $250-$425. Call or write for more information.

Teton Fly Reels
924 A2 Church Hill Rd.
San Andreas, CA 95249
(209) 754-4709
FAX: (209) 754-4716
Owner: Weston H. Ament
Teton Fly Reels are lightweight, strong & durable. The Teton uses 4 different materials and five drag surfaces and feature quick-release spools.

Tibor Reel Company
900 NE 40th Ct.
Oakland Park, FL 33334
(305) 566-0222
FAX: (305) 566-9847
Contact: Tammy Randolph

Valentine Fly Reels
PO Box 95. Chartley, MA 02712
(508) 285-8432
FAX: (508) 285-5510
Contact: Larry Valentine
A revolutionary patented fly reel that features a fully adjustable Teflon disc drag, machined alloy frame, and completely corrosion resistant anodized and stainless steel construction. American made in 3 sizes with handsome leather case Reasonably price: $139-$229. Call or write for more information.

Wathne Collection
1095 Cranbury So. River Rd.
Suite 8, Jamesburg, NJ 08831
(800) 942-1166
FAX: (609) 655-3580
Available: Retail
Produced by the House of Hardy, Wathne offers 2 custom designed high-performance trout and salmon outfits, each an individually numbered limited edition.

J.W. Young & Sons (USA), Inc.
PO Box 288, E. Hartland, CT 06027
(800) 800-3949   (860) 653-0382
FAX: (860) 653-9986
Est.: 1884
VP/Sales & Mktg: Kim Nelson
For over a 100 years offering precision crafted classic British fly fishing reels as well as affordable reels for beginning anglers. Call or write for information.

Zebco
Brunswick Outdoor Recreation Group
PO Box 270, Tulsa, OK 74115
(918) 831-6857
FAX: (918) 831-6938
President: Larry McIsaacs
Unit Mgr: Clifford Ginn
Year after year, more families count on Zebco for rods, reels & combos that offer great performance and advanced features, but are still as easy to use as they are to afford.

RODS

All Star Graphite Rods, Inc.
9817 Whithorn, Houston, TX 77095
(713) 855-9603
FAX: (713) 855-4530
Contact: Tim Grennan
Drawing on years of study and research, All Star offers fly rods designed for the most discerning fly fishing enthusiast and a spectrum of fly fishing applications.

American Rod Co.
American Fly Fishing Co.
3523 Fairoaks Blvd.
Sacramento, CA 95864
(800) 410-1222
FAX: (916) 483-5820
Contact: Gary Eblen
Customer direct only. Best value in 4-piece travel fly rods. Starting at $179. IM6 models include 8' 3/4, 9' 5/6, 9' 7/8, and 9' 9/10.

American Tackle, Ltd.
940 Old Post Rd.,
Cotuit, MA 02635
(800) 516-1750
FAX: (800) 966-9430
Est.: 1984
President: Joe Meehan
CEO: Joe Meehan, Jr.
Importers-exporters of rods, reels & rod building components. Featuring affordable graphite fly reels & rods.

J.P. Apple Rod Company
6245 North Sunny Point Rd.
Milwaukee, WI 53217-4171
(414) 967-9530
Contact: John Apple
Classic graphite fly rods. 7 1/2 and 8 foot light trout rods for 3, 4, and 5 weight lines in several special actions. Send a # 10 self-addressed stamped envelope for information.

L.L. Bean
Casco St., Freeport, ME 04033
(800) 809-7057
FAX: (207) 552-3080
SPT Rods–the power to cast further with better control. Call for more information.

Berkley Rods
1 Berkley Dr., Spirit Lake, IA 51360
(800) 237-5539
(712) 336-1520 (Consumer)
FAX: (712) 336-5183
Berkley's Advanta is a 9 ft. 5 wt. rod that retails for $114.95 with Cordura case and bag.

Biscayne Rod Mfg. Co., Inc.
425 E. 9th St., Hialeah, FL 33010
(305) 884-0808
FAX: (305) 884-3017
Est.: 1948   Staff: 8
President: Kenneth S. Carman
VP: Eddie Carman
Biscayne Rod has manufactured fly rods since 1948 for some of the best fly fishermen in the world. Multiple rod series available for freshwater, saltwater and offshore fishing. Biscayne Rod uses only the highest quality component parts available today on all rod series. "You can't buy a better rod."

Browning Fishing
PO Box 270, Tulsa, OK 74115
(918) 831-6857
FAX: (918) 831-6938
President: Larry McIsaacs
Product Mgr: Andy Carroll
Browning offers a complete line of fishing tackle and accessories; including fly rods and fly reels–fly to baitcast to spinning; accessories–float tubes to waders, wading shoes to tackle systems.

Bruce & Walker
Huntingdon Road, Upwood
Huntingdon, Cambridgeshire
PE17 1QQ England
011-44-171-487-813764
15 ft. Powerlite Speycaster–Developed over a year, the structure of the rod is altered by a different method of wrapping the carbon fibre around the mandrils and is reinforced in strategic places. Made with the amateur in mind.

Cabela's
812 13th Ave., Sidney, NE 69160
(308) 234-5555
FAX: (308) 254-2200

Cape Fear Rod Co.
302 A Raleigh St.
Wilmington, NC 28412
(910) 350-0494   FAX: 2878
Contact: Raiford Trask
Planning on offering a line of quality fly rods in late '97.

Composite Developments
PO Box 100063, N. Shore Mail Ctr.
Auckland 10, New Zealand
Contact: Marty Johanson
Manufacturing the Down Under Series in 11 models (7 1/2 to 9') and the Kiwi Magic IM7 Series in 8', 8 1/2' and 9'. Ten saltwater rods (all 9') are available. Contact Cortland Line Co. (607) 756-2851 for specific availability and pricing.

Cortland Line Co.
3736 Kellogg Rd., PO Box 5588
Cortland, NY 13045
(607) 756-2851
FAX: (607) 753-8835
Contact: Tom McCullough
Nine different series of high quality rods to meet every fly fishing need and every price point from $69.95 to $325. Freshwater and saltwater models in 2 piece and 4 piece designs. Plus the exclusive Down Under Series from New Zealand, found only at Cortland.

Cunningham Mfg. Co.
PO Box 2437
Huntington Beach, CA 92649
(714) 840-3900
FAX: (714) 840-5676
Contact: Wade Cunningham
Wade Rods is a new company making state of the art rods. Designed by Wade Cunningham, a rod builder and blank designer with over two decades of experience. The company makes a full line of rods, however they are most proud of their excellent fly rods. Every Wade rod is distinctive, refined actions, fine components and a rich appearance. Exclusive specialty retailers, superb quality and fair pricing assure success. Call or write for information.

Custom Rod Craft
PO Box 423, Hudson, NH 03051
(603) 889-5963
FAX: (603) 889-1234   Est.: 1993
Contact: James Conrad
Highlander Series–handcrafted fly fishing rods. 65 different models–

graphite, fiberglass, bamboo. Dealer inquiries welcome.

Daiwa Corp.
7421 Chapman Ave.
Garden Grove, CA 92641
(714) 895-6645
FAX: (714) 898-1476
Est.: 1965   Staff: 150
Mktg. Mgr: John C. Weatherell
Product Spec: Adrain Dare
Rods–graphite 6'6", backpack– 8'6" 6-7 wt.

Dennison Fly-Lite Rods
Dennison Research
2220 SW Troy, Portland, OR 97219
(503) 246-6576
FAX: (503) 244-2099
Est.: 1984
Contact: Susan Dennison
Quality 5, Fly-Lite graphite rods, the ultimate answer for light and delicate fishing situations. Small and lightweight, yet strong enough to use 3 and 4 weight lines for plenty of distance. Call or write for more information.

Diamondback Rods
The Diamondback Company
PO Box 308, Stowe, VT 05672
(802) 253-4358
FAX: (802) 253-4570   Est.: 1975
Contact: Barton N. Merle-Smith

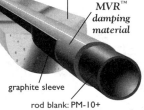

Choosing A Rod

The selection of a rod may be the most important decision you'll make as you enter the sport of fly fishing. Choose wisely and your early angling experiences will be satisfying and leave you craving more; choose badly and you'll feel frustrated and cheated.

But before you purchase a rod or any other equipment for that matter, you'll need to do some homework. First, familiarize yourself with the anatomy of a basic fly rod [see illustration below]. Then give some thought to the kind of fishing you want to do: What kind of fish are you after? And will you be fishing rivers, streams, lakes, or the ocean?

These questions are important because no one fly rod does it all. In fact, each fly rod is designed to work with a specific or very narrow range of line weight. And different fish and different fishing situations demand different line weights.

Matching Rod & Line

How do you match rod to line? Fortunately, the manufacturers have done it for you. Pick up a rod at your local fly shop and look at the shaft, just above the grip. Printed there you might see the code G-85-5. The "G" tells you the rod is graphite; the "85" that its eight and one half feet long; and the "5" that it's designed to cast 5-weight line. [See box, page 103.]

What weight is best for the beginner? Unless you know at the outset that you'll be fishing primarily for large saltwater species requiring a rod/line weight of 9 or more, you'll probably want to buy a #5, #6 or #7 rod to start. (Most experts say that a 4- to 5-weight line is right for pan fish; that a 6-weight outfit works for most trout fishing; 7-weight for trout and bass; 8-weight and up for larger fresh and saltwater fish.) If you're uncertain about what you need, read what you can on the subject and spend a little time chatting up the customers and staff at your local fly shop for additional guidance.

Lengths

Fly rods range in length from novelty rods that are less than 6- feet long to graphite salmon rods as long as 15-feet. Most trout and bass fly rods sold in the United States, however, run from 7 $\frac{1}{2}$ to 8 $\frac{1}{2}$-feet in length. Shorter rods are generally faster and more maneuverable in tight confines; longer rods offer some casting and fly-repositioning advantages. Not surprisingly, the experts differ on the ideal rod length for a beginner, but most recommend a rod in the 8 to 9-foot range.

Actions

Hang around the rod display of any fly shop and before long you'll hear someone describing the feel or "action" of a rod. Simply put, action is the way a rod moves or flexes under stress. A rod's action is determined by its design, length and what it is made of.; it can be categorized as fast, medium or intermediate, or slow. Fast action rods are stiff, tend to flex toward the tip of

continued on page 102>

John Dickson & Son
21 Frederick Street
Edinburgh EH2 2NE, Scotland
011-44-131-225-4218

EAGLE CLAW®

Eagle Claw®
Wright & McGill Co.
4245 E. 46th Ave.
Denver, CO 80216-0011
(303) 321-1481
FAX: (303) 321-4750
Est.: 1925
Product Mgr: Chris Doenges
Granger Medallion and Granger Fly
Rods.

East Branch Rods
43 Aimweg St., Jay, NY 12941
(800) 337-3763
FAX: (518) 946-7413
Est.: 1994
Contact: George "Erik" Jobson
East Branch manufactures and sells
its own blanks, and sells rod building kits and finished rods direct to
customers.

Elkhorn Rod Company
Box 2525, Loveland, CO 80539
(970) 227-4707
FAX: (970) 667-9425
Contact: Tom Clinkenbeard
Complete rod building kits–all components beautifully packaged
together. An easy way to learn rod
building. Four- piece travel rods
available in 3 line weights: 4, 5/6,
7/8. Demo rods available to dealers. Factory built rods also
available.

Empire America, Inc.
1275 Bloomfield Ave.
No. 9–79, Fairfield, NJ 07004
(201) 882-0807
FAX: (201) 882-0803
Contact: David Song
Good selection of graphite fly rods
starting at $30 to $110. Comes in
1, 2 & 4 piece. Blanks available.

Fenwick Corp.
5242 Argosy Dr.
Huntington Beach, CA 92649
(714) 897-1066 Ext. 226
FAX: (714) 891-9610
Est.: 1952
Contact: Dale Barnes
Six different series of graphite rods
for the novice to experienced an-
gler and most fishing situations.

Fin-Nor
5553 Angler Ave.
Ft. Lauderdale, FL 33312

(305) 966-5507
FAX: (305) 966-5509
Est.: 1933
Contact: Bill Preuss

The Fisher Company
Box 3147, Carson City, NV 89702
(702) 246-5220
FAX: (702) 246-5143   Est.: 1922
Contact: Kent Gasch

FLY✦TECH ®

Fly Tech
7450 Whitehall
Ft. Worth, TX 76118
(800) 590-2281
FAX: (817) 590-2053
Est.: 1987   Staff: 23
Sales Mgr: Jesse Shetter
Available: Retail
Offering the two piece Supreme Fly
Rod made of IM6 Hercules Graph-
ite with a rosewood and stainless
steel reel seat available in 7′6" to
9′6". Call for more information.
See Our Ad Above

J. Austin Forbes, Ltd.
24 Pine St.,
East Hartland, CT 06027
(800) 827-6199   (860) 653-5181
FAX: (860) 653-9986
Est.: 1990
Contact: Timothy O'Connor
Compact rods, reels and equipment
for international travelers.
See Our Ad Pg. 95

**Garrison Formula
Graphite Rods**
The Denali Group SSR, Ltd.
3637 Medina Rd.,
Medina, OH 44256
(800) 701-6248
Contact: Art Flynn
Rodmaker: Stephen Roche
Five models designed for fishing
small streams or wherever delicate
presentation is needed.

Glastech Rods
4765 C.T.H. KP,
Cross Plains, WI 53528
(608) 798-3423
Contact: Dennis Franke
Over the last 15 years, glass fiber
and resin technology has continued
to advance, raising fiberglass to the
level of an outstanding rodmaking
material. Glastech believes that
modern glass is now the best material available for making trout rods.
For more information on Glastech's
line of fine glass fly rods, available
in over 30 models, call/write today.

Graphite USA®
by Composite Development Corp.
7569 Convoy Ct.
San Diego, CA 92111
(619) 560-GUSA
FAX: (619) 277-2271   Est.: 1975
Contact: Kit Kantner
The world leader in Dual-Helix
100% graphite blend fly rods and
blanks. Absolutely the strongest

buy is made of is important. Why? Because the material plays a large role in determining the rod's feel, performance, durability and, of course, cost.

Before World War II almost all fly rods were made of "split bamboo," the very best of which came from a special cane grown in Southeast Asia. Quality bamboo rods are expensive and generally heavier and more flexible than their synthetic cousins. Some fly fishing *aficionados* swear by them, especially for trout and pan fish.

Fiberglass was the first synthetic to replace bamboo after the War. Today's fiberglass rods are rugged and good for most types of fishing. Generally the least expensive on the market, they make, in the opinion of many, a fine choice for a first rod.

Back in the mid-70s, fly rods constructed of a synthetic fiber called carbon-graphite made their first appearance. Graphite rods are light and very elastic. They tend to be more forgiving of casting mistakes than bamboo or fiberglass and their elasticity produces greater casting distance. For these reasons and others, graphite rods are favored by many experts.

Boron, another synthetic fiber, made its appearance in the early '80s. Rods made of all-boron or boron-graphite composite rods were very light, very elastic and very expensive. Thought at one time to be the rod "material of the future", boron has been swept from the commercial scene by improvements in graphite technology.

Going to Pieces

Fly rods, even those that come in two sections, are long and difficult to maneuver especially in confined areas. That's why more rods are broken in transit than in catching fish. And why today's three- and four-piece travel rods are growing in popularity.

Years ago the knock on the travel rod was that the ferrules or connections between sections sacrificed "sensitivity." But what was true then is not necessarily so today. Better design and materials make the feel of a travel rod virtually identical to that of a one or two-piece model. So if you're planning to travel to fish—and sooner or later you will—most experts advise spending a bit more up front for a multi-piece travel rod.

the rod and unflex rapidly when stressed; medium or intermediate action rods tend to flex more easily through the upper half of the rod and unflex more smoothly; slow action rods, the most pliable of all, flex quite easily from tip to butt and unflex slowly. With experience, you'll gravitate to the type of action that feels and works best for you. Until then, go with the compromise medium or intermediate action.

Materials

The range of materials used in today's fly rod runs from bamboo to space-age synthetics such as carbon graphite. And knowing what the rod you are going to

Shop Smart

What should you spend on a rod? It depends. There are any number of perfectly good rods on the market for $100 to $150. But there are also top-of-the line rods that cost thousands of dollars. Spend as much as you can reasonably afford, but try not to go over the top, especially if you're a novice.

Whatever you do, don't buy anything the first time you go shopping. Take your time. Read as much as you can about fly fishing in general and fly rods in particular. Seek out experienced fly-fishers and ask their advice. Press them for the names of a trusted dealers. Get some formal instruction—and guidance from the instructor—before you buy. And always try the rod with a matching line before you spend a cent.

ROD/LINE USES & SIZES

Rod/Line Weight	Fish	Fly Sizes
1-2	Trout, panfish	#26 - #18
3-6	Trout, bass, panfish	#26 - #1/0
7-8	Trout, steelhead, bonefish, redfish, Atlantic salmon, bass	#20 - #1/0
9-11	Steelhead, Atlantic salmon, Pacific salmon, bluefish, small tarpon, dorado, stripers	#6 - #2/0
12-15	Tarpon, billfish, tuna	#2/0 - #8/0

blank built in the world today! Performance, durability and value. Call or write today for more information about fly rod blanks factory direct–thank you.

Green River Rodmakers
Green River Rd.
Green River, VT 05301
(800) 859-4553
FAX: (802) 257-4553
Est.: 1989   Staff: 12
Contact: Robert Gorman or Sasha Gorman
Hand-crafted fly rods–graphite and bamboo–that marry the best of traditional craftsmanship and contemporary technology. Green River rods are affordable, functional, durable, maintenance free and beautiful.

W.W. Grigg Co.
Box 204, Lake Oswego, OR 97034
(503) 636-4901
FAX: (503) 636-8942
Contact: Tom Grigg
2 & 4 piece fly rods–wholesale only.

HT PREMIUM FLY TACKLE

HT Enterprises, Inc.
139 East Sheboygan St.
Campbellsport, WI 53010
(414) 533-5080
FAX: (414) 533-5147
Est.: 1974
President: Paul F. Grahl
VP: Kenneth L. Grahl
Sales Mgr: Nate Grahl
Promo. Dir: Thomas C. Gruenwald
HT offers a complete line of affordable, custom-designed fly rods, reels, components and terminal tackle. Our premium rods and reels

range from basic entry-level equipment to high modulus graphites in a variety of lengths and line weights. All HT rods are backed by our unlimited, unconditional lifetime warranty. Dealer inquiries welcome.

Hardy (USA) Inc.
10 Godwin Plaza
Midland Park, NJ 07432
(201) 481-7557
FAX: (201) 670-7190
Contact: Jay White
Split-bamboo and carbon fiber rods in a variety of lengths, styles and line weights from the House of Hardy.

HEXAGRAPH ™

FLY ROD COMPANY

Hexagraph Fly Rod Co.
9919 Hornpipe Lane
Houston, TX 77080
(800) 870-4211
FAX: (713) 464-0505
Est.: 1993   Staff: 4
President: Harry J. Briscoe
Gen. Mgr: Barbara Howard
Hexagraph Fly Rods are unique, built like bamboo of segmented graphite strips, "Hexes" offer what tubular rods cannot; superior strength, exceptional and precise casting accuracy, and an exact replication of the unmistakable feel and action of cane. Available in a variety of lengths, line weights and actions from 7' to 10' and several finish options. Direct sales and dealer inquiries welcome.

Kane Klassics

Kane Klassics Rod Company
PO Box 8124
Fremont, CA 94537
(510) 487-8545 (800) 331-6406
FAX: (510) 487-6448
Est.: 1988
Contact: Doug Kulick
At Kane Klassics Rod Company, owner and maker Douglas Kulick produces superb hand planed bamboo fly rods in sizes from trout to tarpon in one to six piece travel rod variants. As planned in 1996, he released an exquisite line of fine graphite fly rods that will incorporate the design excellence, attention to detail, castability and accuracy that are the hallmarks of his bamboo fly rods. Constructed of "multi-modulus" graphite in taper designs that allow accurate casting in a pleasurable medium-fast action rod. These rods are available in 2-8 wts., 7 1/2' to 9'.
See Our Ad Pg. 100

Kensington/Crystal River
1950 Stanley St.
Northbrook, IL 60065
(708) 564-1900
Kensington/Crystal River–premium rods without the premium price. Grapite rods available in a variety of models, lengths and line weights. Suggested retail prices: $45- $175.

Lamiglas

Lamiglas, Inc.
1400 Atlantic, PO Box U
Woodland, WA 98674
(360) 225-9436
FAX: (360) 225-5050
Contact: Mike Wardian
email: lamiglas@pacifier.com
Fly rods–IM700, LHS2, Pioneer,
Certified Pro, G1000, G500 in
graphite. Brush Creek fly rods in fiberglass.

H.L. Leonard®
Rod Company

H.L. Leonard Rod Company
2 Oak St., PO Box 2797
Kennebunkport, ME 04046
(207) 967-8044
FAX: (207) 967-2671   Est.: 1869
President: Brian J. McGrath
Makers of fine fishing rods and
tackle since 1869.

G. Loomis, Inc.
1359 Down River Rd.
Woodland, WA 98674
(800) 662-8818
FAX: (360) 225-7169
Contact: Kris Leistritz
Exploring the limits of technology
and design so you can explore the
limits of fly fishing, G. Loomis offers 2, 3, and 4 piece graphite rods
in a wide range of lengths and line
weights.

Martin
PO Box 270, Tulsa, OK 74115
(918) 831-6857
FAX: (918) 831-6938
President: Larry McIsaacs
Product Mgr: Bob Scudder
Martin, created in 1884, continues
to apply our years of practical fly
fishing experience to equip value-
conscious anglers with a complete
line of high-quality reels, rods and
pre-packaged fly fishing outfits.

MEC-GAR Fly Rods
998 North Colony Rd.
Meriden, CT 06450
(203) 639-1120
FAX: (203) 639-1236
Contact: Jay Hard

Millcreek Rod Company
5180 S. Commerce Dr.
Suite D, Murray, UT 84107
(801) 265-0392

Est.: 1995   Staff: 2
Owner: Marsh Poulson
As blank manufacturers, we pride
ourselves on their actions, straight-
ness and minimal spine. Rods from
$250.

Mitchell Fly Rods
JWA Fishing & Marine
1326 Willow Rd.
Sturtevant, WI 53177
(800) 227-6433
VP: Bob Reid

ORVIS®

Orvis Company
Rt. 7A, Manchester, VT 05254
(800) 333-1550 (Ext. 844)
(802) 362-3622
Contact: Randy Carlson
Orvis has been building fly rods for
140 years and offers over 105 models to choose from including the
revolutionary Trident Series with
MVR (Maximum Vibration Reduction) technology. Four rod series
over four actions offer every angler
a choice from $115 to $575. For
more information on Orvis rods call
800-333-1550 (Ext. 844).
See Our Ad Pg. 99

Partridge of Redditch
Mount Pleasant, Redditch,
Worcestershire, B97 4JE England
011-44-527-543555
011-44-527-550575
FAX:: 011-44 527 546956
Contact: Ole Bjerke
Hand crafted split cane and greenheart rods available in a wide
variety of models, lengths, line
weights and actions. Uncompro-
mised quality and attention to
detail is evident in every rod. Rod
blanks available in Bamboo and
Greenheart. Call or write for more
information.

E.F. Payne Rod Co.
Box 1994, Sisters, OR 97759
(541) 549-1544
Contact: Dave Holloman
Manufacturers of bamboo and
graphite fly rods

Penn Fishing Tackle Mfg. Co.
3028 W. Hunting Park Ave.
Philadelphia, PA 19132
(215) 229-9415
FAX: (215) 223-3017   Est.: 1932
Contact: Ed Mesunas
Penn offers 40 models of rods–the
Gold Medal (price range: $169.95-

$199.95), and the International
(price range: $189.95-$199.95).

Pflueger Fly Rods
Shakespeare Company
3801 Westmore Dr.
Columbia, SC 29223
(803) 754-7000
Public Relations: Mark Davis
Prices range $35-$89 for rods
alone. Many rod and reel combinations available from $70-$130.

Walton Powell Fly Rods
1329 W. Lindo Ave.,
Chico, CA 95926
(916) 895-8923   FAX: 8946
Contact: Diane Powell

Powell Rod Company
PO Box 4000, Chico, CA 95926
(916) 345-3393
FAX: (916) 345-0567
Est.: 1910   Staff: 10
Mktg: P. Biery
Manufacturers of premium hand-
crafted fly rods and tackle since 1910.
Four generations of rod building.

RST Fishing Tackle
Schwaninger Strasse 31
89352 Ellzee, Stoffenried, Germany
011-49-8283-4612074
FAX: 011-49-8283-461-2054
Contact: Reinhardt Steiner
High-tech precision built, high modulus graphite rods offering splendid
line control and casting qualities.
Available at sporting goods stores
nationwide.

Raven Fly Rods
4436 N. Miller Rd., #200
Scottsdale, AZ 85251
(888) 303-1748
(602) 844-3771 (Voice)
FAX: (602) 844-3771
Est.: 1996   Staff: 4
President: Jim Boydstun
Raven Fly Rods introduces its Advanced Modulus (AM) series of
graphite fly rods in lengths of 7 to
9 1/2 feet. Graphite of 40 to 90 million modulus are blended to
produce this ultralight (11
grams/foot) fishing instrument.
Each Raven comes complete with a
custom sheepskin/leather inner
pouch and a canvas leather outer
carrying tube. Complete at $385,
each Raven includes a lifetime, no-
quibble warranty.
http://www.RavenRods.com

PARTS OF A FLY ROD

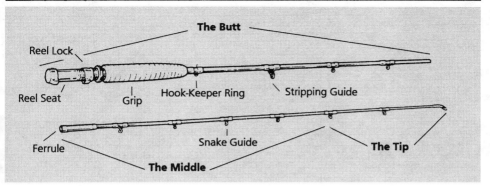

Redington, Inc.
906 S. Dixie Hwy., Stuart, FL 34994
(800) 253-2538   (407) 223-1342
FAX: (407) 220-9957
Contact: Jim Murphy
Durable and accurate fly rods for
freshwater and saltwater angling,
available in wide variety of lengths,
line weights and actions. 1, 2 and 4
piece models. Red.Start rods are
priced at $100 and have a lifetime
guarantee.

Sage
8500 NE Day Rd.
Bainbridge Island, WA 98110
(800) 533-3004   (206) 842-6608
FAX: (206) 842-6830
Est.: 1980   Staff: 150
VP/Sales & Mktg: Marc Bale
Mktg. Mgr: Bill Dawson
Premium producer of high quality,
performance fly rods, reels and ac-
cessories.

Scott Fly Rod Co.
200 San Miguel River Dr.
PO Box 889, Telluride, CO 81435
(800) 728-7208   (970) 728-4191
FAX: (970) 728-5031
Contact: Todd Field
High-performance fly rods of graphite, cane and Fibertouch glass. Over
70 models to choose from, in 2, 3,
4 and 5 piece versions, each recog-
nizably a Scott in craftsmanship
and performance. Scott fly rods are
sold with Unconditional Lifetime
Guarantee. Call our Customer Service Deparment for the location of
your nearest Scott dealer.

Seamaster
16115 S.W. 117th Ave.
Suite A-8, Miami, FL 33177
(305) 253-2408
FAX: (305) 253-5901
Est.: 1950

Contact: Robby Jansen
Custom rod manufacturer.

Shakespeare Co.
3801 Westmore Dr.
Columbia, SC 29223
(800) 334-9105   (803) 754-7000
FAX: (803) 754-7342
Public Relations: Mark Davis

Silstar Corp. of America Inc.
PO Box 6505
West Columbia, SC 29171
(803) 794-8521
FAX: (803) 794-8544
VP/Sales & Mktg: Mark Skrocki
Mktg. Comm: Angelo M. Sireno

South Bend
1950 Stanley St.
Northbrook, IL 60065
(847) 715-1400
FAX: (847) 715-1411
VP/Sales & Mktg: Randy Lemcke
Fly rods and fly rod/reel outfits mar-
keted under the South Bend and
Kensington trade names.

St. Croix Rod
856 4th Avenue North
Park Falls, WI 54552
(800) 826-7042
(715) 762-3226
FAX: (715) 762-3293
Est.: 1948
VP/Sales & Mktg: Jeff Schluter
Manufacturer of high performance
graphite fly rods for fresh and saltwater. St. Croix offers 2, 3 and 4
piece models in a wide range of
lengths and line weights. Excellent
quality, value and service has made
St. Croix a legend in fly fishing.

TKR
Box 1322, High Point, NC 27261
(910) 882-3226
Est.: 1977   Staff: 3
Owner: Tom Kirkman
Thousands of hours of research
and development have gone into
making TKR rods the most innovative and expertly crafted fly rods
available today. Built with an exacting precision unmatched by any
other maker, each TKR rod offers
unmatched performance and appearance. Museum quality
workmanship. Color catalog-$2.00.

**Thomas & Thomas
Rodmakers, Inc.**
2 Avenue A, PO Box 32
Turners Falls, MA 01376
(413) 863-9727
Contact: Rick Smith
T&T makes graphite and split bamboo fly rods in 2, 3 and 7 piece
models in length, line weight and actions to match the fishing you'll be
using them for. Call us for our free
catalog describing all of our rods.

Vaden/French Rod Co.
2041 S. 380th St.
Federal Way, WA 98003
(206) 838-7939
Contact: Charles F. Vaden
Offering the finest bamboo flyrods
at the best prices on earth. Our
rods are sure to please the most discriminating bamboo nut!

Versitex Fly Rods
3545 Schuylkill Rd.
Spring City, PA 19475
(610) 948-4442
FAX: (800) 331-6406
Contact: Fred Claghorn

Single handed and, European two handed fly rods. Reasonably priced models for just about any fishing situation. Made in the USA. Dealer inquiries welcome. Call or write for a free color catalog.
See Our Ad Pg. 102

R.L. Winston Rod Co.
500 S. Main St.
Twin Bridges, MT 59754
(406) 684-5674
FAX: (406) 684-5533
Est.: 1929
Contact: Mike Ewing
Manufacturers of fine graphite and bamboo fly rods. Please call or write for the dealer nearest you.

Zebco
Brunswick Outdoor Recreation Group
PO Box 270, Tulsa, OK 74115
(918) 831-6857
FAX: (918) 831-6938
President: Larry McIsaacs
Unit Mgr: Clifford Ginn
Year after year, more families count on Zebco for rods, reels & combos that offer great performance and advanced features, but are stil as easy to use as they are to afford.

ROD BUILDERS

Marc Aroner Bamboo Rods
PO Box 81, Conway, MA 01341
(413) 773-9920
Contact: Marc Aroner
Makes four series of Tonkin rods, beginning with the Fishing Creek Series at $1,045 and ending with the Aroner Series at $2,500. All rods come with two tips and a brass-topped case.

T. Avery Flyrods
2418 Roanoke Dr., Boise, ID 83712
(208) 389-4667
Contact: Tuck Miller
High-end custom rods...graphite or bamboo.

Bill Ballan Rods
230 Seaman Ave., Bayport, NY 11705
(516) 472-0744
FAX: (516) 472-0744
Est.: 1985
Contact: Gail Ballan
The finest 4-wt. trout rod on the market. A green blank, solid maple insert, slide band. 8 ft. & 7 1/2 ft. Immediate. Call today.

The Bamboo Broker
2041 S. 380th St.
Federal Way, WA 98003

(206) 838-7939
Contact: Charles F. Vaden
Distributor of Paul French custom rod builder.

Biscayne Rod Mfg. Co., Inc.
425 E. 9th St., Hialeah, FL 33010
(305) 884-0808
FAX: (305) 884-3017
Est.: 1948
President: Kenneth S. Carman
VP: Eddie Carman
Designing "custom rods" is nothing new for Biscayne Rods. Each angler today is looking for different rods to meet their specific needs in casting capabilities and fish fighting characteristics. Biscayne Rod takes the time to build the angler what they need around performance and capabilities for their fishing situations.

Bitterroot Rods
W. 3526 Princeton
Spokane, WA 99205
(509) 328-0179
Custom hand-planed split bamboo fly rods.

Lon Blauvelt
15 Town Landing Rd.
Falmouth, ME 04105
(207) 781-5235
Contact: Lou Blauvelt
Bamboo fly rods made to order, appraised; antique rods bought and sold–adjustable metal planing forms. Rod building classes.

Bradford Bamboo Rods
3700 Lawndale
Ft. Worth, TX 76133
(817) 292-3324
FAX: (817) 263-4404
Est.: 1952
Contact: John A. Bradford
Maker and restorer of classic split bamboo fly rods since 1952.

Brandin Split Cane
c/o Bamboo Rod Shop
10254 San Pablo Ave.
El Cerrito, CA 94530
(510) 527-4486   Est.: 1985
Owner: Per Brandin
Maker of 4 and 6 strip bamboo fly rods, baitcasting rods and special tournament rods.

Bud's Bugs
Custom Rods
26183 Chambers Ave.
Sun City, CA 92586
(909) 679-1647
FAX: (909) 679-1647
Est.: 1988
Owner: Robert (Bud) J. Nichols, II
Custom fishing rods and rod repair.

C.F. Burkheimer Fly Rod Designs
372 Laurel Lane
Washougal, WA 98671-7033
(360) 837-2701
FAX: (360) 837-3064
Contact: Kerry Burkheimer
Individualized fly rods designed and meticulously finished. Repair and restoration work done on all Russ Peak "Zenith" glass and graphite rods.

C.W. "Sam" Carlson
971 Rt. 31, Box 322
Greenville, NH 03048
(603) 878-1455
Est.: 1957
Contact: C.W. Carlson
Classic bamboo rod builder

Hoagy B. Carmichael
Crosby Rd., North Salem, NY 10560
(914) 277-8611 (Home)
Contact: Hoagy B. Carmichael

Walt Carpenter, Rodmaker
Box 52, Huntington Mills, PA 18622
(717) 477-3571
FAX: (717) 477-3571
Est.: 1905
Owners: Walt or Marcia Carpenter
The only remaining bamboo rod builder, having worked at both L.F. Payne & H.L. Lenoard in the Hudson Valley/Catskill School of Rodmaking.

W. Cattanach Rod Co.
15315 Apple Ave.
Casnovia, MI 49318
(616) 675-5894
Est.: 1982
Contact: Wayne Cattanach
Handcrafted bamboo fly rods; bamboo rod making classes. Author of "Handcrafting Bamboo Fly Rods".

Croce Rod Company
I-26 Lambert Rd.
Fair Lawn, NJ 07410
(201) 791-1774
Contact: John
Maker of the finest hand planed bamboo flyrods.

Custom Craft
PO Box 2032, Waterloo, IA 50704
(319) 236-0088
FAX: (319) 236-0088
Est.: 1981
Owner: Robert Oaks
Highest quality rod construction of all types. Complete line of components.

Custom Fishing Tackle
190 Parrish St., 71-6A
Canandaigua, NY 14424

The Ulrich Custom Rod™ Is Based On New Design

The search for a better fly rod led Jack Ulrich to invent his own. With greater sensitivity, comfort and performance as his objectives, Jack created the Ulrich Custom Rod, a fishing instrument based on a new design concept that delivers all three qualities.

A resident of Boston, New York, and an avid fly fisherman, Jack noted that the cork or foam that encase the handles of commercially manufactured rods have a dampening effect that diminishes sensitivity and the "feel" of a strike. The solution: a hardwood handle—at times customized to the grip of the individual angler—that results in highly magnified telegraphic properties. Combined with proper guide spacing, the wood handle also contributes to better power transfer for longer, easier and more accurate casting.

Custom grips—an extension of the arm.

Pleased by his prototype, Jack decided to share the advantages of his design, and used it to establish his highly successful custom rod business. But Ulrich Custom Rods are distinguished from others by a great deal more than a superior handle. The production of a rod begins with the customer's selection of the finest graphite rod blanks available. Each blank is tested to determine which is its stiffer side, or spine. Then the spine is positioned for optimal placement of guides and reel seat. This step alone has a significant effect on casting accuracy. If the spine is off to one side, the rod will twist in the hand, spoiling accuracy, presentation and performance.

Forming a Single Unit

Based on a customer's preference, Jack selects wood for the handle to conform to the type and length of the rod. Then he fits the handle to precisely match the diameter and taper of the blank. Next, handle and blank are bonded with an epoxy type adhesive to form a single, solid unit.

Now Jack determines the proper type and placement of guides. He grinds and tapers the guide feet so they will flex with the action of the rod, a step that is omitted with commercial rods and some custom rods. Without this process, which allows windings to be applied smoothly and evenly, the absence of flex causes stress points where rod and guide press together. Performance is lessened and thread damage and breakage can occur.

The final steps in hand-craftsmanship involve the temporary attachment of guides to rod. Then, in a process called "loading," line is run through the guides and a strain is put on the rod. The guides are adjusted for optimal load distribution, then custom-wrapped and triple-coated with an epoxy finish.

An Extension of the Arm

Another service of Ulrich Custom Rod is customized grips that help make a fly rod a veritable extension of the arm. The customer chooses the rod blank and species of wood and sends a tracing of his hand on a piece of paper and indicates if he holds the grip towards the front, back or middle. Jack turns the handle on a lathe for the size of the hand and position of the palm swell. He then returns the partially completed handle to the customer. The customer traces his hand on the handle while holding it as he would while casting or fishing. And when the handle comes back, Jack power carves and hand-sands until the thumb and finger grooves are a perfect match to the individual's hand.

The company also produces spinning and baitcasting rods. Offering customers numerous options, Ulrich Custom Rod prices range from the low hundreds to more than $800. A brochure with price list is available by calling Ulrich Custom Rod at 716-941-5310 or 1-800-255-RODS. Dealer inquiries are welcome.

(716) 396-9706
FAX: (719) 396-9706
Est.: 1996
Owner: David Michaloski
Custom fishing rods, flies, lures &
rod cases.

Drewry Rod Company
3469 Fitzgerald Rd.
Rancho Cordova, CA 96742
(916) 923-0408
Custom fishing rods built to order
for the ultimate fishing experience.

Douglas J. Duck
3821 Hollow Creek Rd.
Ft. Worth, TX 76116
(817) 731-2524
FAX: (817) 731-9038
Contact: Douglas J. Duck
Maker of split bamboo fly rods.

Eilers Rod Shop
938 Fault Line Ave.
North Pole, AK 99705
(907) 488-0469
FAX: (907) 488-0469
Est.: 1978
Contact: Paul or Scott Eilers
Custom built to your specifications.
Built on your choice of blanks,
Loomis, Sage, Pacific Bay cedar.

The Forks Fly Shop
74 McKenzie St.
Inglewood, Ontario
Canada L0N 1K0
(905) 838-3332
Contact: Wayne Martin
Custom built fly rods.

Foss Unlimited
9604 NE Wyant Rd.
Kingston, WA 98346
Contact: Julia Foss

J.W. Gallas Rod Co.
7 Mirijo Rd., Danbury, CT 06811
(203) 790-4188
Contact: John Gallas
Maker of custom cane fly rods
since 1980. Original dry fly and par-
abolic models. Traditional styling.

Ted Godfrey's
3509 Pleasant Plains Dr.
Reisterstown, MD 21136
(410) 239-8468
FAX: (410) 239-8468
Est.: 1972   Staff: 2
Owner: Ted Godfrey
Co-Owner: Faye Godfrey
Custom hand-made reels, rods
(Sage blank); 2-hand rods and flies
for Atlantic salmon, steelhead and
trout.

Golden Witch Rods
4040 8th Ave., Unit #3
Seattle, WA 98105

(206) 545-1974
Rodcrafter: John Gooding

Custom Rods by Grandt
PO Box 4373,
Arlington Heights, IL 60006-4373
(847) 577-0848
FAX: (847) 577-9853
Est.: 1980
Contact: Jim Grandt
Manufacture high end graphite
and bamboo rods. Custom rods by
a 2-time National Rod Building
Champion. Expertly crafted Tonkin
cane and graphite rods. Featuring
fly rods from 5'6" and 2-3 Trout
rods through 15-wt Billfish rods.
Call today.

M. Guido Rod Co.
c/o The Martin Company
PO Box 1461, Kamiah, ID 83536
(800) 705-0367
Contact: Greg Martin
"There is something magical about
shooting a ninety foot fly line to
within inches of a steelhead's
nose." Mel has been making rods
that perform this way for 20 years.
Call for ordering information.

**Duane Hufstedler
Custom Fly Rods**
1409 Glendale Dr.
Abilene, TX 79603
(915) 676-8739
Contact: Duane Hufstedler
Custom split-cane, fiberglass and
Hexagraph® fly rods, and classic
cane rod restoration.

**Interior Alaska
Custom Built Rods**
6399 Cahill Ave., E.
Inver Grove Heights, MN 55076
(800) 455-5593   (612) 455-5583
Est.: 1982
Owner: Cedric A. Knuckey
Custom built fishing rods, accesso-
ries, rod building blanks, and parts.
Over 23 years in the trade. Hand-
crafted graphite rods; hand tied, no
machine used. Lifetime warranty
on all work. All phases of repair.
Free catalogs.

J.C. Rods
PO Box 370, Pine Grove, IA 95665
(209) 223-3217
FAX: (209) 223-3217
Contact: John Christlieb
Private label manufacturer of high-
quality custom fly rods for retailers.

The C.W. Jenkins Fly Rod
5735 S. Jericho Way
Aurora, CO 80015
(303) 699-9128
Est.: 1961

Contact: Steve Jenkins
Finely crafted cane rods for over 30
years. Repair, refinishing and restoration. Quantities limited. Call or
write for a brochure.

H.L. Jennings
3050 Richmond Dr.
Colorado Springs, CO 80922
(719) 573-8923
Est.: 1972
Contact: Homer Jennings
Old world quality. Handcrafted split
bamboo rod maker. Defective parts
replaced or repaired, free of
charge. Custom rod inquiries are
welcome and prices will be quoted
as required.

Kane Klassics

Kane Klassics Rod Company
PO Box 8124, Fremont, CA 94537
(510) 487-8545   (800) 331-6406
FAX: (510) 487-6448
Est.: 1988
Contact: Douglas Kulick
At Kane Klassics Rod Company,
owner and maker Douglas Kulick
produces superb hand planed bamboo fly rods in sizes from trout to
tarpon in one piece rods to six
piece pack rod variants. All bamboo
rods are made from 45-year old
aged Tonkin cane, one at a time.
His taper designs are matched to
today's fly lines offering slow, medium or "graphite-like" fast actions.
All rods carry a lifetime warranty
and are built to the fly fisher's requirements. He performs bamboo
rod restoration on all makes of rods
and, in fact, restored bamboo fly
rods for the movie "The River Runs
Through It".
See Our Ad Pg. 100

Robbie Kerr's Fly Inn
6927 Amherst St., #3
San Diego, CA 92115
(619) 461-6118
Contact: Bob Kerr

King Custom Rod Co.
44 Singer Rd.
New Freedom, PA 17349
(717) 227-0183
FAX: (717) 227-0183
Est.: 1996
Owner: Charles King
Handcrafted graphite rods featur-
ing G. Loomis, Powell, T&T blanks.
Custom nickel silver reel seats. Ex-
ceptional woods.

Kingfisher Custom Rods
4350 Airport Rd., #5-451
Sante Fe, NM 87505
(505) 473-2004
FAX: (505) 471-7010
Contact: David Perlowin
Custom rod builder–graphite only.

Dave Klausmeyer's New England Angler
PO Box 105
Steuben, ME 04680
(207) 546-2018
Est.: 1986   Staff: 2
Contact: Dave Klausmeyer
Specialize in custom split cane and graphite rods.

Loon Custom Fly Rods
133 Safran Ave.
Edison, NJ 08837
(908) 738-9451   (908) 661-1916
Contact: Jerald Smit
Hand-crafted custom built graphite fly rods.

F.D. Lyons Rod Co.
7156 S.E. 118th Dr.
Portland, OR 97266
(503) 760-3933
Contact: Dwight Lyons
Builds, repairs and restores fiber-glass, cane and graphite rods using vintage blanks and components.

Maclin Custom
Box 975, Londonderry, NH 03053
(603) 437-3076
Contact: Ron McKinley
Maker & restorer of fine custom rods.

Maloney Fly Rods
314 Vista Del Mar
Camarillo, CA 92806
(805) 643-2609
Contact: Michael Maloney
Custom rod tuning.

Manhattan Custom Tackle
913 Broadway, 2nd Floor
New York, NY 10010
(800) 219-2000   (212) 505-6690
FAX: (212) 505-1922
Contact: Phil Koenig

T.L. Maxwell Rods
275 Music Mountain Rd.
Falls Village, CT 06031
(860) 824-7349
Contact: Tom Maxwell

Maynard Rods Unlimited
PO Box 54, Sloatsburg, NY 10974
(201) 616-1289   Est.: 1979
Contact: Darren M. Maynard
Fine custom crafted fly rods. A truly exquisite collection of the finest hand finished graphite fly rods. 2

to 12 weight. 6 to 9 feet. 2 to 4 pieces. Custom services available.

Mill Creek Fishing Rods
1007 Goat Trail Loop
Mukilteo, WA 98275
(800) 455-2530   (206) 355-2530
Contact: Kathy Seaman
Heirloom quality rods, individually crafted. Only the finest components used. Custom crafted by Jim & Kathy Seaman.

Tom Morgan Rodsmiths
21505 Norris Rd.
Manhattan, MT 59741
(406) 282-7110
FAX: (406) 282-7167
Contact: Tom W. Morgan
Rodsmiths™ Rods incorporate a lighter and stronger graphite material and new blank taper design. Fly fishers who have fished with Rodsmiths™ prototypes say these are the sweetest casting and best fishing rods they have ever handled. Only 100 rods per year in line sizes 2 - 6. Retail customers only.

Native Custom Rods
10571 Northview Dr.
North Benton, OH 44449
(216) 584-2468   FAX: 2414
Owner: Barry Bonno

**New River
Custom Rodcrafters**
PO Box 1656, Jefferson, NC 28640
(910) 877-3122
Contact: Gregory Hershner
Hand crafted rods built to your
unique specifications. Blanks by
Sage, Powell, and more.

PTM Rod Design
10650 Eagle Rock NE
Albuquerque, NM 87122
(505) 822-1320
Contact: Pete Mocho
Specializes in unique ornamenta-
tion of custom fly rods.

Parker Rods
245 East Line Rd.
Ballston Lake, NY 12019
(518) 899-2629
FAX: (518) 899-2629
Contact: Jon Parker
Maker of hand planed split bamboo fly rods. Call, write or fax for
information.

Performance Fly Rods
Rt. 4, Box 440
Harrisonburg, VA 22801
(540) 867-0856
FAX: (540) 867-0951
Est.: 1988
Contact: Dave Lewis
Custom crafted graphite fly rods by
Dave Lewis. All in-stock rods are
built on Sage, G. Loomis, Pacific
Bay Talon, St. Croix or Performance
blanks. For a truly beautiful fly rod
for about factory prices, consider a
Performance Fly Rod by Dave
Lewis. Satisfaction guaranteed. Call
or write for information.

Walton Powell
1329 W. Lindo Ave.
Chico, CA 95926
(916) 895-8923
FAX: (916) 895-8946
Contact: Diane Powell

**Diane Powell's Graphite
Tubular Fishing Rods**
1329 W. Lindo Ave.
Chico, CA 95926
(916) 343-3769
FAX: (916) 895-8946
Contact: Diane Powell
The ultimate in design and construction, these graphite fishing rods are
made to your specifications (length,
type of action, and weight of line).
Meant to be fished for a lifetime
and then passed on to the next gen-
eration. Write, FAX or call for
further information.

Quilceda Rod Works
928 Marine Dr., NE
Marysville, WA 98271
(360) 652-7204
Est.: 1993
Contact: Steve Gobin
Custom built bamboo fly rods, medium progressive action,
specializing in midge rods 3-5 wt.

Rangeley Rod Co.
PO Box 1270, Rangeley, ME 04970
(207) 864-3898
Contact: Mel Jones
Classic hand planed fly rods ex-
pertly crafted using the finest
bamboo and nickel silver findings.
Call or write for free information.

Raptor Rod
2563 Kennedy Ave., Chico, CA
95973
(916) 894-2062
FAX: (916) 894-1230
Est.: 1995   Staff: 2
Owner: Jim Clarkson
High quality custom rods, glass,
graphite & bamboo. Full service repair & restoration.

Redington Custom Rods
3087 S.E. Dixie Hwy.
Stuart, FL 34997
(407) 220-8108
Contact: Matt Potsko
All types of custom rods, from ultra
light to unlimited. Expert bamboo
restoration 10 years experience. All
work guaranteed.

BJ Reynolds
8172 Ammons Way
Arvada, CO 80005
(303) 421-3287
Custom graphite fly rods, trout to
tarpon. Best components, lifetime
warranty.

Ridgewood Custom Rods
4 Briston Ct., Bedford, NH 03110
(603) 668-4383
Est.: 1987
Contact: Edward Verow
Superior craftsmanship in fine fly
rods. Built to order for the discerning angler. Limited availability.
References available.

Rocky Creek Rods
4566 Bozeman Trail Rd.
Bozeman, MT 59715
(406) 587-7838
(406) 586-4140
Contact: John B. Stewart

Rocky Mountain Kane, Inc.
100 E. Cleveland
Lafayette, CO 80026
(303) 666-7866
FAX: (303) 742-2361

Est.: 1992
President: Joe E. Arguello
Secretary: Verna L. Arguello
Email: rckymtkane@aol.com
Custom handcrafted bamboo fly
rods

Rodmakers, Inc.
7739 Northcross Dr.
Austin, TX 78757
(512) 452-7637
FAX: (512) 452-7902
Contact: Sam Pole

Roth Angling
Box 602,
Manitou Springs, CO 80829
(719) 685-0316
Est.: 1973
Contact: Mark Roth
Fine custom-built Sage, Scott, T&T,
Winston rods at factory prices. Life-
time warranty. References gladly.
Free catalog.

Schaaf Rod Shop
PO Box 535, Concord, CA 94521
(510) 682-9144
Contact: Jim Schaaf

D.G. Schroeder Rod Co.
3822 Brunswick Lane
Janesville, WI 53546
(608) 752-1520
Contact: Don Schroeder
Custom split cane fly rods

Sigman Cane Rods
968 Admiral Callaghan Lane
Suite 182, Vallejo, CA 94591
(800) 292-2840
Contact: Robert Sigman
Custom made cane rods

South Creek Ltd.
PO Box 981, Lyons, CO
80540-0981
(800) 354-5050   (303) 823-6402
FAX: (303) 823-0332
Est.: 1979
Contact: Mike Clark
Custom builder of split bamboo fish-
ing rods...over 19 years experience.
Call or write for more information.

The M.K. Spittler Company
4119 Columbus Ave., S.
Minneapolis, MN 55407
(612) 822-9376
FAX: (612) 822-9376
Contact: Michael Spittler
Available: Direct
Quadrate fly rods featuring fluted
hollow construction. 24 models
priced from $1,295 to $1,495.

R.W. Summers Co.
90 River Rd. East
Traverse City, MI 49686
(616) 946-7923

FAX: (616) 946-7923
Est.: 1956
Contact: Bob Summers
Builder of fine Tonkin cane rods.

Sweet Water Rods
151 Sutter Rd.
Lenhartsville, PA 19534
(610) 756-6385
Contact: George E. Maurer
Hand planed bamboo rods, components & accessories. Bamboo rod building workshops. Models from 6'3" to 8'6", 3-6 wt. Custom tapers available. Call or write for additional information.

Swift River Fly Fishing
RFD1, 25 N. Main St.
New Salem, MA 01355
(508) 544-2582
Contact: Rick Taupier
Exceptional quality fresh and saltwater custom graphite rods at reasonable prices. Fisher, Thomas & Thomas, and Loomis blanks. Call or send for price list.

BAMBOO RODS

A.J. Thramer Bamboo Rod Co.
645 Powers, Unit C,
Eugene, OR 97402
Contact: A.J. Thramer
The A.J. Thramer Rod Co. supplies a high quality line of darkly flamed rods in both 2 and 3 piece configurations. The rods feature 100% nickel silver fittings and modern taper design. The prices start at $695. Request a catalog by mail. Sales and ordering information is being handled exclusively through Len Codella at Heritage Sporting Collectibles, (352) 637-5454.

Randy Towe
Custom Rod Builder
Box 1571, Islamorada, FL 33036
(305) 852-4237
FAX: (305) 852-4480
Contact: Randy Towe

Trela Custom Rods
Div. of D.T. Kustom Tackle
16 Woodland Heights
Ware, MA 01082
(413) 967-3430
Contact: Dan Trela
Custom rods using G. Loomis, Sage Blanks and REC components.

Tuxedo Custom Rod
PO Box 1167, Stockton, CA 95201
(209) 464-6133
FAX: (209) 948-6757
Contact: Don Calcaterra
Quality rods built with your fishing needs in mind.

ULRICH'S CUSTOM RODS

Jack Ulrich's Custom Rods
9167 South Hill Rd.
Boston, NY 14025
(800) 255-7637   (716) 941-5310
Est.: 1990
Contact: Jack Ulrich
Custom rods made with a hardwood handle fitted to the customer's hand with thumb grove and finger groves. Customer chooses wood species. G. Loomis, Sage, St. Croix blanks. Call or write for information.
See Our Ad Pg. 107

Vilord's Custom Rods
215 N. 3700 East, Rigby, ID 83442
(208) 745-0851
Est.: 1985   Staff: 2
Owner: Christopher Vilord
High performance fly rods at a moderate price.

J.D. Wagner
6549 Kingsdale Blvd.
Cleveland, OH 44130
(216) 845-4415
Contact: J.D. Wagner
Fine hand planed split cane rods; repair and restoration.

Art Weiler Rods
313 East St., Bound Brook, NJ 08805
(908) 469-9496
Contact: Art Weiler
Specialty cane rods, graphite UL spin and light-line fly rods and custom rods. Whether you select our fine Heritage Rods Garrison repro-

duction, our faster action Small Stream Rod, or our Custom Graphite Rods, you can rest assured we will do all we can to make sure the rod is "just right" for you. Hand planing fine fly rods for 20 years. We will be happy to discuss with you (call/write) the potential uses and characteristics of each rod.

White River Artisans School
202 South Ave., PO Box 308
Cotter, AR 72626
(501) 435-2600
FAX: (501) 435-1600
Est.: 1992
Contact: Don Cleveland
Bamboo fly rod making workshops

D.L. Whitehead Rod Co.
611 NW 48th St.
Seattle, WA 98107
(206) 781-0133
FAX: (206) 781-0831
Est.: 1987
Contact: Daryll Whitehead
Custom hand planed bamboo fly rods. Presentation grades, hand engraved nickel silver fittings, leather cases.

Whitely Rods
PO Box 1981, Tustin, CA 92681
(714) 832-0089
Contact: Paul L. Whitely
High-quality split-bamboo rods and rod blanks. Handcrafted 6' to 8 1/2', 2 and 3 pieces. Call or write for a free catalog. (Dealers and wholesalers welcome.)

Mario Wojnicki
10254 San Pablo Ave.
El Cerrito, CA 94530
Contact: Mario Wojnicki

The Wright Rod Co.
45 Churchill Rd.
Websterville, VT 05678
(802) 476-6125
Contact: Steve May
High quality, hand crafted graphite rods. Call or write us for more details on the "one rod that covers all situations."

Paul H. Young Rod Co.
535 W. Front St.
Traverse City, MI 49684
(616) 929-4800
FAX: (616) 929-4800   Est.: 1914
Contact: Todd Young
Finest quality split bamboo flyrods. Pre-embargo cane only. Exclusive flame tempering. Restoration on all makes.

ROD BUILDING

Designing a fly rod involves a number of decisions concerning rod length and action, the type of reel seat and the type of guides to be incorporated, the shape of the rod's handle and the color of the thread used for wrapping.

The topics covered in this chart are intended to provide a broad overview of some of these elements. To build your own rod you will need to work with an experienced rod builder, attend a rod building clinic or school or refer to one of the many books on rod building now available, including *Start to Finish Fly Rod Building** from which this material is adapted.

Blank Selection The single most important decision involved in the rod building process, blank selection is really a matter of determining the preferred action, length and line weight rating of the finished rod. [See article on Choosing a Rod for a more detailed discussion of these topics.]

Fly Rod Guides

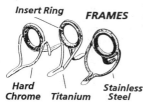

Hard Chrome   Titanium   Stainless Steel

Stripping guides: Most fly rods have one, two or three stripping guides that typically contain an insert ring within the frame. Quality depends on the material used to make the guide and the ring. Sizes run from #8 to # 20, as shown:

Actual Size

⑧ ⑩ ⑫ ⑯ 20

Guide Rings Measured in Millimeters

Wire Guides: Available in double foot ("snake guides") and single foot styles, in a variety of finishes.

Double Foot Snake   Single Foot Wire

Actual Size

2/0 1/0 1 2 3 4 5 6

Numbers assigned to guides by early wire guide manufacturers

Ring

Frame

Single Foot Guides With Inserts: Single foot guides can be used in place of wire guides. Again, quality depends on the composition of the guide frame and insert ring.

Guide Rings Measured in Millimeters   5.5—O ⑥ ⑦ ⑧ ⑩

Actual Size

Tip Tops Wire guides need a traditional fly rod tip top, available in standard or large ring sizes. The tube sizes of these tip tops are given in 1/64ths of an inch and generally range from 3.5 to 7.5. Rods with single foot fly rod guides and inserts use a tip with the same insert and guide frame composition. These tip tops are generally available in size 7 (standard) or size 8 (large).

Tip Tops with Insert Ring

Traditional Tip Tops

measured in 64ths inches   **Large**   **Standard**

• • • • • ● ● ● ●

3.5 4 4.5 5 5.5 6 6.5 7 7.5

Tip tube sizes measured in 64ths of an inch

Reel Seats The basic choice of material (all metal, graphite, and metal with insert material) for a reel seats depends on desired weight, strength, durability, appearance and ultimate cost.

Grip Shapes

Reverse Half Wells: Most popular grip on modern freshwater fly rods.

Cigar: A traditional grip used on freshwater rods.

Half Wells: Generally used on saltwater or heavier freshwater rods.

Full Wells: The most popular grip for saltwater fly rods.

* **Source:** *Start to Finish Fly Rod Building*, Copyright Flex Coat Co., Inc.

ROD BUILDING COMPONENTS

AER Custom Sporting Equip.
6551 Clark Rd., Bath, MI 48808
(800) 532-5481 (Orders)
(517) 641-7277
FAX: (517) 641-6790
Contact: Al Rohen
Manufacturer and distributor of
quality rod building components.
Wholesale only.

American Tackle, Ltd.
940 Old Post Rd.
Cotuit, MA 02635
(800) 516-1750
FAX: (800) 966-9430
Est.: 1984
President: Joe Meehan, III
CEO: Joe Meehan, Jr.
Importers-exporters of rods, reels &
rod building components. Featuring
affordable graphite fly reels & rods.

ANGLER'S Workshop

Angler's Workshop
PO Box 1010, 1350 Atlantic Ave.
Woodland, WA 98674
(360) 225-9445 (Orders)
(360) 225-8641 (Fax-Worldwide)
FAX: (800) 278-1069
Web Site: http://www.an-
glersworkshop.com
Angler's Workshop is celebrating
its 17th year supplying the rod
builder and fly tyer with hard-to-
find materials. Worldwide shipping.
Shop in Angler's Workshop catalog
to find rod blanks, rod kits and components as well as an excellent
supply of fly tying materials, rods,
reels, lines, flies and more. We are
cork import specialists supplying
manufacturers and retailers with
the finest cork rings and preform
handles. As the North American distributors for Hopkins and Holloway,
we supply the best fly guides made
to the largest fly fishing market.
See Our Ad Pg. 61

Anglers World Corp.
PO Box 1377, Foley, AL 36536
(334) 943-4491   (334) 943-4492
FAX: (334) 943-4493
President: Carl Haber
Importers of Fuji rod building com-
ponents, including tips, guides reel
seats, etc.–wholesale only.

C. Beard Co.
Box 2525, Loveland, CO 80539
(970) 227-4707
FAX: (970) 667-9425
Contact: Tom Clinkenbeard
Manufacturer and distributor of fly
rod components, including reel
seats and preformed cork grips.
The best service for custom cork
shapes! Wholesale only.

Bellinger Reel Seats
2017 25th St., S.E.
Salem, OR 97302
(503) 371-6151
FAX: (503) 371-3771
Est.: 1981
Contact: Al Bellinger
Expanded line of reel seats and
choice woods–wholesale only.

Biscayne Rod Mfg. Co., Inc.
425 E. 9th St., Hialeah, FL 33010
(305) 884-0808
FAX: (305) 884-3017
President: Kenneth S. Carman
VP: Eddie Carman
Due to the fact that Biscayne Rod
business is 95% saltwater anglers,
we sell only the highest quality components on the market. Tested and
proven. If we won't put it on our
rods, we don't sell it. We carry
every component needed to build
your own rod. We also have 1
piece, 21' push poles available.

C&D Trading
6451 Lyndale Ave., S.
Richfield, MN 55423
(612) 574-1563
FAX: (612) 572-9876
Est.: 1967
Contact: Chris Kishish
We specialize in high quality cork
handles. Inventory 5 fly fishing handles–and you have the opportunity
to custom order from 100's of patterns in quantities of 250 units.
Please call for information and brochure.

**Classic Sporting
Enterprises, Inc.**
Roaring Brook Rd.
RD#3, Box 3, Barton, VT 05822
(802) 525-3623
FAX: (802) 525-3982
Contact: Bailey Wood
Precision machined reel seats,
Super Swiss & Super S-D nickel sil-
ver ferrules and rod fittings, hook
keepers and other hard to find com-
ponents.

Cork Specialties
1454 N.W. 78 Ave.
Miami, FL 33126

(305) 477-1506
FAX: (305) 591-0593
Contact: Ralph Figueroa
8 styles of fly grips—wholesale
OEM only.

Cortland Line Co.
3736 Kellogg Rd.
PO Box 5588, Cortland, NY 13045
(607) 756-2851
FAX: (607) 753-8835
Contact: Tom McCullough
Over 15 styles of reel seats are available in clear, black, brown and
anodized aluminum models. Large
selection of pre-shaped and pre-
sanded top grade cork grips.
Colorful, polished impregnated
wood spacers and a complete line
of components to give your blank
the look of perfection. Call or write
for free color brochure.

Charles H. Demarest Inc.
Box 238, Bloomingdale, NJ 07403
(201) 492-1414
FAX: (201) 838-6538
Contact: Harold or Eileen Demarest
Importers of Tonkin bamboo

East Branch Rods
43 Aimweg St., Jay, NY 12941
(800) 337-EROD
FAX: (518) 946-7413
Contact: George Erik Jobson
East Branch kits include blank, reel
seat, cork grip, guides, winding
check, winding thread, Flex Coat finish, color preserver, rod bag &
tube.

**"Elephant" Silk Rod
Binding Thread**
Distributed by Belvoirdale
PO Box 176, Wyncote, PA 19095
(215) 886-7211
FAX: (215) 886-1804
President: Grahame Maisey
The only silk thread produced exclu-
sively for rod binding. Limited
stocks of solid and jasper threads.

Elite Products
12 Plants Dam Rd.
East Lyme, CT 06333
(860) 739-8185
FAX: (860) 739-0680
Est.: 1987
Contact: John McBride
Importer of quality 2 pc., 3 pc. & 4
pc. IM6 blanks-6'6" 3 wt.-15'10 wt.

The Fisher Company
Box 3147, Carson City, NV 89702
(702) 246-5220
FAX: (702) 246-5143
Contact: Kent Gasch

ible rod finish epoxy–will not yellow or crack in sunlight. Loon's Rod Bonding Adhesive is a durable, aerospace grade bonding adhesive for securing rod parts. Call or fax for more information.

"S. Maisey" Handmade Rod Components
Distributed by Belvoidale
PO Box 176, Wyncote, PA 19095
(215) 886-7211
FAX: (215) 886-1804
President: Grahame Maisey
Handmade ferrules and reel seats

Osprey Fly Fishers Custom Rods
912 24th Ave., Altoona, PA 16601
(814) 946-8851
Contact: Ralph Diehl
Superb quality blanks, major manufacturers. Fine classic components, finishing materials, complete rod building kits. Catalog available.

Pace Industries, Inc.
6720 NW 15th Way
Ft. Lauderdale, FL 33309
(954) 975-6333
FAX: (954) 975-6422
Contact: Michael Piluso
Supplier of cork handles–wholesale only. All types of cork products.

Pacific Bay Fishing Tackle
540 S. Jefferson St.
Placentia, CA 92670
(714) 524-1778
FAX: (714) 524-2066
Est.: 1976
Contact: Bob Batson
Complete line of rod building components and made in USA graphite rod blanks.

Flex Coat Co., Inc.
Box 190, Driftwood, TX 78619
(512) 858-7742
FAX: (512) 858-7852
Contact: Roger Seiders
Flex Coat is a manufacturer of two-part polymer epoxy rod finishes.

Grand Rod & Tackle Co.
645 W. Oak St.
Oak Harbor, WA 98277
(360) 675-0444
FAX: (360) 679-6681
Contact: Craig Dixon
Fly rod accoutrements. Nickel silver reel seats with highly figured inserts & presentation boxes hand polished, round solid wood rod cases.

Gudebrod, Inc.
PO Box 357, Pottstown, PA 19464
(610) 327-4050
FAX: (610) 327-4588
President: Robert Marquardt
Fly Fishing Sales Mgr: Robert Graham
Gudebrod offers a full line of rod winding threads in various sizes and colors, and chemical rod finishes for the hobbyist and OEM manufacturer.

Lamiglas, Inc.
1400 Atlantic, PO Box U
Woodland, WA 98674
(360) 225-9436
FAX: (360) 225-5050
Sales Mgr: Mike Wardian
email: lamiglas@pacifier.com
Graphite rods available in IM700, LHS2, Certified Pro and G1000 (GF). Fiberglass available in smooth black or "flamed cane" cosmetics.

LOON OUTDOORS
7737 W. Mossy Cup St.
Boise, ID 83709
(800) 580-3811
FAX: (800) 574-0422
Contact: Ken Smith
Envirogloss Rod Finish is a clear, flex-

Perfection Tip Co.
1340 W. Cowles
Long Beach, CA 90813
(310) 491-0076
FAX: (800) 733-5763
Est.: 1917
Customer Svc. Mgr: Larry Jenkins
Perfection Tip Company has an outstanding selection of guides & tops.

Walton Powell Reel Seats
1329 W. Lindo Ave.
Chico, CA 95926
(916) 895-8923
FAX: (916) 895-8946
Contact: Walton Powell

Powell Rod Company
PO Box 4000, Chico, CA 95926
(916) 345-3393
FAX: (916) 345-0567
Est.: 1910   Staff: 10
Contact: P. Biery

REC Components
Research Engineering Company
Harrel St., RR1, Box 1605
Morrisville, VT 05661-9704
(802) 888-7200
FAX: (802) 888-7021
Est.: 1970
Contact: Bill Alley or
Alan Gnann
Complete line of quality fly fishing
components. Specialists in nickel sil-
ver and custom parts.

Rainbow Sports
267 Oliver St.,
N. Tonawanda, NY 14120
(716) 692-7510
FAX: (716) 691-6860
Est.: 1976
Owner: Jack Tessier
Manager: Paul Tessier
Available: Direct
Full line tackle shop–specializing in
components.

Sevier
Manufacturing Inc.
2200 Clermont St.
Denver, CO 80207
(303) 322-3229
FAX: (303) 331-9844
Contact: Ted Sevier
Wholesale supplier of rod building
components, including blanks, tips,
reel seats, etc.
See Our Ad Across, Left

Shikäri

Shikari, Inc.
PO Box 549, Kellyville, OK 74039
(918) 247-3090
FAX: (918) 247-3269
Est.: 1992
Contact: Brian D. Kaupke
Shikari is a rod-blank manufacturer
offering exciting new blank designs
for rod builders. The extensive line
of blanks includes over 70 fly
blanks in standard, intermediate
and high modulus graphite. The
new SHX-HP fast-action blanks feature the latest rod designs and
composite technology. We aren't
your competition...we are your sup-
plier-partner. Call for a free catalog.
See Our Ad Above, Right

St. Croix Rod
856 4th Avenue, N.
Park Falls, WI 54552
(800) 826-7042
(715) 762-3226
FAX: (715) 762-3293
Est.: 1948
VP/Sales & Mktg: Jeff Schluter

Manufacturer of a complete line of
graphite and fiberglass rod blanks.
Distributor of components, handle
kits and rod building accessories.

Glenn Struble
Manufacturing Co.
1382 Duke Ave., PO Box 1370
Sutherlin, OR 97479-1370
(503) 459-1353
FAX: (503) 459-1312
Est.: 1974
Contact: Juanita Struble
Glenn Struble Manufacturing
makes a comprehensive line of reel
seats for fly fishermen. Dealer in-
quiries welcome.

Sully's® North
Columbia Sports
5376 N. Walnut,
Spokane, WA 99205
(509) 328-3585
FAX: (509) 738-6752
Gen. Mgr: Chuck Lindquist, II
An innovative rod-wrapping device
that offers significant advantages
over other such tools. Sully's, for example, maintains constant thread
tension while guides are being
wrapped. The unit is nicely constructed of hardwood, with a slick
waxed finish, and compact. It breaking down in seconds to a box 24"x
5"x 3".

Talon
736 Davidson, PO Box 907
Woodland, WA 98674
(360) 225-8247
FAX: (360) 225-7737
Est.: 1990
Contact: Janis Schmahl
U.S. fishing blank/rod manufac-
turer specializing in private labels,
custom colors, over 400 actions.

U-40 Rod Building Comp.
Trondak Inc., 11710 Airport Rd.
Everett, WA 98204
(800) 878-1492 (206) 290-7530
FAX: (206) 355-9101
Est.: 1971
Cust. Svc: Matt Hulsey
Rod building products for the dis-
criminating craftsman who
demands quality and technical ad-
vancement.

R.L. Winston Rod Co.
500 S. Main St.,
Twin Bridges, MT 59754
(406) 684-5674
FAX: (406) 684-5533
Est.: 1929
Contact: Mike Ewing
Offering a full line of reel seats.

Question or problem?
Give Black's Fly Fishing
a call 9 am - 5 pm E.S.T.
(908) 224-8700.

STORE FIXTURES

Dannick Design
1762 E. State St., Eagle, ID 83616
(208) 939-8275
FAX: (208) 377-4056
Contact: Dan Seniw
Point-of-Sale and trade show display racks for fly rods and rod cases. Sizes range from 12 rods to 60 rods. All display racks are hand finished oak and fine veneers.

The Loomis Co.
3931 1st Ave. S., Seattle, WA 98134
(206) 292-0111
FAX: (206) 292-8688
Contact: Doug Bryan
Manufacturer of custom rod displays, banners and decals for in store fixturing. Horizontal and vertical rod racks.

Muley Brand Inc.
713 Colt Dr., Loveland, CO 80537
(970) 622-0147
FAX: (970) 622-0147
Contact: Dan Mommer
Predesigned and built fly display cases for the fly tackle dealer store.

Signature Concepts
Box 1247, Ballston Lake, NY 12019
(518) 426-3214
FAX: (518) 426-4190
Est.: 1986   Staff: 25
President: Jeffrey R. Henry
Manufacturer of wood products for store fixturing unique to the flyfishing market.

Target Plastics
PO Box 3879, Salem, OR 97302
(503) 399-9710
FAX: (503) 399-0430
Manager: Melissa A. Hescock
Wall shelving, menu boards, point-of-purchase displays and more.

Windy Ridge Wood Design
PO Box 681468
Park City, UT 84068
(800) 262-KNOT   (801) 783-5588
FAX: (801) 783-2579
Contact: Gillian Baty
Design and manufacture P.O.P displays for manufacturers.
Mannequins, in 7 sizes that hold rods (plus dog and cat mannequins) for retailers.

WHOLESALERS

The wholesalers that appear in the following section provide thousands of retailers with fly fishing related products. Each is eager to hear from sporting goods retailers and buyers, tackle stores and bait shops. They are not, however, interested in working with individual consumers. Whenever you call one of the following companies for information or a catalog, please remember to say you saw their name in **Black's Fly Fishing**.

AWR
1437 Fayette St., El Cajon, CA 92020
(619) 448-3960
FAX: (619) 448-3973
Contact: Jack Autry

All Sports
Box 2530, Clackamas, OR 97015
(503) 650-7500
FAX: (503) 650-4191
Sales Mgr: Doug Bellmore

Alpine Tackle Supply, Inc.
15353 E. Hinsdale Circle, Unit I
Englewood, CO 80112
(303) 680-0661
FAX: (303) 766-3305
Contact: Vince Coleman
Full service flyfishing wholesaler. Great service, same day shipping.

American Rod & Gun Co.
Box 2820, Springfield, MO 65801
(800) 332-5377
FAX: (417) 887-9287
President: Burton Steinberg

Angler Accessories USA
4495 Sandpiper Circle
Boulder, CO 80301
(303) 530-1570
FAX: (303) 530-1957
Contact: Lew Erbes
Fly fishing accessories

Angler Sport Group
6619 Oak Orchard Rd.
Elba, NY 14058
(716) 757-9958
FAX: (716) 757-9066

President: Paul Betters
Sole U.S. distributor of Daiichi Hooks, Wheatley boxes and extensive line of fly boxes and related accessories.

Angler's Supply
445 Carmel St.
San Marcos, CA 92069
(619) 736-8229
FAX: (619) 736-4076
Est.: 1995   Staff: 12
Buyer: Mike Battistoni
N.S.M.: Bill Hutcheson
Available: Direct
Wholesaler of a variety of tackle including freshwater, saltwater and fly fishing equipment.

Anglers Image Inc.
5714 Clark Rd., Sarasota, FL 34233
(800) 858-0903
FAX: (941) 927-0560   Est.: 1990
President: Stan Sugerman
VP: Lynne Webb

B-17 Fly Tackle Ltd.
9164 Brady, Redford, MI 48239
(313) 255-2838
FAX: (313) 531-4233
Contact: Thom. Hnizdor

BT's Fly Fishing Products
3020 Secor Ave.,
Bozeman, MT 59715
(406) 585-0745
Contact: Al & Gretchen Beatty
The EZY Product Line–Custom Tied Flies, Materials and Supplies.

Dan Bailey's Fly Shop
Box 1019, Livingston, MT 59047
(800) 356-4052   (406) 222-1673
FAX: (406) 222-8450
Contact: Scott Sanchez
Dan Bailey's is a complete fly fishing supplier. They sell fly lines, waders, fly tying tools and materials, clothing and are the distributors for Dai-Riki hooks & leaders.

BELVOIRDALE

Belvoirdale
PO Box 176, Wyncote, PA 19095
(215) 886-7211
FAX: (215) 886-1804
President: Grahame Maisey
Importer and distributor of the world's finest sporting equipment from England.
-Dinsmores "Green Cushion" tin split and tin and lead split shot
-Dinsmores catch and release landing nets >

-Modular boxes for hooks, fly tying and flyfishing
-Gaelic Supreme premium handmade fly hooks
-Phoenix handmade silk flylines
-Limestoner floating flylines
-S. Maisey handmade rod components
-Elephant silk rod winding thread

Black Arrow, Inc.
2889 Kepler, Sainte-Foy, Quebec
Canada G1X 3V4
(418) 650-1200
FAX: (418) 650-0551
Est.: 1978
Black Arrow distributes a wide range of products–reels, rods, monofilament, waders, tackle boxes, fishing vests, accessories, boots and more–to over 30 different countries. Renowned service and quality products make Black Arrow a leader to thousands of satisfied customers.

Bonitz Brothers
910 Hassler Rd.
Harrisburg, PA 17109
(800) 825-7060
FAX: (717) 545-5250
Contact: Doug Bentzel

Canadian Feather Merchants Ltd.
PO Box 3434
Mission, B.C.
Canada V2V 4J5
(604) 826-2215
FAX: (604) 826-5547
Contact: D. Craig Black

Colorado Angler Supply
Box 471766, Denver, CO 80047
(800) 566-0369   (303) 343-7286
FAX: (303) 343-7429
Est.: 1991   Staff: 5
Contact: Ijaz A. Gureshi
Fly tying tools, material, fishing tools & accessories, feathers. House of Anglerhaus Tools & Zephr Tools.

The Danielson Co.
Box 1917, Auburn, WA 98071
(206) 854-1717
FAX: (206) 852-2794
Est.: 1944   Staff: 14
VP: Robert D. Buchanan
VP: Michael A. Zimmer
Promotional fly reels, flies, leaders, nets, fly boxes, eyewear, fishing vest and extensive terminal tackle.

Del Mar Distributing Co.
Box 270300,
Corpus Christi, TX 78427
(800) 580-8901
FAX: (512) 993-9260
Contact: Nita or Jack

Doug's Bugs
Box 14472, Santa Rosa, CA 95402
(707) 579-3474
FAX: (707) 527-8360
Contact: Doug Brutocao
Fly fishing books, videos, accessories and materials. Catalog for retail dealers only.

Equinox, Ltd.
1307 Park Ave.
Williamsport, PA 17701
(717) 322-5900
FAX: (717) 322-0746
Bags, fishing luggage, rod cases

Fanning Wholesale
Box 1815, 3600 Bombardier
Idaho Falls, ID 83403
(208) 522-8401
FAX: (208) 522-9906
Contact: Roy Leavitt

Fly-Rite, Inc.
7421 S. Beyer
Frankenmuth, MI 48734
(517) 652-9869
FAX: (517) 652-2996
Contact: Judith G. McCann

Folsom LA, Inc.
Box 23710, New Orleans, LA 70183
(504) 733-3142
FAX: (504) 734-7151
Contact: Bob Litt

Folsom of Florida
Box 19157, Tampa, FL 33686
(813) 839-2121
FAX: (813) 837-2217
Contact: Dave Davis

Frank's Tackle Supply
Jobstown-Juliustown Rd.
Jobstown, NJ 08041
(609) 723-0305
FAX: (609) 723-7352
Contact: Frank

Go Sportsmen's Supply
Box 20037, 1535 Industrial
Billings, MT 59104
(406) 252-2109
FAX: (406) 248-7767
Contact: Randy Opp

V.F. Grace
605 E. 13th, Anchorage, AK 99501
(907) 272-6431
FAX: (907) 272-7000
Contact: Chuck Rush

Grizzly Knife & Tackle
1821 Valencia St.
Bellingham, WA 98226
(360) 650-9141
FAX: (360) 676-1075
Est.: 1994   Staff: 5
Nat'l. Sales Mgr: Chris K. McBride
Exec. Ass't: Denise Amos

Wholesaler of fly tying tools, clippers-nipper, reels and fine cutlery.

Gudebrod, Inc.
PO Box 357, Pottstown, PA 19464
(610) 327-4050
FAX: (610) 327-4588
Sales Mgr: Robert Graham

Gunarama Wholesale
Box 3605, E. 4009 Mission Ave.
Spokane, WA 99202
(509) 535-3040
FAX: (509) 534-1399
Contact: Layne McGowan

Hendrix Tackle
570 N. Downs Ln., Fallon, NV 89406
(702) 423-4254
FAX: (702) 423-0458

Henry's
PO Drawer 1107
Morehead City, NC 28557
(919) 726-6186
FAX: (919) 726-7599

Hick's, Inc.
295 W. 3rd St., Luverne, AL 36049
(334) 335-3311
FAX: (334) 335-6243
Contact: Mack Wise

The Hodgson Hook Co.
7116 W. Rowland Ave.
Littleton, CO 80123
(303) 979-5206
FAX: (303) 979-5206
Contact: Bert Hodgson

Inter-Tac/Larva Lace
Box 6340,
Woodland Park, CO 80866
(800) 347-3432
(719) 684-2272
FAX: (719) 687-9820
Contact: Joan or Phil Camera
Fly tying materials and other fly fishing products. Wholesale only.

Hal Janssen Co.
Box 11491,Santa Rosa, CA 95406
(707) 523-4083
FAX: (707) 523-1039
Contact: Hal Janssen
Distributor of a selection of fly fishing tackle.

Mathews and Boucher
1950 Brighton Henrietta Townline Rd.
Rochester, NY 14623
(716) 424-2790
FAX: (716) 424-2797

Maurice Sporting Goods
1910 Techny Rd.
Northbrook, IL 60065
(847) 715-1500
FAX: (847) 715-1419
Contact: Randy Overton

McKenzie Fly Tackle
1075 A Shelley St.
Springfield, OR 97477
(541) 741-8161   FAX: 7565
Est.: 1971   Staff: 20
Sales Mgr: Dale Williams
Manufacturer and distributor of
high-quality flies, materials and fly
tackle. Dealer inquiries only.

Merrick Tackle, Inc.
7349 Rt. 28, HC2
Shandaken, NY 12480
(914) 688-2216
FAX: (914) 688-2329
Est.: 1959   Staff: 12
President: Scott Greenberg
Available: Direct
Email: rroy@internetmci.com
Rod building components & fishing
supplies–worldwide service.

F.J. Neil Co., Inc.
1064 Rt. 109, Box 617
Lindenhurst, NY 11757-0617
(800) 969-6345   (516) 957-1073
Contact: Neil J. Miritello

New England Tackle
North River Co., Inc., 55 Sharp St.,
Unit 2, Hingham, MA 02043
(617) 337-1030
FAX: (617) 331-3501
Contact: Cap

Outdoor Sports HQ
967 Watertower Ln.
Dayton, OH 45449
(800) 444-6744
FAX: (800) 488-6744
Contact: Sales Dept.

Riverborn ™

Riverborn Fly Company, Inc.
Box 65, Wendell, ID 83355
(800) 354-5534
FAX: (208) 536-6103
Est.: 1987   Staff: 6
Pres/Owner: Warren E. Schoth
VP/Owner: Steve Hunter
Riverborn is your distributor of
choice for an extensive line of fresh
and saltwater flies, hooks, hackle,
accessories, equipment and tools.
We feature Riverborn flies and ma-
terials such as our "New Age"
chenille; plus the all new VMC Vana-
dium steel fly hooks, Riverborn and
Keough hackle, and pro products
from Cascade/Crest, Loon, Bug Lug-
gage, Zephr, Anglers Choice and
Von Schlegel.
See Our Ad Pg. 49

Raymond C. Rumpf & Son
PO Box 319, Sellersville, PA 18960
(215) 257-0141
FAX: (215) 453-9758
Est.: 1969   Staff: 14
Contact: Raymond Rumpf
Family owned & operated fly tackle
distributor with over 9,000 sku's.

Shakespeare Co. (UK) Ltd.
PO Box 1, Broad Ground Rd.
Lakeside, Redditch, Worcester
B98 8NQ England
Contact: John Tomsett
Rods, Reels, monofilaments, fly
lines and terminal tackle.

Spirit River
423 Winchester St.
Roseburg, OR 97470
(503) 440-6916
FAX: (503) 672-4309
Contact: Bill Black or Richard Wolfe
SRI are manufacturers and distributors for a wide array of materials,
tools, boxes, flies and organiza-
tional dispensing systems for the
tyer's workbench. 60-page whole-
sale/dealer catalog upon request &
verification. Wholesale only.

Sportsman's Supply
6 Bolte Dr., St. Clair, MO 63077
(314) 629-6100
FAX: (314) 629-1655
Contact: Troy Nogosek

Steve's Wholesale
9102 NE 326th St.
Cameron, MO 64429
(816) 632-5560
FAX: (816) 632-5562

Triple S Sport Supply
325 Creekside Dr.,
Buffalo, NY 14228
(716) 691-3777
FAX: (716) 691-4305
Contact: Peter Schwartz

Troutsmen Enterprises
Box 571326, Murray, UT 84157
(800) 881-0636   (801) 268-0636
FAX: (801) 288-2185
Contact: Tom Nokes
Manufacturer of tying material, rod
cases and related items. Catalog
available.

Umpqua Feather Merchants
PO Box 700, Glide, OR 97443
(800) 322-3218   (541) 496-3512
FAX: (541) 496-0150
Est.: 1972
Nat'l. Sales Mgr: Gus Wunderly
Umpqua Feather Merchants was
founded in 1972 on a simple no-
tion; that fly anglers will always
seek out the highest quality products available.

Universal Telescopic
43 Park Lane, Brisbane, CA 94005
(415) 468-0450
FAX: (415) 468-5147
Contact: Brett Chamberlain

Universal Vise Corp.
PO Box 626, Westfield, MA 01086
(413) 568-0964
FAX: (413) 562-7328
Est.: 1969   Staff: 12
President: Chet Cook
Manufacturer and distributor of fly
tying tools, kits, materials and fly
fishing tackle.

IMPORTERS & EXPORTERS

Vjender International
PO Box 8432, Delhi 110052 India
011-91-11-7428903
FAX: 011-91-11-7252857
Contact: Kishan Singh
Fancy feathers, peacock feathers,
cock necks, saddles, hackles, cock
feathers. Fly tying material, fly tying
tools, Indian flies & fishing flots. Exporter & importer worldwide. Large
stock of feathers for wholesale
only. Call for a free catalog.

Wapsi Fly, Inc.
27 CR 458,
Mountain Home, AR 72653
(501) 425-9500
(800) 425-9599 (FAX)
FAX: (501) 425-9599
Est.: 1945   Staff: 30
G.M.: Karl Schmuecker
Sales Mgr: T.L. Lauerman
Wapsi manufactures and distrib-
utes a complete line of fly tying
materials, tools and accessories.

1997 CALENDAR OF EVENTS

January

Jan. 3-5
Mid West Fly Show
Drury Lane, Oakbrook, IL
(708) 858-7844
Contact: Marcos Vergara
Fly & Field, 560 Crescent Blvd.
Glen Ellywn, IL 60137

Jan. 11-12
The Fly Fishing Show
The Rockford Armory,
University of Maryland,
College Park, MD
(800) 420-7582
FAX: (717) 243-8603
Contact: Barry Serviente &
Chuck Furimsky

The Fly Fishing Show
854 Opossum Lake Rd.
Carlisle, PA 17013

Jan. 17-19
**National Fly Fishing
Show-New England**
Royal Plaza Trade Center,
Marlboro, MA
(207) 594-9544
FAX: (207) 594-5144
Contact: David P. Jackson, Mgr.
Down East Enterprises, Inc.
PO Box 370, Camden, ME 04843

Jan. 24-26
The Fly Fishing Show
Garden State Exhibition Center
Somerset, NJ
(800) 420-7582
FAX: (717) 243-8608
Contact: Barry Serviente or
Chuck Furimsky
The Fly Fishing Show
854 Opossum Lake Rd.
Carlisle, PA 17013

February

Feb. 21-23
**Northeast
Fly Fishing Expo**
Meadowlands Exposition Center,
Secaucus, NJ
(201) 292-2600
(201) 223-1000 (Directions, etc.)
Contact: George Katilus
The Northeast Fly Fishing Expo
92 Bridge Ave., Bay Head, NJ 08742
See Our Ad Below

Feb. 25
A Night to Honor Leigh Perkins
Cosmopolitan Club, New York City
(802) 362-3300
FAX: (802) 362-3308
Contact: Eric Brown, The American
Museum of Fly Fishing, PO Box 42,
Manchester, VT 05254
"By Invitation Only"

March

March 1
Fred Hall Sports Show
Long Beach Convention Center,
Long Beach, CA
(714) 756-9286
Contact: Allan Rohrer
FFF Certification with the Rohrers

March 1
**Atlantic Salmon Federation
Main Council Dinner**
Portland Marriott,
Portland, ME
(207) 725-2833
FAX: (207) 725-2967
Contact: Cheryl Carter, Tickets & Info
Atlantic Salmon Federation
Fort Andorss, Suite 400
14 Main St.
Brunswick, ME 04011

March 8
**Theodore Gordon Flyfishers,
Inc. 35th Annual Exhibition
and Banquet**
Sheraton Crossroads Hotel,
Mahwah, NJ
Fax: (516) 766-3864
Coordinator: Barbara Lituchy
Theodore Gordon Flyfishers
PO Box 978, Murray Hill Station
New York, New York 10156-0603

March 8-9
World Fly Fishing Expo
Shriners Auditorium,
Wilmington, MA
(603) 431-4315
Contact: Paul Fuller
Eastern Fishing & Outdoor
Exposition, Inc.
PO Box 4668
Portsmouth, NH 03802-4660

March 8-9
Midwest Fly Fishing Exposition
Southfield Civic Center,
Southfield, Michigan
(810) 486-4967
Contact: Ron Angove
5300 Seven Mile Rd.
South Lyon, MI 48178-9671

March 21-23
**National Fly Fishing
Show-Midwest**
Navy Pier, Chicago, IL
(207) 594-9544
FAX: (207) 594-5144
Contact: David P. Jackson, Mgr.
Down East Enterprises, Inc.
PO Box 370
Camden, ME 04843

March 22-23
Fly Fishers' Symposium
Seven Springs Mountain Resort,
Champion, PA
(814) 926-2676
FAX: (814) 926-2650
Contact: Chuck Furimsky

March 22-23
**Shallow Water Fishing
Expo-Legends Tour**
Atlanta, GA
(561) 562-5069
FAX: (561) 562-1488
Contact: Mark Castlow, Pres.
Castlow Group, Inc.
2625 Carissa Dr.
Vero Beach, FL 32960

April

April 12-13
Canadian Fly Fishing Forum
Toronto Congress Center,
Toronto, Canada
(905) 855-5420
Contact: Dan Mulvihill
Izaak Walton Fly Fishing Club
2400 Dundas St.
Unit 6, Suite 283, Mississauga,
Ontario, Canada L5K 2R8

May

May 9-10
Annual Festival Weekend
The Equinox and The Museum,
Manchester, VT
(802) 362-3300
FAX: (802) 362-3308
Contact: Eric Brown
The American Museum
of Fly Fishing, PO Box 42
Manchester, VT 05254

May 10
**American Museum of Fly
Fishing Manchester
Dinner Auction**
Equinox Hotel,
Manchester, VT
(802) 362-3300
FAX: (802) 362-3308
Contact: Eric Brown
The American
Museum of Fly Fishing
PO Box 42, Manchester, VT 05254

May 17
**15th Annual Banquet
& Auction**
Rockland House,
Roscoe, NY
(914) 439-4810
FAX: (914) 439-3387
Contact: Mary Fried
Catskill Fly Fishing Center & Museum
PO Box 1295
Livingston Manor, NY 12758

June

June 25-28
**ASA International
Sportfishing Expo**
Las Vegas Convention Center,
Las Vegas, NV
(703) 519-9691
Expo Director: Meg Smith
American Sportfishing Association
1033 N. Fairfax St., Suite 200
Alexandria, VA 22314

June 27-29
**16th European Fishing Tackle
Trade Exhibition (EFTTEX)**
Amsterdam, Holland
011-44-171-606-0555
FAX: 011-44-171-606-0226
EFTTEX '97, 51 Cloth Fair
London EC1A 7JQ England

July

July 31-Aug. 3
**Trout Unlimited's
National Convention**
Knoxville, Tennessee
(703) 522-0200
FAX: (703) 284-9400
Trout Unlimited
1500 Wilson Blvd., #310
Arlington, VA 22209

August

Aug. 5-10
**International Fly
Fishing Show &
Conclave**
Amway Center, Grand Rapids, MI
(406) 585-7592
FAX: (406) 585-7596
Federation of Fly Fishers
Box 1595, Bozeman, MT 59771
See Our Ad, Right

September

Sept. 3-8 Mitsubishi Motors 17th Annual World Fly Fishing Championship & Symposium
Jackson Hole, WY
(307) 733-9619
FAX: (307) 733-0843
Dir. of P.R.: Mike Banville
World Fly FishingChampionship
Box 429, Teton Village, WY 83025

Sept. 18-20 International Fly Tackle Dealer Show
Colorado Convention Center, Denver, CO
(207) 594-9544
FAX: (207) 594-5144
Contact: David P. Jackson, Mgr.
Down East Enterprises, Inc.
PO Box 370, Camden, ME 04843

Sept. 24 8th Annual Congressional Sportsmen's Foundation Banquet
Hyatt Regency on Capitol Hill, Washington, DC
(202) 785-9153
FAX: (202) 785-9155
Contact: Tom Sadler, President
c/o Congressional Sportsmen's Foundation
1730 K St., NW, Suite 1300
Washington, DC 20006
See Our Ad Pg. 23

Sept. 25-28 ASA Fall Expo
McCormick Place, Chicago, IL
(703) 519-9691
Expo Director: Meg Smith
American Sportfishing Association
1033 N. Fairfax St., Suite 200
Alexandria, VA 22314

Sept. 27 National Hunting & Fishing Day
(203) 426-1320
Contact: Chris Chaffin
National Hunting & Fishing Day Headquarters
c/o NSSF, 11 Mile Hill Rd.
Newtown, CT 06470

October

Oct. 11 Shallow Water Fishing Expo-Legends Tour
Houston, TX
(561) 562-5069
FAX: (561) 562-1488
Contact: Mark Castlow, President
Castlow Group, Inc.
2625 Carissa Dr.
Vero Beach, FL 32960

Oct. 18-19 Shallow Water Fishing Expo-Legends Tour
Fort Pierce, FL
(561) 562-5069
FAX: (561) 562-1488
Contact: Mark Castlow, President
Castlow Group, Inc.
2625 Carissa Dr.
Vero Beach, FL 32960

November

Nov. 8-9 International Fly Tying Symposium
Meadowlands Hilton, Secaucus, NJ
(814) 926-2676
FAX: (814) 926-2650
Contact: Chuck Furimsky

Nov. 13 Atlantic Salmon Federation Dinner
Plaza Hotel, New York City, NY
(207) 725-2833
FAX: (207) 725-2967
Contact: Cheryl Carter, Tickets & Info
Atlantic Salmon Federation
Fort Andross-Suite 400
14 Main St.
Brunswick, ME 04011

SCHOOLS & FFF INSTRUCTORS

So you're a natural fly fisher, eh? Good technique is just sort of instinctive with you? Could be. But consider, if you will, the concert pianist who repeats scales for hours a day; the top-flight golf pro who practices the same shot, ball after ball after ball.

You get the point. No matter how good you are, there's always room for improvement. And this is just as true of fly fishing as it is of countless other disciplines.

Fortunately, there is no shortage of professionally run schools, clinics and instructors that can help you hone your skills and break bad habits. The trick is to find the instruction that meets your needs.

Start your search here.

You can start your search right here, with Black's Fly Fishing's detailed listings of shooting schools and instructors. Before you choose, however, a few preliminaries

are called for. First, determine the type of fishing that most interests you. Is it trout or tarpon? Salmon or sailfish? Consider, too, the area of the country you're likely to do most of your fishing in? Write or call the fly fishing schools or instructors that appeal to you and ask for more information.

Is the instruction one-on-one? If not, determine if you'll be in a small class with others of similar ability. And don't be shy about discussing costs. Also, ask about equipment. Is it bring your own or does the school provide what you'll need? Finally, ask for references and contact them before you book a lesson.

A note on the FFF

All of the nearly 500 instructors listed here are sanctioned by the Federation of Fly Fishermen (FFF)—the only organization currently certifying instructors on a national basis. (Schools are independently run and are not affiliated with the FFF unless otherwise noted.)

SCHOOLS & FFF INSTRUCTORS

ALASKA

FFF Instructors
Anchorage: Troy Miller; (907) 561-1939
Eagle River: Paul Rotkis; (907) 696-1501
Eagle River: Tony Weaver; (907) 694-8705
North Pole: Bob Hook; (907) 488-8886

ALABAMA

FFF Instructors
Birmingham: David Diaz; (205) 444-0921
Birmingham: Robert Rogers; (205) 969-3868

ARKANSAS

School

DAVE & EMILY WHITLOCK FLY FISHING SCHOOLS

Dave & Emily Whitlock Fly Fishing Schools
Rt. 1, Box 398, Midway, AR 72651
(501) 481-6120 FAX: (501) 481-6121
Contact: Emily Whitlock
Instructors: Dave & Emily Whitlock
Location: Arkansas Ozark Mountains
Schedule: 1, 2 & 3 day schools: March-Nov; Beginners

thru experienced flyfishers
Private "Day with Dave" available and fly tying classes Classroom and stillwater instruction are on Whitlock's private, springfed lakes at their home/school facility with flowing water instruction on the world-record brown trout waters of the White and Norfork Rivers, and on area spring creeks. Light breakfast and hearty lunch included along with the L.L. Bean Fly Fishing Handbook written by Dave. Tackle and accessories provided by Umpqua, Simms, Scientific Angler and Sage. Maximum of 8 students–learn from a master with 35 years teaching experience.

FFF Instructors
Fort Smith: Duane Hada; (501) 452-1538
Fort Smith: Lee Temple; (501) 452-5818
Jacksonville: Bob Cheatham; 501-982-9280
Little Rock: John Blackwood; (501) 351-4041
Midway: Dave Whitlock; (501) 481-6120
Mountain Home: Dale Fulton; (501) 425-0447

ARIZONA

School

Lees Ferry Anglers
HC67, Box 2, Marble Canyon, AZ 86036
(800) 962-9755 FAX: (520) 355-2271
Contact: Terry & Wendy Gunn
Est.: 1983   9 Instructors/Guides
Hundreds of students/yr.   Location: Vermillion Cliffs/Colorado River 4.5 hrs. from Phoenix/ Las Vegas
Sessions: 1-4 days   Schedule: Year-roundFull Service Tackle Shop   Brochure Available &Equipment Provided

FFF Instructors

Flagstaff: Len Holt; (520) 526-1735
Marble Canyon: Dale Whitmore; (602) 355-2247
Phoenix: Patrick Sullivan; (602) 431-1378
Coquitlam: Peter Morrison; (604) 941-0229
Port Moody: Peter Caverhill; (604) 461-4503
Richmond: Ken Richardson; (604) 876-2022
Sparwood: Ian Ricketts; (604) 425-6614
Vancouver: Denise Maxwell; (604) 945-9002

CALIFORNIA

Schools

California School of Flyfishing
PO Box 8212, Truckee, CA 96162
(800) 58-TROUT FAX: (916) 587-6686
Contact: Ralph and Lisa Cutter
Est.: 1981 Sessions: 1-2 day classes for intermediate through advanced; 2 day classes for beginners
Schedule: May-October Brochure Available
Max. 10 students in intermediate & advanced classes. Max. 3 students in introduction to flyfishing. In these small groups the Cutters will lead you through an intense learning experience on some of the best waters in California.

Clearwater House on Hat Creek
PO Box 90, Cassell, CA 96016
(916) 335-5500 (415) 381-1173
FAX: (916) 335-5500
Owner: Dick Galland   Mgr: Lynn Bedell
Est.: 1980 Location: Clearwater House on Hat Creek, California's only "Orvis Endorsed" lodge
Sessions: Specializing in instruction for beginning, intermediate & advanced skills May thru October
Schedule: Most are five days, including meals & accommodations. Brochure Available
Also offer complete guide service on the finest wild trout rivers in California.

Fly Fishing Outfitters
463 Bush St., San Francisco, CA 94108
(415) 781-3474 FAX: (510) 943-1793
Est.: 1985   Staff: 6
Owners: Peter or Josette Woolley
Instructors: Pete Woolley and Staff
Location: Extensive school program throughout CA
Sessions: 1 day introduction to fly fishing and 2 day schools throughout California
Schedule: All year long
Brochure Available and Equipment Available

The Fly Shop
4140 Churn Creek Rd., Redding, CA 96002
(800) 669-3474 FAX: (916) 222-3572
Contact: Duane Milleman
Est.: 1978   Location: Hat Creek Ranch House & Delta House   Sessions: 2-3 day schools
Schedule: May, June & July
Full service tackle shop
Brochure Available

The Mel Krieger School of Flyfishing
790 27th Ave., San Francisco, CA 94121
(415) 752-0192 FAX: (415) 752-0804
Contact: Mel or Fanny Krieger
Instructors: Certified F.F.F. flycasting instructors
Sessions: One and 2 day seminars
Schedule: Call for '96 schedule
Brochure Available
Equipment Available
Extensive hands-on flycasting sessions are interspersed with lectures and discussions on trout food, artificial flies, equipment, reading water, knots, leaders, fly presentation and more.

Andre' M. Puyans Seminars
1924 C Oak Park Blvd., Pleasant Hill, CA 94523
(510) 939-3113 FAX: (510) 939-3183
Contact: Andre' M. Puyans
FFF Buszek Award recipient. FFF Flycasting Instructor Advisory Committee. FFF Certified Flycasting Instructor. NCC/FFF Hall of Fame recipient. Over 35 years of the highest quality fly casting, fly tying and fly fishing instruction, groups and individuals.
25th Anniversary Year for the Andre' Puyans Idaho-Montana Fly Fishing Seminars. Place: Elk Creek Ranch, Island Park, Idaho. Time: July 13th-20th, 1997. For the beginner or advanced participant. Two to one student to instructor ratio. Fish three states. Twenty-four years of references. Brochure available.

The Reel School of Fly Fishing
PO Box 11377, Truckee, CA 96162
(916) 587-7333
Contact: Frank R. Pisciotta
Est.: 1997   Location: Northern California
Sessions: 2 day basic skills clinics; private groups by arrangement
Schedule: Please inquire about scheduled dates.
Brochure Available

Western Angler
532 College Ave., Santa Rosa, CA 95404
(707) 542-4432 FAX: (707) 542-4437
Contact: Noel Plumb
Est.: 1958   Full service tackle shop
Brochure Available & Equipment Available
Classes offered: Flyfishing 101; Basic and Intermediate Fly Tying; Private Casting Lessons; Rod Building; Flyfishing from a Float Tube; Flyfishing for Female Anglers; Flyfishing for Kids; Saltwater Flyfishing; and The Mel Kreiger School of Flyfishing

Western Sport Shop
902 Third St., San Rafael, CA 94901
(415) 456-5454 FAX: (415) 456-2577
Contact: Gary Vanantwerp
Est.: 1947   Full service tackle shop
Brochure Available & Equipment Available
Classes offered: Flyfishing 101; Basic and Intermediate Fly Tying; Private Casting Lessons; Rod Building; Flyfishing from a Float Tube; Flyfishing for Female Anglers; Flyfishing for Kids; Saltwater Flyfishing; and The Mel Kreiger School of Flyfishing

FFF Instructors

Aptos: Michael Gaines; (408) 688-1624
Auburn: Richard Garland; (916) 888-6276

Auburn: John Hogg; (916) 823-9744
Bellflower: John VanDerHoof; (310) 925-9445
Berkeley: Kimberly Colwell; (510) 845-4342
Bishop: Gary Gunsolley; (619) 872-3581
Brea: Chris Menadier; (310) 697-8870
Burlingame: Floyd Demanes; (415) 508-0666
Coarsegold: Philip Chavez; (209) 323-6643
Concord: Mark Darcy; (510) 370-6604
Concord: Chuck Echer; (510) 689-7195
Concord: John Williams; (510) 686-0232
Culver City: Jim Solomon; (310) 558-1948
Daly City: Alan Schneider; (415) 755-1989
Fall River Mills: Arthur Frey; (916) 336-5574
Foster City: Robert Shadle; (415) 573-9706
Fountain Valley: Daniel Iwata; (714) 965-2008
Fresno: Stuart MacChesney; (209) 229-8395
Hanford: Robin Roberts; (209) 584-9090
King City: Richard McCombs; (408) 385-4778
Lafayette: James Lyle; (415) 728-3086
Lake Arrowhead: Dick Thies; (909) 337-7148
Mammoth Lakes: Don Nelson; (916) 478-9457
Miranda: Michael Foster; (707) 943-3355
Moraga: Al Kyte; (510) 631-0419
Mountain View: Jim Mauch; (415) 960-8519
Napa: Amos Cross; (707) 226-6356
Napa: Phil Ryan; (707) 252-3004
Oakland: Yoshi Miller; (510) 261-7206
Ojai: Ray Johnson; (805) 649-5605
Orleans: Roger Raynal; (916) 469-3492
Petaluma: Paul Wulf; (707) 778-0252
Pleasant Hill: Fred Gomez; (510) 256-7578
Pleasant Hill: Andre Puyans; (510) 938-3113

Pleasant Hill:
Andre Puyans
1924-C Oak Park Blvd., Pleasant Hill, CA 94523
(510) 939-3113
FFF Certified Flycasting Instructor; FFF Flycasting Instructor Advisory Committee; Over 35 years of experience.

Pleasanton: Lois Kilburn; (510) 734-8150
Ridgecrest: Chuck Newmyer; (619) 375-1126
Riverside: Bob Slamal; (909) 784-0205
Sacramento: Bob Giannoni; (916) 927-8383
Salinas: Loren Kitamura; (408) 757-5533
San Carlos: Larry White; (415) 595-5955
San Diego: Gretchen Yearous; (619) 295-6357
San Francisco: Fanny Krieger; (415) 752-0192
San Francisco: Henry Tom; (415) 751-7135
San Jose: Walt Robinson; (408) 268-6968
San Jose: Carol von Raesfeld; (408) 997-7843
San Jose: Robert von Raesfeld; (408) 997-7843
San Mateo: Wayne Taylor; (415) 341-7539
San Pedro: Ed Berg; (310) 547-2444
Santa Clara: Paul Utz; (408) 727-2880
Santa Rosa: Carl Blackledge; (707) 579-2224
Santa Rosa: Charles Cadman; (707) 539-2676
Sonoma: Larry Ginesi; (707) 935-0604
South Lake Tahoe: Nina MacLeod; (916) 573-8940
Stockton: Don Calcaterra; (209) 948-6500
Tahoe City: Bruce Ajari; (916) 587-8152
Torrance: Milton Huber; (310) 324-7748
Truckee: Lisa Cutter; (916) 587-7005

Upland: John Bianco; (909) 982-1405
Upland: Soon Lee; (909) 981-6988
Visalia: Dan Busby; (209) 636-8907
Visalia: Stuart Garrison; (209) 733-5222
Walnut: John Williams; (909) 598-7905
Walnut Creek: Jannifer Lee; (510) 939-3113
Yosemite: Chris Otterbein; (209) 372-8613
Oakville, ON L6J 1T1: Gary Whittles; (905) 842-2227
Brampton, Ontario: Murray Abbott; (905) 846-8254
Etobicoke, Ontario: Dan Mulvihill; (416) 234-9701
Edmonton, AB: Barry White; (403) 475-8139

COLORADO
Schools

The Flyfisher Ltd.
252 Clayton St., Denver, CO 80206
(303) 322-5014　FAX: (303) 322-3053
Contact: Ren Cannon
Est.: 1973　Sessions: 3 day school; 2 day classroom, 1 day on stream　Schedule: April through September
Full service tackle shop
15 students maximum per school.

Scott Fly Rod Co. Fly Fishing School
200 San Miguel River Dr., PO Box 889
Telluride, CO 81435
(800) 728-7208　FAX: (970) 728-5031
Contact: John Duncan　Est.: 1996
Location: Nationwide　Sessions: 1/2 day casting clinics; 1 day fly fishing schools　Schedule: Year-round

FFF Instructors

Arvada: Mike Bostwick; (303) 423-7829
Avon: Orb Greenwald; (970) 845-7770
Basalt: Willard Clapper; (303) 927-3502
Basalt: Patrick McCord; (303) 927-3030
Boulder: Eugene Shimel; (303) 440-3554
Denver: Darrel Sickmon; (303) 934-7066
Denver: Terrie Yamagishi; (303) 744-6468
Dillon: Dale Fields; (303) 468-8945
Englewood: James Lane; (303) 721-6216
Fort Collins: Brian Shipley; (303) 484-6272
Grand Jct: Pat Oglesby; (970) 434-3912
Grand Junction: Jack Sherrill; (970) 434-1221
Hayden: Chuck Grobe; (303) 276-3683
Lakewood: Rhonda Sapp; (303) 232-8298
Littleton: Gerald Bliss; (303) 730-9896
Littleton: Lyle Ockander; (303) 770-8608
Littleton: Jim Tate; (303) 798-9653
Lyons: Vince Zounek; (303) 823-5888

Lyons:
Vince Zounek
455 Old St. Vrain Rd., Lyons, CO 80540
(303) 823-5888
Old Saint Vrain School of Fly Fishing,
415 Main St., Lyons, CO, 80540, (303) 823-5888.
Contact Vince Zounek, FFF Certified Fly Casting Instructor. Personalized casting and fly tying instruction, all levels, equipment provided. Casting, video taping and critiquing offered, brochure available upon request.

New Castle: Tim Jacobs; (303) 984-2924

CONNECTICUT

Schools

Flyfishing Charters-
Northeast Saltwater Flyfishing
PO Box 2540, 520 Riverside Ave.
Westport, CT 06880
(203) 226-1915 (203) 222-0058
Est.: 1968   Contact: Capt. Jeff A. Northrop

Northeast Flyfishing Schools
PO Box 315, East Hartland, CT 06027
(880) 318-7971 (860) 653-9986
FAX: (860) 653-9986
Contact: Terrence O'Connor
Est.: 1994   Staff: 6
Instructors: FFF Certified
Sessions: 1 & 2 day classes
Accommodations Available
Equipment Available
Full Service Tackle Shop
Classes on the Farmington River or Caribbean location

Sportsmen's Den of Greenwich, CT
Calf Island Outdoor Adventures
33 River Rd., Cos Cob, CT 06807
(203) 869-3234 (914) 967-8246
FAX: (203) 661-6242
Contact: Michael Noyes   Est.: 1990
Instructors: Capt. Bill Herold; Joe Santora
Location: Greenwich, CT
Sessions: Evening seminars; 2 day group classes
Schedule: Year-round
Full service tackle shop
Brochure Available & Equipment Available
Seminars also available for corporations and clubs

FFF Instructors

Danbury: Scott Bennett; (203) 778-2496
East Hartland: Terrence O'Connor; (860) 653-9498

Granby:
Mark Philippe
62 Creamery Hill Rd.
Granby, CT 06035
(860) 653-7544
Professional educator. 22 years experience teaching fly casting and fly fishing. Individuals or small groups. Fresh/saltwater. Guiding available. FFF Certified Instructor. Reasonable rates.

Kensington: Brian Owens; (860) 828-3354
Westport: Christopher Valante; (203) 226-1649

DELAWARE

Rehoboth Beach
Tom Sisson
5 Pennsylvania Ave., Rehoboth Beach, DE 19971
(302) 227-7067
Master FFF Instructor and member APGAI (British angling instructors). Beginning through advanced single and double-handed fly rod casting instruction. May through November.

FLORIDA

Schools

Boca Grande Fly Fishing School
2416 Parson Lane, Sarasota, FL 34239
(941) 923-6095 FAX: (941) 925-9483
Email: capt.petegreenan@worldnet.att.net
Owner: Capt. Pete Greenan
Est.: 1980   Location: Uncle Henry's Marina Resort, Boca Grande, FL, 30 min. so. of Sarasota
Sessions: 3 day schools on weekends
Brochure Available
All levels: novice to experienced. 4 students per instructor.

Boca Grande Saltwater Fly Fishing School
PO Box 1407, Boca Grande, FL 33921
(800) 4-TARPON
(941) 964-0907 FAX: (941) 964-1611
Contact: Capt. Sandy Melvin or
Capt. Phil O'Bannon
1 hour from Ft. Myers or Sarasota
Schedule: Year-round
Orvis Authorized Dealer
Brochure available & Rate Sheet
Group size: 12 students maximum to provide you with individualized "hands-on" instruction.

The Bonefish School
PO Box 500937
Marathon, FL 33050-0937
(305) 743-0501 FAX: (305) 743-5007
Contact: Jake Jordan
Est.: 1990
Location: Peace & Plenty Beach Inn, Exuma Island, Bahamas   Sessions: 7 day residential classes
Schedule: Dec. 1-8, 1996; April 27-May 4, 1997; Nov. 30-Dec. 7, 1997; April 26-May 2, 1998.

The Florida Keys Fly Fishing
School & Outfitters, Inc.
PO Box 603, Islamorada, FL 33036
(305) 664-5423 FAX: (305) 664-5501
Contact: Sue Moret
Instructors: Steve Huff; Sandy Moret; Flip Pallot; Steve Rajeff; Rick Ruoff; Chico Fernandez; Associate Instructors: Craig Brewer and Tim Klein Location: Cheeca Lodge, Islamorada, Florida Keys
2 hours from Miami Int'l. Airport
Sessions: 2 day schools
Schedule: 6 times per year
Full service tackle shop
Several packages available in addition to the 2 day schools.   Group Size: 5 max. per instructor
Films, slide presentations, discussion and field exercises are mixed to give broad coverage to the material under study. Brochure Available
See Our Ad Pg. 126

The Fly Fishing Institute
130 Old Mims Rd., Geneva, FL 32732
(407) 349-2614
Contact: Jon B. Cave
Est.: 1975 Location: Saltwater Flats of the Indian
River Lagoon System and the St. John's River. 30 mins.
northeast of Orlando, FL.
Sessions: 2 day schools for beginning and
experienced anglers
3 comprehensive schools: The Saltwater Fly Fishing
School; The Warmwater Fly Fishing School; The
Compleat Fly Fishing School.

Bob Marvin and Doug Swisher
Fly Fishing & Fly Casting Schools
3620 23rd Ave., SW
Naples, FL 33964
(941) 455-7548
Contact: Capt. Bob Marvin or Doug Swisher
Est.: 1972 Location: Naples, FL Schedule: Year round
Equipment Available
Saltwater fly fishing & casting instruction.

The Outdoors Shops
2555 North Monroe St.
Tallahassee, FL 32303
(904) 386-4181 FAX: (904) 386-1952
Contact: John Underwood
Est.: 1977

FFF Instructors
Boca Grande: Christopher Brown; (941) 964-0907
Boca Grande: Capt. Sandy Melvin; (813) 964-0907
Bonita Springs: Frank Ogden, DVM; (941) 992-6297
Clearwater: George Hunt III; (813) 797-7874
Duck Key: Steve Huff; (305) 743-4361
Fern Park: John Kumiski; (407) 839-2954
Fort Lauderdale: Jody Moore; (954) 321-9667
Fort Myers Beach: Ike Hays; (813) 466-9682
Ft. Lauderdale: Michael Rosa; (954) 726-8817
Geneva: Jon Cave; (407) 349-2614
Gulf Breeze: Tom Springer; (904) 934-2743
Hollywood: Jon Dee; (305) 920-3556
Islamorada: Capt. Gary Ellis; (305) 664-2002
Islamorada: Capt. Chuck Nolan; (305) 852-7520
Islamorada: Tom Redden; (305) 664-4303
Islamorada: Rick Ruoff; (305) 664-2511
Maitland: Joseph Mulson; (407) 834-2932
Marathon: Jake Jordan; (305) 743-0501
Marco Island: D. Clark Everest, Jr.; (813) 642-9717
Marco Island: Don Phillips; (941) 642-7696
Melbourne: James Buckingham; (407) 729-3970
Melbourne: Bill Emrick; (407) 255-6505
Naples: Tom Shadley; (941) 793-3370
North Fort Myers: David Westra; (941) 995-2280
Pensacola: Lance Davis; (904) 434-0111

Pensacola:
Matthew Richardson
211 E Brent Lane, Pensacola, FL 32503
(904) 476-8688
Certified FFF Casting Instructor. Individual instruction or small groups. Emphasis on fly fishing the Gulf Coast–saltwater/freshwater. Tips on rigging, fly selection, fly tying.

Pensacola Beach: Vance Cook; (904) 932-5793

Ponte Vedra Beach:
Capt. Jerry F. Knight
101 Cordova Reina Ct.,
Ponte Vedra Beach, FL 32082
(904) 285-5411
Ponte Vedra Beach is home to the PGA, American Tennis Professional Assoc., and the famous Tournament Players Championship. It is also home of some of the greatest inshore fishing for huge redfish, sea trout and manty others. Learn fly casting and try your skill with this instructor on our waterways.

Ponte Vedra Beach: Eric Wall; (904) 273-8626
Port Charlotte: Capt. Dennis Blue; (941) 624-2923
Punta Gorda: Jack Montague; (813) 639-4007
Raiford: Ron Davis; (904) 431-1812

Rotonda West:
Capt. Richard Hyland
54 Bunker Ct., Rotonda West, FL 33947
(941) 697-2190　　(Boca Grande Area)
FFF Master Instructor. Fly fish Boca Grande for tarpon, snook, redfish. Private instruction on land or learn while you fish. Orvis tackle provided. Please visit my web site: http://www.charterboats.com/rhyland.htm

Sanibel Island: Capt. Chris Dotson; 941-395-9647
Sanibel Island: Michael Rehr; (813) 472-3308
Satellite: Rodney Smith; (407) 773-2955
St. Augustine: Russell Tharin; (904) 825-7982
Stuart: Warren Gorall; (407) 288-3996
Tallahassee: Lee Avirett; (904) 224-7425
Tampa: Bill Miller; (813) 935-3141
Tavernier: Richard Miller; (305) 852-7612
Venice: Walt Jennings; (941) 488-1522

Vero Beach:
Eric Davis
2855 Ocean Dr., Suite A-1,
Vero Beach, FL 32963
(561) 589-1404
Professional guided fishing trips on Florida's central east coast. The area's finest fly shop "The Back Country". Private and group classes with FFF Certified Instructors. Free brochure.

Yulee: Michael Leary; (904) 261-7144

GEORGIA
Schools

Little St. Simons Island
Saltwater Fly Fishing School
PO Box 21078-BFF, St. Simons Island, GA 31522
(912) 638-7472　FAX: (912) 634-1811

Est.: 1980　　Staff: 17
Contact: Kevin or Debbie McIntyre
Location: Little St. Simons Island, GA
Sessions: 2 day schools for any level/saltwater fly fishing on Georgia's coast
Schedule: Aug. thru November

FFF Instructors
Lafayette: Thomas Rueping; (706) 764-1779

Marietta:
Robert S. Hafner, Jr.
4600 C Woodchase Ln #C, Marietta, GA 30067
(770) 951-8479
FFF Certified Fly Casting Instructor. Learn basic and advanced casting with emphasis on techniques. Also, tips on rigging, knot tying and fly selection.

Marietta: Ron Hickman; (770) 977-5627
Savannah: Craig Ficklin; (912) 353-7451
St. Simons Island: Larry Kennedy; (912) 638-3214

IDAHO
Schools

Silver Creek Outfitters
PO Box 418, 500 N. Main, Ketchum, ID 83340
(208) 726-5282　FAX: (208) 726-9056
Est.: 1994
Contact: Roger Schwartz
Location: Ketchum, ID
Sessions: 2 day classes
Schedule: Mid-June thru Aug.
Full service tackle shop
Brochure Available
Equipment Available

FFF Instructors
Boise: Ken Folwell; (208) 343-9689
Boise: Barbara Folwell; (208) 343-9689
Boise: Don Knickrehm; (208) 939-6718
Boise: Don Pape; (208) 344-6986
Carmen: Kirk Eberhard; (208) 756-4132
Coeur d'Alene: Skip Quade; (208) 667-9243
Eagle: Joy Knickrehm; (208) 939-6718
Ketchum: Jim Curran; (208) 726-7279
Ketchum: Mark Harbaugh; (208) 726-9538
Ketchum: Mike Riedel; (208) 726-9666
Ketchum: Ford Rollo; (208) 726-9675
Ketchum: Roger Schwartz; (208) 726-9452
Moscow: Dave Engerbretson; (208) 882-1687
Mountain Home: J. Lee Banks; (208) 832-7201
Rexburg: Paul Bowen; (208) 356-6760
Sandpoint: Gary Carlson; (604) 229-5611
Shelley: Buck Goodrich; (208) 357-7328

Wendell:
Warren E. Schoth
Box 65, Wendell, ID 83355
(208) 536-2355
Thirty years experience conducting dealer clinics, public seminars, schools and private lessons for casters of all skill levels.

ILLINOIS

Schools

Trout and Grouse
300 S. Happ Rd., Northfield, IL 60093
(847) 501-3111   FAX: (847) 501-5246
Est.: 1976   Staff: 4
Pres/G.M.: Peter Sykes
Ass't. Mgr: Curt Schlesinger
Location: North shore of Chicago
Sessions: 1 day classes
Schedule: April through August
Trout and Grouse proudly provides complete
professional fly fishing outfitting and instruction.

Davy Wotton
1098 Randville Dr., Palatine, IL 60067
(847) 359-0297   FAX: (847) 359-0297
Instructor: Davy Wotton
Sessions: 2 hours, 1/2 day & full day
These courses are designed to cover all aspects of fly
fishing for various species of freshwater fishes on
streams, lakes and stillwaters, as well as saltwater fly
fishing.

FFF Instructors

Countryside: Richard Klemme; (708) 482-4990
Joliet: Dr. David F. Filak; (815) 729-9020 Ext. 2535
Spring Grove: Kevin Barry; (815) 675-2730
Springfield: Thomas Yocom; (217) 544-7218
Wheaton: Arthur Mazzier; (708) 653-2271

INDIANA

Schools

FlyMasters of Indianapolis
8232 Allisonville Rd., Indianapolis, IN 46250
(317) 570-9811 FAX: (317) 570-9812
Contact: Jon Widboom
Est.: 1989 Students/yr: 200+
Location: Indianapolis, IN
Sessions: 1-3 day schools by appointment
Schedule: Year-round
Full Service Tackle Shop
Brochure Available & Equipment Available
Complete schooling for beginners through expert.
One-on-one beginning fly fishing school. Individual
casting and fly tying lessons also are available.

IOWA

FFF Instructors

Des Moines: Kennan Arp; (515) 251-8911
Des Moines: Jene Hughes; (515) 282-4217
Marion: Jeff Moore; (319) 373-0735
Muscatine: John Rigler; (319) 263-4243
Polk City: Landon Morris; (515) 984-6992
Solon: Jeff Johnson; (319) 848-4478
Waukee: Tony Nevshemal; (515) 987-1832

KANSAS

FFF Instructors

Overland Park: Kevin Kurz; (913) 341-8118

LOUISIANA

FFF Instructors

Baton Rouge:
Glen "Catch" Cormier
2014 Timberwood, Baton Rouge, LA 70816
(504) 751-6848
Instructor for LSU and Nature Conservancy. Innovative
tier; unorthodox pursuer of all species. Specialties: club
and youth programs, computer and internet consulting.

Kenner: Kirby LaCour; (504) 464-1697
LaPlace: Tom Tripi; (504) 651-9093
New Orleans: Tom Jindra; (504) 392-7511
New Orleans: Thomas Piccolo; (504) 524-2768
New Orleans: Richard Whitner; (504) 524-3767
River Ridge: Rene Larriviere, Jr.; (504) 737-7388

MASSACHUSETTS

Schools

Excellent Anglers' Seminars, Inc.
PO Box 730, 11-A Schossett St., Pembroke, MA 02359
(617) 829-9090
Location: Saltwater School-Boston's South Shore
Contact: Bill Bois
Sessions: Two day school for novices, also multi-day
experts' program.   Schedule: May thru September
Brochure Available
Equipment: All provided

Fishing the Cape
Harwich Commons
Box 1552, East Harwich, MA 02645
(508) 432-1200   FAX: (508) 430-1184
Contact: Bob Benson
Est.: 1994 Students/yr: 300+
Location: Wequassett Inn,
Chatham, MA
Sessions: 2 1/2 days beginning Friday morn.
Schedule: May 17 thru Aug
Full service Orvis fly shop
Brochure Available
Equipment Available
The Orvis Cape Cod Saltwater Fly Fishing School–Our
school is dedicated to introducing new anglers, and
reinforcing experienced anglers to the exciting world
of saltwater fly fishing.

Points North Fly Fishing School
PO Box 146, Adams, MA 01220
(413) 743-4030   FAX: (413) 743-4030
Contact: Fred Moran; Marilyn Moran; or Kevin Moran
Est.: 1985   Location: Northern Berkshires
2 1/2 hrs. from Boston
Sessions: 1 day and 2 day schools
Schedule: April through June
Full service tackle shop   Brochure Available
Shop Location: Jiminy Peak Resort, Hancock, MA

FFF Instructors

Adams: Marilyn Moran; (413) 743-5126
Belchertown: Brad Gage; (413) 253-3643
Boylston: Kenneth Gaucher; (508) 869-0310
East Bridgewater: Clarence Lovell; (508) 378-3550

Marblehead:
Fred Christian
Goodwin's Landing, Marblehead, MA 01945
(617) 631-1879
Fred is a full time instructor and guide with over 20 years of experience and welcomes anglers of all experience levels. Instruction for both individuals and groups. Conducts both saltwater and freshwater schools. FFF Certified fly casting instructor.

Milford: Margaret Charles; (508) 473-4613
Monson: Scott Trainor; (413) 267-4472
Newbury: David Rimmer; (508) 463-3378
South Dartmouth: David Cornell; (508) 636-2769
Vineyard Haven: Arthur Silvia; (508) 693-1270

MARYLAND
Schools

Mark Kovach Fly Fishing Schools
406 Pershing Dr., Silver Spring, MD 20910
(301) 588-8742   Contact: Mark Kovach
Instructors: Mark Kovach/Peter Yarrington
Location: Theurmont, MD–trout; Harper's Ferry,
WV–bass   Sessions: 1 day basic or advanced
Schedule: Apr-Oct   Brochure & Equipment Available
Basic class covers tackle, equipment, knots, entomology, fly selection, coached fly casting and stream fishing. Advanced class focuses on casting. Video tape analysis of student's current technique is followed by the application of new casting techniques while fishing.

Pintail Point
511 Pintail Point Farm Lane, Queenstown, MD 21658
(410) 827-7029   FAX: (410) 827-7052
Contact: Carol Johnson or Sara Gardner
Est.: 1995   Instructors: Sarah Gardner
Location: Eastern Shore of Maryland
15 minutes east of Bay Bridge
Sessions: Private, group–half, full and 2 day classes
Schedule: March - November   Brochure Available
Equipment, license and guide trips are available. Small classes are held on farm ponds and the Wye River. Our Chesapeake Bay location is great for saltwater fly fishing instruction.
See Our Ad Below

The Rod Rack Fly Fishing School
181 Thomas Johnson Dr., Frederick, MD 21702
(301) 694-6143   FAX: (301) 663-4880
Contact: Rob Gilford
Est.: 1965   50 mi. from Baltimore
Sessions: 2 day schools   Schedule: March thru Sept.
Full service tackle shop   Brochure Available

FFF Instructors

Ellicott City: Philip Krista; (410) 461-3007
Pylesville: Peter McCall; 410-836-1602

Silver Spring:
Mark Kovach
737 Thayer Ave.
Silver Spring, MD 20910
(301) 588-8742
Mark's been a professional fly fishing instructor since 1979. His basic classes have provided hundreds of anglers with a strongfoundation in the sport. All classes incorporate classroom, casting field, and fishing experiences. In the advanced classes, video taping is used to critique student's casting. Mark stresses development of each student's personal casting style. He receivesnumerous compliments from both male and female clients on his animated and congenial class environment. See ad in Maryland Outfitter/Guide section.

MAINE

Schools

Barnes' Outfitters Saltwater
Fly Fishing School
305 Commercial St., Portland, ME 04101
(207) 772-4222
Contact: Capt. Pat Keliher
Est.: 1993

L.L. Bean Fly Fishing School
Outdoor Discovery Program
Casco St., Freeport, ME 04033
(800) 341-4341 Ext. 2666   FAX: (207) 865-4761
Contact: Sim Savage
Location: Freeport, Maine; Labrador; Paradise Valley, Montana; Grand Lake Stream, Maine
Sessions: 1 day to 7 day courses
Schedule: May through September
Full Service Tackle Shop   Brochure Available
L.L. Bean offers 9 fly fishing schools: Introductory Fly Fishing; Intermediate Fly Fishing; Parent and Child Fly Fishing; Northeastern Saltwater; Atlantic Salmon; Western Trout; Introductory Fly Fishing Workshop; Introductory Fly Casting; and Women's Introductory Fly Casting Schools.

FFF Instructors

Brunswick: Glenn Johsson; (207) 725-8227
Brunswick: Macauley Lord; (207) 729-3737
Durham: Paul Dolbec; (203) 353-6948
Falmouth: Van Blauvelt; (207) 781-8052
Falmouth: Scott Timothy; (207) 797-7431
Falmouth: Harvey Wheeler; (207) 781-3908

Greenville:
Bud Fackelman
Little Lyford Pond Camps
Greenville, ME 04441
(207) 534-2284
Private lessons in a wilderness setting. Instruction at the casting pool, on the ponds or on stream–just a stone's throw from your own log cabin.

New Gloucester: Samuel Flick; (207) 926-4424
New Gloucester: Ellen Peters; (207) 926-4806
Portland: Jim Kaiser; (207) 774-4070

Presque Isle:
Bill Brown
21 Howard St.
Presque Isle, ME 04769
(207) 764-3372
FFF Certified Flycasting Instructor, Registered Maine Guide. Complete instructional programs for beginners–specialized for "seasoned" citizens 55+. Elderhostel Instructor. bbrown31@maine.maine.edu
URL: http//maine.maine.edu/~bbrown31/

South Portland: Simmons Savage III; (207) 767-3881
South Portland: Francis Tiene; (207) 799-5101
Topsham: Tom Ackerman; (207) 729-1795
Westbrook: Brian Golden; (207) 856-9983
Yarmouth: Patrick Jackson; (207) 846-5472

MICHIGAN

Schools

FIELDSPORT Fly Fishing School
3313 W. South Airport Rd.
Traverse City, MI 49684
(616) 933-0767 FAX: (616) 933-0768
Contact: Bryan Bilinski

The Thornapple Angling School
c/o Thornapple Orvis Shop
1200 East Paris
Grand Rapids, MI 49546
(616) 975-3800   FAX: (616) 975-3855
Owner: Dick Pobst
Est.: 1975   Staff: 5
Store/School Mgr: Wade Seley
Instructors: Dick Pobst, Wade Seley, Jason Kuipers, Jay Allen, Dick Nelson
Location: In-store and stream work at the Rogue River
Sessions: 1 day schools; 2 day schools; Individual instruction & women's clinic
Schedule: April and May
Full service tackle shop
Brochure Available
We have developed special techniques for teaching the three skills every angler needs: 1. Fly casting; 2. Which fly to use; 3. On-stream experience.

FFF Instructors

Ann Arbor: Mike Traugott; (313) 665-3197
Baldwin: John Kluesing; (616) 745-3792
Flint: Butch Mayer; (810) 232-3879
Grayling: John Norcross; (517) 348-5336
Grosse Pte. Woods.: Pat Gossman; (313) 885-7436
Midland: John Johnson; (517) 835-6047
Midland: George Killat; (517) 835-3793
Midland: John Van Dalen; (517) 631-6873
Northville: John Long; (313) 235-8691
Owosso: Terry Bevington; (517) 723-5738
Pentwater: Dorothy Schramm; (616) 869-5487
Saginaw: Jac Ford; (517) 781-0997
Saginaw: Peter Jones; (517) 791-6000
Traverse City: Dave Leonhard; (616) 938-5337
Wellston: Ray Schmidt; (616) 848-4191

MINNESOTA

Schools

Fish Tech Institute
Box 807, Walker, MN 56484
(218) 547-1882   FAX: (218) 547-1882
Est.: 1991   Staff: 10
Director: Reggie Thiel
Sessions: 6-day residential schools
Instructional fishing camp for youth includes fly fishing course and freshwater species.

FFF Instructors

Duluth: John Sharkey; (218) 525-9267
Lakeville: John Kline Jr.; (612) 435-7532
Mahtomedi: Bill Hinton; (612) 429-2820

MISSISSIPPI

FFF Instructor

Biloxi: Reed Guice; (601) 374-4509

MISSOURI

FFF Instructors

Ballwin: Jack Birkner; (314) 296-0302
Ballwin: Tom Timmerberg; (314) 227-0028
Carthage: Joe Butler; (417) 358-2900
Columbia: Thomas Ziegler; (573) 443-3461
Fenton: Bill Armon; (314) 349-3141
St. Ann: Jerry Clark; (314) 423-1489
St. Louis: Jeff Grodin; 314-963-7876
St. Louis: Ed Story; (314) 963-7876
St. Louis: Robert Story; (314) 963-7876
St. Louis: Robyn Story; (314) 963-7876
St. Louis: Robert Temper; (314) 894-0319

Tecumseh:
Shawn Taylor
HC1 Box 1755, Tecumseh, MO 65760
(417) 284-3055
Taylormade River Tactics Flyfishing School offers one or two day on-stream instruction on the North Fork River. Guide trips on surrounding Ozark rivers.

MONTANA

Schools

George Anderson's Yellowstone Angler
PO Box 660, Hwy. 89 South
Livingston, MT 59047
(406) 222-7130   FAX: (406) 222-7153
Contact: George Anderson
Est.: 1983   Staff: 8
Guide Bookings: Brant Oswald
Location: Yellowstone River and private spring creeks
25 miles east of Bozeman
Sessions: 1-2 days; tailored to customer's needs
Full service tackle shop
Guided wade & float trips. Yellowstone River, Spring Creeks, Bighorn. Extensive selection of flies & tackle.

Dan Bailey's Fly Fishing School
PO Box 1019, Livingston, MT 59047
(800) 356-4052   FAX: (406) 222-8450
Contact: Tim Williams
Est.: 1938   25 miles east of Bozeman, MT
Sessions: Hourly; 1 day; 2 day
Schedule: 1st wk July thru Sept
Full service tackle shop
Brochure Available & Equipment Available
Our school is a comprehensive course designed for the beginner or those wishing to fine-tune their already acquired basic skills.

Bob Jacklyn's Fly Shop
105 Yellowstone Ave., PO Box 310
West Yellowstone, MT 59758
(406) 646-7336   FAX: (406) 646-9729
Owner: Bob Jacklyn
Est.: 1974
Location: Yellowstone Park, Madison River, and Henry's Fork of the Snake River in Idaho
90 mi. from Bozeman, MT
Sessions: Ind. and group lessons with on stream instruction
Schedule: June through September
Full Service Tackle Shop
Brochure Available & Equipment Available

Greg Lilly Fly Fishing Services
234 Mill Creek Rd.
Sheridan, MT 59749
(406) 684-5960
Contact: Greg Lilly or Janet Lilly
Instructors: Greg Lilly and Annette Lilly-Russ

Madison River Fishing Company
Fly Fishing Schools
109 Main St., P.O. Box 627
Ennis, MT 59729
(800) 227-7127   FAX: (406) 682-4744
Manager: Eric Swedman
Est.: 1987
Location: Spring creeks, Blue Ribbon Gallatin and the Madison Rivers.
Sessions: 3 day schools
Call for 1997 dates

Maggie Merriman Fly Fishing Schools
PO Box 755, West Yellowstone, MT 59758
(406) 646-7824
Est.: 1975
Contact: Maggie Merriman
Location: In the Western states
Sessions: 1-4 day
Beggining to Advanced
Schedule: May-October
Brochure & Equipment Available
Special Schools for Women
Winter months call (818) 282-3173

Montana State University
Fly Fishing Institute
204 Culbertson, Bozeman, MT 59717
(406) 994-4820   FAX: (406) 994-6546
Contact: Marilyn Jarvis
2 classes available in '97: Beginner: 7/9-12/97
Intermediate: 7/23-26/97

Montana Troutfitters
1716 West Main St.
Bozeman, MT 59715
(800) 646-7847   (406) 587-4707
FAX: (406) 586-0724
Est.: 1978   Staff: 12
Owner: David L. Kumlien
Location: Bozeman, MT   Sessions: 2 day "mini school instruction". 4 day schools. Schedule: 2 day-Bozeman; 4 day at Gallatin Gateway Inn
Full service tackle shop
Brochure Available and Equipment Available

Parade Rest Ranch Fly Fishing School
7979 Grayling Creek Rd.
West Yellowstone, MT 59758
(406) 646-7217   (800) 753-5934 Gen'l Info
Est.: 1988   Instructor: Jim Danskin

FFF Instructors

Bigfork: Jim Johnson; (406) 837-3210
Bozeman: Al Beatty; (406) 585-0745

Bozeman:
Denise Durham
24 E Main
Bozeman, MT 59715
(406) 587-9111
FFF Certified Instructor.
Private lessons available. Fly-
fishing guide of Montana's
Blueribbon trout streams. Trips available at RJ Cain and Co. Outfitters. Women's weekend retreat available August 1997. Call for free brochures on retreats and guided trips.

Bozeman: Bob Frey; (406) 585-9235
Bozeman: Lars-Ake Olsson; (406) 587-5140
Bozeman: Jennifer Olsson; (406) 587-5140
Bozeman: J. Kern Stevenson; (406) 586-5750
Bozeman: Eric Troth; (406) 582-7600
Columbia Falls: Jerry Smalley; (406) 892-4785
Corvallis: Sharon Chaffin; (406) 961-4416
Great Falls: Patti Madsen; (406) 761-6313
Hamilton: Darryl Osburn; (406) 363-2398

Harrison:
Guy Tillotson
P.O. Box 131, Harrison, MT 59735
(406) 685-3655
Specializing in individual instruction of basic techniques necessary for successful fly casting and fly fishing. Special emphasis with youth instruction. Experienced since 1979, saltwater,warmwater or coldwater. Former Flordia guide. Also available, fly fishing adventures arranged to Florida and Montana. References available. FFF life member. Walk/ wade Montana's lesser known streams with me.

Helena: Art Keeler; (406) 443-2978
Kalispell: Jim Tilmant; (406) 756-5860
Libby: Dave Blackburn; (406) 293-7578
Livingston: John Bailey; (406) 222-1623
Livingston: Rod Walinchus; (406) 222-8054
Marion: Bob Elias; (406) 854-2805

Missoula: Rich Ward; (406) 543-5842
Nye: Randy Turpin; (406) 328-6355
Polson: Chance Cole; (406) 883-6673
Red Lodge: Ernest Strum; (406) 446-2514
Stevensville: Dave Rice; (406) 777-5043
Superior: Thomas Yost; (406) 822-3340
Twin Bridges: Greg Lilly; (714) 289-1034
West Yellowstone: Bob Jacklin; (406) 646-7336
W. Yellowstone: Maggie Merriman; (406) 646-7824
Whitefish: Tim Joern; (406) 862-1490

NEVADA
School

Reno Fly Shop
294 E. Moana La., #14
Reno, NV 89502
(702) 825-3474   FAX: (702) 825-5610
Est.: 1983   Staff: 8
Owner: Dave Stanley
Mgr: Jeff Cavender
6-8 fly fishing schools per year
Full service tackle shop

FFF Instructor

Lincoln: Jay Callahan; (402) 489-9179

NEW HAMPSHIRE
Schools

Hunters North Country Angler
PO Box 516, Rt. 116, North Main St.
North Conway, NH 03860
(603) 356-6000
Est.: 1972   Staff: 5
Licensed Guide/Mgr: Jon Howe
Location: White Mountains of NH
2 hrs. north of Manchester, NH
Sessions: 2 1/2 day school beginning Friday evenings
Schedule: Memorial Day weekend through July Full service tackle shop
Brochure Available Saltwater school dates also available, located on the New Hampshire coast.

Dick Munroe
1 Bill St., Derry, NH 03038
(603) 432-3520
Est.: 1969   Students/yr: 30
15 minutes from Manchester, NH
Sessions: 2 students per session. Beginner to master level programs.
Equipment Available
28 years experience. Satisfaction guaranteed.

FFF Instructors

Bedford:
Stan Fudala
412 New Boston Rd., Bedford, NH 03110
(603) 472-5002
Individual or small group instruction. Fly casting or fly tying seminars in both fresh and saltware techniques. Contact Golden Demon Fly Shop, Hudson, NH (603) 598-6518.

Laconia: Jerry T. Gray; (603) 524-4165
Meredith: Richard Secord; (603) 253-8575
Salem: David Beshara; (603) 893-3333

NEW JERSEY

FFF Instructors

Bay Head: George Katillus III; (908) 892-8008
Clark: John Gayewski; (908) 382-0548
Hazlet: Stanley Jurecki Jr.; (908) 739-2371
Jersey City: Daniel Lancefield; (201) 963-2411
Rahway: Richard Kress; (908) 388-3086

Toms River:
Capt. Dick Dennis
501 Midship Drive, Toms River, NJ 08753
(908) 929-0967
Back Cast Enterprises, Fly Tying Saltwater, FFF Fly Casting Instructor, U.S.C.G. Licensed Captain. Beach Tours, Fly Fishing, Light Tackle Fishing–inshore and offshore.

NEW MEXICO

Schools

The Santa Fe Flyfishing School/Guide Service
PO Box 22957
Santa Fe, NM 87502-2957
(800) 555-7707   (505) 986-3913
Est.: 1991   Staff: 5
Contact: Dirk Kortz/Hugh Ableson
Instructors: Hugo Ableson, Ed Adams Dirk Kortz, Barrie Bush,
Location: Most classes are held on the Pecos River, although other locations are offered as well
Sessions: 1 day classes
Schedule: May thru September
Brochure Available
Equipment Rental Available

FFF Instructors

Albuquerque: Dick Blumershine; (505) 268-4959
Albuquerque: Bob Pelzl; (505) 884-7501

Albuquerque:
Bob Pelzl
3214 Matthew, NE
Albuquerque, NM 87107
(505) 884-7501
Casting and fly tying instruction for individuals and small groups. Casting and fly tying schools. Beginning to advanced. FFF Master Certified Casting Instructor.

Albuquerque: Robert Stehwien; (505) 266-6044
Albuquerque: Robert Widgren; (505) 299-6988
Brookfield: Blair Fleming; (902) 673-2413
Brookfield: Verlie Grant; (902) 673-2590
Brookfield: Dennis Grant; (902) 673-2590
Halifax: Ann Morrison; (902) 429-2027
Halifax County: George MacQuarrie; (902) 384-2378
Middle Musquodoboit: S. Matheson; (902) 384-2397

Oakfield: Harold Coe; (902) 883-1444
Reno: Jeff Cavender; (702) 329-8315
Reno: Dave Stanley; (702) 827-0600

NEW YORK

Schools

Adirondack Sport Shop
Rt. 86
Wilmington, NY 12997
(518) 946-2605
Est.: 1964   Staff: 2
President: Fran Betters
CEO: Jan Betters
Schedule: May through September
Full Service Tackle Shop
Brochure Available

Beaver Kill Angler
Stewart Ave., PO Box 198
Roscoe, NY 12776
(607) 498-5194   FAX: (607) 498-4740
Est.: 1980   Staff: 3
Owner: John E. McCullough
Mgr: Joan Barnicott

Catskill Fly Fishing Center and Museum
PO Box 1295, 5447 Old Rt. 17
Livingston Manor, NY 12758
(914) 439-4810   FAX: (914) 438-3387
Est.: 1981
Sessions: Year round programs
Brochure Available
The Catskill Fly Fishing Center & Museum takes an active role in education with a variety of programs throughout the year. Courses include stream ecology and angling, fly tying, and rod building.

Ephemera
PO Box 629
Roscoe, NY 12776
(607) 498-4508   FAX: (607) 498-4740
Proprietor: Floyd N. Franke
Location: Southern Catskills
Brochure Available
Private and small group instructors at all levels, beginner to advanced. Workshops and clinics in casting, fly fishing and fly tying.

Fly Fishing with
Bert & Karen
1070 Creek Locks Rd.
Rosendale, NY 12472
(914) 658-9784
Contact: Bert Darrow or
Karen Graham
Location: Rosedale, NY; Catskill Mountains Area 90 miles from NYC
Sessions: 2 day schools, April thru June; Private hourly instruction and licensed guide service
Brochure Available
Equipment Available

Indian Springs Flyfishing Camp
Upper Delaware River
RR1, Box 200AA, Warren Rd.
Hancock, NY

(215) 679-5022   (717) 224-2708 (In season)
FAX: (215) 679-4536
Est.: 1991
Contact: Lee Hartman
Instructors: Lee Hartman/Joe DeMarkis/Scot Brown
Location: Lordville, NY
50 miles from NYC–50 miles from Binghampton
Sessions: One-on-one schools by appointment (May 1st to Sept. 30th)
Schedule: 2 day course; 3 day course includes lodging and meals
Brochure Available
Equipment Available

Reed's Orvis Shop
5655 Main St.
Williamsville, NY 14221
(716) 631-5131 FAX: (716) 633-8903
Contact: Bill Reed
Est.: 1970
10 mi. from Buffalo, NY
Sessions: 1/2 day clinics to full day schools–trout classes; salmon/steelhead schools
Schedule: May through October
Full Service Tackle Shop
Brochure Available
Equipment Available

The Royal Coachman Ltd.
PO Box 642, 1410 E. Genesse St.
Skaneateles, NY 13152
(315) 685-0005
Contact: Michael DeTomaso
Est.: 1990   Location: Central N.Y. State–Finger Lake Region   20 mi. SW of Syracuse
Sessions: 1 day intro to fly fishing; 1 1/2-2 day advanced schools
Schedule: May & June (1 day); July & August (advanced)
Full service tackle shop
Brochure Available
Ladies only classes available

Mark Sedotti Fly Casting
59 South Regent St.
Port Chester, NY 10573
(914) 939-5960
Contact: Mark Sedotti
One day casting schools, May thru October; Hourly private lessons; seminars for fly shops, clubs and corporations.

The Wulff School of Fly Fishing
HCR1, Box 70
Lew Beach, NY 12758
(914) 439-4060 FAX: (914) 439-8055
Contact: Jane Mann
Est.: 1979
Instructors: Joan Wulff and Staff
Location: Catskills, on the Beaverkill River
100 miles NW of NYC
Sessions: 2 1/2 day courses
Schedule: Late April through June
Brochure Available
Two courses offered in weekend schools: all encompassing trout fishing or focus on fly casting.

FFF Instructors
Airmont: George Spector; (914) 357-8025
Homer: Leon Chandler; (607) 749-2324
Lew Beach: Joan Wulff; (914) 439-4060
Long Eddy: Francis Davis; (914) 887-5164
Manorville: Glen Mikkleson; (516) 878-0883
McDonough: Gary Sweet; (607) 647-5598

New York:
David Blinken
131 E 81st St. #2
New York, NY 10028
(212) 517-3474
Exciting fly fishing on the Eastend of Long Island. Fishing the waters of Easthampton & Montauk. Full and half day charters available.

New York: Gerald Wolland; (212) 662-0509
New York: Nancy Zakon; (212) 289-3439
Pound Ridge: Michael Milstein; (914) 764-1310

Roscoe:
Floyd Franke
P.O. Box 629
Roscoe, NY 12776
(607) 498-4508
Quality instruction by one of the East's most experience fly fishing instructors. FFF Master Certified and Instructor at the Wulff Fly Fishing School. Free brochure available.

Stillwater: Edward Michaels, II; (518) 587-5056

NORTH CAROLINA
Schools

McLeod's Highland Fly Fishing, Inc.
191 B Wesser Heights Dr., Bryson City, NC 28713
(704) 488-8975
Contact: Mac Brown
Est.: 1987
Location: Within 2 hr. drive of Asheville & Atlanta
Sessions: 2 1/2 day school; private instruction available
Schedule: March- August, weekends Brochure Available
Fly tying clinics and guide service also available.

FFF Instructors

Asheville:
Alan Geer
278 Independence Blvd.
Asheville, NC 28805
(704) 299-3995
Experience instructor and guide. Individual instruction or seminars for small groups. Guided fishing trips in Pisgah National Forest or Great Smoky Mountains National Park.

Asheville: Bruce Harang; (704) 299-3230
Asheville: Richard Phillips; (704) 667-3550
Barnardsville: Bruce Van Deuson; (704) 626-3679
Boone: Haden Copeland; (704) 963-5050
Boone: Mark Gould; (704) 963-8576
Chapel Hill: Richard Kurczak; (919) 489-4925

Chapel Hill: John Martyn; (919) 403-1604
Charlotte: James Dickinson; (704) 533-7393
Hendersonville: Timothy Asbury; (704) 697-6188
Highlands: T.M. Le Gardeur; (704) 526-5298
Spruce Pine: David Duffy; (704) 765-8239

OHIO

FFF Instructors

Archbold: Ron Dilbone; (419) 445-4993
Salem: Dick Owsley; (216) 332-0024

Strongsville:
Gerald Darkes
13098 Tradewinds Dr.
Strongsville, OH 44136
(216) 846-8877
FFF Certified. 30 years plus experience. Instruction for individuals, couples, groups. Experience with all ages and skill levels. Guiding service for Lake Erie and tributary stream.

Tallmadge: John T. Truex; (330) 633-7437
Toledo: Lee Faber; (419) 536-4067

Williamsburg:
Will Gray
5303 Glancy Corner Rd.
Williamsburg, OH 45176
(513) 724-7403
Fly fishing instruction for everyone–individuals, groups, community centers. FFF Certified with strict adherence to FFF casting essentials. All equipment, texts and supplies provided.

OKLAHOMA

FFF Instructors

Oklahoma City: Reece Lansberg; (405) 843-6009
Tulsa: Jack Wadlin; (918) 583-5208
Ancaster: Ted Knott; (905) 304-0388
Burlington: Barney Jones; (905) 336-8821
Don Mills: Keith Weeks; (416) 445-5957
Fergus: Ken Collins; (519) 787-4359
North York: Chris Seipio; (416) 221-9002
Ottawa: Denis Landreville; (613) 236-6443
Scarborough: Bill Wattie; (416) 284-6342
Stoney Creek: Rick Whorwood; (905) 662-8999
Waterdown: John Valk; (905) 689-0880

OREGON

Schools

The Fly Box Fishing School
1293 NE 3rd St.
Bend, OR 97701
(541) 388-3330 FAX: (541) 388-3330
Contact: Alan Stewart
Est.: 1982
Location: Deschutes River; Crooked River; Private lakes
Sessions: 1, 2 & 3 day schools
Schedule: Year-round
Full service tackle shop
Schools can be tailored to the customer's needs.
Individual instruction or groups of any size: 1-3

students per instructor. Floating classrooms are 2 students per instructor.

Kaufmann's Fly Fishing Expeditions, Inc.
PO Box 23032
Portland, OR 97281-3032
(800) 442-4359   (503) 639-6400
FAX: (503) 684-7025   http://www.kman.com
Contact: Kevin Erickson
Location: Deschutes River, Maupin
2 hrs. from Portland, OR
Sessions: 3 day schools
Schedule: May through September
Full service tackle shop
Brochure Available   Fly fishing, fly tying and steelhead schools are based at our completely modern, riverside house in Maupin.

FFF Instructors

Bend: Dave Heimes; (541) 382-0275
Bend: Rick Wren; (503) 382-1264
Enterprise: Mac Huff; (541) 426-3493
Eugene: Cliff Adams; (503) 345-0827
Gresham: Donna Teeny; (503) 667-6602
Gresham: Jim Teeny; (503) 667-6602
Hood River: Travis Duddles; (503) 386-6977
Keizer: Alvin Buhr; (503) 393-6965
Madras: Bill Howland; (541) 553-1549
McKenzie Bridge: Jim Berl; (541) 822-6003
Milwaukie: Leroy Teeple; (503) 659-8094

Portland:
Jack Hagan
17302 NE Halsey
Portland, OR 97230
(503) 492-3016
FFF Certified Casting Instructor. Licensed Guide. President N.W. Fly Fisher's Club. Fly Casting, Fly Fishing and Fly Tying Classes.Beginner through Advanced.

Portland: Scott Stoughton; (503) 291-1871
Reedsport: Michael DuVal; (503) 271-4463
Salem: Keith Burkhart; (503) 363-8324
Springfield: Stan Stanton; (503) 746-6080
Sunriver: Fred Foisset; (503) 593-5935
Welches: Brian Silvey; (503) 622-4329
West Linn: James Coulthurst; (503) 655-4797

PENNSYLVANIA

Schools

A.A. Pro Shops Fly Fishing Schools
RD1, Box 78, White Haven, PA 18661
(717) 443-8111
Est.: 1971
Location: Private waters
Sessions: Private lessons with one-on-one instruction
Schedule: March through October
Full service tackle shop
Brochure Available & Equipment Available
The schools at A.A. Pro Shop provide individual attention by working with small groups. Our program is designed for all ages.

Al Caucci Fly Fishing School
Al Caucci Fly Fishing Ent., Inc.
RD1, Box 102
Tannersville, PA 18372
(717) 629-2962 FAX: (717) 629-2962
Contact: Al or Betty Caucci
Est.: 1984

Fishing Creek Outfitters
RD#1, Box 310-1
Benton, PA 17814
(800) 548-0093   (717) 925-2225
FAX: (717) 925-5644
Contact: Dave & Donna Colley
Location: Benton, PA
25 min. from I-80, Exit 35
Sessions: 1 day schools for beginners & advanced fly
fishers   Full service tackle shop
Brochure Available & Equipment Available
Basic instruction: 3 students per instructor.
Intermediate instruction: tailored to the individual.

Joe Humphreys Fly Fishing Schools
Allenberry Resort Inn and Playhouse
Box 7, Boiling Springs, PA 17007
(717) 258-3211 FAX: (717) 258-1464
Contact: Jere Heinze
Est.: 1989
Instructors: Joe Humphreys, Ed Shenk, Norm Shires
Location: Allenberry Resort Inn in central Pennsylvania
Sessions: 2 day schools beginning Friday evenings
Schedule: April through October
Brochure Available
Weekend packages available

Yellow Breeches Outfitters
Fly Fishing Schools
2 First St., Boiling Springs, PA 17007
(717) 258-6752 FAX: (717) 258-9364
Est.: 1993
Contact: Bill Zeiders
Location: At shop and on Yellow Breeches
20 miles from Harrisburg
Sessions: 1 day classes; private instruction and casting
clinics   Schedule: March through October
Full service tackle shop
Brochure Available

FFF Instructors
Benton: Barry Beck; (717) 925-2392

Hatfield:
Jonathan Greaser
715 A Forty Foot Road
Hatfield, PA 19440
(215) 393-5721

FFF Certified Fly Casting In-
structor/Keystone Aquatic
Resource Education Instruc-
tor/I.G.F.A. Fly Rod World
Record Holder. Owns and operates Flyfishing Forever,
Inc., a full service flyfishing store located in Worcester
Township, PA.

Orwigsburg: Joseph DeMarkis; (717) 366-0165
Selinsgrove: Karl Gebhart; (717) 374-6955
State College: Daniel Shields; (814) 234-4189
Tannersville: Al Caucci; (717) 629-2962

RHODE ISLAND
Coventry: Stan Sugerman; (401) 828-0666
Westerly: Lawrence Maderia; (401) 596-3204

SOUTH CAROLINA
School

Classic Sports International
Spring Valley West
217 S. Shields Rd.
Columbia, SC 29223
(800) 375-5692 FAX: (803) 699-2477
Director: John R. Cornetti
Location: Worldwide
Continuing post-graduate education seminars
designed for physicians, dentists, attorneys and other
professionals concerned with current medical-legal
issues. Ten seminars are planned for 1997 at locations
featuring flyfishing, wingshooting and big game
hunting. Classic Sports International represents choice
locations for individual and group bookings.

FFF Instructors

Beaufort:
Wanda Taylor
P.O. Box 1837
Beaufort, SC 29901
(803) 524-0681 (Winter)

First (and possibly still the
only) woman FFF Certified
Master Flycasting Instructor.
Wanda conducts private in-
struction for individuals, couples or groups. She
welcomes the novice,intermediate or advanced caster
preparing for fresh or saltwater fly fishing adventures.

Inman:
Thomas J. Theus
114 Pinebrook Dr.
Inman, SC 29349
(864) 599-7402
Experienced Certified FFF
Casting Instructor. Member of
Joan Whitlock's Speakers
Bureau. Conducts freshwater
and saltwater fly fishing schools for individuals,
groups, corporations, clubs, demos and clinics. Slide
shows: "Fly Fishing Florida's Fabulous West Coast", "Fly
Fishing the Carolinas from Freshwater to Saltwater"
and "Fly Fishing the 4 Seasons of the Davidson River".
Offers selective fly fishing destination trips.

Summerville: Charles Giet; (803) 873-1169

TENNESSEE

School

Smokey Mountain Field School
University of Tennessee
600 Henley St., #105
Knoxville, TN 37996
(423) 974-0150
Est.: 1991
Program Coordinator: Meg Mabbs
Instructor: Jim Casada
Location: Sugarlands Visitor Center, Gatlinburg, TN
45 mins. from Knoxville
Sessions: 1 and 2 day sessions for beginners and
intermediate skill levels
Schedule: 1 day: 7/19/97; 2 day: 5/17-18; 5/31-6/1;
10/11-12.
Brochure Available and Equipment Available

FFF Instructors

Benton:
Wanda Taylor
P.O. Box 618
Benton, TN 37307
(423) 338-6283 (Summer)
First (and possibly still the only) woman FFF Certified
Master Flycasting Instructor. Wanda conducts private
instruction for individuals, couples or groups. She
welcomes the novice, intermediate or advanced caster
preparing for fresh or saltwater fly fishing adventures.

Memphis: Dan Berry; (901) 398-8012
Memphis: James Cowan; (901) 527-4443
Nashville: Charles Robinson; (615) 370-1090

TEXAS

School

Angler's Edge
Saltwater Fly Fishing School
3926 Westheimer
Highland Village
Houston, TX 77027
(713) 993-9981   FAX: (713) 993-9972
Contact: Brooks Bouldin

FFF Instructor

Austin: Raye Carrington; (512) 502-9670
Austin: Joe Robinson; (512) 477-7870
Baytown: Bill Gammel; (713) 424-8638
Colleyville: James Linn; (817) 581-6070
Dallas: Cary Marcus; (214) 350-7530
Dripping Spring: Terry Manning; (512) 858-4205
Fort Worth: Andrea Thomas; (817) 924-6073
Ft. Worth: Ronald Norman; (817) 738-1801
Galveston: James Doggett; (409) 737-3652
Hext: Leonard Wilson; (915) 396-2265
Houston: James Bridges; (713) 771-7977
Houston: Kim Helms Kennedy; (713) 669-8687
Houston: Greg Mason; (713) 664-1584

Houston:
Phil Shook
5739 Rutherglenn Drive
Houston, TX 77096
(713) 723-3275
Learn basic flycasting skills with emphasis on techniques for area saltwater flats and and bass ponds.
Instruction includes tips on rigging, knot tying and fly
selection.

Houston: Scott Surprise; (713) 480-3458
McAllen: Bud Rowland; (210) 682-0104

Rockport:
Kenneth Callaway
2321 Harbor Dr.
Rockport, TX 78382
(512) 729-7475
FFF Certified Master Flycasting Instructor. Teach, Beginners, Intermediate, Advanced–All Phases of flycasting,
including Terminal tackle knots, etc. Individuals or
Groups, Demo's or Clinics.

San Antonio:
Raymond Chapa
8927 Rustling Branches
San Antonio, TX 78250
(210) 680-0912
Basic flycasting instruction for individuals or small
groups. Taylor made classes for Texas hill country
streams, saltwater coast, or vacation destinations.
Equipment provided. Since 1994.

San Antonio: Raymond Chapa; (210) 680-0912
San Antonio: Jimmy Cook; (210) 828-1868
San Antonio: Thomas Howell; (210) 344-1060
San Antonio: Ken Rupkalvis; (210) 622-6468
San Antonio: William West; (210) 824-5162
Spring: Barkley Souders; (281) 370-9491

UTAH

FFF Instructors
Dutch John: Robb Carter; (801) 889-3727

Dutch John:
Lyle Waldron
25 Flaming Gorge Meadows
Dutch John, UT 84023
(801) 889-3807
10 years guiding on the famous Green River. Certified
FFF, October 1993 by Mel Krieger. I'm also on the Flycasting Advisory Committee, (801) 889-3807.

Park City: Berris Samples; (801) 658-0107
Sandy: Mickey Anderson; (801) 566-9744
Sandy: Byron Gunderson; (801) 942-2563

VERMONT

Schools

The Battenkill Anglers
RR#1, Box 2303, Manchester Center, VT 05255
(802) 362-3184   Contact: Tom Goodman
Est.: 1990   Schedule: May 1-Oct. 31
Sessions: 1/2 to 2 days
On-stream private instruction on the Battenkill and
Mettowee Rivers.

Fly Fish Vermont
804 S. Main St.-#4, Stowe, VT 05672
(802) 253-3964
Contact: Bob Shannon
Est.: 1983 Location: The Commodores, Stowe, VT
45 min. from Burlington, VT
Sessions: 1 day classes for groups of 1-4 students
Schedule: May through October
Full service tackle shop
Brochure Available
Equipment Available
Drift boat guide service available

Orvis Fly-Fishing Schools
Historic Rt. 7A, Manchester, VT 05254
(802) 362-8616
Contact: Dan O'Connor
Full Service Tackle Shop
Brochure Available & Equipment Available
Orvis Fly-Fishing Schools offer 7 locations to choose
from: Manchester, VT; Millbrook, NY; Colorado; Cape
Cod; Key Largo; Mays Pond, FL; England. At each
location, different angling styles are pursued. All Orvis
Fly-Fishing Schools include comprehensive instruction,
a non-resident fishing license where required, lunches,
the use of an Orvis rod, reel, line, leaders and flies,
and your choice of one of our fly-fishing guide books.
For reservations or more information on a specific
Orvis Fly-Fishing School, call (800) 235-9763, ext. 844.

Woodstock Outfitters
20 Central St.
Woodstock, VT 05095
(802) 457-2007
Contact: Jack
Est.: 1991 Location: Killington Ski Resort
Sessions: 2 1/2 day-all inclusive
Schedule: End of May through July
Full service tackle shop
Brochure Available
"Orvis Endorsed" outfitter and dealer. Guide Service
Available

**The Wright Schools of
Fly Fishing & Rod Building**
The Wright Rod Co.
PO Box 27, 45 Churchill Rd.,
Websterville, VT 05678
(802) 476-6125
Contact: Steve May
Location: Barre, VT area
Sessions: 3 day fly fishing school: Friday through
Sunday; 2 day rod building school
Brochure Available
Equipment Available

FFF Instructors

Dorset: Leigh Oliva; (802) 867-0244
Manchester Ctr.: Gwenn Perkins; (802) 362-3502
Newport Center: Jerry Gibbs; (802) 334-8831
Reading: Susan Damone Balch; (802) 484-9791
South Royalton: Erin Curpier; (802) 763-7038

VIRGINIA

School

Murray's Fly Shop
PO Box 156, 121 Main St., Edinburg, VA 22824
(540) 984-4212 FAX: (800) 984-4895
Est.: 1962   Staff: 4
President: Harry Murray
Location: Bass School-Edinburg, VA; Trout
School-Madison, VA
Sessions: Bass-2 day schools; Trout-1 day schools
Schedule: March through October
Full service tackle shop
Brochure Available & Equipment Available
19 schools will be offered in 1997. Class size is
restricted in order to provide the maximum time with
each student.

FFF Instructors

Arlington:
Phil Gay
3488 N Emerson St, Arlington, VA 22207
(703) 536-2726
Phil is a Federated Fly Fishers Master Certified Casting
Instructor. His company, Trout & About, provides guid-
ing, teaching and package trips within the
Washington, DC area.

McLean: Arthur Hendrick; (703) 821-3144

Middleburg:
Rhea Ann Topping
P.O. Box 1831, Middleburg, VA 20118
(540) 592-3006
1st Joan Wulff Eastern Instructor's School 1996. Win-
ner Rohrer Cup Casting Competition, 1996 Montana.
FFF Certified–one of the best female instructors in the
East–D.C. area.

Roanoke: M. Lanier Woodrum; (703) 774-2798
Vienna: Rick Larkin; (703) 938-0153

WASHINGTON

School

**Sage Fly Fishing Schools and
Fly Casting Clinics**
8500 NE Day Rd., Bainbridge Island, WA 98110
(800) 533-3004 (206) 842-6608
FAX: (206) 842-6830
School Director: Randi Swisher
Location: Nationwide
Sessions: 1 day schools
Schedule: Spring through Fall
Call for our complete schedule.
Sage Fly Fishing Schools and Casting Clinics are held

throughout the United States in cooperation with the Sage dealers in your area. A complete list of schools can be obtained by writing Sage.

FFF Instructors

Auburn: Mike Duey; (206) 833-5495
Auburn: Greg Tompkins; (206) 839-3635
Bainbridge Island: Randi Swisher; (206) 842-0546
Battle Ground: Robin White; (503) 223-4700
Battle Ground: Tom White; (360) 687-6390
Bothell: Larry Iwafuchi; (206) 402-1055
Bothell: Peg Van Natter; (206) 485-1410
Bothell: Bill Van Natter; (206) 486-5011
Bremerton: James Sisson; (360) 377-9228
Clinton: Gilbert Nyerges; (360) 341-5313
Duvall: Gary Todd; (206) 788-1610
Edmonds: Robert McLaughlin; (206) 776-1141
Hansville: Ray Bianco; (360) 638-2137
Packwood: Mark Raisler; (509) 672-3112
Poulsbo: James Birkholm; (360) 697-3905
Poulsbo: Deanna Birkholm; (206) 697-3905
Pullman: Andrew Parker; (509) 334-2472
Seattle: Andy Hall; (206) 363-3962
Seattle: John Olson; (206) 782-3735
Seattle: Don Simonson; (206) 932-4925
Snohomish: Kevin Sack; (360) 668-9228
Tacoma: Darrel Martin; (206) 531-6480
Vashon Island: Cam Sigler; (206) 567-4839

WISCONSIN

FFF Instructors

River Falls: Tom Andersen; (715) 381-5234
Wausau: Gary Borger; (715) 842-9879

Wausau:
Jason Borger
PO Box 2166
Wausau, WI 54402
(715) 843-7878
Come to understand the mechanics of fly casting with the "Shadow Caster" in "A River Runs Through It": Offering seminars, schools, and private instruction.

WYOMING

Schools

Jack Dennis Fly Fishing
PO Box 3369
Jackson, WY 83001
(307) 733-3270 FAX: (307) 733-4540
Contact: Bruce James
Sessions: 2 hour lesson-minimum

High Country Flys
PO Box 3432
185 North Center St.
Jackson, WY 83001
(307) 733-7210 FAX: (307) 733-5382
Contact: Howard Cole or Jim Jones
Est.: 1988   Location: Jackson, WY
Sessions: 1 day instructional trips
Schedule: Mid-June through Mid-September
Full service tackle shop
Flyer Available and Equipment Available

Westbank Anglers
Fly Fishing Schools and Clinics
PO Box 523, Teton Village, WY 83025
(800) 922-3474   (307) 733-6483
Contact: Stephen & Kim Vletas or Reynolds Pomeroy

FFF Instructors

Buffalo: David Todd; (307) 684-7549
Casper: Bill Mixer; (307) 234-0647
Jackson: Paul Bruun; (307) 733-5173
Jackson: Howard Cole; (307) 733-1957
Jackson: Bill Klyn; (307) 739-9818
Saratoga: John Dobson; (307) 326-8002
Wilson: A.J. DeRosa; (307) 733-3061

CANADA

Schools

Murray's Fly Fishing School
30 Evalene Ct.
Brampton, Ontario, Canada L6Z 3A3
(905) 846-8254
Contact: Murray Abbott
Est.: 1992
Instructors: FFF Certified
Location: Toronto area
Sessions: 1 day courses for beginners & intermediate
Schedule: Every weekend: last weekend March until October
Brochure Available and Equipment Available

Rocky Mountain Institute of Fly Fishing
8403 145 Ave., Edmonton, AB
Canada T5E 2J1
(403) 475-8139   FAX: (403) 473-6327
Contact: Barry White
FFF Master certified flycasting instructor.
Destination Fly Fishing Schools from 1 to 3 days or private instruction available.

FFF Instructors

Calgary, AB,: Richard Mercer; (403) 287-2604
St. Albert, AB Roman Scharabun; (403) 973-5259
Hamilton, Ontario: Bill Spicer; (905) 529-0212

How To Use The Destination Directory

It is safe to say that no one really knows how many fly lodges, outfitters and guides are out there. Thousands, for sure. Thankfully, you don't have to have a list of every single one to book the fishing excursion you're looking for. What you need is a list ample enough to allow you to shop wisely.

Where do you find such a list? Right here Black's Destination directory. More than a mere list, however, the section provides a profile of 450-plus lodges, outfitters and guides worldwide. Each profile contains enough information for you to "get a feel" for what an individual operator has to offer, and, of course, details on how to contact him. [See the explanation of a **Typical Listing** below.]

In addition, many state sections begin with a short list of fly tackle dealers, which in addition to providing a place to purchase equipment, often offer guide and outfitting services of their own.

Ads Provide Valuable Information

The advertisements and listing enhancements that appear in the Destinations section provide even more information to help you find the fishing experience you're after. In short, those ads are an operator's way of telling you that he or she is eager for your business.

Contacting a lodge, outfitter or guide by phone can be tricky. In some remote areas, no one may be manning the phones for extended periods of time. Often, outfitters and guides will be away from their phones doing what they love to do—outfit and guide! Don't be put off, however. Check the seasonal phone and fax numbers listed and try again. Or write and ask for a flyer, brochure or, when available, a video.

When you call an owner, manager, guide or outfitter talk to them about your fishing plans. Listen to their advice. Get their brochures and flyers. Ask for references—and call them.

Say You Saw it in Black's

Black's Fly Fishing would not be published without the advertising support of fly fishing companies and destinations trying to reach and influence you, the angler. So whenever you contact one of them, tell them that you have benefited from seeing their ad or listing. And don't forget to say that you "saw it in Black's."

TYPICAL DESTINATION LISTING

1 —— **Eagle Nest Lodge**
PO Box 577, Hardin, MT 59034
2 —— (406) 665-3711 Fax (406) 665-3711
Contact Keith or Alan Kelly
3 —— Area Big Horn River
Services Lodge, Accommodations, Fly
Shop, School; Est. 1981; Waters Public;
4 —— Type Walk/Wade, Boat; Fish Rainbow,
Brown; Packages 1 Day, up to 14 anglers

How The Directory Is Organized

Black's Fly Fishing's U.S., Canadian and International Listings are organized alphabetically by state, province and country name. Each U.S. state section begins with an alphabetized list of fly tackle dealers and lodges (when available), followed by an alphabetized list of outfitters and guides.

1 & 2 Dealer, Lodge, Outfitter/Guide Contact Information Operation and contact names, addresses (physical, Email and web site, when available), telephone and fax numbers and seasonal calling information useful in gathering flyers, brochures and additional information.

3 Area A brief description of the geographic area, sometimes including the names of well recognized rivers, lakes, national parks or regions in which the lodge, outfitter/guide operates.

4 Description In the case of fly tackle dealers, a narrative about the range of products and services provided. Whenever possible, Black's offers detailed information about the lodges and outfitter/guides listed. This information is provided by the operator and is not verified by Black's. Listings may include the following:

Est. The year the lodge, outfitter/guide began operation.

Services A list of services and amenities offered by the operator.

Season The months of the year during which the lodge, outfitter/guide operates.

Waters An indication of whether the access to waters fished by the operator is public or private.

Type The "type" of fishing offered, specifically Float Tube, Walk/Wade, or Boat.

Fish A listing of up to five species of fish offered by the operator. (Some operators offer many more than five varieties of fish; call for info.)

Packages Indicates the shortest duration fishing package available, usually 1/2 to 1 day in length. Longer packages are almost always offered. The number of anglers indicated is the maximum number the operator can handle at any one time.

ALABAMA

Fly Tackle Dealers

The Deep South Fly Shop
3431 Colonnade Pkwy., Suite 300
Birmingham, AL 35243
(205) 969-3868   FAX: (205) 969-1339
Contact: Rob Rogers
Sage, Orvis, Winston, Abel. Instruction, guide service available.

North Alabama Outdoors
7540-B So. Memorial Pkwy
Huntsville, AL 35802
(205) 882-2236
Contact: Bernie Parr
Full service fly shop; booking trips to Canada, South America and the Bahamas.

ALABAMA
Outfitters/Guides

Capt. Jimbo Meador
17105 Scenic Hwy 98, PO Box 995,
Point Clear, AL 36564
(205) 990-9067
Contact Capt. Jimbo Meador
Area Near Mobile;   **Services** Guide;   **Waters** Public;
Type Walk/Wade, Boat;   **Fish** Largemouth, Sea Trout

ALASKA

Lodges

Alagnak Lodge
17105 Scenic Hwy. 98, PO Box 995,
Point Clear, AL 36564
(800) 877-9903
Area Alagnak;   **Services** Lodge, Accommodations;
Waters Public;   **Type** Walk/Wade;   **Fish** Rainbow,
Salmon, Grayling

Alaska Rainbow Lodge
PO Box 39, King Salmon, AK 99613
(800) 451-6198   **Contact** Ron Hayes
Services Lodge, Accommodations;   **Waters** Public

Alaska's Fishing Unlimited Lodge
PO Box 190301, Anchorage, AK 99519
(907) 243-5899   **Fax** (907) 243-2473
Contact Lorane Owsichek or Brenda Bowles
Area Bristol Bay;   **Services** Lodge, Accommodations;
Est. 1976;   **Season** Jun-Oct;   **Waters** Public;   **Type**
Walk/Wade, Boat;   **Fish** Trout, Salmon, Char, Pike,
Grayling;   **Packages** 3 Days, up to 16 anglers
O 21 years of fly-out fishing in Bristol Bay
O Your pilot/guide & plane stay with you all day
O Fishing famous Iliamna trophy Rainbow area
O Beautiful lodge with hot tubs, saunas, &
   cabins for two
O Five species of Pacific Salmon
O Five species of fresh water fish

Alaska's Rainbow River Lodge
4127 Raspberry Rd., Anchorage, AK 99502
(907) 243-7894 or (907) 571-1210
Fax (907) 248-1726 **Contact** Chris Goll, Master Guide
Area Iliamna/Bristol Bay; **Services** Lodge,
Accommodations, Fly Shop, School; **Est.** 1980;
Season Jun-Oct; **Waters** Public/Private; **Type** Float
Tube, Walk/Wade, Boat; **Fish** Rainbow, Steelhead,
Salmon, Char, Pike, Grayling; **Packages** 3 Days, up to
12 anglers

▼ ORVIS ENDORSED ▼

ALASKA'S

Valhalla
Lodge

Alaska's Vahalla Lodge
PO Box 190583, Anchorage, AK 99519
(907) 243-6096 **Fax** (907) 243-6095
Contact Kirk & Sarah Gay   **Area** Lake Clark &
Katmai Nat'l Parks; **Services** Lodge,
Accommodations; **Est.** 1939; **Season** Jun-Oct;
Waters Public; **Type** Walk/Wade, Boat; **Fish**
Rainbow, Salmon; **Packages** 3 Days, up to 12 anglers
See Our Ad Across

▲ ORVIS ENDORSED ▲

Angler's Paradise Lodges
4550 Aircraft Dr., Anchorage, AK 99502
(800) 544-0551 or (907) 243-5448
Fax (907) 243-0649 **Contact** Sonny Petersen
Area Katmai Ntl. Park; **Services** Lodge, Accom-
modations, Fly Shop; **Est.** 1950; **Season** Jun-Oct;
Waters Public; **Type** Walk/Wade, Boat; **Fish** Rainbow, Lake Trout, Salmon, Char, Dolly Varden, Pike,
Grayling; **Packages 3, 4 or 7 Days** up to 20 anglers
O The Best Fishing
O The Best Guides
O The Best Locations
O The Best Since 1950
Our reputation as Alaska's finest sportfishing Lodges is
the result of the quality of our service. Professional
guides and experienced Alaska pilots are the key to
your satisfaction and safety. The knowledge of the fish-
ing waters and terrain accumulated by our staff since
1950 assures you an exceptional fishing experience.

Baranof Wilderness Lodge
at Warm Springs Bay
PO Box 2187, Sitka, AK 99835
(916) 582-8132   **Area** S.E. Alaska & Kanektok River;
Services Lodge, Accommodations; **Waters** Public;
Type Walk/Wade, Boat; **Fish** Rainbow, Cutthroat,
Salmon, Dolly Varden, Halibut **Packages** 6 Day, 5
Night or 8 Day, 7 Night

▼ ORVIS ENDORSED ▼

ORVIS
ENDORSED
LODGE

Boardwalk
Wilderness Lodge
PO Box 19121, Cook's Cove, Thorne Bay, AK 99919
(907) 828-3918 or (907) 828-3980
Fax (907) 828-3367   **Contact** Douglas Ibbetson
Area Thorne & Staney Rivers; **Services** Lodge,
Accommodations, Fly Shop; **Est.** 1985; **Season**
Apr-Sep; **Waters** Public; **Type** Float Tube,
Walk/Wade, Boat; **Fish** Cutthroat, Steelhead,
Salmon, Dolly Varden, Grayling; **Packages** 3 Days, up
to 12 anglers
See Our Ad Pg. 145

▲ ORVIS ENDORSED ▲

Bristol Bay Lodge
PO Box 1509, Dillingham, AK 99576
(907) 842-2500 Oct-May Call: (509) 964-2094
Fax (509) 964-2269 **Contact** Maggie & Ron McMillan
Services Lodge, Accommodations; **Est.** 1972;
Season Jun-Sep; **Waters** Public/Private; **Type**
Walk/Wade, Boat; **Fish** Trout, Salmon, Char, Dolly
Varden, Grayling; **Packages** up to 20 anglers
O ORVIS Endorsed
Three hundred fifty miles west of Anchorage lies Bris-
tol Bay Lodge and its vast watershed home of the
finest freshwater fishing in North America. BBL is a full
service fly out fishing lodge with 25 years of same man-
agement experience, catering to sportsmen who
desire only the best.

Chelatna Lake Lodge
3941 Float Plane Dr., Anchorage, AK 99502
(800) 999-0785 or (907) 243-7767
Fax (907) 248-5791   **Contact** Duke Bertke
Area Denali Nat'l Park;   **Services** Lodge;   **Season**
Jun-Sep;   **Waters** Public;   **Fish** Rainbow, Lake Trout

Crystal Creek Lodge
PO Box 3049, Dillingham, AK 99576
(800) 525-3153 **Fax** (907) 245-1946
Contact Dan Michels   **Area** Bristol Bay area;
Services Lodge, Accommodations;   **Season**
Jun10-Sep25;   **Waters** Public;   **Type** Walk/Wade;
Fish Rainbow, Salmon, Char, Dolly Varden, Grayling;
Packages 7 Days, up to 22 anglers
O ORVIS Endorsed

Goodnews River Lodge
Alaska River Safaris
4909 Rollins Dr., Anchorage, AK 99508
(800) 274-8371 Jun 22-Sep 9 Call: (907) 967-8526

Fax (907) 338-5356   **Contact** Capt. Ron Hyde
Area Togiak Nat'l Wildlife Refuge;   **Services** Lodge,
Accommodations;   **Est.** 1974;   **Season** Year-round;
Waters Public;   **Type** Boat;   **Fish** Rainbow, Salmon,
Char, Dolly Varden, Grayling

Great Alaska Fish Camp & Safaris
HC, Box 218, Sterling, AK 99672
(800) 544-2261 **Fax** (907) 262-8789
Contact John Lawrence
Services Lodge, Accommodations;   **Season**
May15-Oct.15;   **Waters** Public;   **Type** Walk/Wade;
Fish Rainbow, Steelhead, Salmon, Dolly Varden,
Grayling;   **Packages** up to 40 anglers

Kachemak Bay Wilderness Lodge
Box 956, Homer, AK 99603
(907) 235-8910 **Fax** (907) 235-8911
Contact Michael & Diane McBride
Services Lodge, Accommodations;   **Season**

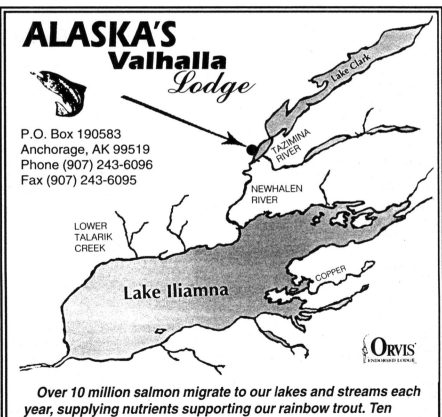

ALASKA'S
Valhalla
Lodge

P.O. Box 190583
Anchorage, AK 99519
Phone (907) 243-6096
Fax (907) 243-6095

LOWER
TALARIK
CREEK

TAZIMINA RIVER

NEWHALEN RIVER

Lake Clark

COPPER

Lake Iliamna

ORVIS
ENDORSED LODGE

Over 10 million salmon migrate to our lakes and streams each year, supplying nutrients supporting our rainbow trout. Ten species of sportfish are abundant in our area. Come explore and fish wild, remote streams for an unforgettable experience.

May-Oct15; **Waters** Public; **Type** Walk/Wade;
Fish Trout, Rainbow, Salmon, Char; **Packages** 5
Days, up to 12 anglers

Katmai Lodge, Ltd.
2825 90th St., SE, Dept. BFF, Everett, WA 98208
(206) 337-0326 **Fax** (206) 337-0335
Area Alagnak River, Bristol Bay; **Services** Lodge,
Accommodations, Fly Shop; **Est.** 1979; **Season**
Jun-Oct; **Waters** Public; **Type** Walk/Wade, Boat;
Fish Rainbow, Salmon, Char, Dolly Varden, Grayling;
Packages 3 Days, up to 45 anglers

Kodiak Island River Camps
Box 1162, Kodiak, AK 99615
(907) 486-5310 **Contact** Daniel Busch
Area Kodiak & Afogniak Islands; **Services** Lodge,
Accommodations; **Est.** 1989; **Season** Jun-Oct;
Waters Public; **Type** Float Tube, Walk/Wade, Boat;
Fish Trout, Steelhead, Salmon; **Packages** 6 Days

Lions Den Wilderness Lodge
PO Box 29, Port Lions, AK 99550
(907) 454-2301 **Fax** (907) 454-2301
Contact Kevin & Kathy Adkins
Services Lodge, Accommodations; **Season**
June1-Nov1; **Waters** Public; **Type** Walk/Wade;
Fish Rainbow, Salmon, Dolly Varden

Maurice's
Alaskan Floating Lodge
PO Box 1261, Dillingham, AK 99576
(800) 356-2844 **Contact** Capt. Maurice Bertini
Area Remote Bristol Bay Waters; **Services** Lodge,
Accommodations; **Season** Jun-Sep30; **Waters**
Public; **Type** Walk/Wade, Boat; **Fish** Rainbow,
Salmon, Char, Dolly Varden, Grayling; **Packages** up
to 6 anglers
Picture this: a floating five-star hotel designed and built
by the owner, Maurice Bertini, which draws one foot
of water and is fully equipped with skiffs, hand-picked
guides and a gourmet chef, situated in the renowned
Bristol Bay/Wood/Tikchik State Park. Our discriminating anglers enjoy unsurpassed salmon, trophy
rainbows, grayling, and char fishing literally at their
doorstep. No more "rainy day poker parties" to mar
this trip of a lifetime. All weather lodge places you "on
the fish" at the peak of the runs–rain or shine. Fish 24
hours a day–sleep is optional. Ask about our September, "Cast 'n Blast" specials. Call or write today!
See Our Ad Pg. 141

No See Um Lodge, Inc.
PO Box 382, King Salmon, AK 99613
(907) 439-3070 or (916) 241-6204
Fax (916) 244-4618 **Contact** John Holman
Area Iliamna-Katmai, N.P. of S.W. Alaska; **Services**
Lodge, Accommodations, Fly Shop, School; **Est.**
1975; **Season** June8-Oct.1; **Waters** Public/Private;
Type Boat; **Fish** Rainbow, Salmon, Char, Dolly
Varden, Grayling; **Packages** 7 Days, up to 10 anglers

Northwoods Lodge
PO Box 56, Skwentna, AK 99667
(800) 999-6539 or (907) 733-3742
Fax (907) 733-3742 **Contact** Eric & Shan Johnson
Area Yentna River; **Services** Lodge,
Accommodations; **Season** May25-Oct1; **Waters**
Public; **Type** Walk/Wade, Boat; **Fish** Rainbow,
Salmon, Pike, Grayling; **Packages** 7 Days, up to 15
anglers

Ole Creek Lodge
506 Ketchikan St., Fairbanks, AK 99701
(907) 452-2421 or (907) 533-3474
Fax (907) 452-2421 **Contact** Donald Haugen
Area Lake Iliamna; **Services** Lodge,
Accommodations; **Season** Jun-Oct; **Waters** Public;
Type Boat; **Fish** Rainbow, Salmon, Pike

Quinnat Landing Hotel
Katmai Adventures
5520 Lake Otis, Ste. 101, Anchorage, AK 99507
(907) 561-2310 or (800) 770-FISH
Fax (907) 561-1700 **Contact** Joe Cantrell
Services Lodge, Accommodations; **Waters** Public;
Type Walk/Wade

Saltery Lake Lodge
1516 Larch St. #1, Kodiak, AK 99615
(800) 770-5037 or (907) 486-7083
Fax (907) 486-3188 **Contact** Doyle Hatfield
Area Eastern side of Kodiak Island; **Services** Lodge,
Accommodations; **Season** Apr15-Nov30; **Waters**
Public; **Type** Walk/Wade, Boat; **Fish** Trout,
Steelhead, Salmon, Dolly Varden

Silver Salmon Creek Lodge
PO Box 3234, Soldotna, AK 99669
(902) 262-4839
Services Lodge, Accommodations; **Waters** Public;
Type Walk/Wade; **Fish** Salmon, Dolly Varden;
Packages 3 Days

Talaview Lodge
PO Box 190088, Anchorage, AK 99519
(907) 733-3447 **Fax** (907) 733-3447
Contact Steve & Louise Johnson
Services Lodge, Accommodations; **Est.** 1978;
Season Jun15-Sep15; **Waters** Public; **Type**
Walk/Wade; **Fish** Rainbow, Salmon, Grayling;
Packages up to 14 anglers

Tikchik Narrows Lodge
PO Box 220248, Anchorage, AK 99522
(907) 243-8450 **Fax** (907) 248-3091
Contact Bud Hodson
Services Lodge, Accommodations; **Est.** 1969;
Season Jun-Oct; **Waters** Public; **Type** Walk/Wade,
Boat; **Fish** Trout, Salmon, Char, Dolly Varden,

Todd's Igiugig Lodge
PO Box 871395, Wasilla, AK 99687
(907) 376-2859 or (907) 533-3216
Fax (907) 373-0298 **Contact** Larry or Elizabeth Todd
Area Lake Iliamna; Bristol Bay Area; **Services** Lodge,

Accommodations, Fly Shop; **Est.** 1973; **Season**
June10-Sept.30; **Waters** Public/Private; **Type**
Walk/Wade, Boat; **Fish** Trout, Rainbow, Lake Trout,
Salmon, Char, Whitefish, Dolly Varden, Pike, Grayling;
Packages 7 Days, up to 8 anglers

Whalers Cove Lodge
Box 101, Angoon, AK 99820
(800) 423-3123 or (907) 788-3123
Fax (907) 788-3104
Contact Richard & Sharon Powers
Area Southeast Alaska; **Services** Lodge,
Accommodations, Fly Shop; **Est.** 1980; **Season**
Jun-Oct; **Waters** Private; **Type** Walk/Wade, Boat;
Fish Trout, Steelhead, Salmon, Dolly Varden, halibut,
red snapper, long cod, king, silver, pink and chum;
Packages up to 50 anglers
○ Guided & self guided trips
○ Clear, easily wadeable streams
○ Fantastic Meals/Lodging
○ Success Guaranteed

Wilderness Place Lodge
PO Box 190711-BF, Anchorage, AK 99519
(907) 733-2051 or (907) 248-4337
Area Lake Creek; **Services** Lodge, Accommodations;
Waters Public; **Type** Walk/Wade; **Packages** up to
15 anglers

ALASKA
Outfitters/Guides

Alaska Rainbow Adventures
PO Box 456, Anchor Point, AK 99556
(907) 235-2647   **Contact** Paul Hansen
Area Bristol Bay, Togiak, Alagnak & Tirchik Rivers;
Services Outfitter/Guide, Accommodations; **Season**
Jun-Oct; **Waters** Public; **Type** Boat; **Fish** Trout,
Salmon, Char, Grayling

Alaska Trophy Fishing Safaris
PO Box 670071, Chugiak, AK 99567
(907) 696-2484 **Fax** (907) 696-2484
Contact Dennis Harms
Services Guide; **Est.** 1970; **Waters** Public; **Fish**
Steelhead, Salmon, Char

Alaska Wilderness Expeditions
Box 237, RD 5, Coatesville, PA 19320, AK
(610) 380-0103   **Contact** Tim or Marsha White
Area American Creek, Talachulitna & Mulchatna
Rivers; **Services** Outfitter/Guide, Accommodations;
Est. 1989; **Season** Jun-Aug; **Waters** Public; **Type**
Walk/Wade, Boat; **Fish** Rainbow, Lake Trout, Dolly
Varden, Pike; **Packages** 6 Days, up to 8 anglers

Brightwater Alaska, Inc.
PO Box 110796, Anchorage, AK 99511
(907) 344-1340   **Contact** Chuck Ash
Services Outfitter/Guide; **Est.** 1975; **Waters** Public;
Type Walk/Wade, Boat; **Fish** Rainbow, Salmon,
Char, Grayling

Eruk's Wilderness Float Tours
12720 Lupine Rd., Anchorage, AK 99516
(888) 212-2203 **Fax** (907) 345-7678
Contact Eruk Williamson
Area SW Alaska; **Services** Guide, Accommodations;
Est. 1988; **Season** Jun-Aug; **Waters** Public; **Type**
Walk/Wade, Boat; **Fish** Rainbow, Salmon, Char, Pike;
Packages 5 Days, up to 6 anglers

Ouzel Expeditions Inc.
PO Box 935, Girdwood, AK 99587
(907) 783-2216 **Fax** (907) 783-3220
Contact Paul & Sharon Allred
Services Outfitter/Guide, Accommodations; **Est.**
1978; **Waters** Public; **Type** Boat; **Fish** Rainbow,
Steelhead, Salmon, Char

Togiak River Fishing Adventures
PO Box 329, Togiak, AK 99678
(907) 493-5744 (Summer); (208) 558-7587 (Winter)
Contact David Lovegren
Area Togiak River, Bristol Bay Alaska; **Services**
Outfitter/Guide, Accommodations, Fly Shop, School;
Est. 1992; **Season** June-Sept.; **Waters** Public;
Type Walk/Wade, Boat; **Fish** Trout, Rainbow,
Salmon, Char, Dolly Varden, Pike, Grayling; **Packages**
3 Days, up to 12 anglers

ARIZONA
Fly Tackle Dealers

Canyon Creek Anglers
21 W. Camelback Rd., Phoenix, AZ 85013
(602) 277-8195   FAX: (602) 277-0127
Contact: Carmine Isgro
A full service outfitter with a complete line of all major
products. Connection to a large network of guides
throughout Arizona.

Lees Ferry Anglers
HC67, Box 2, Marble Canyon, AZ 86036
(800) 962-9755   FAX: (520) 355-2271
Contact: Terry & Wendy Gunn
Full service fly shop. Year round fly fishing school; and
guide service on the Colorado River.

ARIZONA
Outfitters/Guides

Ambassador Guide Service
PO Box 735, Prescott, AZ 86302
(520) 771-8627   **Fax** (520) 778-5050
Contact Bill McBurney
Area Lee's Ferry & Grand Canyon; **Services** Guide;
Waters Public; **Type** Walk/Wade; **Fish** Rainbow

Lees Ferry Anglers

HC 67 - Box 2, Marble Canyon, AZ 86036
(800) 962-9755 (520) 355-2261
Fax (520) 355-2271   **Contact** Terry Gunn
Area Colorado River;   **Services** Outfitter/Guide, Fly
Shop;   **Season** Yr.Round;   **Waters** Public/Private;
Type Walk/Wade, Boat;   **Fish** Rainbow;   **Packages** 1
Day, up to 20 anglers
Challenging Tailwater Catch 'n' Release Trophy Rainbow Trout. Below Glen Canyon Dam on the the
Colorado River at the entrance to Grand Canyon. Rainbow trout, gin clear water and majestic scenery. Fish
365 days a year with one of our eight full-time USCG-li-
censed boat or walk/wade fly-fishing guides. A
comfortable drive from Las Vegas or Phoenix. Full service fly shop. Call or write for information. E-Mail:
anglers@leesferry.com Web Site:
http://www.leesferry.com
See Our Ad, Right

ARKANSAS

Outfitters/Guides

John Gulley

Box 3012, River View Rd., Norfolk, AR 72658
(501) 499-7517   **Contact** John Gulley
Area Norfolk River, No. Arkansas;   **Services** Guide;
Est. 1973;   **Waters** Public;   **Type** Walk/Wade;   **Fish**
Bass, Rainbow, Brook, Brown, Cutthroat

The Ozark Angler

659 Wilburn Rd., Hwy 110 E.,
Herber Springs, AR 72543
(501) 362-3597 or (501) 225-6504;
Email: Ozarkflys@aol.com   **Fax** (501) 362-3597
Contact Tom Hawthorne
Area Little Red River;   **Services** Outfitter/Guide,
Accommodations, Fly Shop;   **Est.** 1988;   **Season**
Year-round;   **Waters** Public/Private;   **Type** Float
Tube, Walk/Wade, Boat;   **Fish** Smallmouth, Rainbow,
Brook, Brown, Cutthroat;   **Packages** 1 Day, up to 12
anglers
O ORVIS Endorsed
World-class fly fishing for brown, rainbow, cutthroat,
and brook trout. Float or wade one of Arkansas' fine
tailwaters for trout or choose an Ozark Mountain
stream for native smallmouth. Guide services include
float trips, walk/wade trips, and fly fishing schools.
Guests can arrange daily guide trips or select a full
package. The full service fly shop offers a complete selection of Orvis tackle, trout, and bass flies. Let the
experienced staff of The Ozark Angler help you plan
an Arkansas fly fishing trip.

CALIFORNIA

Fly Tackle Dealers

Brock's Fly Fishing Specialists

100 N. Main, Bishop, CA 93514
(888) 619-3581   (619) 872-3581
FAX: (619) 872-6003   Contact: Gary Gunsolley
We are a full service fly shop with a large selection of
flies, rods, reels and up-to-date fishing information.
Instruction/guide service available.

Fishermen's Spot!

14423 Burbank Blvd., Van Nuys, CA 91401
(818) 785-7306   FAX: (818) 785-7069
Contact: Steve Ellis   Internet: Ken Lindsay
Fishermen's Spot! has been supplying a full line of fly
fishing and tying equipment, travel, collectibles and
instruction for over 25 years.

High Sierra Flyfisher

337 W. Ridgecrest Blvd., Ridgecrest, CA 93555
(619) 375-5810   Contact: Chuck Newmyer
A full service fly fishing shop. Instruction available.

Pacific Coast Anglers
2005 Crow Canyon Pl., #140, San Ramon, CA 94583
(510) 830-8791 FAX: (510) 830-8791
Contact: Bob Searle
PCA is a full service fly fishing specialty shop that provide a large range of glasses for both the novice and expert. We specialize in saltwater travel/guide service.

San Diego Fly Shop
4401 Twain Ave., #6, San Diego, CA 92120
(800) 363-FISH FAX: (619) 283-3472
Contact: Jeff Solis
Full service fly shop and your gateway to Baja. Featuring classes, schools, guide service & worldwide travel!

Mike Scott's Hackle, Tackle & Flies
2324 N. Batavia St., Suite 116, Orange, CA 92865
(714) 998-9400 FAX: (714) 998-6176
Contact: Mike & Regina Scott
Full service fly shop, schools, travel. Huge selection feathers & materials. Loomis, Diamondback, Powell, Fisher, Fenwick, Abel, Gatti, Teton, Aaron, Fin Nor, Ryall.

The Selective Angler
2215 Larkspur Landing Circle, Larkspur, CA 94939
(415) 461-6655 FAX: (415) 461-6656
Contact: Larry Kovi
Marin's only fly fishing specialist–Sage, Loomis, Redington, Sci-Angler, Ross.

CALIFORNIA
Lodges

Clearwater House on Hat Creek
PO Box 90, Cassel, CA 96016
(415) 381-1173 or (916) 335-5500
Fax (916) 335-5500 **Contact** Dick Galland, Owner
Area Northern California; **Services** Lodge, Accommodations, School; **Est.** 1980; **Waters** Public; **Type** Walk/Wade, Boat; **Fish** Trout

The Fly Shop
4140 Churn Creek Rd., Redding, CA 96002
(800) 669-FISH **Contact** Duane Milleman, Mgr.
Area Northern California; **Services** Outfitter/Guide, Accommodations, Fly Shop, School; **Season** Year-round; **Waters** Public/Private; **Type** Walk/Wade, Boat; **Fish** Rainbow, Brown, Steelhead
If catching large to huge rainbows and browns in beautiful surroundings captures your imagination give us a call. With seven private ranches under lease we can customize an unforgettable fly fishing experience for you. Our private fishing program is the most comprehensive of its kind anywhere, with lodges and housekeeping cabins on some of the West's very best lakes and streams.

Lava Creek Lodge
PO Box 2132, Santa Rosa, CA 95405
(707) 539-3366 or (800) 950-4242
Fax (707) 539-1320   **Contact** Bob Nauheim
Area Shasta County's Fall River Valley; **Services** Lodge, Accommodations; **Waters** Public; **Type** Float Tube, Walk/Wade, Boat; **Fish** Trout

Sorensen's
14255 Hwy. 88, Hope Valley, CA 96120
(800) 423-9949 or (916) 423-9949
Contact Patty & John Brissenden
Area Hope Valley, Northern CA; **Services** Lodge, Accommodations; **Waters** Public; **Type** Walk/Wade; **Fish** Trout

CALIFORNIA
Outfitters/Guides

Capt. Don Haid
2524 Fordham, Costa Mesa, CA 92626
(714) 578-1880 or (800) 543-0282
Contact Capt. Don Haid   **Services** Guide

Frank Holminski
PO Box 128, Mt. Shasta, CA 96067
(916) 926-6648   **Contact** Frank Holminski
Area Northern CA; **Services** Guide; **Waters** Public; **Type** Walk/Wade

Mt. Lassen Trout
28125 Hwy. 36 E, Red Bluff, CA 96080
(916) 597-2222 **Fax** (916) 597-2068
Area 4 hours north of San Francisco; **Services** Guide; **Season** Oct15-May15; **Waters** Private; **Type** Float Tube, Walk/Wade; **Fish** Rainbow

Mark Pinto
1445 San Juan Ave., Stockton, CA 95203
(209) 948-FISH   **Contact** Mark Pinto
Area 1 Hr North of San Fransisco; **Services** Guide; **Waters** Public; **Fish** Trout, Steelhead

Dean Schubert
713 Wildwood Trail, Santa Rosa, CA 95409
(707) 537-0736   **Contact** Dean Sschubert
Area Pit & Hat Creek, northern CA; **Services** Guide; **Season** May-Nov; **Waters** Public; **Type** Walk/Wade; **Fish** Trout

Thy Rod & Staff
PO Box 10038, Truckee, CA 96162
(916) 587-7333 Dec-Apr Call: (510) 798-8692
Contact Frank Pisciotta   **Area** Northern California; **Services** Guide; **Waters** Public; **Type** Float Tube, Walk/Wade; **Fish** Trout

Murrey Wolfe
2874 Old State Hwy, Alton, CA 95540
(707) 725-1955 **Area** Klamath River, northern CA; **Services** Guide; **Waters** Public; **Type** Walk/Wade; **Fish** Steelhead

COLORADO

Fly Tackle Dealers

Alpine Angler
13720 E. Quincy Ave., Aurora, CO 80015
(888) 694-1020   Contact: Derek Blea
Full service, excellent service. Custom rods/flies.
Instruction & guiding. Free newsletter. Ask about
being our field staff.

Angler's Covey
917 W. Colorado Ave., Colorado Springs, CO 80905
(719) 471-2984   FAX: (719) 471-9527
Full service fly shop.

Arkansas River Fly Shop
7500 Hwy. 50, Salida, CO 81201
(719) 539-3474   Contact: Rod Patch
Located on the Arkansas River in Colorado, Arkansas
River Fly Shop has all the fly tackle you need. Guide
Service.

Cowdrey Store and Trout Camp
Box 37, Cowdrey, CO 80434
(970) 723-8248   Contact: Jay Edwards
Wonderful North Platte headwaters flyfishing. Fly
shop, cafe, cabins, bookstore. Bamboo fly rods hand
built, restored, consignment sales.

Dragonfly Anglers
307 Elk Ave., PO Box 1116
Crested Butte, CO 81224
(970) 349-1228   FAX: (970) 349-0737
Contact: Rod Cesario
Dragonfly Anglers is an established full service fly shop
and guide service; walk/wade Black Canyon & drift
boat local waters.

Duck Creek Sporting Goods
400 S. Boulder Rd., Lafayette, CO 80026
(303) 665-8845   Contact: Denny McDaniels
Bamboo (new & used), Diamondback, Sage rods.
Instruction/guiding on private mountain resort.
Upland, waterfowl and big game hunting supplies.

Oxbow Outfitting Co.
623 E. Durant, Aspen, CO 81611
(970) 925-1505   Contact: Jonathan or Mike
Full service fly tackle dealer and guide service offering
wade and float trips on the Roaring Fork, Frying Pan
and Colorado Rivers.

Ramble House
PO Box 116, Creede, CO 81130
(719) 658-2482   FAX: (719) 658-2482
Contact: Shane Birdsey
Forty years of fishing on the Rio Grande. All your
fishing and souvenir needs.

Rocky Mountain Kane, Inc.
100 E. Cleveland, Lafayette, CO 80026
(303) 666-7866   FAX: (303) 742-2361

Contact: Joe E. Arguello
Full service fly shop featuring brand names and
hand-crafted bamboo fly rods by Joe E. Arguello.

Royal Gorge Anglers
1210 Royal Gorge Blvd., Canon City, CO 81212
(719) 269-3474   FAX: (719) 269-3474
Contact: Bill Edrington or Jan Carson
Full service flyfishing shop; tackle; clothing;
books/videos/software; guide service; flyfishing/fly
tying instruction; Wyoming pack trips; Internet sales.

Sangre de Cristo Fly Shop
104 Main St., Westcliffe, CO 81252
(719) 783-2313

Uncle Milty's Tackle Box
4811 South Broadway, Englewood, CO 80110
(303) 789-3775   Contact: Milt or Ray
Flies & related gear for the Rocky Mountains and listen
to KHOW Radio, 630 AM, Saturday mornings 6-7am
Fishing Show.

COLORADO
Lodges

Elk Creek Lodge
PO Box 130, 1111 CR 54, Meeker, CO 81641
(970) 878-4565 **Fax** (970) 878-5311
Area White River, NW CO; **Services** Lodge,
Accommodations, Fly Shop; **Est.** 1988; **Season**
Jun-Oct; **Waters** Private; **Type** Float Tube,
Walk/Wade, Boat; **Fish** Rainbow, Brook, Brown,
Cutthroat; **Packages** 5 Days, up to 16 anglers

Elktrout Lodge
PO Box 614, Kremmling, CO 80459
(970) 724-3343
Area Colorado and Blue Rivers; **Services** Lodge,
Accommodations, Fly Shop; **Waters** Private; **Type**
Float Tube, Walk/Wade, Boat; **Fish** Trout;
Packages 3 Days, up to 22 anglers

Fryingpan River Ranch
32042 Fryingpan River Rd., Meredith, CO 81642
(970) 927-3570   **Contact** Jim Rea
Area Fryingpan River,175 Mi SW of Denver; **Services**
Lodge, Accommodations; **Waters** Public; **Type**
Walk/Wade, Boat; **Fish** Brook, Cutthroat

Mt. Blanca
Game Bird & Trout
PO Box 236, Blanca, CO 81123
(719) 379-3825 **Fax** (719) 379-3589
Contact Bill Binnian
Area 150 mi. SW of Colorado Springs; **Services**
Lodge, Accommodations, Fly Shop; **Est.** 1987;
Season Apr-Nov; **Waters** Private; **Type**
Walk/Wade; **Fish** Trout, Rainbow, Brook, Brown;
Packages 1/2 Day, up to 250 anglers
See Our Ad Pg. 151

Seven Lakes Lodge
738 CR 59, Meeker, CO 81641
(970) 878-4772   **Contact** Steve Herter
Area White River, NW CO;   **Services** Lodge,
Accommodations;   **Waters** Public;   **Type**
Walk/Wade;   **Fish** Rainbow, Cutthroat;   **Packages** 5
Days, up to 22 anglers

Sylvan Dale Guest Ranch
2939 N. County Rd., 31D, Loveland, CO 80538
(970) 667-3915   **Contact** Darlys Koschel
Area Thompson River, 40 Mi N of Denver;   **Services**
Lodge, Accommodations;   **Waters** Private;   **Type**
Walk/Wade;   **Fish** Rainbow, Brown

COLORADO
Outfitters/Guides

Anasazi Angler
607 Sunnyside, Durango, CO 81301
(970) 385-HOOK   **Contact** Jerry Freeman
Area San Juan River, SW CO;   **Services**
Outfitter/Guide;   **Waters** Public/Private;   **Type**
Walk/Wade, Boat;   **Fish** Trout

Angler's Covey, Inc.
917 W. Colorado Ave., Colorado Springs, CO 80905
(800) 753-4746   **Fax** (719) 471-9527
Area South Platte & Arkansas Rivers;   **Services** Guide,
Fly Shop;   **Waters** Public;   **Type** Walk/Wade

Blue Quill Angler
1532 Evergreen Pkwy., Evergreen, CO 80439
(303) 674-4700   **Fax** (303) 674-4791
Area Near Denver;   **Services** Outfitter/Guide;
Waters Public;   **Type** Walk/Wade, Boat;   **Fish** Trout

Colorado Fishing Adventures
6421 Pulpit Rock Dr., Colorado Springs, CO 80918
(888) 540-3474   or (719) 532-9880
Fax (719) 262-0738   **Contact** Gary or Joan Willmart
Area San Juan, South Platte & Rio Grande Rivers;
Services Outfitter/Guide, Accommodations, Fly Shop;
Est. 1990;   **Season** AllYear;   **Waters** Public/Private;
Type Float Tube, Walk/Wade;   **Fish** Trout, Rainbow,
Brook, Brown, Cutthroat, Pike;   **Packages** 1 Day, up
to 12 anglers

Fish breathtaking sections of Colorado and New Mexico streams and lakes. The San Juan River below
Navajo Dam for trophy rainbows, with access to private waters for large browns and rainbows. Private
waters on the upper San Juan and Rio Grande Rivers.
A magnificent 32,000 acre ranch at Chama, NM. The
South Platte near Colorado Springs for large rainbows.
Friendly, experienced guides, Colorado Outfitter
#1031. No experience required, all equipment fur-
nished at no charge.

Colorado Fishing Guides
PO Box 3417, Eagle, CO 81631
(800) 461-5267   or (970) 328-5267
Fax (970) 328-5267   **Contact** Scott Taylor
Area Roaring Fork, Eagle & Colorado Rivers;   **Services**
Guide, Accommodations;   **Est.** 1992;   **Season**
Apr-Nov;   **Waters** Public/Private;   **Type** Walk/Wade,
Boat;   **Fish** Rainbow, Brook, Brown, Cutthroat,
Whitefish;   **Packages** 1/2 Day, up to 20 anglers

Fly Fishing Outfitters
PO Box 2861, Vail, CO 81658
(970) 845-8090   or (800) 595-8090
Fax (970) 845-8025   **Contact** Bill Perry/Steve Litt
Area Colorado and Eagle Rivers;   **Services** Outfitter,
Accommodations, Fly Shop, School;   **Est.** 1990;
Season Yr.Round;   **Waters** Public/Private;   **Type**
Float Tube, Walk/Wade, Boat;   **Fish** Rainbow, Brown,
Cutthroat;   **Packages** 1/2 Day, up to 50 anglers
○ ORVIS Endorsed, Outfitter Lic. 1337
Nestled along the Eagle River, minutes from Vail and
Beaver Creek ski areas, sits our full line Orvis shop. Our
store is open year round with the best fishing opportu-
nities from March to November. Whether your choice
is fishing a pristine alpine lake, a gin clear freestone
headwater or floating one of several "Gold Medal" rivers, Fly Fishing Outfitters' Orvis-endorsed guides will
help you get the most out of your trip.

The Flyfisher Guide Service
252 Clayton St., Denver, CO 80206
(303) 322-5014   **Fax** (303) 322-3053
Contact Vance Watson
Area South Platte & Colorado Rivers;   **Services**
Outfitter/Guide;   **Est.** 1973;   **Season** Year-round;
Waters Public/Private;   **Type** Walk/Wade, Boat;
Fish Rainbow, Brown, Cutthroat;   **Packages** 1 Day,
up to 3 anglers

Gorsuch Outfitters
263 E. Gore Creek Dr., Vail, CO 81657
(970) 476-2294   or (970) 476-2880 Ext. 333
Fax (970) 476-4323
Contact David Bishop, John or Marianne Cochran
Services Outfitter, Accommodations, Fly Shop, School;
Est. 1992;   **Season** Year-round;   **Waters**
Public/Private;   **Type** Float Tube, Walk/Wade, Boat;
Fish Trout, Rainbow, Brook, Brown, Whitefish;
Packages 1/2 Day, up to 24 anglers
○ Area: Colorado River, Roaring Fork, Eagle, Piney
River, Sweetwater Creek
○ Worldwide Web: http://vail.net/gorsuch-outfitters

Trophy Trout, Scenic Splendor and Western Hospitality

— Colorado's Mt. Blanca Lodge —

Book trout ... Rainbows ... Browns ... even Steelheads. They all await you, in abundance, at Mt. Blanca Lodge.

Situated amid 6,000 privately owned acres in the splendor of the Colorado Rockies, Mt. Blanca offers three wooded lakes whose natural feed and aquatic growth produce trout that redefine trophy fishing.

Other features that make Mt. Blanca fishing a genuine pleasure include expert guides who are pleased to share advice on techniques and equipment...a wide selection of boats, float tubes and waders at your disposal...and pure relaxation in a lodge celebrated for its food, lounge, gift shop, sauna and hot tub.

Mt. Blanca is the summit for other sports, too: the very best in upland game and migratory bird hunting...sporting clays fields that challenge and delight...and golf, skiing, horseback riding and scenic tours arranged at your request.

Mt. Blanca. Renowned as one of Colorado's finest fishing sites, it provides scenery, comfort—and trout—in an experience you're unlikely to forget.

No licenses required for upland game and fishing.

Please contact us for complete information, or to make your reservation.

Mt. Blanca Lodge
PO Box 236 • Blanca, CO 81123-0236
Tel: (719) 379-3825
Fax: (719) 379-3589

Gunnison River Telluride Flyfishers

PO Box 315, Montrose, CO 81402
(970) 249-4441 or (800) 828-7547
Area 60 Mi SE of Grand Junction;   **Services**
Outfitter/Guide;   **Waters** Public;   **Type** Walk/Wade,
Boat;   **Packages** 1 Day

Mountain Angler

PO Box 467, Breckenridge, CO 80424
(303) 453-4665
Area 80 Mi SW of Denver;   **Services** Outfitter/Guide,
Accommodations, Fly Shop;   **Waters** Public;   **Type**
Walk/Wade

Old Glendevey Ranch Ltd.

G.W. Peterson Outfitting
Glendevey CO Rt., 3219 Cty. Rd. 190,
Jelm, WY 82063
(800) 807-1444 Winter Call: (970) 490-1444
Contact Garth or Olivia Peterson
Area Rawah Wilderness Area, Laramie River;
Services Lodge, Accommodations;   **Est.** 1972;
Season Jun-Sep;   **Waters** Public/Private;   **Type** Float
Tube, Walk/Wade;   **Fish** Trout, Brook, Brown,
Cutthroat;   **Packages** 3 Days, up to 10 anglers

Roaring Fork Anglers

2022 Grand Ave., Glenwood Springs, CO 81601
(970) 945-0180 **Fax** (970) 945-6894
Contact Craig Chisesi
Area Roaring Fork, Frying Pan & Colorado Rivers;
Services Guide, Accommodations, Fly Shop;   **Est.**
1980;   **Season** Year-round;   **Waters** Public/Private;
Type Walk/Wade, Boat;   **Fish** Rainbow, Brook,
Cutthroat, Whitefish;   **Packages** 1/2 Day, up to 16
anglers

Summit Guides

Box 2489, Dillon, CO 80435
(970) 468-8945
Area 60 Mi W of Denver;   **Services** Guide, Fly Shop,
School;   **Waters** Public;   **Type** Walk/Wade;
Packages 1/2 Day

Taylor Creek Fly Shops

PO Box 799, Basalt, CO 81621
(970) 927-4374
Area Basalt & Aspen, CO;   **Services** Guide, Fly Shop,
School;   **Waters** Public;   **Type** Walk/Wade;   **Fish**
Trout

West Fork Outfitters

PO Box 300, Dolores, CO 81323
(970) 882-7959   **Contact** Eugene Story
Area Dolores, Telluride, SW CO;   **Services** Guide;
Waters Public;   **Type** Walk/Wade;   **Fish** Trout

CONNECTICUT

Fly Tackle Dealers

The Compleat Angler

987 Post Rd., Darien, CT 06820
(203) 655-9400   FAX: (203) 655-9400
Contact: Scott Bennett
full service fly shop

Mill River Fly Shop

3549 Whitney Ave., Hamden, CT 06518
(203) 248-7850   Contact: Gabriel Macare
Sage, Winston, Scott, Powell, Redington, Cortland,
Abel, ATH, Lamson, Ross, Ryall, Bauer, Tibor, Pate,
Simms, Bare, Metz, Hoffman, Herbert, Daiichi

Rivers End Tackle

141 Boston Post Rd., Old Saybrook, CT 06475
(860) 388-2283   Contact: Pat Abate or Mark Lewchik
Full service shop, Orvis, Abel and more. Great selection
of tying materials. Information our specialty.

Sportsman's Den of Greenwich, CT

33 River Rd., Cos Cob, CT 06807
(203) 869-3234   FAX: (203) 661-6242
Contact: Michael Noyes
Fly fishing pro shop (Orvis, Loomis, Abel, Charlton),
individual/group fly casting instruction–guided trips
(salt/freshwater).

CONNECTICUT
Outfitters/Guides

Connecticut Woods & Water Guide Service

6 Larson St., Waterford, CT 06385
(860) 442-6343   **Contact** Capt. Dan Wood
Area Scenic Long Island Sound;   **Services** Guide;
Est. 1979;   **Season** May-Nov;   **Waters** Public;   **Type**
Boat;   **Fish** Bass, Bluefish, Bonito, False Albacore;
Packages 1/2 Day, up to 4 anglers
O ORVIS Endorsed

Fly Guy

25 Smith Ave., Niantic, CT 06357
(860) 739-7419 or (860) 739-9761
Contact Capt. Dan Wood
Area Long Island Sound;   **Services** Guide, Fly Shop;
Est. 1972;   **Season** May-Nov;   **Waters** Public;   **Type**
Boat;   **Fish** Bass, Bluefish;   **Packages** 1/2 Day, up to
2 anglers

"Say you saw it in Black'sFly Fishing!"

This publication wouldn't be possible without the support of hundreds of fly fishing industry companies listed and advertising in this edition.

Whenever you contact one of these companies, please remember to tell them that you benefitted from the information you found here. And don't forget to say: "I saw it in Black's Fly Fishing."

Capt. Bill Herold

ORVIS ENDORSED GUIDE

15 Walker Avenue, Rye, NY 10580
(914) 967-8246   **Contact** Capt. Bill Herold
Area Western Long Island Sound, N.Y.C.;   **Services**
Guide;   **Est.** 1974;   **Season** Yr.Round;   **Waters**
Public;   **Type** Walk/Wade, Boat;   **Fish** Bass, Bluefish;
Packages 1/2 Day, up to 2 anglers
○ ORVIS Endorsed
Capt. Bill Herold, is a full-time professional who owns
and operates a unique guide service in Greenwich, CT.
He has earned a richly-deserved reputation as a dedi-
cated fly fishing expert; holding numerous I.G.F.A.
world fishing records. Capt. Herold maintains an active
year-round education schedule, operating seminars,
clinics and fly fishing schools.

Northrop's Landing

521 Riverside Ave., Westport, CT 06880
(203) 226-1915 or (203) 222-0058
Fax (203) 454-0857   **Contact** Capt. Jeff A. Northrop
Area Norwalk Islands, Long Island Sound;   **Services**
Guide, Fly Shop;   **Est.** 1968;   **Season** Mar-Dec;
Waters Public;   **Type** Walk/Wade, Boat;   **Fish** Bass,
Bluefish;   **Packages** 1/2 Day, up to 3 anglers

Brandywine Outfitters

2000 Pennsylvania Ave., Wilmington, DE 19806
(302) 656-6008   **Contact** Peter Cooper
Area PA trout, DE smallmouth & mid-Atlantic coastal;
Services Outfitter/Guide, Fly Shop;   **Est.** 1990;
Season Yr.round;   **Waters** Public;   **Type**
Walk/Wade;   **Fish** Smallmouth, Striped Bass, Trout,
Bluefish, Striped Bass;   **Packages** 1/2 Day, up to 16
anglers

FLORIDA

FLY TACKLE DEALERS

Everglades Angler, Inc.

810 12th Ave., S., Naples, FL 34104
(941) 262-8228   Contact: Mark Ward
Full service Orvis fly shop and outfitter. Top guides in
SW Florida, fishing Naples, Marco Island and the
Everglades National Park.

Fishing Unlimited
Outfitters & Fly Shop

PO Box 1407, 370 E. Railroad Ave.
Boca Grande, FL 33921
(800) 4TA-RPON   (941) 964-0907
FAX: (941) 964-1611
Contact: Capt. Sandy Melvin or Robin Melvin
Full Orvis dealership. Handling charters for
Backcountry & tarpon. Full range of outdoor apparel
for men & women.

Sanibel Fly Shop

2340 Periwinkle Way
Sanibel Island, FL 33957
(941) 472-8435   FAX: (941) 472-8685
Contact: Keith Owens
A fly shop for the saltwater angler. Saltwater fly rod
rentals, guide referrals and quality equipment

FLORIDA
Lodges

Bienville Plantation

1111 Orange St., # 101, Macon, GA 31201, FL
(912) 755-0705 **Fax** (912) 744-9672
Contact Steve Barras
Area Suwannee River, N. FL;   **Services** Lodge,
Accommodations;   **Est.** 1994;   **Season** Year-round;
Waters Private;   **Type** Boat;   **Fish** Bass, Crappie,
Bream, Bream;   **Packages** 2 Days, up to 40 anglers
See Our Ad Pg. 155

Cheeca Lodge

Mile Marker 82, Islamorada, FL 33036
(800) 327-2888 or (305) 664-4651
Fax (305) 664-2893   **Contact** Julie Perrin, Dir/PR
Area Florida Keys;   **Services** Lodge,
Accommodations, School;   **Est.** 1946;   **Season**
Year-round;   **Type** Boat;   **Fish** Trout, Sea Trout,
Bonefish, Tarpon, Baracuda, Permit, Sailfish, Billfish,
Redfish;   **Packages** 1/2 Day

FLORIDA
Outfitters/Guides

A Sportfishing
Guide Services, Inc.
14913 Warman St., Tampa, FL 33613
(813) 962-1435 Email: DMarkett@aol.com
Fax (813) 961-3474 **Contact** Capt. Dave Markett
Area West Central Florida; **Services** Outfitter/Guide;
Est. 1978; **Season** Year-round; **Waters** Public;
Type Boat; **Fish** Bass, Tarpon, Redfish; **Packages**
1/2 Day, up to 100 anglers
Florida Sun Coast's oldest charter service specializing
in light tackle, salt and fresh water angling for groups
and individuals.

The Back Country, Inc.
2855 Ocean Dr., Ste. A-1, Vero Beach, FL 32963
(561) 231-9894 **Fax** (561) 231-9885
Contact Capt. Eric T. Davis
Area Vero Beach, Indian River, Sebastian Inlet;
Services Outfitter/Guide, Fly Shop, School; **Est.**
1993; **Season** Year-round; **Waters** Public/Private;
Type Walk/Wade, Boat; **Fish** Largemouth, Sea
Trout, Bluegill, Tarpon, Redfish, Snook; **Packages**
1/2 Day, up to 3 anglers
O Vero Beach's Finest Fly Shop
The Back Country, Inc. is a diverse fly fishing outfitter,
specializing in fishing the beautiful Indian River and
neighboring largemouth bass impoundments. Game
fish species include snook, redfish, spotted sea trout,
and tarpon. Our guides are top professionals, licensed
by the Coast Guard, fully insured, and equipped with
state of the art equipment. We run a full service fly
shop and offer casting and fly tying instruction. Half
and full day trips available. Call today for brochure!
F.F.F. Certified.

Capt. Simon Becker
PO Box 6565, Key West, FL 33041
(305) 745-3565 **Contact** Capt. Simon Becker
Area Key West; **Services** Guide; **Season** Yr.round;
Waters Public; **Type** Boat; **Fish** Bonefish, Tarpon,
Permit; **Packages** up to 2 anglers

Capt. Michael Bednar
Box 452, Long Key, FL 33001
(305) 664-8408 **Contact** Capt. Michael Bednar
Area Middle Florida Keys; **Services** Guide; **Waters**
Public; **Type** Walk/Wade, Boat; **Fish** Bonefish,
Tarpon, Permit

Capts. Mark & Jenni Bennett
5809 Consuello Dr., Holliday, FL 34690
(813) 848-8747 **Fax** (813) 848-8747
Contact Capt. Mark Bennett

Area Tampa Bay/Boca Grande; **Services** Guide;
Waters Public; **Type** Boat; **Fish** Tarpon, Redfish

Boca Grande Guide Service
54 Bunker Ct., Rotonda West, FL 33947
(941) 697-2190 **Contact** Capt. Richard Hyland
Area Boca Grande, Charlotte Harbor; **Services**
Guide, Fly Shop, School; **Est.** 1985; **Season**
Year-round; **Waters** Public; **Type** Walk/Wade, Boat;
Fish Bonefish, Tarpon, Permit, Redfish, Snook;
Packages 1/2 Day, up to 6 anglers

C.B.'s Saltwater Outfitters
1249 Stickney Point Rd.,
Siesta Key, Sarasota, FL 34242
(941) 349-4400 **Fax** (941) 346-1148
Contact Aledia Tush/Chris Campbell
Area Sarasota, South Tampa Bay, Boca Grande area;
Services Outfitter/Guide, Accommodations, Fly Shop,
School; **Est.** 1976; **Season** Year-round; **Waters**
Public; **Type** Walk/Wade, Boat; **Fish** Sea Trout,
Bluefish, Tarpon, Baracuda, Redfish, Snook;
Packages 1 Day, up to 4 anglers

Captain Rod's Guidelines
PO Box 373257, Satellite Beach, FL 32937
(407) 777-2773 **Fax** (407) 779-9151
Contact Rodney Smith
Area 1 Hr. east of Orlando Intn'l Airport; **Services**
Guide, Accommodations, School; **Est.** 1990;
Season Year-round; **Waters** Public; **Type** Float
Tube, Walk/Wade, Boat; **Fish** Largemouth, Sea Trout,
Tarpon, Redfish; **Packages** 1/2 Day, up to 12 anglers
Fish Florida's Space Coast, located one hour east of Or-
lando. Enjoy the famous flats of the Banana, Indian
River and Mosquito Lagoons, catching redfish, tarpon,
and snook. Sight fish for cobia, tripletail, jack, tarpon
etc. outside Sebastian and Port Canaveral. Beginners
and experts welcome. Trips include tackle, transportation, licenses, flies, food & drink. Call today!
See Our Ad Pg. 153

Capt. Mike Conner
4641 SW 135 Ave., Miami, FL 33175
(305) 552-8457 **Contact** Capt. Mike Conner
Area Biscayne Bay, Florida Bay; **Services** Guide;
Waters Public; **Type** Boat; **Fish** Trout, Bonefish,
Tarpon, Permit, Redfish

The Everglades Angler
810 12th Ave. S., Naples, FL 34102
(941) 262-8228 or (800) 573-4749
Contact Capt. Mark Ward
Area Naples/SW Florida; **Services** Outfitter/Guide;
Waters Public; **Type** Boat; **Packages** 1/2 Day

ORVIS® Endorsed Wingshooting Lodge

Spans 20,000 Acres in North Florida

60 Miles West of Jacksonville Airport

TROPHY BASS • BREAM • CRAPPIE
<u>Also:</u> Quail, Dove, Duck & Deer

Over 6,000 acres in lakes that derive from
the "famous phosphate pits."

Fish for trophy bass, bream or crappie.

The natural and man-made managed lakes hold some of
the highest concentrations of waterfowl in Florida and the
Plantation's open land creates an excellent dove habitat.

1997 New Facilities Will Include:
5 (5-bedroom) Cabins • Main Lodge With Meeting Rooms
Restaurant • Bar • Recreation Room • Pro Shop

For information & reservations

– 912-755-0705 –

**Bienville Plantation
111 Orange St., Suite 101
Macon, GA 31201**

Floriday's Fishing Excursions

380 Otter Blvd., New Smyrna Beach, FL 32168
(904) 428-8530 or (800) 368-8340
Contact Capt. Mike Hakala
Area Indian River, Mesquito Lagoon, Canaveral
Seashore; **Services** Guide; **Est.** 1993; **Season**
Year-round; **Waters** Public; **Type** Boat; **Fish** Sea
Trout, Redfish, Snook; **Packages** 1/2 Day, up to 3
anglers

Fly Fishing Paradise

PO Box 145, Sugarload Shores, FL 33044
(305) 745-3304 **Fax** (305) 745-3304
Contact Capt. Dexter Simmons
Area Key West, Marquesas & Lower Keys; **Services**
Guide, Accommodations; **Est.** 1991; **Season**
Year-round; **Waters** Public; **Type** Boat; **Fish**
Bonefish, Tarpon, Baracuda, Permit; **Packages** 1/2
Day, up to 3 anglers

Capt. Warren L. Gorall

6122 S.E. Landing Way #4, Stuart, FL 34997
(407) 288-3996   **Contact** Capt. Warren L. Gorall
Area West Palm Beach; **Services** Guide; **Waters**
Public; **Type** Boat; **Fish** Trout, Tarpon

Grand Slam Outfitters, Inc.

100 Anchor Dr., Suite 391, North Key Largo, FL 33037
(305) 367-5000 **Fax** (305) 367-4340
Contact Capt. Bruce Miller
Area North Key Largo & Biscayne Bay; **Services**
Outfitter, Accommodations, Fly Shop; **Est.** 1975;
Season Yr.Round; **Waters** Public; **Type** Boat; **Fish**
Bonefish, Tarpon, Permit, Snook; **Packages** 1/2 Day,
up to 20 anglers
O ORVIS Endorsed
In a serene, protected area just an hour south of
Miami Airport lies a stretch of isolated, unspoiled,
lightly fished waters. On turquoise flats along this
beautiful mangrove coast are bonefish, tarpon, permit
and snook, while in the deeper water just offshore
swim sailfish, dolphin and barracuda. This is a fitting
home for Orvis's Key Largo saltwater fly fishing school.
As a full-line Orvis dealer and outfitter we can accom-
modate all your fishing needs. We have eight captains
who will provide you with tackle and lunch along with
the most exciting fly fishing in the U.S. Learn how to
stalk the world's hardest fighting gamefish, how to
tempt them to strike, and how to catch them. Call or
write today!

CAPTAIN JOHN HOLAHAN
LIGHT TACKLE & FLY SPECIALIST

Capt. John Holahan
PO Box 1184, Islamorada, FL 33036
(800) 521-1348 or (305) 664-8212
Fax (305) 664-8212   **Contact** Capt. John Holahan
Area Florida Keys & Everglades Nt'l Park; **Services**
Guide; **Est.** 1989; **Season** Year-round; **Waters**
Public; **Type** Boat; **Fish** Sea Trout, Bonefish, Tarpon,
Permit, Redfish, Snook; **Packages** 1/2 Day, up to 3
anglers

Jake Jordan Fishing Adventures

Mean Marlene Sportfishing
PO Box 500937, Marathon, FL 33050
(305) 743-0501 **Fax** (305) 743-5007
Contact Capt. Jake Jordan   **Area** Marathon/Florida
Keys; **Services** Guide; **Est.** 1979; **Season**
Year-round; **Waters** Public; **Type** Boat; **Fish**
Bonefish, Tarpon, Baracuda, Permit; **Packages** 1/2
Day, up to 4 anglers

Capt. Joe M. Kalman

795 Fernwood Rd., Key Biscayne, FL 33149
(305) 361-5155 or (305) 542-7493
(305) 531-2981   **Contact** Capt. Joe M. Kalman
Area Biscayne Bay, Florida Keys, West Coast;
Services Guide; **Waters** Public; **Type** Boat; **Fish**
Bonefish, Tarpon, Permit

Capt. Allen C. Kline

5590 W. Oaklawn St., Homosassa, FL 34446
(352) 628-5381 or (352) 628-7907
Contact Al Kline   **Area** Homosassa area, No. Gulf
Coast; **Services** Guide, Accommodations; **Est.**
1972; **Season** Year-round; **Waters** Public; **Type**
Boat; **Fish** Sea Trout, Tarpon, Redfish; **Packages**
1/2 Day, up to 4 anglers

Double Haul Ltd.

Capt. Jerry F. Knight

101 Cordova Reina Ct., Ponte Vedra Beach, FL 32082
(904) 285-5411 **Fax** (904) 285-5411
Contact Capt. Jerry F. Knight
Area Ponte Vedra Beach, NE Florida Inside & Flats;
Services Guide; **Est.** 1976; **Season** Year-round;
Waters Public; **Type** Boat; **Fish** Sea Trout, Tarpon,
Redfish; **Packages** 1/2 Day, up to 2 anglers

Capt. Mike Locklear

PO Box 900, Homosassa, FL 34487
(352) 628-4207 **Fax** (352) 628-4207
Contact Capt. Mike Locklear
Area Homosassa Flats & River; **Services** Guide,

Accommodations; **Est.** 1976; **Season** Year-round; **Waters** Public; **Type** Boat; **Fish** Sea Trout, Bluefish, Tarpon, Permit, Redfish; **Packages** up to 4 anglers

Capt. Dan Malzone - Saltwater Outfitters
4709 Cherokee Rd., Tampa, FL 33629
(813) 831-4052   **Contact** Capt. Dan Malzone
Area Tampa; **Services** Guide; **Waters** Public; **Type** Boat; **Fish** Redfish

MANGROVE FISHING ADVENTURES
with Captain Chris Dotson

Mangrove Fishing Adventures with Capt. Chris Dotson
PO Box 1712, Sanibel Island, FL 33957
(941) 395-9647   **Contact** Capt. Chris Dotson
Area J.N. "Ding" Darling Nt'l Wildlife Refuge; **Services** Guide, Accommodations; **Season** Year-round; **Waters** Public; **Type** Boat; **Fish** Sea Trout, Tarpon, Redfish, Snook; **Packages** 1/2 Day, up to 3 anglers

A sanctuary where tranquil natural beauty is punctuated only by violent aquatic aggression. Environmentally friendly Sanibel's 5,000-acre island refuge offers protected backwaters and abundant wildlife. Glide in a unique electric 20-foot sneakboat, putting flycasters near shallow gamefish in comfort. Chris is an experienced guide, FFF Certified Instructor and writer.

Mangrove Outfitters
4111 East Tamiami Tr., Naples, FL 34112
(941) 793-3370   **Fax** (941) 793-3370
Contact Capt. Tom Shadley   **Area** Everglades & Gulf; **Services** Outfitter/Guide, Accommodations, Fly Shop; **Est.** 1995; **Season** Nov-May; **Waters** Public; **Type** Walk/Wade, Boat; **Fish** Tarpon, Redfish; **Packages** 1/2 Day, up to 2 anglers

Capt. Dick Martin
579 Lake Ashley Circle, West Melbourne, FL 32904
(407) 768-8847   **Fax** (407) 768-8847
Contact Capt. Dick Martin   **Area** Sebastian Inlet/Sebastian River, Indian Rvr Lagoon; **Services** Guide; **Est.** 1992; **Waters** Public; **Type** Boat; **Fish** Trout, Tarpon, Redfish

Capt. Bruce Miller
100 Anchor Dr.- Ste 391 Ocean Reef Club, North Key Largo, FL 33037
(305) 367-5000   **Fax** (305) 367-4340
Contact Capt. Bruce Miller   **Area** FL Keys; **Services** Guide; **Est.** 1975; **Season** Year-round; **Waters** Public; **Type** Boat; **Fish** Bonefish, Tarpon, Permit

Capt. Jim Nickerson
3100 4th St., NE, Naples, FL 34120
(941) 353-5448   **Fax** (941) 353-5879
Contact Capt. Jim Nickerson
Area Everglades Nat'l. Park, 10,000 Islands; **Services** Guide; **Est.** 1989; **Season** Year-round; **Waters** Public; **Type** Boat; **Fish** Tarpon, Redfish, Snook; **Packages** 1/2 Day, up to 3 anglers

Capt. Darrick Parker
6491 SW 74th St., Miami, FL 33143
(305) 669-8477   **Contact** Capt. Darrkick Parker
Area Miami; **Services** Guide; **Season** Year-round; **Waters** Public; **Type** Boat; **Fish** Bonefish, Tarpon,

Capt. Terry Parsons
141 Easy St., Sebastian, FL 32958
(561) 589-7782   **Contact** Capt. Terry Parsons
Area Vero Beach; **Services** Guide; **Waters** Public; **Type** Boat; **Fish** Bass

Capt. Mike Rehr
1155 Buttonwood, Sanibel, FL 33957
(941) 472-3308   **Contact** Capt. Mike Rehr
Area Sanibel, near Ft. Meyers; **Services** Guide; **Waters** Public; **Type** Boat; **Fish** Tarpon

Capt. Frank Salomonsen
701 Lot No. 114 Spanish Main Dr., Summerland Key, FL 33042
(305) 745-9089   **Contact** Capt. Frank Salomonsen
Area Lower Florida Keys; **Services** Guide; **Waters** Public; **Type** Boat; **Fish** Bonefish, Tarpon, Baracuda,

Sanibel Light Tackle Outfitters, Inc.
2025 Periwinkle Way, Sanibel Island, FL 33957
(941) 472-2002   **Fax** (941) 472-8180
Contact Capt. Al Helo, Tom Rizzo
Services Outfitter/Guide

Sporting Classics Outfitters
1702 S. Dale Mabry, Tampa, FL 33629
(813) 254-5627   **Contact** Capt. Dan Malzone
Area Tampa; **Services** Outfitter, Fly Shop; **Waters** Public; **Type** Boat; **Fish** Largemouth, Sea Trout, Tarpon; **Packages** 1/2 Day

Capt. W.J. Torpey
1349 Bay Dr., Sanibel, FL 33957
(941) 472-2082   Summer Call: (508) 228-0546
Contact Cap. W.J. Torpey   **Area** Near Ft. Myers; **Services** Guide; **Season** Sep-May; **Waters** Public; **Type** Boat; **Fish** Bass, Bluefish, Tarpon, Redfish

Capt. Mike Ware
PO Box 16021, Panama City, FL 32406
(904) 785-6216   or Cellular (904) 866-6216
Contact Capt. Mike Ware   **Area** St. Andrews Bay & Inshore Gulf of Mexico; **Services** Guide; **Est.** 1987; **Season** Year-round; **Waters** Public; **Type** Boat; **Fish** Trout, Sea Trout, Bluefish, Redfish; **Packages** 1/2 Day, up to 2 anglers

GEORGIA

Fly Tackle Dealers

Athens Fly Fishing
1764 S. Lumpkin St., Athens, GA 30606
(706) 369-1797 FAX: (706) 369-3114
Contact: Barry Crume
Fully stocked fly shop, regional guide service & fly
fishing schools and instruction.

GEORGIA
Lodges

Burnt Pine Plantation
2941 Little River Rd., Madison, GA 30650
(706) 342-7202 **Fax** (706) 342-2170
Contact Steve Spears
Area 60 mi. E of Atlanta; **Services** Lodge,
Accommodations; **Est.** 1973; **Waters** Private;
Type Walk/Wade, Boat; **Fish** Bass, Largemouth
Burnt Pine Plantation offers premier largemouth bass
and bream fishing on a dozen private lakes. All waters
are managed for actually catching fish, not just wetting a line. This 8000 acre plantation is the ideal
getaway for fly and spin fishermen alike, so come for
the day or stay for the weekend. Guided or unguided
fishing available.

Callaway Gardens Resort
U.S. Hwy 27, Pine Mountain, GA 31822
(706) 663-5142 **Fax** (706) 663-5004
Contact Carter Nelson
Area 76 Miles south of Atlanta; **Services** Lodge,
Accommodations; **Est.** 1994; **Season** Year-round;
Waters Private; **Type** Float Tube, Boat; **Fish**
Largemouth, Rainbow; **Packages** 1/2 Day, up to 10
anglers

GEORGIA
Outfitters/Guides

Capt. Larry Kennedy
511 Marsh Villa Rd., St. Simon's Island, GA 31522
(912) 638-3214 **Contact** Capt. Larry Kennedy
Area Sea Island area; **Services** Guide; **Waters**
Public; **Type** Boat; **Fish** Sea Trout, Tarpon

Stouffe-Waiohai
Cast N' Catch Guide Service
PO Box 1371, Koloa, Kauai, HI 96756
Services Lodge, Accommodations; **Waters** Public;
Type Boat; **Fish** Bass; **Packages** 1/2 Day, up to 2
anglers

The Lodge at Little St. Simons Island
PO Box 21078-BFF, St. Simons Island, GA 31522
(912) 638-7472 **Fax** (912) 634-1811
Contact Debbie or Kevin McIntyre
Area Barrier island off the Georgia coast; **Services**
Lodge, Accommodations, Fly Shop; **Est.** 1980;
Season Yr.round; **Waters** Public/Private; **Type**
Walk/Wade, Boat; **Fish** Trout, Sea Trout, Bluefish,
Tarpon, Redfish; **Packages** 2 Days, up to 30 anglers
○ ORVIS Endorsed
Little St. Simons Island is a unique, privately owned,
10,000-acre barrier island located off Georgia's coast.
Untouched wilderness and seven miles of pristine Atlantic beach are the backdrop for excellent saltwater
fishing. Custom tailored excursions to the surf and
tidal creeks are arranged for both the experienced and
the novice fly fisher, with someone on board to both
guide and instruct in angling for tarpon, shark, speck-
led trout, reds, jacks and flounder. The Orvis Endorsed
Lodge at Little St. Simons Island also offers interpretive
naturalist programs, horseback riding, birding, canoeing, boating, shelling, swimming and hiking in
maritime forests. Comfortable accommodations for
only 30 overnight guests, delicious regional cuisine
and an attentive staff round out a complete island experience. Open year round, with flyfishing programs
from mid-August through early November. We welcome the entire family. Visit our web page at
http://www.pactel.com.au/lssi

HAWAII

Outfitters/Guides

Bass On Kauai
PO Box 143, Hanalei, Kauai, HI 96714
(808) 826-2566 **Contact** Erik Brandsen or Mike Mraz
Services Guide; **Est.** 1995; **Waters** Public; **Type**
Boat; **Fish** Bass; **Packages** 1/2 Day, up to 4 anglers

Fishing Hawaii
PO Box 2731, Kamuela, HI 96743
Contact Steven Bowles
Area Puu Iki Pond; **Services** Guide; **Waters** Private;
Type Walk/Wade, Boat; **Fish** Rainbow

Ken Takashima c/o Robalo-One
PO Box 10253, Lahaina, HI 96761
(808) 661-0480 **Contact** Ken Takashima
Area Maui - Inshore light tackle and fly fishing;
Services Guide; **Est.** 1987; **Waters** Public;
Packages 1 Day, up to 4 anglers

IDAHO

FLY TACKLE DEALERS

Howard's Fly Shoppe
1663 Garrity Blvd., Nampa, ID 83637
(208) 465-0946   FAX: (208) 467-3055
Contact: Jean Davis   G-Loomis, St. Croix, STH,
Cortland. Fly tying materials, Mustad, Tiemco & more.

Howard's Tackle Shoppe
1707 Garrity Blvd., Nampa, ID 83687
(208) 465-0946   FAX: (208) 467-3055
Contact: Jean Davis
G-Loomis, St. Croix, STH, Cortland. Fly tying materials,
Mustad, Tiemco & more.

IDAHO
Lodges

Flying B Ranch
PO Box 400, Grangeville, ID 83530
(208) 983-3410 **Fax** (208) 983-1516
Contact Rand Yager   **Area** Lochsa and Selway
Rivers; **Services** Lodge, Accommodations, Fly Shop;
Est. 1986; **Season** Apr-Dec; **Waters** Public/Private;
Type Float Tube, Walk/Wade, Boat; **Fish** Rainbow,
Cutthroat, Steel head, Sturgeon; **Packages** 1 Day, up
to 4 anglers

South Fork Lodge
PO Box 22, Swan Valley, ID 83449
(208) 483-2112 or (800) 483-2110
Fax (208) 483-2121   **Contact** Spence & Linda Warner
Area Snake River in Swan Valley; **Services** Lodge,
Accommodations, Fly Shop; **Est.** 1935; **Waters**
Public; **Type** Walk/Wade, Boat; **Fish** Rainbow,
Brown, Cutthroat

Wapiti Meadow Ranch
H.C. 72, Cascade, ID 83611
(208) 633-3217 **Contact** Diana Swift
Area Middle Fork, Salmon River; **Services** Lodge,
Accommodations, Fly Shop; **Est.** 1987; **Season**
Jul-Sep; **Waters** Public/Private; **Type** Float Tube,
Walk/Wade; **Fish** Rainbow, Brook, Cutthroat, Dolly
Varden; **Packages** 3 Days, up to 12 anglers

IDAHO
Outfitters/Guides

Hyde Outfitters
1520 Pancheri, Idaho Falls, ID 83402
(800) 445-4933 **Fax** (208) 529-4397
Contact Lynn Sessions
Services Outfitter/Guide, Accommodations, Fly Shop;
Est. 1989; **Season** May-Nov; **Waters** Public; **Type**
Walk/Wade, Boat; **Fish** Rainbow, Brook, Brown,
Cutthroat; **Packages** 1/2 Day, up to 24 anglers
○ Area: Henry's Fork, South Fort Snake, Teton River &
   Yellowstone National Park

Last Chance Outfitters
HC 66, Box 482, Island Park, ID 83429
(800) 428-8338 or (208) 558-7068
Fax (208) 558-7075   **Area** Henry's Fork of the
Snake; **Services** Guide, Accommodations, Fly Shop;
Waters Public; **Type** Walk/Wade, Boat; **Fish** Trout

Solitude River Trips
PO Box 907, Merlin, OR 97532, ID
(800) 396-1776 or (541) 476-1876
Fax (541) 471-2235   **Contact** Al or Jeana
Area Idaho's Middle Fork of Salmon River; **Services**
Outfitter/Guide, Accommodations; **Est.** 1976;
Season Jun-Aug; **Waters** Public; **Type** Walk/Wade,
Boat; **Fish** Trout, Cutthroat, Dolly Varden;
Packages 6 day dry fly fishing trips
○ 100 miles of wilderness
○ Everything furnished
○ Deluxe camp accommodations
○ ORVIS Endorsed Expedition Outfitter
America's premeire fly fishing and whitewater river.
The Middle Fork is the rare place where you can fly
fish while the non fisher people in your family enjoy
whitewater rafting, hiking and hot springs. Our guides
have years of experience teaching fly fishing to people
of all ages, from beginner to advanced.

St. Joe Hunting & Fishing Camp
HCR 1 Box 109A, St. Maries, ID 83861
(208) 245-4002 **Fax** (208) 245-4002
Contact Will & Barbara Judge   **Area** St. Joe River;
Services Lodge, Accommodations; **Est.** 1983;
Season Jul-Sep; **Waters** Public; **Type** Walk/Wade;
Fish Cutthroat; **Packages** 4 Days, up to 10 anglers

ILLINOIS

Fly Tackle Dealers

Dan's Tackle Service
2237 W. McLean Ave., Chicago, IL 60647
(773) 276-5562   FAX: (773) 276-5590
Contact: Dan Pieczonka
Sage rods & blanks, Mastery, Cortland, Abel, Tibor,
Ross, Umpqua, Tiemco, DaiRiki, rod building and fly
tying supplies and instruction.

Orvis Chicago
142 E. Ontario at Michigan Ave., Chicago, IL 60611
(312) 440-0662   FAX: (312) 587-8713
Fly Fishing Mgr: Jim Budelman
Orvis Chicago is a complete fly shop located in the
heart of Chicago's shopping district. Schools and
instruction are available.

INDIANA

Fly Tackle Dealers

FlyMasters of Indianapolis
8232 Allisonville Rd., Indianapolis, IN 46250
(317) 570-9811 FAX: (317) 570-9812
Contact: Jon Widboom   Fly Masters is a full service fly shop catering to the discriminating fisher and fly tyer. FlyMasters stocks all major rods, reels and tying supplies year-round. Instruction available.

KENTUCKY

Outfitters/Guides

Krugercraft Guide Service
14022 US Hwy 68 East, Benton, KY 42025
(800) 354-8027   Contact Ron Kruger   Area Kentucky Lake, Western KY; Services Guide; Waters Public; Type Walk/Wade, Boat; Fish Largemouth, Smallmouth; Packages 1 Day, 2 anglers

LOUISIANA

Fly Tackle Dealers

Lafayette Shooters Wilderness Westernwear
3520 Ambassador Caffery Pkwy.
Lafayette, AL 70503
(318) 988-1193 FAX: (318) 984-5553
Contact: Buddy Sparks   Southwest Louisiana's fly fishing/tying headquarters. G. Loomis, St. Croix, Redington, STH, Cortland, Penn, Scientific Angler. Ghee-Noe/Chief Canoes, outdoor apparel.

The Ouachita River Co.
312 Trenton St., West Monroe, LA 71291
(800) 935-FLYS   Contact: Tim Cotita or Gabe Ables
Full Orvis dealer–guided trips–Arkansas trophy trout fishing–instruction.

LOUISIANA
Outfitters/Guides

The Geaux Geaux
Dancer Charters
200 Lodge Dr. #812, Lafayette, LA 70506
(318) 288-5010 Days; (318) 988-9226 Eve.
Fax (318) 988-9225   Contact Captain Troy D. Nash
Area Marsh Island & Vermillion Bay; Services Outfitter/Guide, Fly Shop; Est. 1982; Season Mar-Oct; Waters Public; Type Walk/Wade, Boat; Fish Sea Trout, Redfish; Packages 1/2 Day
o Inshore shallow water sight-fishing for tailing redfish and schooling sea trout
o Professional guide service with national endorsements
o 14 years charter experience
o USCG Licensed & Insured; Louisiana State Licensed Guide
o All Inclusive–2 anglers max–guide, fuel, sandwiches, fly tackle & flies

MAINE

Lodges

▼ ORVIS ENDORSED ▼

Libby Camps
PO Box V-B, Ashland, ME 04732
(207) 435-8274 or (207) 435-6233
Fax (207) 435-3230   Contact Matt & Ellen Libby
Area Aroostook River, northern ME; Services Lodge, Accommodations; Est. 1890; Season May-Oct; Waters Public; Type Walk/Wade; Fish Salmon
o ORVIS Endorsed
The Libby family has operated a lodge and guide service since 1890. Located in the heart of a 4 million acre wilderness you can "fish a different remote pond or wild river every day for trophy squaretails or land-locked salmon." Day trips or overnighters via the camp's seaplane, 4 x 4s or boats to one of dozens of fisheries or nine outlying spike camps. Fly fishing for the beginner to the most advanced fisherman for pan sized to trophy native trout. The six guest cabins are comfortable, clean, spacious and private. The food is homecooked and served family style in the dining room overlooking the lake. Perfect accommodations for families, business groups or honeymooners. Sea-ane or 4 x 4 shuttle from anywhere in Maine.
See Our Ad Right, Top

▲ ORVIS ENDORSED ▲

Tim Pond
Wilderness Camps
PO Box 22, Eustis, ME 04936
(207) 897-4056 Camp Call: (207) 243-2947
Fax (207) 897-6892   Area Rangeley Lake region, Sugarloaf Ski area; Services Lodge, Accommodations, Fly Shop, School; Est. 1850; Season May-Nov; Waters Public/Private; Type Walk/Wade, Boat; Fish Trout, Brook; Packages 2 Days, up to 40 anglers
"The Place You've Been Looking For–But Didn't Know How To Find" - Nestled in the breathtaking beauty of the Maine wilderness, Tim Pond is the oldest sporting camp in New England. A scenic two-hour trip from Portland or Bangor, the camp is perfectly suited for a weekend getaway or a relaxing week-long vacation. The fishing season typically runs from early May to the end of September. Those new to the sport, or eager to improve their skills, are invited to attend Tim Pond's fly fishing school. The camp offers 11 comfortable cabins, complete with daily maid service. Three delicious homecooked meals are served. Tim Pond's offers a plentiful supply of native square tailed brook trout. Utilizing classic Rangeley boats and canoes, the camp's guests are able to fish every inch of the mile-long pond. Gated access to the pond allows guests the privacy and seclusion needed for a quality fly fishing experience. Call or write today for more information.
See Our Ad Right, Below

Weatherby's

The Fisherman's Resort
RR 1, Box 69, Grand Lake Stream, ME 04673
(207) 796-5558 **Fax** (207) 796-5558
Area North of Bangor; **Services** Lodge,
Accommodations; **Waters** Public; **Type**
Walk/Wade, Boat; **Fish** Smallmouth, Salmon

Wheaton's Lodge

HC 81, Box 120, Forest City, ME 04413
(207) 448-7723 Winter Call:(207) 843-5732
Contact Dale & Jana Wheaton
Area East Grand & Spednic Lakes, Upper St. Croix
region; **Services** Lodge, Accommodations, Fly Shop;
Est. 1952; **Season** May-Oct; **Waters** Public; **Type**
Walk/Wade, Boat; **Fish** Bass, Smallmouth, Salmon,
Pickerel; **Packages** 3 Days, up to 28 anglers

MAINE
Outfitters/Guides

Capt. Doug Jowett

61 Four Wheel Dr., Brunswick, ME 04011
(207) 725-4573 **Contact** Capt. Doug Jowett
Area Kennebec River & Cape Cod; **Services** Guide;
Season May-Oct; **Waters** Public; **Type** Boat; **Fish**
Bass; **Packages** 1 Day, up to 2 anglers

Capt. Pat Keliher

157 Durham Rd., Freeport, ME 04032
(207) 865-6561 **Contact** Capt. Pat Keliher
Area Kennebec River, Casco Bay; **Services** Guide;
Waters Public; **Type** Boat; **Fish** Bass, Striped Bass,
Bluefish, Striped Bass

Maine Outdoors

PO Box 401, Union, ME 04862
(207) 785-4496 **Fax** (207) 785-4496
Contact Capt. Don Kleiner
Area Mid-coast Maine; **Services** Guide; **Est.** 1986;
Waters Public; **Type** Boat; **Fish** Largemouth,
Smallmouth, Brown, Pickerel, Bluefish

Carroll Ware

16 Greenwood Ave., Skowhegan, ME 04976
(207) 474-5430 **Fax** (207) 474-5430
Contact Carroll Ware **Services** Guide

MARYLAND

Outfitters/Guides

Check Your Fly
3141 Beaver Lane, Trappe, MD 21673
(410) 476-3342 **Contact** Capt. Steve Culver
Area Chesapeake Bay & Tributaries; **Services**
Outfitter/Guide; **Waters** Public; **Type** Walk/Wade,
Boat; **Fish** Bass, Trout, Bluefish

Mark Kovach
Fishing Services
406 Pershing Dr., Silver Spring, MD 20910
(301) 588-8742 **Contact** Mark Kovach
Area Potomac River; **Services** Guide, School; **Est.**
1979; **Season** Apr-Nov; **Waters** Public; **Type**
Walk/Wade, Boat; **Fish** Smallmouth, Trout;
Packages 1 Day, up to 4 anglers
See Our Ad, Right

On The Fly
538 Monkton Rd., Monkton, MD 21111
(410) 329-6821 **Area** Gunpowder River, north of
Baltimore; **Services** Guide, Fly Shop; **Waters** Public;
Type Walk/Wade; **Fish** Trout

Pintail Point
511 Pintail Point Farm Lane, Queenstown, MD 21658
(410) 827-7029 **Fax** (410) 827-7052
Contact Carol Johnson & Sarah Gardner
Area Annapolis and Eastern Shore; **Services** Guide,
School; **Season** Apr-Dec; **Waters** Public/Private;
Type Walk/Wade, Boat; **Fish** Bass, Largemouth,
Trout, Crappie, Bluefish; **Packages** 1/2 Day, up to 7
anglers
See Ad Below & Our School Ad Pg. 129

MASSACHUSETTS

Fly Tackle Dealers

The Lower Forty
134 Madison St., Worcester, MA 01610
(508) 752-4004   FAX: (508) 752-4004
Contact: Jim Bender   Full service pro shop. Instruction/guiding services, Home of "The Schoolie School".

Rivers Edge Trading Co.
50 Dodge St., Beverly, MA 01915
(508) 921-8008   FAX: (508) 921-8008
Contact: David Griskevich

Henry Weston Outfitters, Inc.
15 Columbia Rd., Rt. 53, Pembroke, MA 02359
(617) 826-7411   FAX: (617) 826-9140
Contact: Jim McKay   South of Boston's largest fly shop, a full line Orvis dealer featuring clothing, flies, tackle, guides from Boston-Cape Cod.

MASSACHUSETTS
Outfitters/Guides

Capt. Rich Benson
77 Cemetery Rd., E. Harwich, MA 02645
(508) 432-6264   **Contact** Capt. Rich Benson
Area Cape Cod; **Services** Guide; **Est.** 1987; **Season** May-Oct; **Waters** Public; **Type** Boat; **Fish** Bass, Bluefish; **Packages** 1 Day, up to 2 anglers
○ ORVIS Endorsed

▼ ORVIS ENDORSED ▼

Boston Fly Fishing Company
with Capt. Fred Christian
Goodwin's Landing, Marblehead, MA 01945
(617) 631-1879 **Fax** (617) 631-6796
Contact Capt. Fred Christian
Area Boston Harbor to Cape Ann; **Services** Guide, School; **Est.** 1971; **Season** May-Oct; **Waters** Public; **Type** Walk/Wade, Boat; **Fish** Bass, Striped Bass, Bluefish; **Packages** 1/2 Day, up to 3 anglers
From Boston Harbor to Gloucester, you'll find some of the most exciting Striped Bass and Bluefish fishing on the New England coast. This is structure fishing at its best. At the Boston Fly Fishing Company, we offer the finest guiding and school services and welcome anglers of all experience levels. We will tailor the fishing or learning experience to your individual needs, with your safety and comfort foremost.
See Our Ad Above

▲ ORVIS ENDORSED ▲

Capt. Barry Clemson
Box 24, North Thetford, VT 05054, MA
(802) 333-4600 Summer Call: (508) 463-9249
Contact Capt. Barry Clemson
Area Plum Island, NE MA; **Services** Guide; **Season** May-Oct; **Waters** Public; **Type** Boat; **Fish** Bass, Bluefish

Fishing the Cape
Rts 137 & 39, Harwich Commons,
East Harwich, MA 02645
(508) 432-1200   **Contact** Bob Benson
Area Cape Cod; **Services** Outfitter/Guide, Fly Shop, School; **Waters** Public; **Type** Walk/Wade, Boat; **Fish** Bass, Striped Bass, Bluefish, Bonito, Striped Bass
○ ORVIS Endorsed

Cooper Gilkes
RFD, Box 19, Edgartown, MA 02539
(508) 627-3909   **Contact** Cooper Gilkes
Area Martha's Vineyard;   **Services** Outfitter/Guide,
Accommodations;   **Season** May-Oct;   **Waters** Public;
Type Walk/Wade, Boat;   **Fish** Bass, Bluefish;
Packages 2 Days

Capt. Bob McAdams
PO Box 600, Orleans, MA 02653
(508) 240-0420   **Contact** Capt. Bob McAdams
Area Cape Cod;   **Services** Guide;   **Waters** Public;
Type Walk/Wade, Boat;   **Fish** Bass, Bluefish

Capt. Jon Perette
28 Regatta Rd., N. Weymouth, MA 02191
(617) 331-7328   **Contact** Capt. Jon Perette
Services Guide

Points North
PO Box 146, Adams, MA 01220
(413) 743-4030 or Email: pointsnrth.@aol.com
Fax (413) 743-4030   **Contact** Fred Moran
Area NW Massachusetts;   **Services** Guide, Fly Shop,
School;   **Est.** 1985;   **Season** Apr-Oct;   **Waters**
Public;   **Type** Walk/Wade;   **Fish** Rainbow, Brook,
Brown;   **Packages** 1/2 Day, up to 4 anglers

Rivers Edge Trading Company
50 Dodge St., Beverly, MA 01915
(508) 921-8008   **Contact** Rick Green/David Griskevich
Services Outfitter/Guide, Fly Shop, School;   **Type**
Walk/Wade, Boat;   **Fish** Bluefish, Offshore Sharks
❍ ORVIS Endorsed
❍ Area: Massachusetts North Shore, Merrimack River,
   Plum Island Sound, Ipswich Bay, Cape Ann
❍ Orvis Fly Rods and Reels
❍ Over 40,000 Flies in Stock
❍ Fly Tying Tools and Materials
❍ Technical Clothing
❍ Waders and Wading Gear
Rivers Edge is an Orvis Endorsed outfitter offering
guided trips for stripers, blues and offshore sharks,
May thru October. Visit our store in Beverly for all your
fly fishing needs.

Capt. Dave Tracy
PO Box 6041, N. Plymouth, MA 02362
(800) 320-3252   **Contact** Capt. Dave Tracy
Area Boston Harbor to Duxbury Bay;   **Services** Guide;
Waters Public;   **Type** Boat;   **Fish** Bass, Bluefish

MICHIGAN

Fly Tackle Dealers

Backcast Fly Shop
1675 US 31, Box 377, Benzonia, MI 49616
(800) 717-5222   (616) 882-5222
Contact: Steve Forrester
Near Betsie & Platte Rivers. Rod building, fly tying, fly
fishers steelhead/salmon supplies, clothing, books,
bait and tackle. Free brochure, mail order, guide
service.

The Great Lakes Fly Fishing Company
2775 10 Mile Rd., Rockford, MI 49341
(800) 303-0567   FAX: (616) 866-6756
Contact: Glen R. Blackwood
A full service fly shop serving Western Michigan.
Quality guides, instruction, equipment and sporting
literature. Call for a free catalog.

MICHIGAN
Lodges

Gates Au Sable Lodge
471 Stephan Bridge Rd., Grayling, MI 49738
(517) 348-8462   **Contact** Rusty Gates
Area Au Sable River, Northern Michigan;   **Services**
Lodge, Accommodations, Fly Shop;   **Waters** Public;
Type Walk/Wade;   **Fish** Brown

Streamside Orvis - Grand Traverse Resort
4400 Grand Traverse Village, Blvd E-4,
Williamsburg, MI 49690
(616) 938-5337
Area Traverse City, NW MI;   **Services** Lodge,
Accommodations, Fly Shop;   **Season** Year-round;
Waters Public;   **Type** Walk/Wade, Boat;   **Fish**
Rainbow, Brook, Brown, Steelhead, Salmon

MICHIGAN
Outfitters/Guides

Johnson's Pere Marquette
Rt. 1, Box 1290 S-M37, Baldwin, MI 49304
(616) 745-3972
Area Pere Marquette River, 60 Mi N of Grand Rapids;
Services Outfitter/Guide, Fly Shop;   **Season**
Year-round;   **Waters** Public;   **Type** Walk/Wade;
Fish Brown, Steelhead, Salmon

Matthew A. Supinski
7616 S. Hazelwood, Newaygo, MI 49337
(616) 652-2868
Contact Matthew A. Supinski
Services Outfitter, Accommodations; **Est.** 1995;
Season Yr.round; **Waters** Public/Private; **Type**
Walk/Wade, Boat; **Fish** Rainbow, Brown, Steelhead,
Salmon; **Packages** 1 Day, up to 6 anglers
O ORVIS Endorsed
Located on Michigan's famous Muskegon River, one
of the hottest growing tailwaters in the country. Hook
and land brown and rainbow trout, salmon and steel-
head year round on a tremendous variety of caddis fly,
mayfly and stonefly hatches. Call today for informa-
tion.
See Our Ad, Right

MINNESOTA

Lodge

Gunflint Lodge
750 Gunflint Trail, Grand Marais, MN 55604
(800) 328-3325 or (888) GUNFLINT
Fax (218) 388-9429　**Contact** Bruce Kerfoot
Area Boundary waters country of N.E. Minnesota;
Services Lodge, Accommodations, Fly Shop, School;
Est. 1927; **Season** May15-Oct.15; **Waters** Public;
Type Boat; **Fish** Largemouth, Smallmouth, Rainbow,
Brook, Lake Trout, Pike, Pickerel; **Packages** 1 Day, up
to 50 anglers

MISSOURI

Fly Tackle Dealers

Backcountry Outfitters
1316 E. Battlefield Rd., Springfield, MO 65804
(417) 889-6548　FAX: (417) 889-5862
Contact: Jack Nickols
Fly fishing, Sage, Orvis, Scott, Winston, Simms,
Lamson, Ross, Abel. Fly tying and fly casting instruction,
guide trips. Largest selection of flies in the area.

Hawthorn Galleries
PO Box 6071, Branson, MO 65615
(417) 335-2170　FAX: (417) 335-2011
Contact: Stephen D'Lack
Fine art gallery featuring custom hand made fly rods
and reels.

MISSOURI
Outfitters/Guides

BackCountry Outfitters
1316 Battlefield, Springfield, MO 65804
(417) 889-6548　**Contact** Jack Nickols
Area Arkansas White River; **Services**
Outfitter/Guide, Fly Shop, School; **Waters**
Public/Private; **Type** Walk/Wade; **Fish** Bass, Trout

MONTANA

Fly Tackle Dealers

Blackbird's Fly Shop & Lodge

1754 Hwy. 93, PO Box 998, Victor, MT 59875
(800) 210-8648   FAX: (406) 642-6375
Contact: Mark Bachik
Premier "One Party Only" lodge featuring 2,000 sq. ft.
fly shop offering quality merchandise, instruction and
guide service.

Dave Blackburn's Kootenai Angler

115 W. 2nd St., Libby, MT 59923
(406) 293-7578   FAX: (406) 293-7578
Contact: Dave Blackburn   Full service fly shop
featuring Orvis, Sage and T&T. Guide service and
riverfront lodge on Kootenai River in NW Montana.

Fishaus Fly Fishing

702 N. 1st St., Hamilton, MT 59804
(406) 363-6158   FAX: (406) 363-6158
Contact: Bill Bean   Full service fly shop, catalog,
outfitter/guide, accommodations, Western Montana
Rivers, fish rainbow, cutthroat, brook

MONTANA
Lodges

Battle Creek Lodge

Box 670, Choteau, MT 59422
(406) 466-2815 or (406) 799-0499
Fax (406) 466-5510   **Contact** Jack
Area East slope of the Rockies in Northwest Montana;
Services Lodge, Accommodations, Fly Shop;   **Est.**
1991;   **Season** Jun-Sep15;   **Waters** Public/Private;
Type Float Tube, Walk/Wade, Boat;   **Fish** Rainbow,
Brook, Brown, Cutthroat;   **Packages** 5 Days, up to 8
anglers

Bear Creek Lodge

1184 Bear Creek Trail, Victor, MT 59875
(406) 642-3750 or (800) 270-5550
Fax (406) 642-6847
Contact Roland & Elizabeth Turney
Area Western Montana, Bitterroot Valley;   **Services**
Lodge, Accommodations;   **Est.** 1991;   **Season**
Mar-Dec;   **Waters** Public/Private;   **Type** Walk/Wade,
Boat;   **Fish** Trout, Rainbow, Brook, Brown, Cutthroat;
Packages 3 Days, up to 16 anglers
Fish for wild, native trout in the Bitterroot, Big Hole,
Clark Fork, or Blackfoot Rivers. Return to our exquisite
log lodge at the edge of the Wilderness for cocktails &
a scrumptious dinner. Only eight guest rooms, all with
private bath. Great retreat for non-anglers as well. Call
for brochure or visit our home page at http://www.rec-
reate. com/bcl/

Bighorn River Lodge

PO Box 7756, Fort Smith, MT 59035
(800) 235-5450 or (406) 666-2368
Fax (406) 666-9109   **Contact** Phil & Patty Gonzalez
Area Bighorn River;   **Services** Lodge,
Accommodations;   **Est.** 1969;   **Waters** Public/Private;
Type Walk/Wade

The Blue Winged Olive

PO Box 1551, Livingston, MT 59047
(800) 471-1141 or (406) 222-8646
Fax (406) 222-8646   **Contact** Joan Watts
Area Paradise Valley's Spring Creeks & Yellowstone;
Services Lodge, Accommodations;   **Est.** 1995;
Season Apr-Oct;   **Waters** Public/Private;   **Type** Float
Tube, Walk/Wade, Boat;   **Fish** Rainbow, Brown,
Cutthroat;   **Packages** 1 Day, up to 10 anglers

CB Cattle and Guest Ranch

Box 604, Cameron, MT 59720
(406) 682-4954 Winter Call: (619) 723-1932
Fax (619) 723-1932   **Contact** Sandy Vander Lans
Area Madison River;   **Services** Lodge,
Accommodations;   **Season** Jul-Sep;   **Waters** Public;
Type Walk/Wade, Boat;   **Fish** Rainbow, Brown;
Packages up to 14 anglers

Canyon Creek Ranch

PO Box 126, Melrose, MT 59743
(800) 291-8458 Ranch Call: (406) 496-9155
Contact Dave Duncan
Area 55 mi. SW of Butte;   **Services** Lodge,
Accommodations;   **Est.** 1945;   **Season** Jun-Sep;
Waters Public;   **Type** Walk/Wade, Boat;   **Fish** Trout,
Rainbow, Brook, Brown, Cutthroat;   **Packages** 2
Days, up to 20 anglers
See Our Ad Pg. 3 & 169

Crane Meadow Lodge

Box 303, Twin Bridges, MT 59754
(406) 684-5773 **Fax** (406) 684-5772
Contact Bob Butler   **Area** Southwest Montana;
Services Lodge, Accommodations;   **Season** Apr-Oct;
Waters Public;   **Type** Walk/Wade;   **Fish** Trout

Diamond J Guest Ranch

PO Box 577F, Ennis, MT 59729
(406) 682-4867   **Contact** Tim Combs
Area Madison, Beaverhead, Big Hole & Yellowstone
Rivers;   **Services** Lodge, Accommodations;   **Est.**
1959;   **Season** Jun-Oct;   **Waters** Public/Private;
Type Walk/Wade, Boat;   **Fish** Rainbow, Brown;
Packages 1 Day, up to 36 anglers

Eagle Nest Lodge: Great Fishing on the Bighorn

Trout in abundance. Scenic splendor. Restful accommodations. Sumptuous meals. They all contribute to the allure of one of fly fishing's most popular destinations, Eagle Nest Lodge. Fifty five miles from Billings, Montana, Eagle Nest lodge is situated on the Bighorn River, indisputably one of the nation's best trout fisheries.

Providing mile upon mile of blue ribbon water, the Bighorn is renowned for the quality and quantity of its rainbow and brown trout. So it's not unusual for the average angler, assisted by one of the lodge's professional guides, to land 20 fish between 16 and 22 inches in a single day.

What's more, the same guides who know just where the trout are rising are also qualified instructors, eager to teach beginners the fundamentals of fly fishing, to help intermediate anglers improve their skills, and to show experts new and exciting ways to take trophy trout.

Exceptional wingshooting, too.

But Eagle Nest Lodge, owned since its inception by Alan and Wanda Kelly and their sons, Keith and Matthew, offers more than fabulous fishing. The surrounding hills, coulees and stubble fields are rich in game birds, and present some of the finest wingshooting in the West. From September through early December, guests enjoy outstanding grouse and partridge hunting on a sprawling ranch open only to them. In October, pheasants provide an additional challenge.

Bird hunts at Eagle Nest are conducted in traditional Western style, over both flushing and pointing dogs. Guides and dog handlers are experienced in locating birds, so shotgunners' game bags are often filled.

Not the least of Eagle Nest's attractions is the lodge itself, a well planned combination of rustic beauty and modern comfort. Six spacious guest rooms, each with two single beds and a full bath, are designed for rest and relaxation. The great trophy room includes a huge screened in porch with rockers and a swing. And the lodge's dining room features fresh Montana meats and wild game delicacies, complemented by salads and side dishes that are meals in themselves.

Eagle Nest's Lodge combines rustic beauty with the comforts of the modern age.

The lodge also operates its own tackle shop with a full line of fishing and hunting gear.

A choice of packages

Eagle Nest offers a trout fishing package from May through Mid-October; a bird-hunting package from mid-October through early December; and a combination package from September through October. Custom packages and exclusive stays are available.

The lodge recommends making reservations well in advance of a desired stay. Write or phone A. Keith Kelly, Eagle Nest Lodge, PO Box 509, Hardin, Montana 59034; (406) 665-3711.

A Lodge of Distinction

Secluded on the banks of the legendary Bighorn River and surrounded by hills and valleys that harbor abundant populations of grouse, partridge and pheasants, Eagle Nest Lodge enjoys the distinction of being the first in the world to achieve an Orvis endorsement for both fly fishing and wingshooting.

The credit for that achievement goes to the Kelly family who has owned Eagle Nest Lodge since its inception. Alan Kelly, the former U.S. Fish & Wildlife biologist on the Bighorn, and his wife, Wanda, built the business in the early eighties. Now their sons and their wives—Keith and Erika, Matt and Lisa—continue the Eagle Nest tradition of excellence. Together they invite you to join them for "the experience of a lifetime, in what has been called 'The Last Best Place: Montana'."

▼ ORVIS ENDORSED ▼

AN ORVIS®
Double Endorsed Lodge

Eagle Nest Lodge
PO Box 509, Hardin, MT 59034
(406) 665-3711   **Contact** Keith Kelly
Area Bighorn River; **Services** Lodge,
Accommodations, Fly Shop, School; **Est.** 1981;
Season Apr-Oct; **Waters** Public; **Type** Walk/Wade,
Boat; **Fish** Rainbow, Brown; **Packages** 2 Days, up
to 12 anglers
Eagle Nest Lodge is one of the world's Premiere fly-fishing and bird hunting destinations. The service, lodging
and dining of this family-owned and operated sporting
lodge, secluded on the banks of the legendary Bighorn
River, has satisfied even the most discerning
sportspersons for more than a decade. Call today!
See Our Ad Pg. 167

▲ ORVIS ENDORSED ▲

Craig Fellin's Big Hole River Outfitters
PO Box 156, Wise River, MT 59762
(406) 832-3252   **Contact** Craig Fellin
Area Wise River, SW MT; **Services** Lodge,
Accommodations; **Waters** Public/Private; **Type**
Float Tube, Walk/Wade, Boat; **Fish** Rainbow, Brook,
Brown, Cutthroat, Grayling; **Packages** up to 10
anglers

Firehole Ranch - West Yellowstone
PO Box 6868, West Yellowstone, MT 59758
(406) 646-7294   **Contact** Stan Klassen
Area Madison & Yellowstone Rivers; **Services** Lodge,
Accommodations, Fly Shop; **Est.** 1982; **Waters**
Public; **Type** Float Tube, Walk/Wade, Boat; **Fish**
Rainbow, Brook, Brown, Lake Trout, Cutthroat;
Packages up to 20 anglers

Five Rivers Lodge
13100 Hwy. 41 N., Dillon, MT 59725
(406) 683-5000 or (800) 378-6470
Contact Jay Burgin   **Area** Beaverhead, Bighole, Ruby
& Jefferson Rivers; **Services** Lodge,
Accommodations, Fly Shop; **Season** Apr-Nov;
Waters Public/Private; **Type** Walk/Wade, Boat;
Fish Rainbow, Brown; **Packages** 2 Days, up to 30
anglers

Fly Fishers' Inn
2629 Old US Hwy 91, Cascade, MT 59421
(406) 468-2529   **Contact** Lynne & Rick Pasquale
Area Missouri River; **Services** Lodge,
Accommodations, Fly Shop; **Est.** 1991; **Season**
March-Nov.; **Waters** Public; **Type** Walk/Wade,
Boat; **Fish** Trout, Rainbow, Brown; **Packages** 1 Day,
up to 14 anglers

Hubbard's Yellowstone Lodge
RR 1, Box 662, Emigrant, MT 59027
(406) 848-7755 **Fax** (406) 848-7471
Contact Matt Greenmore
Area Yellowstone Park; **Services** Lodge,
Accommodations, School; **Season** Jun-Sep; **Waters**
Public/Private; **Type** Walk/Wade, Boat

Last Stand Outfitters
Star Rt. Box 2131, Hardin, MT 59034
(406) 665-3489 **Fax** (406) 665-3492
Contact Dave & Kim Egdorf
Area Big Horn River, Lakes, Private Streams; **Services**
Lodge, Accommodations; **Est.** 1991; **Season**
Sep-May; **Waters** Public/Private; **Type** Walk/Wade,
Boat; **Fish** Rainbow, Brown; **Packages** 1 Day, up to
6 anglers

Little Blackfoot Retreat Center
PO Box 1251, Helena, MT 59624
(406) 442-3045   **Contact** Margaret or Carroll Jenkins
Area Missouri & Blackfoot Rivers; **Services** Lodge,
Accommodations, Fly Shop; **Est.** 1986; **Season**
Year-round; **Waters** Public/Private; **Type** Float
Tube, Walk/Wade, Boat; **Fish** Trout, Rainbow, Brook,
Brown, Cutthroat; **Packages** 1/2 Day, up to 16
anglers

Lone Mountain Ranch
PO Box 160069, Big Sky, MT 59716
(406) 995-4644 or (800) 514-4644
Fax (406) 995-4670   **Contact** Gary Lewis
Area Gallatin & Madison Rivers; **Services** Lodge,
Accommodations, Fly Shop; **Est.** 1977; **Season**
Jun-Oct15; **Waters** Public/Private; **Type** Float Tube,
Walk/Wade, Boat; **Fish** Rainbow, Brook, Brown,
Golden, Cutthroat, Grayling
○ Packages: 1 day or 1 week
○ ORVIS Endorsed
○ Family Vacations for Fly Fishermen
○ Gallatin & Madison River and Yellowstone Park
○ Internet: www.lone.mountainranch.com

Lost Fork Ranch
11-12 Hwy. 287 N., Cameron, MT 59720
(406) 682-7690 **Fax** (406) 682-7515
Area Madison & Gallatin Rivers; **Services** Lodge,
Accommodations, Fly Shop; **Est.** 1988; **Season**
MidJun-Oct; **Waters** Public; **Type** Walk/Wade,
Boat; **Fish** Trout, Rainbow, Brown, Golden,
Cutthroat; **Packages** 3 Days, up to 22 anglers

Madison Valley Ranch
Jeffers Rd. 245, Ennis, MT 59729
(406) 682-7497   **Contact** Gary Gustafson
Area Madison River; **Services** Lodge,
Accommodations; **Est.** 1878; **Waters** Public; **Type**
Walk/Wade

CANYON CREEK · GUEST RANCH

AT ROAD'S END FIND TRUE PEACE AND QUIET.

If fly fishing is your dream, Canyon Creek Guest Ranch, in the awesome beauty of Montana Beaverhead National Forest, is the place for you.

Lakes and streams abound throughout this majestic, rugged wilderness area. Our guides know where the trout are "really jumpin" in this legendary fishing region.

There are few places remaining in the world where you can find the variety of Mountain Trout fishing opportunities that are available at Canyon Creek. Depending on where you fish, Native Brown, Rainbow, Cutthroat, Grayling and Brook trout, average anywhere from 8 to 24 inches.

A fly fisherman will relish the diversity of wading the Big Hole River one day and stalking the brushy narrows of a mountain stream the next. Our secluded alpine lakes provide another spectacular dimension for the fly fisherman.

Canyon Creek is the perfect place to take a trail ride. Our private log cabins have showers and baths, wood-burning fireplaces and comfortable beds. Meals are served family style in the main lodge.

You will enjoy the finest fishing and hunting in Montana amid scenery so breathtaking that you will never forget the experience.

Please don't forget your camera. Do make reservations and arrangements well ahead of time. We'll pick you up in Butte.

Canyon Creek Guest Ranch "where at road's end, you'll find true peace and quiet."

CANYON CREEK · GUEST RANCH

"The only one of its kind in all outdoors."
For brochure, information & reservations:

800-291-8458

P.O. Box 126 • Melrose, Montana 59743

**Eastern Coordinator
FRANK EICHMAN
610-436-0336**

Montana Trout Club
on the Diamond "O" Ranch
PO Box 411, Twin Bridges, MT 59754
(406) 683-4950 **Fax** (406) 683-4148
Area Southwest Montana; **Services** Lodge,
Accommodations; **Season** Jun-Sep; **Waters**
Public/Private; **Type** Walk/Wade; **Fish** Rainbow,
Brown, Grayling; **Packages** up to 21 anglers

Sixty-Three Ranch
Box 979-BFF, Livingston, MT 59047
(406) 222-0570 or (406) 222-6963
Contact Sandra or Jeff Cahill   **Area** Yellowstone
River; **Services** Lodge, Accommodations; **Est.** 1930;
Season Jun15-Oct15; **Waters** Public/Private; **Type**
Float Tube, Walk/Wade, Boat; **Fish** Rainbow, Brook,
Brown, Cutthroat; **Packages** 7 Days, up to 30 anglers

Spotted Bear Ranch
2863 Foothill Rd., Kalispell, MT 59901
(800) 223-4333 or (406) 755-7337
Contact Kirk Gentry
Area Flathead River; **Services** Lodge,
Accommodations; **Waters** Public; **Type**
Walk/Wade, Boat; **Fish** Cutthroat; **Packages** 3
Days, up to 14 anglers

Tamarack Lodge
32855 South Fork Rd., Troy, MT 59935
(888) 295-1822 **Fax** (406) 295-1022
Contact Bill or Judy McAfee
Area Lincoln County, Yaak Valley; **Services** Lodge,
Fly Shop; **Est.** 1981; **Season** Jul-Oct15; **Waters**
Public/Private; **Type** Float Tube, Walk/Wade, Boat;
Fish Rainbow, Brook, Cutthroat; **Packages** 1 Day, up
to 22 anglers

Upper Canyon Ranch
PO Box 109, Alder, MT 59710
(800) 735-3973 **Area** Ruby River; **Services** Lodge,
Accommodations; **Waters** Public

Yaak River Lodge
27744 Yaak River Rd., Troy, MT 59935
(800) 676-5670
Area Purcell Mountains, NW MT; **Services** Lodge,
Accommodations; **Waters** Public; **Type**
Walk/Wade, Boat; **Fish** Rainbow, Brook, Cutthroat

Yellowstone Mt. Guides
9250 Thorpe Rd., Bozeman, MT 59718
(406) 388-0148 **Fax** (406) 587-0472
Contact Steve Gamble
Services LodgeOutfitter/Guide, Accommodations, Fly
Shop, School; **Est.** 1983; **Season** AllYear; **Waters**
Public/Private; **Type** Float Tube, Walk/Wade, Boat; .
Fish Rainbow, Brook, Brown, Golden, Cutthroat,
Grayling; **Packages** 1 Day, up to 16 anglers
O email: sgaymg@gomontana.com
O http://www.gomontana.com/ymg.html
O Area: Yellowstone National Park, Southwest
  Montana Rivers: Madison, Gallatin, Yellowstone

MONTANA
Outfitters/Guides

George Anderson's Yellowstone Angler
Hwy 89 South, PO Box 660, Livingston, MT 59047
(406) 222-7130 **Fax** (406) 222-7153
Contact George Anderson
Area Spring Creeks, Yellowstone River; **Services**
Outfitter/Guide, Fly Shop, School; **Est.** 1980;
Season Year-round; **Waters** Public/Private; **Type**
Walk/Wade, Boat

Angling Specialties
3731 Stucky Rd., Bozeman, MT 59715
(406) 587-7246 **Fax** (406) 587-7246
Contact Bob or Jean Granger
Area Rivers, streams, spring creeks & lakes of SW
Mont.; **Services** Guide; **Season** Yearround;
Waters Public/Private; **Type** Float Tube, Walk/Wade;
Fish Trout; **Packages** 1/2 Day

Beartooth Plateau
Outfitters, Inc.
PO Box 1127, 320 Main St., Cooke City, MT 59020
(406) 838-2328 or (800) 253-8545
Area Yellowstone Park; **Services** Outfitter/Guide, Fly
Shop; **Season** Jun-Sep; **Waters** Public; **Type**
Walk/Wade
O ORVIS Endorsed
O Horseback Pack Trips
O Horseback Day Trips
O Absaroka-Beartooth Wilderness
O Yellowstone Park
O Exclusive Beartooth Lodge/Orvis Fly Shop

Big Sky Flies & Guides
PO Box 4, Emigrant, MT 59027
(406) 333-4401 **Fax** (406) 333-4716
Contact Garry E. McCutcheon
Area Yellowston & Madison Rivers; **Services**
Outfitter/Guide, Fly Shop; **Waters** Public/Private;
Type Walk/Wade; **Fish** Trout

Bighorn River Shop
PO Box 470, Hardin, MT 59034
(800) 665-3799   **Contact** Nick C. Forrester
Services Outfitter/Guide

Diamond N Outfitters
PO Box 1982, Missoula, MT 59806
(800) 308-FISH **Fax** (800) 543-3887
Contact Brian D. Nelson
Area 8 Montana Rivers; **Services** Outfitter/Guide,
Accommodations; **Est.** 1986; **Season** Year-round;
Waters Public; **Type** Walk/Wade, Boat; **Fish** Trout,
Rainbow, Brown, Cutthroat; **Packages** 1 Day, up to
12 anglers

Gary Evans Madison River Guides
PO Box 1456, Ennis, MT 59729
(406) 682-4802 **Fax** (406) 682-7889
Contact Gary or Jill Evans

Area Madison, Yellowstone Rivers & Yellowstone Nat'l Pk; Services Outfitter/Guide, Accommodations, Fly Shop; Est. 1988; Season Apr-Oct; Waters Public; Type Walk/Wade, Boat; Fish Rainbow, Brown, Cutthroat; Packages 1 Day, up to 12 anglers

Gallatin Riverguides
Hwy. 191, Box 160212, Big Sky, MT 59716
(406) 995-2290 Fax (406) 995-4588
Contact Steven French
Area S.W. & S.C. Montana; Services Outfitter/Guide, Accommodations, Fly Shop; Est. 1984; Season Year-round; Waters Public/Private; Type Float Tube, Walk/Wade, Boat; Fish Rainbow, Brook, Brown; Packages 1/2 Day

Grizzly Hackle
215 West Front St., Missoula, MT 59802
(800) 297-8996 or (406) 721-8996
Contact Jim Toth
Area Blackfoot; Services Outfitter/Guide, Accommodations; Waters Public; Type Walk/Wade

Headwaters Guide Service
Box 311, Gallatin Gateway, MT 59730
(406) 763-4761 Fax (406) 763-5548
Contact Robin Cunningham
Area Gallatin, Yellowstone, Madison Rivers; Services Outfitter/Guide; Est. 1983; Season May-Oct; Waters Public/Private; Type Float Tube, Walk/Wade, Boat; Fish Rainbow, Brown, Cutthroat; Packages 1 Day, up to 4 anglers

Bob Jacklyn's Fly Shop
105 Yellowston Ave, PO Box 310, West Yellowstone, MT 59758
(406) 646-7336 Contact Bob Jacklyn
Area Yellowstone Nt'l Park & Idaho & Montana; Services Outfitter/Guide; Est. 1974; Waters Public; Type Float Tube, Walk/Wade

Kootenai Angler
13546 Hwy. 37, Libby, MT 59923
(406) 293-7578 or (406) 293-5140
Contact Dave Blackburn
Area Kootenai River and tributaries, northwest Montana; Services Outfitter/Guide, Accommodations, Fly Shop; Est. 1984; Waters Public; Type Float Tube, Walk/Wade, Boat; Fish Rainbow, Brook, Cutthroat; Packages up to 14 anglers

Bud Lilly's Trout Shop
39 Madison Ave., West Yellowstone, MT 59758
(800) 854-9559 or (406) 646-7801
Fax (406) 646-9370 Contact Dick Greene
Area Madison River, Yellowstone Nat'l Pk, Henry's Fork; Services Outfitter/Guide, Fly Shop, School; Waters Public; Type Float Tube, Walk/Wade; Fish Trout

Linehan Outfitting Company
472 Upper Ford Rd., Troy, MT 59935
(406) 295-4872 Contact Tim & Joanne Linehan

Area Kootenai River, Northwest Montana; Services Outfitter/Guide; Est. 1993; Season May-Oct; Waters Public; Type Float Tube, Walk/Wade, Boat; Fish Trout, Rainbow, Brook, Cutthroat; Packages up to 6 anglers

Lower Clark Fork River Outfitters
85 Donlan Flats, St. Regis, MT 59866
(800) 745-3933 Cellular Call: (406) 250-6299
Area 85 mi. West of Missoula; Services Outfitter/Guide, Accommodations; Waters Public/Private; Type Float Tube, Walk/Wade, Boat

James Marc
PO Box 1551, Livingston, MT 59047
(800) 471-1141 Fax (406) 222-8646
Contact James Marc
Area Paradise Valley's Spring Creeks & Lakes; Services Guide; Est. 1994; Season May-Oct; Waters Public/Private; Type Float Tube, Walk/Wade; Fish Rainbow, Brown, Cutthroat; Packages 1 Day, up to 3 anglers

Medicine Lake Outfitters
PO Box 3663-BFF, Bozeman, MT 59772
(406) 388-4938 Contact Tom Heintz
Area Yellowstone backcountry; Services Outfitter/Guide, Accommodations; Est. 1977; Waters Public; Type Walk/Wade; Fish Trout; Packages 4 Days

Missoulian Angler
420 N. Higgins, Missoula, MT 59802
(800) 824-2450 Area Western Montana; Services Outfitter/Guide, Accommodations, Fly Shop, School; Waters Public; Type Walk/Wade, Boat

Montana River Outfitters
1401 5th Ave.S., Great Falls, MT 59405
(406) 761-1677 or (800) 800-8218
Fax (406) 452-3833
Contact Craig Madsen or Neale Streekes
Area Missouri, Smith, Blackfoot & South Fork Flathead
Services Outfitter/Guide, Accommodations, Fly Shop; Est. 1977; Season Yr.round; Waters Public; Type Walk/Wade, Boat; Fish Rainbow, Brook, Brown, Cutthroat, Grayling; Packages 1/2 Day, up to 12 anglers
The Smith & Missouri River Pros since 1977. Montana' finest trout fishing and bird hunting. One-half to 7-day float trips on the Missouri, Smith and Blackfoot; Housepack/float trips on Wilderness Rivers. Fly shop with sales and rentals of boats and fishing gear. Cabins and R.V. park, too. Two locations–Great Falls and Wolf Creek. Free Color Brochure. Video Available.

Montana Troutfitters
1716 West Main St., Bozeman, MT 59715

(800) 543-4665 or (406) 222-2273
Fax (406) 222-9433   **Contact** Tom Travis
Area Yellowstone Nt'l Park;   **Services**
Outfitter/Guide, Fly Shop;   **Est.** 1987;   **Season**
Year-round;   **Waters** Public/Private;   **Type** Float
Tube, Walk/Wade, Boat;   **Fish** Rainbow, Brown,

John Perry's Montana Fly Fishing
PO Box 20080, Missoula, MT 59801
(406) 258-2997 or (800) 580-9703
Fax (406) 549-5352   **Contact** John Perry
Area Rock Creek;   **Services** Outfitter/Guide;   **Waters**
Public;   **Type** Walk/Wade

Quill Gordon Fly Fishers
PO Box 597, Fort Smith, MT 59035
(406) 666-2253   **Contact** Gordon S. Rose
Area Big Horn River;   **Services** Outfitter/Guide,
Accommodations, Fly Shop;   **Waters** Public;   **Type**
Walk/Wade, Boat

Paul Roos Outfitters
PO Box 621, 326 N. Jackson, Helena, MT 59624
(406) 442-5489 or (800) 858-3497
Fax (406) 449-2293   **Contact** Paul Roos
Area Smith, Missouri, Blackfoot & Rock Creek Rivers;
Services Lodge, Accommodations, Fly Shop;   **Est.**
1970;   **Season** Mar-Nov;   **Waters** Public/Private;
Type Float Tube, Walk/Wade, Boat;   **Fish** Rainbow,
Brown, Cutthroat;   **Packages** 1 Day, up to 12 anglers

Running River Fly Guide
113 W. Villard, Bozeman, MT 59715
(800) 763-3474 or (406) 586-1758
Contact Stuart Howard
Area Yellowstone & Madison Rivers;   **Services**
Outfitter/Guide;   **Est.** 1984;   **Season** Apr-Oct;
Waters Public/Private;   **Type** Walk/Wade, Boat;
Fish Rainbow, Brown, Cutthroat;   **Packages** 1 Day

Schneider's Guide Service
St. Xavier, MT 59075
(406) 855-1978 or (406) 666-2460
Contact Gary H. Kidder
Area The Bighorn River, Afterbay to Two Leggins;
Services Guide;   **Season** AllYear;   **Waters** Public;
Type Float Tube, Walk/Wade;   **Fish** Rainbow, Brown

The Tackle Shop
PO Box 625, Ennis, MT 59729
(406) 682-4263
Area Madison River;   **Services** Outfitter/Guide,
Accommodations, Fly Shop;   **Est.** 1937;   **Waters**
Public;   **Type** Float Tube, Walk/Wade, Boat

NEVADA

Outfitters/Guides

Capt. Lex Moser
14752 Rim Rock Rd., Reno, NV 89511
(702) 852-3474   **Contact** Capt. Lex Moser
Area Pyramid Lake;   **Services** Guide;   **Waters** Public;
Type Walk/Wade, Boat

Reno Fly Shop
294 E. Moana Ln. # 14, Reno, NV 89502
(702) 825-3474   **Fax** (702) 825-5610
Contact Dave Stanley
Area Reno;   **Services** Guide, Fly Shop;   **Est.** 1983;
Waters Public;   **Type** Walk/Wade

NEW HAMPSHIRE

Lodges

The Glen
First Connecticut Lake, Pittsburg, NH 03592
(800) 445-4536 or (603) 538-7121
Contact B.H. Falton
Area First Connecticut Lake;   **Services** Lodge,
Accommodations;   **Est.** 1963;   **Waters** Public;   **Type**
Walk/Wade

Hidden Meadow Farm
Land Resource Management
PO Box 64, Temple, NH 03084
(603) 924-6030   **Contact** Martin Connolly
Area Boston

Lopstick Lodge & Cabins
1st Connecticut Lake, Pittsburg, NH 03592
(800) 538-6659 In-state Call: (603) 538-6659
Contact Chuck & Lisa Hopping
Area CT Lakes Region of NH;   **Services** Lodge,
Accommodations;   **Est.** 1920;   **Waters** Public;   **Type**
Float Tube, Walk/Wade, Boat;   **Fish** Rainbow, Brook,
Brown, Lake Trout, Salmon

Tall Timber Lodge
231 Beach Rd., Pittsburg, NH 03592
(800) 835-6343 In-state Call: (603) 538-6651
Contact The Caron Family
Area Connecticut Lakes;   **Services** Lodge,
Accommodations, Fly Shop;   **Est.** 1946;   **Season**
Apr-Oct15;   **Waters** Public;   **Type** Walk/Wade, Boat;
Fish Rainbow, Brook, Brown, Lake Trout, Salmon;
Packages up to 55 anglers

The Timberdoodle Club
One Webster Hwy., Temple, NH 03084
(603) 654-9510   **Fax** (603) 654-5964
Contact Randall Martin
Area Boston;   **Services** Lodge, Accommodations, Fly
Shop;   **Waters** Public/Private;   **Type** Float Tube;
Fish Trout

Timberland Lodge & Cabins
1st Connecticut Lake, Pittsburg, NH 03592
(800) 545-6613 In-state Call: (603) 538-6613
Contact Linda & Doug Feltmate
Area 1st Connecticut Lake;   **Services** Lodge,
Accommodations;   **Est.** 1925;   **Season** Apr15-Sep30;
Waters Private;   **Type** Walk/Wade, Boat;   **Fish**
Rainbow, Brook, Brown, Salmon;   **Packages** 1 Day,
up to 110 anglers

NEW JERSEY

Fly Tackle Dealers

Bay Head Outfitters
92 Bridge Ave., Bay Head, NJ 08742-4753
(908) 892-8008   FAX: (908) 892-2208
Contact: George Katilus
Est.: 1994 Full service fly shop

Sportsmen's Center
U.S. Hwy. 130, Bordentown, NJ 08505
(609) 298-5300   FAX: (609) 298-6137
Contact: Tony Gullo

Streams of Dreams
324 Rt. 17 North
Upper Saddle River, NJ 07458
(201) 934-1138   FAX: (201) 934-1180
Est.: 1994   Contact: Harry Huff

NEW JERSEY
Outfitters/Guides

Bayhead Outfitters
92 Bridge Ave., Bay Head, NJ 08742
(908) 892-8008 **Fax** (908) 892-2208
Contact Capt. Dick Dennis
Area Barnegate Light & Manasquan; **Services** Outfitter/Guide, Fly Shop; **Est.** 1994; **Season** Apr-Dec; **Waters** Public; **Type** Walk/Wade, Boat; **Fish** Bass, Bluefish; **Packages** 1 Day, up to 4 anglers

Ed Broderick
11 Hawthorne Dr., Westfield, NJ 07090
(908) 789-3382   **Contact** Ed Broderick
Area New Jersey Coast; **Services** Guide; **Waters** Public; **Type** Boat; **Fish** Bass, Bluefish

The Fly Hatch
90 Broad St., Red Bank, NJ 07701
(908) 530-6784 **Fax** (908) 530-6784
Contact Dave Chouinard
Area Sandy Hook, NJ; **Services** Guide

NEW MEXICO

Fly Tackle Dealers

Los Rios Anglers, Inc.
226 C North Pueblo Rd., Taos, NM 87571
(800) 748-1707   FAX: (505) 758-2798
Contact: Jack Woolley
Full service fly shop and fly fishing guide service.

NEW MEXICO
Lodges

Rizuto's San Juan River Lodge
PO Box 6309, Navajo Dam, NM 87419
(505) 632-3893
Area San Juan River; **Services** Lodge, Accommodations, Fly Shop; **Waters** Public; **Type** Walk/Wade

Step Back Inn
103 W. Aztec Blvd., Aztec, NM 87410
(505) 334-1200 or (800) 334-1255
Fax (505) 334-9858   **Contact** T. Blancett
Area 4 Corners, San Juan River; **Services** Lodge; **Est.** 1995; **Season** Year-round; **Waters** Public/Private; **Type** Float Tube, Walk/Wade, Boat; **Fish** Bass, Trout, Salmon; **Packages** 1 Day, up to 40 anglers

NEW MEXICO
Outfitters/Guides

Ken Armenta's New Mexico Trout Anglers
PO Box 340, Capitan, NM 88316
(505) 354-3187   **Contact** Ken Armenta
Area Wilderness Pack Trips in Northern NM; **Services** Guide; **Est.** 1974; **Season** Year-round; **Waters** Public; **Type** Walk/Wade; **Fish** Rainbow, Brown, Cutthroat; **Packages** 2 Days, up to 3 anglers

"Born 'n' Raised" on the San Juan River
San Juan River, Navajo Dam, NM 87419
(505) 632-2194 or (505) 632-0492
Contact Tim R. Chavez
Area San Juan River; **Services** Outfitter, Accommodations, Fly Shop; **Waters** Public; **Type** Walk/Wade; **Fish** Rainbow

Cottonwood Anglers
PO Box 405, Blanco, NM 87412
(505) 632-8639   **Contact** Paul (Dave) Jacquez
Area San Juan River; **Services** Guide; **Waters** Private; **Type** Walk/Wade

High Desert Angler, Inc.
435 S. Guadalupe, Sante Fe, NM 87501
(505) 988-7688 **Fax** (505) 988-7688
Contact Jan Crawford
Area Northern New Mexico, San Juan River; **Services** Guide, Fly Shop, School; **Est.** 1985; **Season** Yr. round; **Waters** Public/Private; **Type** Float Tube, Walk/Wade, Boat; **Fish** Largemouth, Rainbow, Brook, Cutthroat, Pike; **Packages** 1 Day, up to 20 anglers
Pro fly shop, guide service statewide, year round fly fishing. Wide variety of water. Equipment rental, books, quality tackle, gifts and gift certificates, outdoor clothing. Fly fishing casting, fly tying classes, private & semi-private instruction. Enjoy Santa Fe's history, scenary, cultural events, restaurants & fly fish too!

The Reel Life/Orvis Endorsed Outfitters
1100 San Mateo Blvd. Ste. 10,
Albuquerque, NM 87110
(888) 268-FISH or (505) 268-1693
Fax (505) 268-1667   **Contact** Manuel Monasterio
Area San Juan River and Statewide; **Services**
Outfitter/Guide, Fly Shop, School; **Est.** 1995;
Season Year-round; **Waters** Public/Private; **Type**
Float Tube, Walk/Wade, Boat; **Fish** Rainbow, Brook,
Brown, Cutthroat

Rocky Mountain Anglers
PO Box 6306, Navajo Dam, NM 87419
(505) 632-0445   **Contact** Paul Faust
Area San Juan River; **Services** Guide; **Waters**
Public; **Type** Walk/Wade, Boat

San Juan Troutfitters
PO Box 243, Farmington, NM 87499
(800) 848-6899   **Contact** Harry Lane
Area San Juan River; **Services** Guide, School;
Waters Public; **Type** Walk/Wade

GUIDE SERVICE

**Santa Fe Flyfishing
School & Guide Service**
PO Box 22957, Santa Fe, NM 87502
(800) 555-7707 or (505) 986-3913
Contact Dirk Kortz/Hugo Ableson
Area Santa Fe, Taos & the San Juan River; **Services**
Outfitter/Guide, School; **Est.** 1991; **Season**
Year-round; **Waters** Public/Private; **Type**
Walk/Wade, Boat; **Fish** Trout; **Packages** 1/2 Day,
up to 20 anglers   Fish with experienced guides and
instructors who know:
○The waters throughout northern New Mexico
○ The right flies (provided free)
○Proven techniques
Buffet lunch included. Rental equipment and private
waters available. Find out why our clients keep coming
back! Call (800) 555-7707 or (505) 986-3913.

NEW YORK

Fly Tackle Dealers

Jones Outfitters, Ltd.
37 Main St., Lake Placid, NY 12946
(518) 523-3468   FAX: (518) 523-3468
Contact: Chris Williamson
Full service Orvis store since 1958. The most complete
fly fishing shop in the Adirondacks. Schools, private
lessons, guide service.

Manhattan Custom Tackle, Ltd.
913 Broadway, New York, NY 10010
(212) 505-6690   FAX: (212) 505-1922
Contact: Phil Koenig

Custom rods, rod building components, fly tying
materials. Website: http://fishdoc.com

Orvis New York
355 Madison Ave., New York, NY 10017
(212) 697-3133   Contact: Tom Lenz

NEW YORK
Lodges

The Altmar Smokehouse & Lodge
PO Box 260, #3 Pulaski St., Altmar, NY 13302
(315) 298-2993 **Fax** (315) 298-2993
Contact Malinda Barna
Area Salmon River; **Services** Lodge,
Accommodations, Fly Shop; **Season** Year-round;
Waters Public/Private; **Type** Float Tube, Walk/Wade,
Boat; **Fish** Smallmouth, Rainbow, Brown, Lake Trout,
Steelhead, Salmon

Battenkill Lodge
Hickory Hill Rd., Box 111, Shushan, NY 12873
(516) 671-7690 In-season Call: (518) 854-9840
Contact Capt. Bob Storc
Area Battenkill River, NE NY; **Services** Lodge,
Accommodations; **Season** Apr-Oct; **Waters** Public;
Type Walk/Wade; **Fish** Brown

Fish Inn Post
2035 Co. Rt. 22, Altmar, NY 13302
(315) 298-6406   **Contact** Dave Barbe
Area Salmon River & Lake Ontario Tributaries;
Services Lodge, Accommodations, Fly Shop; **Season**
Sept.-May15; **Waters** Public/Private; **Type**
Walk/Wade, Boat; **Fish** Rainbow, Brown, Steelhead,
Salmon; **Packages** 1 Day, up to 24 anglers

Indian Springs Flyfishing Camp
RR 1 Box 200AA, Hancock, NY 13783
(215) 679-5022 In Season Call: (717) 224-2708
Fax (215) 679-4536   **Contact** Lee Hartman
Area Upper Delaware River System; **Services** Lodge,
Accommodations, School; **Est.** 1991; **Season**
May-Oct.; **Waters** Public; **Type** Walk/Wade, Boat;
Packages 1 Day, up to 4 anglers
○ Fish: Trout, Shad
○ Specialized 2-Day Float Package
○ Private Cabins
○ Experienced Guides
○ Casting Pond
○ Great Food

Wild River Inn
7743 State Route 3, Pulaski, NY 13142
(315) 298-4195
Contact Capt. Todd & Ann Marie Sheltra
Area Salmon River & Lake Ontario; **Services** Lodge,

Accommodations; **Season** Yr.Round; **Waters** Public; **Type** Walk/Wade, Boat; **Fish** Bass, Trout, Salmon; **Packages** 1 Day, up to 10 anglers

NEW YORK
Outfitters/Guides

Adirondack Fishing Adventures
with Pete Burns
Box 96, Wevertown, NY 12886
(518) 251-3394   **Contact** Pete Burns
Area Hudson River Gorge; **Services** Guide, Fly Shop; **Waters** Public; **Type** Walk/Wade, Boat; **Fish** Smallmouth, Trout; **Packages** 1 Day

Beaverkill Angler
PO Box 19P Roscoe, NY 12776
(607) 498 5194 **Fax** (607) 498-4740
Area Catskills; **Services** Guide, Fly Shop, School; **Waters** Public; **Type** Walk/Wade

Delaware River Tackle
816 Victory St., Johnson City, NY 13790
(607) 729-4009   **Contact** Walt Mercincavage, Jr.
Area West, East & Main Delaware Rivers; **Services** Outfitter/Guide; **Est.** 1988; **Season** May-Oct.; **Waters** Public; **Type** Walk/Wade, Boat; **Fish** Trout, Rainbow, Brown,Shad; **Packages** 1/2 Day, up to 2 anglers

ENDORSED GUIDE

Capt. Paul Dixon
74 Montauk Hwy., #9, E. Hampton, NY 11937
(516) 324-7979 **Fax** (516) 324-7928
Contact Capt. Paul Dixon
Area Montauk Point & Gardiners Bay; **Services** Guide, Accommodations, Fly Shop; **Est.** 1993; **Season** May-Dec; **Waters** Public; **Type** Boat; **Fish** Striped Bass, Bluefish, Bonito, False Albacore, Striped Bass; **Packages** 1/2 Day, up to 3 anglers
O ORVIS Endorsed
Fly fish the fabled waters of Montauk and Gardiners Bay on the east end of Long Island. Sight fish the flats for striped bass and bluefish in spring and summer. Chase false albacore and giant striped bass in the fall. Two hours from N.Y.C. Call today for information.

Capt. Bill Herold
15 Walker Ave., Rye, NY 10580
(914) 967-8246   **Contact** Capt. Bill Herold
Area Western Long Island Sound, N.Y.C.; **Services** Guide; **Est.** 1974; **Season** Yr.Round; **Waters** Public; **Type** Walk/Wade, Boat; **Fish** Bass, Bluefish; **Packages** 1/2 Day, up to 2 anglers

Capt. Barry Kanavy
3944 Beacon Rd., Seaford, NY 11783
(516) 785-7171 **Contact** Capt. Barry Kanavy

Area Long Island's South Shore; **Services** Guide; **Season** Apr-Nov; **Waters** Public; **Type** Boat; **Fish** Bass, Bluefish

Matterhorn Country Sport Shop
227 Summit Park Rd., Spring Valley, NY 10977
(914) 354-5986 **Fax** (914) 354-8984
Area Rockland County; **Services** Guide, Fly Shop; **Waters** Public; **Type** Walk/Wade

Glen Mikkleson
PO Box 368, Manorville, NY 11949
(516) 878-0883   **Contact** Glen Mikkleson
Area East End of Long Island; **Services** Guide; **Est.** 1995; **Season** May-Nov; **Waters** Public; **Type** Walk/Wade; **Fish** Bass, Bluefish; **Packages** 1/2 Day, up to 2 anglers

The Montana Guide
PO Box 264, Stone Ridge, NY 12484
(914) 687-0869   **Contact** Ray Ottulich
Area Catskill Rivers & Delaware River; **Services** Guide, Accommodations, School; **Est.** 1989; **Season** Apr-Nov; **Waters** Public; **Type** Walk/Wade; **Fish** Largemouth, Smallmouth, Rainbow, Brook, Brown; **Packages** 1/2 Day, up to 2 anglers
24 years of experience in Montana. 8 years as a professional guide on the Kootenai, the state's largest and most demanding "Blue Ribbon" stream. You'll leave with insights most anglers never understand. Let me help you master and enjoy the magical sport of fly fishing. Call or write for brochure.

Orvis New York
355 Madison Ave., New York, NY 10017
(212) 697-3133 **Fax** (212) 697-5826
Area Catskill Waters, Long Island Sound; **Services** Outfitter/Guide, Fly Shop, School; **Waters** Public; **Type** Walk/Wade; **Fish** Bass, Trout, Brown, Bluefish

Anthony Ritter

PO Box 230, Lake St., Narrowsburg, NY 12764
(914) 252-3657 or (212) 866-6398
Contact Anthony Ritter
Area Upper Delaware River; **Services** Guide;
Season Apr-Nov; **Waters** Public; **Type** Walk/Wade,
Boat; **Fish** Smallmouth, Trout; **Packages** 1/2 Day,
up to 2 anglers
Welcome! My name is Tony Ritter and I'm a New York
State Licensed Guide with over ten years experience
on the main stem of the Delaware River. My company,
Gone Fishing Guide Service, operates from Narrowsburg, NY, just a two hour drive from the George
Washington Bridge. I invite you to fish the nationally
recognized Delaware River with me aboard my McKenzie drift boat. Whether you're a novice or a
dyed-in-the-wool fisherman, Gone Fishing Guide Service will do our best to provide you with a day you'll
remember for many years to come! Call today.
See Our Ad Pg. 175

Tony's Salmon
Country Sports

3790 St. Rt. 13, Pulaski, NY 13142
(315) 298-4104 **Fax** (315) 298-3721
Services Guide, Accommodations, Fly Shop; **Waters**
Public; **Type** Walk/Wade, Boat
○ Tackle, Gift Shop
○ Fish Smoking
○ Free River Access

NORTH CAROLINA

Fly Tackle Dealers

IntraCoastal Angler
6303 Oleander Dr., #102, Wilmington, NC 28403
(888) 325-4285   Contact: Tyler Stone
One of the mid-Atlantic's finest full service fly shop.
Instruction/guiding services available.

NC Anglers & Outfitters
714 Ninth St., Durham, NC 27705
(800) 454-6657   Contact: Jan Hackett
NC Anglers is a full service shop offering Orvis fly
tackle and clothing. Casting and tying instruction
along with guiding services.

TKR
1706 C English Rd., High Point, NC 27262
(910) 882-3226   Contact: Tom Kirkman
Full service fly shop, including rod manufacturing,
restoration and repair services.

NORTH CAROLINA
Outfitters/Guides

Appalachian Angler Guide Service
174 Old Shulls Mill Rd., Boone, NC 28607
(704) 963-7474   **Contact** Theo Copeland
Services Guide, Fly Shop; **Season** Apr-Nov; **Waters**
Public; **Type** Walk/Wade, Boat; **Fish** Smallmouth,
Rainbow, Brown; **Packages** 1/2 Day, up to 12 anglers

McLeod's Highland Fly Fishing
191 Wesser Heigts Dr., Bryson City, NC 28713
(704) 488-8975   **Contact** Mac Brown
Area Great Smoky Mtns./Back Country Overnights;
Services Guide, School; **Est.** 1987; **Season**
Year-round; **Waters** Public; **Type** Walk/Wade, Boat;
Fish Smallmouth, Rainbow, Brook, Brown; **Packages**
1 Day, up to 6 anglers
○ Back Country Trips
○ Over 25 years experience
Mac's innovative techniques, lectures, and articles
have been well received from anglers worldwide. His
unique teaching methods and programs have been
praised repeatedly in numerous publications as simply
the best in the nation. McLeod's also offers quality destination trips here and abroad for that angling
adventure of a lifetime.

Outer Banks Fly Angler
Nags Head, NC 27959
(800) 368-0807 or (919) 441-2200
Area Cape Hatteras; **Services** Outfitter/Guide, Fly
Shop, School; **Waters** Public; **Type** Walk/Wade,
Boat; **Fish** Bluefish, Redfish

OHIO

Fly Tackle Dealers

Mad River Outfitters
779 Bethel Rd., Columbus, OH 43214
(888) 451-0363 (614) 451-0363
FAX: (614) 451-0709
Contact: Brian Flechsig or Tom Frick
Everything for the fly fisher, upland hunter and
sporting clays shooter. Full line Orvis dealer. Guide
service/classes.

TMF Sport Shop
4081 Sandy Lake Rd., Ravenna, OH 44266
(330) 296-2614   FAX: (330) 296-7248
Contact: Frank Navarrete
Orvis rods #2-#12. Ohio's largest selection of fly tying
materials. Filson, Barbour, Lewis Creek clothing. FFF
certified casting instruction available.

OKLAHOMA

Fly Tackle Dealers

River's Edge
10904 N. May, Oklahoma City, OK 73120
(403) 748-3900   FAX: (403) 748-3986
Contact: Reece Lansberg
Full service fly shop and guide service.

OREGON

Fly Tackle Dealers

Fly Country Outfitters
3400 State St., Suite G-704, Salem, OR 97301
(503) 585-4898   FAX: (503) 581-7720
Contact: George Hadley
Worldwide service, fly shop, regional Orvis dealer, guides, schools

Northwest Flyfishing Outfitters
17302 NE Halsey, Gresham, OR 97230
(503) 252-1529   Contact: John Hagan
Full service fly shop, 10 minutes from the Portland International Airport, on the way to the Deshutes, Sandy and John Day Rivers. Guided trips and on river classes.

The Valley Flyfisher
153 Alice Ave., S., Salem, OR 97302
(503) 375-3721 FAX: (503) 375-0070
Contact: Keith A. Burkhart
Full service fly shop featuring presentation quality custom Sage and Winston fly rods, Bellinger classic reels and reel seats.

OREGON
Lodges

The Big K Guest Ranch
20029 Hwy 138 W., Elkton, OR 97436
(800) 390-2445
Area Umpqua River;   **Services** Lodge, Accommodations;   **Waters** Private;   **Type** Walk/Wade, Boat;   **Fish** Smallmouth, Steelhead, Salmon

Morrison's Rogue River Lodge
8500 Galice Rd., Merlin, OR 97532
(541) 476-3825 Or 800-826-1963
Fax (541) 476-4953   **Contact** Michelle Hanten,
Area Rogue River, southern OR;   **Services** LodgeOutfitter/Guide, Accommodations, Fly Shop;
Est. 1946;   **Waters** Public;   **Type** Walk/Wade, Boat;   **Fish** Rainbow, Steelhead, Salmon

Rainbow King Lodge
1527 Lake Front Rd., Lake Oswego, OR 97034
(800) 458-6539 or (503) 697-4415
Fax (503) 635-3079   **Contact** Tom Robinson
Area Lake Iliamna; **Services** Lodge,
Accommodations; **Season** May15-Oct.1; **Waters**
Public; **Type** Walk/Wade, Boat; **Fish** Rainbow, Lake
Trout, Salmon, Char, Pike

Steamboat Inn
42705 N. Umpqua Hwy., Steamboat, OR 97447
(800) 840-8825
Area North Umpqua River; **Services** Lodge,
Accommodations; **Waters** Public; **Type**
Walk/Wade; **Fish** Steelhead

Yamsi Ranch
PO Box 371, Chiloquin, OR 97624
(541) 783-2403   **Contact** Gerda Hyde
Area Upper Williamson; **Services** Lodge,
Accommodations, Fly Shop; **Est.** 1980; **Season**
May-Nov; **Waters** Private; **Type** Float Tube,
Walk/Wade; **Fish** Rainbow, Brook; **Packages** 3
Days, up to 10 anglers

OREGON
Outfitters/Guides

Ashland Fly Shop Guide Service
PO Box 864, Ashland, OR 97520
(541) 482-1430   **Contact** Mark Swisher
Area Rogue & John Day Rivers; **Services**
Outfitter/Guide, Fly Shop; **Est.** 1979; **Season**
Feb-Nov; **Waters** Public; **Type** Walk/Wade, Boat;
Fish Bass, Smallmouth, Trout, Rainbow, Cutthroat,
Steelhead; **Packages** 5 Days, up to 14 anglers

The Fly Fishing Shop
PO Box 368, Welches, OR 97067
(503) 622-4607
Area Sandy & Deschutes Rivers; **Services** Guide, Fly
Shop; **Waters** Public; **Type** Walk/Wade, Boat;
Fish Trout, Steelhead

High Desert Drifters Guides & Outfitters
721 N.W. Ogden, Bend, OR 97701
(541) 389-0607 or (800) 685-FISH
Contact Rick or Kim Killingsworth
Area Deschutes River; **Services** Outfitter/Guide,
Accommodations; **Est.** 1986; **Season** Apr-Dec;
Waters Public; **Type** Walk/Wade, Boat; **Fish** Trout,
Rainbow, Steelhead; **Packages** 1 Day, up to 9 anglers

Jim's Oregon Whitewater
56324 McKenzie Hwy., McKenzie Bridge, OR 97413
(541) 822-6003 or (800) 254-JIMS
Fax (541) 822-3149   **Contact** Jim Berl
Area Deschutes & McKenzie Rivers; **Services** Guide,
Accommodations; **Est.** 1984; **Season** May-Oct;
Waters Public; **Type** Walk/Wade, Boat; **Fish** Trout,
Rainbow, Cutthroat, Steelhead; **Packages** 1/2 Day,
up to 10 anglers

Northwest Flyfishing Adventures
PO Box 68739, Portland, OR 97268
(800) 359-7330 **Fax** (503) 659-0969
Area NW OR; **Services** Outfitter/Guide; **Season**
Year-round; **Waters** Public; **Type** Walk/Wade;
Fish Trout, Steelhead, Salmon

Silvey's Flyfishing Guide Service
PO Box 681, Welches, OR 97067
(800) 510-1702 or (503) 622-4329
Contact Brian & Lisa Silvey
Area Deschutes & Sandy Rivers; **Services** Guide,
Accommodations; **Est.** 1984; **Season** Year-round;
Waters Public; **Type** Walk/Wade, Boat; **Fish** Trout,
Rainbow, Steelhead; **Packages** 1 Day, up to 3 anglers

Stringham Outfitters, Inc.
61535 S. Hwy 97 #9-274, Bend, OR 97702
(800) 999-5524 or (541) 385-0903
Fax (541) 330-1940   **Contact** Steve Stringham
Area Deschutes & Crooked Rivers; **Services** Guide,
Accommodations; **Season** Mar-Dec; **Waters**
Public/Private; **Type** Float Tube, Walk/Wade, Boat;
Fish Trout, Rainbow, Steelhead; **Packages** 1 Day, up
to 9 anglers

PENNSYLVANIA
FLY TACKLE DEALERS

Flyfisher's Paradise
2603 E. College Ave., State College, PA 16801
(814) 234-4189 FAX: (814) 238-3686
Contact: Dan or Steve
Orvis, Cortland, Sage, G. Loomis, Metz, Umpqua,
Instructional Services, Ross, Thompson, Richardson,
LaCrosse, Flies, Books, Fly Tying Accessories,
Information. Catalog: $1.

Flyfishing Forever
Germantown Pike & Valley Forge Rd.
Fairview Village, PA 19409
(610) 631-8990 FAX: (610) 631-8991
Contact: Jonathan Greaser
Full service flyfishing store. FFF Certified Casting
Instructor providing Saturday morning no charge
casting instruction.

Old Village Fly Shop
23 S. Main St., Shrewsbury, PA 17361
(717) 235-9020 FAX: (717) 227-0183
Contact: Charles King
Fly shop/guiding service; custom rod building;
premium fly tying materials and rod building supplies;
G. Loomis; Powell; T&T; Ross; J. Ryall

The Sporting Gentleman
306 E. Baltimore Pike, Media, PA 19063
(610) 565-6140 FAX: (610) 565-6140
Contact: Barry Staats
The Sporting Gentleman is an Orvis store. We offer fly
tying and fly fishing instruction.

Yellow Breeches Outfitters
PO Box 200, 2 E. First St.
Boiling Springs, PA 17007
(717) 258-6752   FAX: (717) 258-9364
Contact: Bill Zeiders
Complete line of fly fishing & fly tying equipment and clothing. Specializing in fly fishing schools and instruction.

PENNSYLVANIA
Lodges

Angling Fantasies
Box 1294, RR 2, Port Royal, PA 17082
(717) 527-2805 or (717) 543-5481
Fax (717) 527-2805
Contact Jim Gilson
Area Central PA Limestoners, Spruce Creek; Services Lodge, Accommodations, School; Est. 1982; Season Mar-Nov; Waters Public/Private; Type Walk/Wade; Fish Trout, Rainbow, Brown; Packages 1 Day, up to 14 anglers

Big Moore's Run Lodge
R.D.#3, Box 204A, Coudersport, PA 16915
(814) 547-5300 Fax (814) 647-9928
Contact Bill Haldaman
Area 6 1/2 hrs from NYC; Services Lodge, Accommodations, Fly Shop; Est. 1987; Waters Public/Private; Type Walk/Wade, Boat; Fish Rainbow, Brook, Brown

Al Caucci's Delaware River Club
HC-1 Box 1290, Starlight, PA 18461
(800) 6MA-YFLY or (717) 635-5880
Fax (717) 635-5844
Contact Bob Wills, Mgr.
Services Lodge, Accommodations, Fly Shop, School; Est. 1994; Waters Public; Type Float Tube, Walk/Wade

PENNSYLVANIA
Outfitters/Guides

Angling Adventures
328 Zion Rd., Mt. Holly Springs, PA 17065
(717) 486-7438   Contact Tom Baltz
Area South Central PA; Services Guide; Season Year-round; Waters Public; Type Walk/Wade, Boat; Fish Largemouth, Smallmouth, Trout; Packages 1 Day, up to 3 anglers
O Member National Assn. of Fly-Fishing Guides
Instruction/guiding; South Central PA's Yellow Breeches, Letort, other limestone trout streams. Summer/Fall river smallmouth bass. Custom Flies. Brochure.

Ed Carbonneau
PO Box 116, Starlight, PA 18461
(908) 995-4894 Fax (908) 995-4795
Contact Ed Carbonneau
Area Delaware River; Services Guide; Waters Public; Type Walk/Wade; Fish Smallmouth, Rainbow, Brown

Cold Spring Anglers
419 East High St., Suite A, Carlisle, PA 17013
(800) 248-8937 or (717) 245-2646
Fax (800) 553-9943
Contact Herb & Kathy Weigl
Area Cumberland Valley; Services Guide, Fly Shop; Est. 1986; Waters Public; Type Walk/Wade; Fish Trout; Packages 1/2 Day
O Catalog, Classes
O Guided fly fishing for trout on Letort, Yellow Breeches, Big Spring, Clark's Creek, etc.
O All-day or half-day trips available
O Easy access from I-81 or Pennsylvania Turnpike (I-76)

Falling Spring Outfitters
PO Box 35, 3813 Old Main St., Scotland, PA 17254
(717) 263-7811 Contact Mark Sturtevant
Area Falling Spring, Letort; Services Outfitter/Guide, Fly Shop; Est. 1993; Season Year-round; Waters Public; Type Walk/Wade; Fish Rainbow, Brook, Brown

Fishing Creek Outfitters
RD 1, Box 310-1, Benton, PA 17814
(717) 925-2225 Fax (717) 925-5644
Contact Dave & Donna Colley
Area NE PA; Services Outfitter/Guide, Fly Shop; Waters Private; Type Walk/Wade

Northeast Flyfishers
923 Main St., Honesdale, PA 18431
(717) 253-9780 Fax (717) 253-9450
Contact Rick Eck   Area Upper Delaware River; Services Outfitter/Guide, School; Waters Public; Type Walk/Wade, Boat; Fish Bass, Largemouth, Trout, Rainbow, Brook, Brown

Norther Tier Outfitters
15 Fairview Ave., Galeton, PA 16922
(814) 435-6324 Contact Brad Bireley
Area North central PA; Services Guide, Fly Shop; Est. 1995; Waters Public; Type Walk/Wade; Fish Rainbow, Brook, Brown; Packages 1/2 Day

Matt Zito
PO Box 221, Boiling Springs, PA 17007
(800) 258-1639 or (717) 258-8344
Fax (717) 258-9882 Contact Matt Zito
Area Yellow Breeches & Letort; Services Guide; Est. 1994; Season Apr-Nov; Waters Public; Type Walk/Wade; Fish Rainbow, Brook, Brown; Packages 1 Day, up to 6 anglers

RHODE ISLAND

Outfitters/Guides

Capt. Ed Hughes
28 W. Castle Way, #D, Charlestown, RI 02813
(401) 783-5912   **Contact** Capt. Ed Hughes
Services Guide;   **Waters** Public;   **Type** Walk/Wade,
Boat;   **Fish** Bass, Bluefish

The Saltwater Edge Fly Fishing Co.
561 Thames, Newport, RI 02840
(401) 842-0062   **Contact** Gregg Weatherby
Area Rhode Island Bays & Rivers;   **Services** Guide, Fly
Shop;   **Waters** Public;   **Type** Walk/Wade, Boat;
Fish Bass, Bluefish, Bonito, False Albacore;   **Packages**
1/2 Day
The spectacular coastal beaches and inshore reefs of
Rhode Island are the summer home to Striped Bass,
Bluefish, Bonito, and False Albacore. The Saltwater
Edge provides a guide service taking you where the
fish are with it staff of highly experienced and profes-
sional guides. From May to November our guides track
the schools of fish as they enter our bays and rivers
and will take you to the most recently active areas.

SOUTH CAROLINA

Fly Tackle Dealers

Luden's
Concord & Charlotte Sts., Charleston, SC 29401
(803) 723-7829
Full service authorized Orvis shop. Guiding services can
be arranged.

SOUTH CAROLINA
Lodges

Brays Island Plantation
PO Box 30, Sheldon, SC 29941
(803) 846-3100   **Fax** (803) 846-3154
Area Coastal Beaufort;   **Services** Lodge,
Accommodations;   **Waters** Private;   **Type**
Walk/Wade, Boat

Broxton Bridge Plantation
PO Box 97, Ehrhardt, SC 29081
(803) 267-3882   or (800) 437-4868
Fax (803) 267-3241   **Contact** G.D. "Jerry" Varn, Jr.
Area Low country coastal area of South Carolina;
Services Lodge, Accommodations, Fly Shop, School;
Est. 1988;   **Season** Year-round;   **Waters**
Public/Private;   **Type** Walk/Wade, Boat;   **Fish** Sea
Trout, Tarpon, Redfish;   **Packages** 1/2 Day

SOUTH CAROLINA
Outfitters/Guides

Bay Street Outfitters
815 Bay St., Beaufort, SC 29902
(803) 524-5250   **Fax** (803) 524-9002
Contact Jason Farmer
Area Beaufort County;   **Services** Outfitter/Guide, Fly
Shop;   **Season** Year-round;   **Waters** Public/Private;
Type Walk/Wade, Boat;   **Fish** Trout, Tarpon;
Packages 1/2 Day, up to 8 anglers

Capt. Bramblett Bradham
PO Box 1248, Charleston, SC 29402
(803) 870-4688   **Contact** Capt. Bramblett Bradham
Services Guide

Calvin Guide Service
107 Brookside Ave., Greenville, SC 29607
(864) 370-0720   or (864) 235-4289
Contact John Calvin
Area North & South Carolina;   **Services** Guide,
Accommodations;   **Est.** 1994;   **Season** Yr.round;
Waters Public;   **Type** Walk/Wade;   **Fish** Trout;
Packages 1 Day, up to 15 anglers
O ORVIS Endorsed
O 1 Day to 1 Week Packages
O Guiding on 60+ Streams in North and
   South Carolina
O 3 Generations of Fly-fishing Experience
O Instructional Trip for Beginner or Expert Guiding for
   Advanced Fly Fisherman
O Lodging and Meals–No Extra Charge!
   (for overnight packages)

Dry Flyer Outfitters
PO Box 1837, Beaufort, SC 29901
(423) 338-6263   **Contact** Tony Wilson
Services Outfitter;   **Waters** Public

Mike Hester
12 W. Lewis Plaza, Greenville, SC 29605
(803) 235-0981   or (704) 692-4719
Contact Mike Hester
Area Blue Ridge & Smoky Mts.;   **Services** Guide;
Waters Public;   **Type** Walk/Wade;   **Fish** Rainbow,
Brown;   **Packages** 1 Day

The Lodge at Lofton's Landing
PO Box 245, Charleston, SC 29402
(803) 720-7332 email: makairal1@aol.com
Fax (803) 853-7586   **Contact** Pam McConnell
Area Cape Romain Wildlife Refuge north of
Charleston; **Services** Lodge, Accommodations, Fly
Shop, School; **Est.** 1996; **Season** Year-round;
Waters Public/Private; **Type** Walk/Wade, Boat;
Fish Sea Trout, Tarpon, Redfish; **Packages** 2 Days,
up to 14 anglers
This spectacular 16th Century Japanese style pole
home overlooking the marsh is located on 210 acres
just 35 minutes north of Charleston. Perfect for corporate retreats, The Lodge offers catered meals and
recreational services designed to meet clients' specific
requests. The house is also available on a straight
rental basis. Fish, bird or kayak in the vast tidal
saltmarsh flats of the Cape Romain Wildlife Refuge or
freshwater streams and swamps. Sporting clays/lim-
ited hunting can be arranged. Call for free brochure.

David Murray
100 Grayson St., Beaufort, SC 29902
(803) 525-6820   **Contact** David Murray
Area Port Royal & St. Helena Sound, Inshore Waters;
Services Guide; **Season** Year-round; **Waters** Public;
Type Boat; **Fish** Sea Trout, Redfish

Capt. Richard Stuhr
547 Sanders Farm Lane, Charleston, SC 29492
(803) 881-3179   **Contact** Capt. Richard Stuhr
Area Charleston, Kiawah, Isle of Palms; **Services**
Guide; **Waters** Public; **Type** Walk/Wade, Boat;
Fish Sea Trout, Bluefish; **Packages** 1/2 Day, up to 3
anglers
O Red Drum, Cravalle Jacks, Lady Fish,
   Spanish Mackeral
O ORVIS Endorsed
The Charleston area offers year round angling for red
drum, with some of the best red drum and sea trout
fishing available in fall and winter. Summer is the sea-
son for tailing reds, world class cravalle jacks and a
variety of other species.

Captain Gary Taylor
1993 Orvis Guide of the Year
PO Box 1837, Beaufort, SC 29901
(803) 846-3100 or (803) 524-0681
Contact Gary Taylor
Area Hilton Head; **Services** Outfitter/Guide;
Season Year-round; **Waters** Public; **Type**
Walk/Wade, Boat; **Fish** Rainbow, Brown

TENNESSEE

Fly Tackle Dealers

Hiwassee Outfitters
Ellis Creek Rd., PO Box 62
Reliance, TN 37369
(800) 338-8133   FAX: (423) 338-1261
Contact: C.J. Jaynes
Fly fishing guide service, full line fly shop, riverside
cabins and campground, boat rentals and shuttle
service.

TENNESSEE
Outfitters/Guides

Chris Nischan
2807-C West End Ave., Nashville, TN 37203
(615) 327-0557   **Contact** Chris Nischan
Area Caney Fork & Elk Rivers; **Services** Guide;
Waters Public/Private; **Type** Walk/Wade, Boat;
Fish Bass, Rainbow, Brown

Old Smoky Outfitters
511 Parkway #201, Gatlinburg, TN 37738
(423) 430-1936   **Contact** Jack Snapp
Area Smokies, Clinch River, Nantahala River;
Services Outfitter, Accommodations, Fly Shop, School;
Est. 1991; **Season** Year-round; **Waters**
Public/Private; **Type** Walk/Wade, Boat; **Fish** Bass,
Largemouth, Smallmouth, Striped Bass, Trout,
Rainbow, Brook, Brown, Striped Bass; **Packages** 1/2
Day, up to 12 anglers

South Harpeth Outfitters
PO Box 218226, Nashville, TN 37221
(615) 952-4186   **Contact** Ernie Paquette
Area Middle Tennessee rivers & streams; **Services**
Guide; **Waters** Public/Private; **Type** Walk/Wade,
Boat; **Fish** Bass, Smallmouth, Rainbow, Brook, Brown

Captain Gary Taylor
1993 Orvis Guide of the Year
PO Box 618, Benton, TN 37307
(423) 338-6263   **Contact** Gary Taylor
Services Outfitter/Guide; **Season** May-June;
Waters Public; **Type** Walk/Wade, Boat; **Fish**
Rainbow, Brown

TEXAS

Fly Tackle Dealers

H&E Sports
410 N. Main, Midland, TX 79701
(915) 682-2473   FAX: (915) 684-7691
Contact: Jim Henderson   Orvis Dealer

Pico Outdoor Company
1600 Harper Rd., Kerrville, TX 78028
(800) 256-5873   FAX: (210) 895-4344
Contact: R.B. Miller
Warm water fly fishing headquarters for Texas Hill country. 1/2 day to 3 day trips available. Rentals & instruction.

Westbank Anglers-Dallas
5370 West Lovers Lane, #320, Dallas, TX 75209
(214) 350-4665   FAX: (214) 350-4667
Contact: David & Cathie Coleman

TEXAS
Lodges

Joshua Creek Ranch
PO Box 1946, Boerne, TX 78006
(210) 537-5090   **Contact** Ann Kercheville
Area 25 mi. NW of San Antonio;   **Services** Lodge, Accommodations;   **Est.** 1990;   **Type** Walk/Wade, Boat;   **Fish** Bass, Rainbow
○ Exceptional hunting for quail, pheasant, duck, dove, turkey & deer
○ Rainbow trout and guadalupe bass fishing
○ World Class Sporting Clays
○ Excellent dining, lodging & conference facilities
○ Less than 45 minutes north of San Antonio

TEXAS
Outfitters/Guides

Cypert's Guide Service, Inc.
PO Box 73, Aquilla, TX 76622
(817) 694-3422   **Contact** Charlie Cypert
Area Central Texas Lakes & Rivers;   **Services** Guide, School;   **Est.** 1989;   **Waters** Public;   **Type** Walk/Wade, Boat;   **Fish** Bass, Largemouth, Smallmouth, Black Bass, Striped Bass, Striped Bass, White Bass;   **Packages** 1/2 Day, up to 3 anglers
○ ORVIS Endorsed
○ 40+ Years Fishing Experience
○ Fly Fishing & Fly Tying Schools & Seminars
○ Techniques to Catch More & Larger Fish
○ Retail & Wholesale Warm Water Flies
○ High Quality Foil Poppers (fresh & saltwater)

Curtis McNabb
PO Box 1362, Rockport, TX 78381
(512) 729-5382   **Contact** Curtis McNabb
Services Guide;   **Type** Walk/Wade;   **Fish** Trout, Redfish

Chuck Naiser
PO Box 100, Fulton, TX 78358
(512) 729-9314   **Contact** Chuck Niser
Area Rockport area;   **Services** Guide;   **Est.** 1993;   **Season** Year-round;   **Waters** Public;   **Type** Walk/Wade, Boat;   **Fish** Trout, Redfish;   **Packages** 1 Day, up to 2 anglers

Sycamore Creek Ranch
4703 Greatland Dr., San Antonio, TX 78218
(210) 661-5346   **Fax** (210) 661-9128
Contact Dave Terk
Services Lodge, Accommodations;   **Season** Year-round;   **Type** Boat;   **Fish** Black Bass

UTAH

Fly Tackle Dealers

Willow Creek Outfitters
424 E. 12300 South, Draper, UT 84020
(801) 576-1946
Contact: David Curneal or   Andrew Benson
Full line of fly fishing, local tied flies, guide services, private waters & mail order.

UTAH
Lodges

Falcon's Ledge
PO Box 67, Altamont, UT 84001
(801) 454-3737   **Fax** (801) 454-3392
Contact Howard Brinkerhoff
Area 2 hours from Salt Lake City;   **Services** Lodge, Accommodations, Fly Shop, School;   **Est.** 1993;   **Season** Mar-Nov;   **Waters** Public/Private;   **Type** Float Tube, Walk/Wade;   **Fish** Trout, Rainbow, Brook, Brown, Cutthroat;   **Packages** 1 Day, up to 20 anglers

Flaming Gorge Lodge
Greendale, US 191, Dutch John, UT 84023
(801) 889-3773   **Fax** (801) 889-3788
Contact Craig W.Collett
Area Green River & Flaming Gorge Res.;   **Services** Lodge, Accommodations;   **Est.** 1971;   **Season** Year-round;   **Waters** Public;   **Type** Walk/Wade, Boat;   **Fish** Rainbow, Brown, Lake Trout, Cutthroat;   **Packages** 1/2 Day

UTAH
Outfitters/Guides

Anglers' Inn
2292 Highland Dr., Salt Lake City, UT 84106
(801) 466-3921   **Fax** (801) 483-1885
Area Green River;   **Services** Outfitter/Guide, Fly Shop;   **Waters** Public;   **Type** Walk/Wade, Boat

ONSTREAM OUTFITTERS

Onstream Outfitters
945 West 200 S., Provo, UT 84601
(801) 371-0891   **Contact** Jeff Bird
Area Provo River; High Country Fly Fishing;   **Services**
Guide;   **Est.** 1993;   **Season** Yr.Round;   **Waters**
Public;   **Type** Walk/Wade, Boat;   **Fish** Rainbow,
Brown, Cutthroat;   **Packages** 1/2 Day, up to 6 anglers
o Quality Equipment Provided Just For You
o Seasoned Guides
o McKenzie Drift Boats
o Trophy Browns and Big Rainbows
o Special Winter Midge Fishing

Spinner Fall Fly Shop
1450 S. Foothill Dr., Salt Lake City, UT 84108
(801) 583-2602 or 800-959-3474
Fax (801) 583-5445
Area Green River;   **Services** Outfitter/Guide, Fly
Shop;   **Waters** Public;   **Type** Walk/Wade;   **Fish**
Rainbow, Brown, Cutthroat

Trout Creek Flies
PO Box 247, Dutch John, UT 84023
(801) 889-3735 or (800) 835-4551
Contact Dennis & Grace Breer
Area Green River;   **Services** Outfitter/Guide,
Accommodations;   **Season** Year-round;   **Waters**
Public;   **Type** Walk/Wade, Boat;   **Fish** Rainbow,
Brown, Cutthroat;   **Packages** 1 Day, up to 20 anglers

Western Rivers Flyfisher
867 E. 900 St., Salt Lake City, UT 84105
(800) 545-4312 or (801) 521-6424
Area Green River;   **Services** Guide, Fly Shop;
Waters Public/Private;   **Type** Walk/Wade

Wild Country Outfitters & Fly Shop
4304 -5 Harrison Blvd., Ogden, UT 84403
(801) 479-1194 **Fax** (801) 479-1195
Services Outfitter/Guide, Accommodations, Fly Shop;
Waters Public;   **Type** Walk/Wade;   **Fish** Rainbow,
Cutthroat

VERMONT

Lodges

Seymour Lake Lodge
RR1, Box 61, Morgan, VT 05853
(800) 207-2752   **Contact** Dave Benware
Area Seymour Lake;   **Services** LodgeGuide,
Accommodations, School;   **Est.** 1971;   **Waters**
Public;   **Type** Walk/Wade, Boat;   **Fish** Smallmouth,
Trout, Brook, Brown, Lake Trout, Salmon

VERMONT
Outfitters/Guides

David L. Deen
RFD 3, Box 800, Westminster, VT 05346
(802) 869-3116   **Contact** David L. Deen
Area Connecticut River;   **Services** Guide;   **Est.** 1983;
Waters Public;   **Type** Walk/Wade;   **Fish** Rainbow,
Salmon

Fly Fish Vermont
804 S. Main St. Unit 4, Stowe, VT 05672
(802) 253-3964   **Contact** Bob Shannon
Services Outfitter/Guide, Accommodations, Fly Shop,
School;   **Waters** Public;   **Type** Walk/Wade, Boat;
Fish Steelhead, Salmon

Chuck Kashner
PO Box 156, Pawlet, VT 05761
(800) 682-0103   **Contact** Chuck Kashner
Area Battenkill & Southern VT;   **Services** Guide;
Waters Public/Private;   **Type** Walk/Wade;   **Fish**
Rainbow, Brook, Brown;   **Packages** 1/2 Day

Three Forks Flyfisher
PO Box 611, East Middlebury, VT 05740
(802) 388-6575   **Contact** Justin Rogers
Area Vermont & Adirondack Park of NY;   **Services**
Outfitter/Guide, School;   **Est.** 1996

Uncle Jammer's Guide Service
RR #1, Box 6910, Underhill, VT 05489
(800) 805-6495 **Fax** (802) 899-5019
Contact James Ehlers
Area Winooski, Lamoille, and Upper Connecticut
Rivers;   **Services** Guide, Accommodations, School;
Est. 1994;   **Season** Apr-Oct;   **Waters** Public;   **Type**
Walk/Wade, Boat;   **Fish** Rainbow, Brook, Brown;
Packages 1/2 Day, up to 8 anglers
Experience New England's finest fly fishing. Cast to ris-
ing rainbows from a driftboat while floating Vermont's
pastoral valley rivers. Wade into position for a chance
at feisty browns. Stalk richly colored brook trout on secluded mountain streams. The popular all-inclusive
school packages prepare you for a future of certain
success. Call for a free brochure or visit us at
http://pobox.com/~uncle or e-mail VTFLYF-
ISH@juno.com

Vermont Bound Outfitters
HCR 34 Box 28, Killington, VT 05751
(800) 639-3167 or (802) 773-0736
Contact Jack Sapia   **Area** White River;   **Services**
Guide;   **Waters** Public;   **Type** Walk/Wade;   **Fish**
Rainbow, Brown;   **Packages** 1/2 Day

VIRGINIA

Outfitters/Guides

Bob Cramer
Rt. 3 PO Box 238-A, Dayton, VA 22921
(540) 867-9310   **Contact** Bob Cramer
Area Shenandoah Vlaley; **Services** Guide, School;
Waters Public/Private; **Type** Float Tube, Walk/Wade;
Fish Smallmouth, Trout

Murray's Fly Shop
PO Box 156, 121 Main St., Edinburg, VA 22824
(540) 984-4212 **Fax** (800) 984-4895
Contact Harry W. Murray
Area Shenandoah River; **Services** Guide, Fly Shop,
School; **Est.** 1962; **Season** Mar-Oct; **Waters**
Public/Private; **Type** Walk/Wade, Boat; **Fish**
Smallmouth, Rainbow, Brook, Brown, Bluegill;
Packages 1 Day, up to 10 anglers

Orvis Roanoke
Market Square, 19 Campbell Ave., Roanoke, VA 24010
(703) 345-3635   **Area** Smith River; **Services**
Outfitter/Guide, Fly Shop; **Waters** Public; **Type**
Walk/Wade; **Fish** Smallmouth, Trout

Trout & About
3488 N. Emerson St., Arlington, VA 22207
(703) 536-7494 **Fax** (703) 536-0017
Contact Phil Gay
Area 2 Hours from Washington D.C.; **Services**
Guide, School; **Season** Year-round; **Waters** Public;
Type Walk/Wade; **Fish** Smallmouth, Trout;
Packages 1/2 Day, up to 4 anglers

WASHINGTON

Fly Tackle Dealers

Yakima River Outfitters
1210 W. Lincoln, Yakima, WA 98902-2536
(509) 457-3474   FAX: (509) 457-1810
Contact: Gary
Eastern Washington's most complete fly fishing specialty shop. Blue Ribbon Yakima River fly fishing guides.

WASHINGTON
Outfitters/Guides

Herb Jacobsen
PO Box 1485, Forks, WA 98331
(800) 307-1074 or (360) 374-5135
Contact Herb Jacobsen
Area Olympic Peninsula; **Services** Guide; **Waters**
Public; **Type** Walk/Wade; **Fish** Cutthroat,
Steelhead, Salmon, Dolly Varden

Jeff Martin
865 NW 73rd St., Seattle, WA 98117
(206) 781-8915   **Contact** Jeff Martin
Services Guide

Bob Pigott
208344 Hwy. 101, Port Angeles, WA 98363
(360) 327-3554   **Contact** Bob Pigott
Area Olympic Peninsula; **Services** Guide; **Est.** 1966;
Waters Public; **Type** Walk/Wade; **Fish** Trout,
Steelhead, Salmon, Dolly Varden

Capt. Keith A. Robbins
2318 Viewmont Way W., Seattle, WA 98199
(206) 283-6680 Pager: (206) 918-0707
Contact Capt. Keith A. Robbins
Area Puget Sound; **Services** Guide; **Est.** 1990;
Season Year-round; **Waters** Public; **Type** Boat;
Fish Cutthroat, Salmon

Ron Romig
4702-361 St. S.E., Fall City, WA 98024
(206) 222-7654   **Contact** Ron Romig
Area Seattle; **Services** Guide; **Waters** Public;
Type Walk/Wade; **Fish** Rainbow, Cutthroat

Jim Shuttleworth
4730 228th SE, Bothell, WA 98024
(206) 487-3645   **Contact** Jim Shuttleworth
Area Yakima River; **Services** Guide; **Season**
Year-round; **Waters** Public; **Type** Walk/Wade, Boat;
Fish Rainbow, Steelhead, Salmon

Whitewater Travel, Inc.
The Professional's Choice
109 Ankrom St., Fayetteville, WV 25840
(800) 723-8982 or (304) 574-1298
Fax (304) 574-1298 **Contact** Kyle L. Coon
Area New River, Gateway River; **Services**
Outfitter/Guide, Accommodations, Fly Shop, School;
Est. 1993; **Season** March-Nov.; **Waters**
Public/Private; **Type** Boat; **Fish** Smallmouth, Black
Bass, Rainbow, Brook, Brown, Golden; **Packages** 1
Day, up to 40 anglers

WISCONSIN

Fly Tackle Dealers

The Fly Fishers
8601 W. Greenfield Ave., West Allis, WI 53214
(414) 259-8100   FAX: (414) 259-8100
Contact: Pat Ehlers   The Fly Fishers is a full service
specialty shop. Fresh & saltwater specialists. Classes,
guiding & travel services available.

WISCONSIN
Outfitters/Guides

Wisconsin John Guides Again
336 Chute St., Menasha, WI 54952
(414) 722-4004   **Contact** John Nebel
Area Wolf, Oconto & Waupaca Systems; **Services**
Outfitter/Guide, Fly Shop; **Est.** 1982; **Season**
Yr.round; **Waters** Public; **Type** Walk/Wade; **Fish**
Rainbow, Brook, Brown, Steelhead, Salmon;
Packages 1/2 Day, up to 4 anglers

WYOMING

Fly Tackle Dealers

Orvis Jackson Hole
485 W. Broadway, PO Box 9029
Jackson, WY 83002
(307) 733-5407 FAX: (307) 733-7158
Contact: Dave Fallon

....

Platte River Fly Shop
7400 Alcova Hwy. 220, Casper, WY 82604
(307) 237-5997 FAX: (307) 265-6152
Contact: Mark or Ron
Guided fly fishing trips; locally tied flies; custom rods & repairs; casting, tying & rod building classes. Open year-round.

....

Sports Lure
66 S. Main, Buffalo, WY 82834
(800) 684-7682   (307) 684-7682
FAX: (307) 684-7165 Contact: David Todd
Full line sporting goods with complete fly shop, lessons, guided trips.

....

Wind River Sporting Goods
420 Vinta Dr., Green River, WY 82935
(800) 568-5115   Contact: Jack Ely
Orvis dealer. Outfitter on the Wyoming Green River.

WYOMING
Lodges

Brush Creek Ranch
Star Route Box 10, Saratoga, WY 82331
(307) 327-5241 or 800-726-2499
Fax (307) 327-5384 **Contact** Kinta Blumenthal
Area Snowy Range Mts.; **Services** Lodge, Accommodations, Fly Shop, School; **Est.** 1993;
Season May-Nov; **Waters** Public/Private; **Type** Walk/Wade, Boat; **Fish** Rainbow, Brook, Brown, Cutthroat; **Packages** 3 Days, up to 6 anglers

....

Crescent H Ranch
PO Box 347, Wilson, WY 83014
(307) 733-2841 or (307) 733-3674
Area Jackson Hole; **Services** Lodge, Accommodations, School; **Est.** 1927; **Waters** Public/Private; **Type** Walk/Wade, Boat

....

Shirley Mountain Lodge
PO Box 2850, Casper, WY 82644
(307) 266-1470 or (307) 235-0899
Services Lodge

WYOMING
Outfitters/Guides

Aune's Absaroka Angler
1390 Sheridan Ave., Cody, WY 82414
(307) 587-5105 or (307) 527-7868
Services Outfitter/Guide; **Waters** Public; **Type** Walk/Wade, Boat; **Packages** 1/2 Day

....

Bressler Outfitters, Inc
Box 766, Wilson, WY 83014
(307) 733-6934 **Contact** Joe Bressler
Area Jackson Hole; **Services** Outfitter/Guide, Fly Shop; **Waters** Public; **Type** Walk/Wade, Boat; **Packages** 1 Day

....

Jack Dennis Sports
Box 3369, Jackson Hole, WY 83001
(307) 733-3270 or (800) 570-3270
Fax (307) 733-4540 **Contact** Bruce James
Area Snake; **Services** Outfitter/Guide, Fly Shop;
Est. 1969; **Season** Apr-Oct; **Waters** Public; **Type** Float Tube, Walk/Wade, Boat; **Fish** Brown, Lake Trout, Cutthroat; **Packages** up to 22 anglers

....

Fatboy Fishing
PO Box 121, Wilson, WY 83014
(307) 733-3061 **Contact** A.J. DeRosa
Area Montana, Wyoming, Yellowston Nt'l Park;
Services Outfitter/Guide, School; **Est.** 1974;
Season Apr-Nov; **Waters** Public/Private; **Type** Float

Float Tube, Walk/Wade, Boat;   **Fish** Trout, Rainbow, Brook, Cutthroat;   **Packages** 1 Day, up to 4 anglers

Five Star Expeditions
PO Box 582, 431 Main St., Lander, WY 82520
(307) 332-3197 **Fax** (307) 332-3198
Contact Ed Beattie
Area Green River, New Fork River, North Platte River;
Services Outfitter/Guide, Accommodations;   **Est.** 1980;   **Waters** Public;   **Type** Walk/Wade, Boat;
Fish Rainbow, Brown, Cutthroat;   **Packages** 3 Days

Great Rocky Mountain Outfitters
216 E. Walnut, Box 1636, Saratoga, WY 82331
(307) 326-8750 **Fax** (307) 326-5390
Contact Robert Smith
Area Upper North Platte & Encampment River;
Services Outfitter/Guide, Fly Shop, School;   **Est.** 1981;   **Season** May-Oct.;   **Waters** Public/Private;
Type Float Tube, Walk/Wade, Boat;   **Fish** Rainbow, Brook, Brown, Golden, Cutthroat;   **Packages** 1/2 Day, up to 20 anglers

George H. Hunker
Sweetwater Fishing Expeditions
PO Box 524, Lander, WY 82520
(307) 332-3986   **Contact** George H. Hunker
Area Wind River Mountains;   **Services** Outfitter/ Guide;   **Waters** Public;   **Type** Walk/Wade;   **Fish** Rainbow, Brook, Golden, Cutthroat;   **Packages** 1 Day

Medicine Bow Drifters, Inc.
PO Box 1642, 120 E. Bridge St., Saratoga, WY 82331
(307) 326-8002 **Email:**/Home page
www.MedBow.com **Fax** (307) 326-8003
Contact John Dobson & Rod Merritt
Area Upper North Platte, Encampment, Miracle Mile;
Services Guide, Fly Shop, School;   **Season** Apr-Nov;
Waters Public/Private;   **Type** Float Tube, Walk/Wade;
Fish Rainbow, Brook, Brown, Cutthroat;   **Packages** 1/2 Day, up to 8 anglers
○ Undiscovered wild trout fishing 3 1/2 hrs. from Denver
○ Professional fly fishing guides utilizing McKenzie style drift boats
○ Tailwater fishing on the Miracle Mile
○ Custom trips to fit your schedule
○ FFF certified casting instructors

Reel Women Fly Fishing
Adventures Women Only
PO Box 20202, Jackson, WY 83001
(307) 733-2210 **Fax** (307) 733-8655
Contact Christy Ball
Services Outfitter/Guide;   **Waters** Public;   **Type** Walk/Wade, Boat;   **Fish** Trout, Bonefish

South Fork
Fly Fishing Float Trips
PO Box 1385, Jackson, WY 83001
(307) 733-5173 **Fax** (307) 733-4607
Contact Paul Bruun
Area Snake & Green Rivers;   **Services** Outfitter/Guide;   **Est.** 1974;   **Season** MidJul-MidOct;
Waters Public;   **Type** Boat;   **Fish** Trout, Cutthroat;
Packages 1 Day, up to 2 anglers

Westbank Anglers
PO Box 523, Teton Village, WY 83025
(307) 733-6483 or (800) 922-3474
Fax (307) 733-9382 **Area** Jackson Hole;   **Services** Guide;   **Waters** Public;   **Type** Walk/Wade

Wilderness Discovery Youth Program
HC 63-347, Jackson Hole, WY 83001
(307) 733-7745 **Fax** (307) 733-1403
Contact Randy Foster   **Area** Wind River & Wyoming Range;   **Services** Outfitter/Guide, Accommodations;
Est. 1987;   **Season** Jun-Sep;   **Waters** Public;   **Type** Float Tube, Walk/Wade, Boat;   **Fish** Rainbow, Brook, Brown, Golden, Lake Trout;   **Packages** 2 Days, up to 12 anglers

Yellowstone Outfitters
PO Box 1156, Afton, WY 83110
(800) 447-4711
Contact Everett D. Petersen or Lynn D. Madsen
Area Jackson Hole;   **Services** Outfitter/Guide, Accommodations;   **Waters** Public;   **Type** Walk/Wade;   **Fish** Cutthroat
○ ORVIS Endorsed
Deluxe 6 Day Horseback Pack-In Fly Fishing on the headwaters of the Yellowstone and Thorofare Rivers, north of Jackson Hole, Wyoming next to Yellowstone Park in the most remote area of the Teton Wilderness. For the experienced or novice angler. Fish for trophy Wild Breed Cutthroat Trout in the 16-20 inch (3-4 pound) class...Catch & Release...Truly a Fly Fisherman's Paradise...Deluxe tent camps...A treasured trip you will always remember. Call or write today!
See Our Ad Pg. 185

CANADA - ALBERTA

Lodges

Frontier Fishing Lodge
Box 32008, Edmonton, Alberta, Canada T6K 4C2
(403) 465-6843 **Fax** (403) 466-3874
Contact Wayne Witherspoon **Area** Great Slave
Lake; **Services** Lodge, Accommodations; **Est.** 1965;
Season Jun15-Sept15; **Waters** Public; **Type** Boat;
Fish Lake Trout, Whitefish, Pike, Grayling

Kingfisher Drifting
2219 Paliswood Bay S.W., Calgary, AB,
Canada T2V 4Y7 (403) 281-2322
Contact Michael Truch **Area** Bow River; **Services**
Guide; **Waters** Public; **Type** Boat; **Fish** Rainbow,

Barry White's Bow River Angler
8403-145 Ave., Edmonton, Alberta, Canada T5E 2J1
(403) 475-8139 **Fax** (403) 473-6327
Contact Barry White **Area** Bow River; **Services**
Guide, Accommodations; **Est.** 1977; **Waters** Public;
Type Walk/Wade, Boat; **Fish** Rainbow, Brown;
Packages 1 Day

BRITISH COLUMBIA

Lodges

Caverhill Lodge
PO Box 190, Barriere, B.C., Canada V0E 1E0
(250) 672-9806 **Contact** Larry & Marlene Loney
Area Southern British Columbia; **Services** Lodge,
Accommodations; **Est.** 1947; **Season** Jun1-Sep30;
Waters Public; **Type** Boat; **Fish** Rainbow;
Packages 3 Days, up to 14 anglers

Eureka Peak Lodge & Outfitters
Box 1332B, 100 Mile House, B.C., Canada V0K 2E0
(250) 397-2445 Autotel Call: (250) 398-1104
Fax (250) 397-2445 **Contact** Stuart & Joyce Maitland
Area Cariboo Region; **Services** Lodge,
Accommodations; **Waters** Public; **Type** Walk/
Wade, Boat; **Fish** Trout, Rainbow, Lake Trout, Kokanee
Join us for a professionally guided fly fising adventure
in a secluded setting. We specialize in an all inclusive
American Plan angling experience from our Gotchen
Lake Lodge. We provide: angling guides; accommoda-
tion in private, modern log cabins; hearty
home-cooked meals; boats, motors and transportation
by vehicle and/or horseback to quality lakes, rivers and
streams for wild rainbow trout, lake trout and
kokanee.

Lac Le Jeune Resort
650 Victoria St., Kamloops, B.C., Canada V2C 2B4

(800) 561-5253 **Fax** (604) 374-9997
Area Lac Le Jeune Lake; **Services** Lodge,
Accommodations; **Waters** Public; **Type**
Walk/Wade, Boat; **Fish** Rainbow

McLeans Ts'yl-os Park Lodge & Adventures
PO Box 2560, Williams Lake, Canada, B.C. V2G 4P2
(604) 398-7755 or (604) 394-4103
Fax (604) 398-7738 **Contact** McLean Family
Area Chilko Lake; **Services** Lodge, Accommodations;
Waters Public; **Type** Walk/Wade

Moose Lake Lodge
Box 3310, Anahim Lake, B.C., Canada V0L 1C0
(250) 742-3535 (250) 742-3749
Contact John & Mary Lou Blackwell
Area Dean & Blackwater Rivers; **Services** Lodge,
Accommodations; **Season** May10-Oct15; **Waters**
Public; **Fish** Rainbow, Cutthroat, Steelhead, Salmon,
Dolly Varden; **Packages** 3 Days

Northland Steelhead Lodge
PO Box 2666, Smithers, B.C., Canada V0J 2N0
(250) 847-9234 or (250) 847-0259
Fax (250) 847-9234 **Contact** Jim & Kathy Ismond
Area Canada, British Columbia; **Services** Lodge,
Accommodations, School; **Est.** 1981; **Season**
May-Nov.; **Waters** Public; **Type** Walk/Wade; **Fish**
Trout, Rainbow, Cutthroat, Steelhead, Salmon;
Packages 1 Day, up to 8 anglers

Stewart's Lodge & Camps
Box 19, Nimpo Lake,, B.C., Canada, V0L 1R0
(800) 668-4335 or (800) ON-THE-FLY
Fax (604) 932-0288 **Contact** Ronda Stewart
Area Blackwater & Dean; **Services** Lodge,
Accommodations; **Season** May-Sep; **Waters** Public;
Type Walk/Wade; **Fish** Rainbow, Cutthroat;
Packages up to 16 anglers

The Blackwater Company
PO Box 4084, Williams Lake, B.C. V2G 2V2
(604) 392-5081 **Fax** (604) 392-1143
Contact Ron Thompson
Area Blackwater River, Cariboo Chilcotin Region;
Services Outfitter/Guide, Accommodations; **Est.**
1971; **Season** Jun15-Sep; **Waters** Public; **Type**
Boat; **Fish** Rainbow, Steelhead; **Packages** 6 Days,
up to 12 anglers
O Over 25 yrs. quality float trip
O Ideal for private groups to 12 anglers
O Private, secluded waters
O Unlimited walk/wade water available
O Many remote, productive area lakes

Columbia River Outfitters
Box 495 Trail,, B.C., Canada V1R 4L7
(800) 667-2311 **Area** Columbia River; **Services**
Outfitter/Guide; **Season** Apr-Oct; **Waters** Public;
Type Walk/Wade, Boat; **Fish** Rainbow

Dirty Harry Guide Service
632 Erickson Rd., Campbell River, B.C.,
Canada V9W 5N9
(250) 923-2236 **Fax** (250) 923-5744
Area Campbell River, Vancouver Island; **Services**
Guide; **Waters** Public; **Type** Walk/Wade, Boat;
Fish Steelhead, Salmon

Northwest Fishing Guides
PO Box 434, Terrace, B.C., Canada V8G 4B1
(604) 635-5295 **Fax** (604) 635-5295
Area Skeena & Kalum Rivers; **Services** Guide;
Waters Public; **Type** Boat; **Fish** Steelhead, Salmon

MANITOBA

Lodge

Plummer's Artic Fishing Lodges
950 Braford St., Winnipeg, Man., Canada R3H 0N5
(204) 774-5775 or (800) 665-0240
Fax (204) 783-2320 **Contact** Irene Landry
Area Great Slave & Great Bear Lakes; **Services**
Lodge, Accommodations; **Season** Jun-Sep; **Waters**
Public; **Type** Boat; **Fish** Lake Trout, Pike, Grayling

NEW BRUNSWICK

Lodges

Miramichi Gray Rapids Lodge
326 MacDonald Ave., Oromocto,
New Brunswick, Canada E2V 1A7
(800) 261-2330 **Fax** (506) 357-9733
Contact Guy A. Smith
Area Main SW Miramichi, Blackville; **Services** Lodge,
Accommodations; **Season** Apr-Oct; **Waters** Private;
Type Walk/Wade; **Fish** Trout, Salmon; **Packages**
up to 12 anglers

Miramichi Inn
RR #2,, Red Bank, N.B., Canada E0C 1W0
(506) 836-7452 **Fax** (506) 836-7805
Contact Andre Godin
Area Little South West Miramichi; **Services** Lodge,
Accommodations; **Season** Apr15-Oct15; **Waters**
Public; **Type** Walk/Wade, Boat; **Fish** Salmon

Pinkham's Fishing Lodge
PO Box M, Ashland, ME 04732
(207) 435-6954 **Fax** (207) 435-2451
Contact Virginia Pinkham
Area Restigouche River, New Brunswick; **Services**
Lodge, Accommodations; **Season** May-Aug.;
Waters Private; **Type** Boat; **Fish** Trout, Atlantic
Salmon; **Packages** up to 10 anglers

Pond's Resort
Porter Cove Rd., Ludlow, N.B. Canada E0C 1N0
(506) 369-2612 **Fax** (506) 369-2293

Area Miramichi River; **Services** Lodge,
Accommodations; **Est.** 1925; **Season** Apr-Sep;
Waters Public/Private; **Type** Walk/Wade, Boat;
Fish Brook, Atlantic Salmon; **Packages** up to 20
anglers

Wades Fishing Lodge
Box K472, RR#10, Moncton, N.B. Canada E1C 9J9
(506) 384-2229 or (506) 843-6416 (Summer)
Fax (506) 858-1996 **Contact** Joyce Holmes
Area Miramichi & Cains Rivers; **Services** Lodge,
Accommodations, Fly Shop; **Est.** 1933; **Season**
Apr15-Oct15; **Waters** Private; **Type** Walk/Wade,
Boat; **Fish** Trout, Sea Trout, Salmon, Atlantic Salmon;
Packages 3 Days, up to 16 anglers

Katamaran Tours
RR 2, Red Bank, NB, Canada E0C 1W0
(506) 836-7682 **Fax** (506) 836-7102
Contact Johnny E. Holmes
Area Miramichi River; **Services** Guide,
Accommodations; **Season** Apr15-Oct; **Waters**
Public; **Type** Walk/Wade, Boat; **Fish** Bass, Trout,
Salmon

NEWFOUNDLAND

Lodges/Outfitters/Guides

Awesome Lake Lodge, Labrador
PO Box 320, Clarenville, NF A0E 1J0
(709) 466-2413 **Fax** (709) 466-2413
Contact Len Rich **Services** Lodge, Accommodations;
Waters Public; **Type** Walk/Wade; **Fish** Trout, Brook

Big River Camps, Inc.
PO Box 250, Pasadena, NF, Canada A0L 1K0
(709) 686-2242 **Fax** (709) 686-5244
Contact R.W. Skinner
Services Lodge, Accommodations; **Season**
Jul10-Aug30; **Waters** Public; **Type** Walk/Wade,
Boat; **Fish** Trout, Salmon, Atlantic Salmon

Chute Pool Lodge
12 Birchdale Ave., Dartmouth, N.S., Canada B2X 1E5
(902) 435-1560 Summer Call: (709) 551-5333
Fax (902) 435-1560 **Contact** Al Rothwell
Area Pinware River; **Services** Lodge,
Accommodations; **Waters** Public; **Fish** Salmon

Cooper's Minipi Camps
Box 340, Sta. B, Happy Valley,
Labrador, Newf. Canada A0P 1E0
(709) 896-2891 or (709) 896-3024
Fax (709) 896-9616 **Contact** Jack Cooper
Services Lodge, Accommodations; **Season**
Jun-Sep15; **Waters** Public; **Type** Walk/Wade; **Fish**
Brook, Char, Pike

Lucky Strike Lodge
Box 27, L'Anse au Loup, LB, NF, Canada A0K 3L0
(709) 927-5520 or (709) 454-3803
Contact Denis & Lorne Normore
Area Pinware River; **Services** Lodge,

Accommodations; **Est.** 1965; **Waters** Public; **Type** Walk/Wade; **Fish** Brook, Lake Trout, Char, Pike

Northern Labrador Outdoors
PO Box 89, Jay, ME 04239
(207) 897-4056 or (207) 243-2947
Fax (207) 897-6892 **Contact** Harvey Calden
Area Torngat Mountains, Labrador; **Services** Lodge, Accommodations, Fly Shop; **Est.** 1991; **Season** Aug-Sep; **Waters** Public; **Type** Walk/Wade, Boat; **Fish** Trout, Brook, Sea Trout, Char; **Packages** 7 Days, up to 6 anglers

Pinware River Lodge
L'Anse au Loup, LB, NF A0K 3L0
(709) 927-5785 **Fax** (709) 927-5869
Contact Arthur Fowler **Services** Lodge, Accommodations; **Waters** Public; **Type** Walk/Wade; **Fish** Brook, Lake Trout, Atlantic Salmon

Riverkeep Camp
PO Box V, Ashland, ME 04732
(207) 435-8274 or (207) 843-5515
Fax (207) 435-3230 **Contact** Matt & Ellen Libby
Area Atikonak River; **Services** Lodge, Accommodations; **Waters** Public; **Type** Walk/Wade, Boat; **Fish** Trout, Salmon; **Packages** up to 8 anglers

ONTARIO

Lodges

Hawk Lake Lodge
Box 142, Kenora, Ont. Canada P9N 3X1
(800) 528-9045 or (807) 226-1228
Contact Garry Delton **Area** Northwest, Ontario; **Services** Lodge, Accommodations; **Season** May15-Sep; **Waters** Public; **Type** Boat; **Fish** Smallmouth, Lake Trout, Pike; **Packages** 1 Day

Canoe Canada Outfitters
PO Box 1810, Atrikokan,, Ontario, Canada P0T 1C0
(807) 597-6418 **Fax** (807) 597-5804
Contact Jim Clark & Bud Dickson
Area Quetico Park; **Services** Outfitter/Guide, Accommodations; **Season** May-Sep; **Waters** Public; **Type** Walk/Wade, Boat; **Fish** Smallmouth, Lake Trout, Pike; **Packages** up to 8 anglers

George River Lodge
PO Box 88, Saint-Augustin, Quebec, Canada G3A 1V9
(418) 877-4650 or (800) 473-4650
Fax (418) 877-4652 **Contact** Jean or Pierre Paquet
Area Ungava Northern Quebec; **Services** Lodge, Accommodations; **Est.** 1965; **Season** Jul-Sep; **Waters** Private; **Type** Walk/Wade, Boat; **Fish** Brook, Lake Trout, Atlantic Salmon, Char; **Packages** 6 Days, up to 12 anglers

SASKATCHEWAN

Lodge

Scott Lake
Lodge & Outposts
17-1802 Centennial St.., Whitehorse, YT Y1A 3Z4
(403) 668-2600 **Fax** (403) 668-6368
Contact Blaine Anderson
Area Located on the border of Sask./NW Territories; **Services** Lodge, Accommodations, School; **Est.** 1985; **Season** Jun-Sep; **Waters** Private; **Type** Walk/Wade, Boat; **Fish** Lake Trout, Pike, Grayling; **Packages** 7 Days, up to 18 anglers
See Our Ad Above

ARGENTINA

Lodges/Outfitters/Guides

Argentina Estancias
C.C.#25, 8370 San Martin De Los, Andes,
Prov. Del Neuquen Argentina
Tel 54-972-28641 Fax 54-972-27111
Services Lodge, Accommodations; **Est.** 1965;
Season Nov-Mar; **Waters** Private; **Type** Walk/Wade

AUSTRALIA

Lodge

Ken Orr's Tasmanian Trout Expeditions
Brady's Lake, c/o Post Office,
Tarraleah, Tasmania 7140, Tel/Fax 011-61-362-891191
Contact Ken & Marea Orr   **Area** Bronte Lagoon & Central Highlands; **Services** Guide, Accom-
modations; **Season** Oct-Mar; **Waters** Public; **Type** Walk/Wade; **Fish** Brown

BAHAMAS

Lodge

Deep Water Cay Club
Grand Bahama Island
1100 Lee Wagener Blvd. Ste. 352,
Fort Lauderdale, FL 33315
(954) 359-0488 Bahamas Tel/Fax: (809) 353-3073
Fax (954) 359-9488
Services Lodge, Accommodations; **Est.** 1959;
Season Mid-Sept-Aug.1; **Waters** Public; **Type** Walk/Wade, Boat; **Fish** Bonefish, Permit

Peace & Plenty Bonefish Lodge
PO Box EX29173, Georgetown, Exuma, Bahamas
(242) 345-5555 **Fax** (242) 345-5556
Contàct Bob Hyde
Services Lodge, Accommodations; **Waters** Public;
Type Walk/Wade, Boat; **Fish** Bonefish, Baracuda,
Permit

Commander Charters
PO Box 4263, Key West, FL 33041
(305) 294-9693   **Contact** Admiral Busby
Area Acklins Island; **Services** Outfitter/Guide,
Accommodations; **Type** Boat; **Fish** Bonefish, Permit

BELIZE

Lodges

Turneffe Flats
PO Box 36, Deadwood, SD 57732
(800) 815-1304 or (605) 578-1304
Services Guide, Accommodations; **Waters** Public;
Type Walk/Wade, Boat; **Fish** Bonefish, Tarpon,
Permit

CHILE

Lodges

Estancia de Los Rios
PO Box 558, Puerto Varas, Chile
(800) 288-0886 or (503) 297-2468
Fax (503) 297-3048
Contact John Eustice & Assoc. Ltd.
Area Patagonia; **Services** Lodge, Accommodations,
School; **Waters** Private; **Type** Walk/Wade

jim REPINE'S
ANGLING ADVENTURES

Futaleufu World Class Trout Fishing
Casilla 1238, Vina del Mar, Chile
Phone/Fax: 011-56-32-812-659
Contact Sonia & Jim Repine, Hosts
Area Chile/Patagonia; **Services** Lodge,
Accommodations; **Season** Jan-Apr; **Waters** Public;
Type Walk/Wade; **Fish** Rainbow, Brown; **Packages**
7 Days, up to 4 anglers
O Horseback, Floating, 4-Wheel Drive
Idyllic fly fishing retreat. Enchanted valley in southern
Andes, 10 miles from village. Superb rainbow/brown
trout fishing. Wading, horseback, floating. Caring at-
tention best cuisine/wine, 4 guests per week, English
speaking guides, ideal for couples, Jan-March.
See Our Ad, Right

Rio Baker Lodge
PO Box 1551, Livingston, MT 59047
(800) 471-1141 **Fax** (406) 222-8646
Contact James Marc
Area Patagonia; **Services** Lodge, Accommodations;
Est. 1994; **Season** Oct15-Apr7; **Waters** Public;
Type Float Tube, Walk/Wade, Boat; **Fish** Rainbow,
Brown; **Packages** up to 6 anglers

Rio Palena Lodge
1520 Pancheri, Idaho Falls, ID 83429
(800) 444-4933 **Fax** (208) 529-4397
Contact Lynn Sessions
Area Palena River S. of Puerto Montt; **Services**
Lodge, Fly Shop; **Est.** 1981; **Season** Nov-Apr;
Waters Public; **Type** Float Tube, Walk/Wade; **Fish**
Rainbow, Brook, Brown; **Packages** 7 Days, up to 8
anglers
O Rio Palena Lodge-Chile
O Superb Lodging & Meals
O Expert Guides
O Float & Wade Fishing
O Browns-Rainbows-Brook Trout

Posada de los Farios
Casilla 104, Coyhaique, XI Region, Chile
(800) 669-3474 or 011-56-67-236402; Fax:
011-56-67-232500
Contact Rex Bryngelson/Mike Michalak
Area Rio Cisnes (River of the Swans); **Services**
Outfitter/Guide, Accommodations; **Est.** 1994;
Season Oct-April; **Waters** Public; **Type** Float Tube,
Walk/Wade, Boat; **Fish** Trout, Rainbow, Brown,
Salmon; **Packages** 4 Days, up to 6 anglers

COSTA RICA

Lodge

Archie Fields' Rio Colorado Lodge
PO Box 5094-1000, San Jose, Costa Rica
(800) 243-9777 Costa Rica: 011-506-232-8610
Fax (813) 933-3280
Contact Archie Field
Area Costa Rica's San Juan River; **Services** Lodge,
Accommodations; **Season** Year-round; **Waters**
Public; **Type** Walk/Wade, Boat; **Fish** Tarpon;
Packages up to 38 anglers

HONDURAS

Lodge

Posada del Sol Resort
Guanaja, Bay Islands, Honduras
1201 US Hwy. 1, Ste. 210, N. Palm Beach, FL 33408
(800) 642-3483 or (407) 624-3483
Fax (407) 624-3225
Contact Sandra Cundiff
Area Guanaja Island;   **Services** Lodge,
Accommodations, Fly Shop;   **Waters** Public;   **Type**
Walk/Wade, Boat;   **Fish** Bonefish, Permit

IRELAND

Lodge

Clonanav Fly Fishing Centre
Nire Valley, Ballymacarbry, Co., Waterford, Ireland
Tel/Fax 011-353-52-36141
Area River Suir and river Blackwater;   **Services**
Outfitter/Guide, Accommodations, Fly Shop;   **Waters**
Private;   **Type** Walk/Wade;   **Fish** Brown, Salmon

NEW ZEALAND

Lodges/Outfitters/Guides

Louie the Fish/Parklands Lodge
PO Box 192, Turangi, Lake Taupo, New Zealand
(800) 605-6265 Tel/Fax: 011 647 386 7953
Services Outfitter/Guide, Accommodations;   **Est.**
1981;   **Waters** Public;   **Type** Walk/Wade;   **Fish**
Trout, Rainbow, Brown

New Zealand Fishing
PO Box 315, Montrose, CA 81402
(800) 297-4441 or (303) 249-4441
Fax (800) 297-4441
Contact Hank Hotze
Services Lodge, Accommodations;   **Waters** Public;
Type Walk/Wade, Boat;   **Fish** Rainbow, Brown,
Salmon

South Island Fishing Tours
42 Maces Rd., Christchurch, New Zealand
011-64-3-3265611 (Tel/Fax)
Area South Island of New Zealand

NORWAY

Lodge

Norwegian Fly Fisher's Club
N-7090, Storen, Norway
Tel 47-94-72-98-43 Fax 47-72-43-11-01
Contact Manfred Raguse
Services Outfitter/Guide, Accommodations;   **Season**
Jun-Aug;   **Waters** Private;   **Type** Walk/Wade, Boat;
Fish Salmon

UNITED KINGDOM

Lodge

The Orvis Co., Inc.
The Mill,Nether Wallop,Stockbridge, Hampshire,
England SO20 8ES, Andover   011-44-264-781212
Area Test & Itchen Rivers;   **Services** Outfitter/Guide,
Fly Shop, School;   **Waters** Public;   **Type** Walk/Wade;
Fish Trout

Black's 1998 Fly Fishing - *FREE BASIC EQUIPMENT CO. LISTING*

Complete and return this form by mail or fax to request a free profile of your company in next year's edition.

EQUIPMENT COMPANY INFORMATION

Name:

Address:

City: State: Zip:

Phone: FAX:

Year Established: No. of Employees:

Contact/Title:

PRODUCT or SERVICE DESCRIPTION

Please briefly describe your primary product, product line, or service in the space provided below. (Limit descriptions to 15 words or less. Expanded listings containing logos and longer product descriptions are available. See Advertising Rates or call for information.)

Signature: Date:

P.O. BOX 2029, RED BANK, NJ 07701 • TEL: 908-224-8700 • FAX: 908-741-2827

Make Your Advertising Dollars Work Harder & Longer In. . . Black's 1998 Fly Fishing

Space Reservations: September 30, 1997
Material Deadline: October 31, 1997
Publication Date: December, 1997

Your advertising expenditures work overtime for you in **Black's Fly Fishing.** Why? Because **Black's Fly Fishing** is not just another magazine that's read and discarded, but a buyer's guide to fly fishing equipment, services and destinations. An annual directory that places your marketing message in front of your best prospects for a full year.

Black's Fly Fishing reaches fly and tackle shops . . . sporting goods stores . . . professional buyers . . . lodge operators . . . guides and outfitters . . . outdoor writers . . . and thousands of free-spending fly fishing enthusiasts. 20,000 copies distributed. Circulation that's 50% industry, 50% consumer and 100% effective.

Best of all, the cost of advertising in **Black's Fly Fishing** will barely be noticed in your promotional budget, as this rate sheet demonstrates.

Advertising Sizes & Rates:

ITEM		— COST—	
SIZE	**B&W**	**4-COLOR**	**LOGOS**
Full page	$1,290	B&W + $390	3 Free
1/2 page	$690	B&W + $290	2 Free
1/3 page	$490	B&W + $190	1 Free
COVERS			
Inside Front	na	$2,750	3 Free
Inside Back	na	$2,550	3 Free
Back	na	$2,950	3 Free
SPECIAL POSITIONS			
Page 1 (opposite inside front cover)	na	$1,980	2 Free
Opposite Table of Contents	na	$1,890	2 Free
LISTING ENHANCEMENT PACKAGES			
Logo & 50 Word Product Description (50% off additional logos)	$129	na	na
Photo Listing & 50 Word Description	$199	na	na

Multiple Ad Discount

The above display rates are based on a single advertising purchase. Advertiser's who run more than one ad in each annual edition of **Black's Fly Fishing** are entitled to a 5% discount on the second ad; 10% on each additional ad. (Ad sequence determined by ad size—largest ads first.)

Corporate Advertiser Distribution Programs

Black's Fly Fishing corporate distribution program offers advertisers an opportunity to purchase—at deeply discounted rates—hundreds or thousands of copies of *Black's Fly Fishing* for use as premiums, sales incentives or gifts.

Questions?

For more information about **Black's Fly Fishing** call or write: James F. Black, Jr., Publisher, P.O. Box 2029, Red Bank, NJ 07701; (908) 224-8700; fax: (908) 741-2827.

(F:\USERS\FLYFISH\ADRATE.CHP)